Mediating the World in the Novels of Iain Banks

MEDIATED FICTIONS

STUDIES IN VERBAL AND VISUAL NARRATIVES

Series Editors: Artur Blaim and Ludmiła Gruszewska-Blaim

VOLUME 1

Katarzyna Pisarska

Mediating the World in the Novels of Iain Banks

The Paradigms of Fiction

PETER LANG
EDITION

Bibliographic Information published by the Deutsche Nationalbibliothek
The Deutsche Nationalbibliothek lists this publication in the Deutsche Nationalbibliografie; detailed bibliographic data is available in the internet at http://dnb.d-nb.de.

Library of Congress Cataloging-in-Publication Data
Pisarska, Katarzyna, 1977-
 Mediating the world in the novels of Iain Banks : the paradigms of fiction / Katarzyna Pisarska.
     pages cm – (Mediated fictions ; volume 1)
 Includes bibliographical references and index.
 ISBN 978-3-631-62614-6
 1. Banks, Iain, 1954-2013–Criticism and interpretation.
 2. Mediation in literature. I. Title.
 PR6052.A485Z83 2013
 823'.914–dc23

                              2013048324

This publication was financially supported by
Maria Curie-Skłodowska University, Lublin.

Cover illustration printed with kind permission of Jerzy Durczak.

Reviewed by Zofia Kolbuszewska.

ISSN 2194-5918
ISBN 978-3-631-62614-6 (Print)
E-ISBN978-3-653-02006-9 (E-Book)
DOI 10.3726/978-3-653-02006-9

© Peter Lang GmbH
Internationaler Verlag der Wissenschaften
Frankfurt am Main 2013
All rights reserved.

Peter Lang Edition is an Imprint of Peter Lang GmbH.

Peter Lang – Frankfurt am Main · Bern · Bruxelles · New York · Oxford · Warszawa · Wien

This book is part of the Peter Lang Edition list and was peer reviewed prior to publication.

www.peterlang.com

For my parents

Contents

Acknowledgements

I would like to express my gratitude to Professor Ludmiła Gruszewska-Blaim and Professor Artur Blaim, the general editors of the series, for their invaluable help and support in the preparation and publication of this book. I owe special gratitude to Professor Andrzej Zgorzelski (University of Gdańsk), who read the first draft of this book and offered illuminating comments and criticism. I would also like to thank Professor Zbigniew Mazur (Maria Curie-Skłodowska University of Lublin) for his kind assistance in my mediation studies. I am grateful to Professor Andrew Milner (Monash University, Melbourne), Professor Zofia Kolbuszewska (John Paul II Catholic University of Lublin) as well as the members of the Editorial Board of the series, Professor Joanna Durczak, Professor Fátima Vieira, Professor Antonis Balasopoulos, and Professor David Malcolm, for their kind suggestions which helped me to improve this book. I should express special thanks to Professor William Sullivan (Maria Curie-Skłodowska University of Lublin), without whose help the book as it is now would be impossible. I must not forget the kindness of my colleagues from the Department of English Literature at Maria Curie-Skłodowska University, Dr Justyna Galant, Dr Marta Komsta, Dr Urszula Terentowicz-Fotyga, Dr Andrzej Sławomir Kowalczyk, as well as Professor Anna Kędra-Kardela from the Department of Anglo-Irish Literature, who always lent a sympathetic ear. Last but not least, I would like to thank Jorge for his unwavering love, support, and encouragement, which helped me weather the crises and complete this book.

Special thanks to Maria Curie-Skłodowska University for funding this publication.

Introduction:
The Case of Iain (M.) Banks

Iain Banks, an internationally recognized, contemporary British novelist, whose death on 9 June 2013 interrupted his successful career, had never forgotten his Scottish roots. In an interview for *Spike Magazine* in 1996, he admitted: "I'm Scottish and a writer so I'm a Scottish writer" (Mitchell). The statement may come across somewhat as a syllogism; however, it gives us an insight into the author's own idea of his Scottishness and of the place he occupied on his country's literary scene. In his view, both questions seemed to be linked, first and foremost, with his provenance and the place of residence rather than with his close affiliation with the prevailing trends and the climate of literary changes in Scotland. This view is perhaps not surprising, as Iain Banks regarded himself primarily as a writer of science fiction, who usually spent his time with other SF writers (Mitchell 1996), and whose main objective was the rehabilitation of science fiction. In his opinion, this aim would be attained once a science fiction novel was shortlisted for the Booker Prize (Alegre 2000: 198).

Another yardstick for measuring Banks's contribution to Scottish literature was, he suggested, the degree to which he employed Scottish settings and characters and addressed particularly Scottish themes and concerns in his books. Asked to determine his own place among contemporary Scottish writers, he offered rather commonsensically:

> I think it's more of a sliding scale, a spectrum of Scottishness, someone like James Kelman or Alasdair Gray at one end and somebody like Candia McWilliam perhaps at the other end, who is certainly a Scottish writer but not one who necessarily writes about Scotland. Or Alasdair McLean maybe, who has maybe written one or two books set in Scotland but is not what

you think of as a Scottish writer. I think I'm probably somewhere in the middle. (Kelman 1998: 19)

By his own standards, Banks was a Scottish writer, being firmly rooted in his country's landscape and social fabric. He lived in North Queensferry, not far from the Forth Rail Bridge, whose towering silhouette provided the imaginative context for *The Bridge*, his most complex novel. The Scottish setting appears in one way or another in practically all his mainstream novels, even those most surreal or set in an unspecified place or time like *A Song of Stone* (see Kelman 1998: 21). His characters, in their overwhelming majority, come from Scotland and are preoccupied with their Scottish roots, family relationships, and the issue of the country's existence within the larger space of Great Britain. "I prefer writing in Scottish context," Banks explained, "because it is what I am used to, so I don't have to do any research. [. . .] I write about Scotland because I have a Scottish background" (Kelman 1998: 19).

Hailed as "the Tarantino of the book world" (Hoggard 2007), a comparison which well conveys his penchant for grotesqueness, graphically described violence, and black humour, Iain Banks achieved something few authors have managed so far. Being, in his own view, "an SF writer who happens to write mainstream" (McKenzie 1995), he published his literary fiction as Iain Banks and his science fiction as Iain M. Banks, enjoying immense popularity among lay readers as well as the recognition of literary critics and academia for both strands of his novelistic production. Since the publication of his highly controversial first novel, *The Wasp Factory* (1984), Banks's *oeuvre* steadily expanded to comprise in the end twenty-nine books: fifteen mainstream novels, twelve science fiction novels, one collection of short stories, and a non-fiction travelogue through Scotland and its distilleries.

From the ghoulish grotesqueness of *The Wasp Factory*, whose male protagonist discovers himself to be a woman, followed by the postmodernist games and allegories in *Walking on Glass* (1985) and *The Bridge* (1986), Banks took his readers over the years on regular journeys through time, space, and genre. Among these we can count: a fictional autobiography-cum-Künstlerroman of a Scottish rock star in the 1970s world of drugs, sex, and rock'n'roll in *Espedair Street* (1987); a political thriller set in post-war Japan and 1980s Panama in *Canal Dreams* (1989); a Scottish family saga and novel of development in *The Crow*

Road (1992), *The Steep Approach to Garbadale* (2007), and *Stonemouth* (2012); a noir thriller addressing the abuses of power in the bleak reality of Thatcher's aftermath in *Complicity* (1993); a quest narrative about the vicissitudes of a member of a religious sect in *Whit* (1995); an apocalyptic allegory in *A Song of Stone* (1997); a techno-thriller set in the world of financial circles in *The Business* (1999); a caper story and popular romance rolled into one, developing in the media world after the collapse of the World Trade Center in *Dead Air* (2002); and an autistic youth's first-person account of his life in the north of England in *The Quarry* (2013). Not to mention inter-dimensional travel in *Transition* (2009) and the extrapolated future canvas of his science fiction novels, in which he explores the subgenre of space opera.

The variety of settings and Banks's use of multifarious genre conventions go hand in hand with such technical ploys as intertextual allusions, competing or alternating narratives, elements of fantasy and dream being introduced into the framework of the mimetic narrative (Watson 2007: 255), as well as linguistic experiments with English and Scots. The technical artistry of Banks's fiction is accompanied by what MacGillivray calls

> the scintillating range of Banks's humour and ludic inventiveness. Jokes in abundance, constant playing upon words and ideas, puzzles and riddles for the reader, the creation and description of games of all kinds, good humour and black comedy, even sick humour: all these and more enliven a Banks novel. (1996)

As noted by Douglas Gifford, when it comes to Scottish identity-making, there has been a marked drive in contemporary Scottish fiction "in the direction of synthesis, but a synthesis which is permissive of multiple perspectives and a plurality of approaches through different genres" (1996: 37). It has resulted in the literary presentations of multiple visions of Scotland, limited neither by time, place, nor tradition, a heterogeneity which can be noticed also in Banks's novels. In Banks, the urban and the rural Scotland, the Lowlands and the Highlands, exist side by side, "the Scotland of oilrigs and technology" looks to "the Scotland of tradition, with its mountains and historical relics" (Gifford 1996: 43), the Scotland of Gothic horrors and the uncanny intertwines with the Scotland of materialism and pop culture, and the exclusive environments of family or religious order are exploded by the inclusive and all-embracing power of globalized community and the Internet. All Banks's fiction is, using Gifford's phrase, "about *Scotlands*, about possibilities" (1996: 42), with the characters being forced to acknowledge and mediate between their multiple identities in the changing Scotland, Britain, and the world.

This hybridity of representations which contests the uniformity of the dominant English culture, in opposition to which Scottish national identity has been reforging itself (cf. Head 2002: 147), can be seen as a manifestation of postcolonial consciousness. Randall Stevenson comments on the ambiguity of Scotland's postcolonial status, at the same time noting typically postcolonial sensibilities in Scottish literature:

> As a primary agent in the construction of the British Empire, and on the whole one of its beneficiaries, Scotland clearly cannot be assumed to share uncomplicatedly in the conditions of colonies or former colonies abroad. [. . .] Yet, illuminating coincidences and homologies remain visible between Scotland's situation – within a waning but long-endured form of English empire – and the experiences postcolonial theory analyses. In belonging to a small country, of many internal divisions, still dominated by London-centred media and institutions, Scottish writers experience 'strange fusions' and plural hybridised forms of imagination without ever having to migrate from home. (2004: 224)[1]

---

1   In his article "Democracy and Scottish Postcoloniality" (1996), Michael Gardiner makes the following distinction between the terms *post-colonial* and *postcolonial* while discussing the Scottish context: "*Post-colonial* describes a situation where a power has retreated after a colonial period; *postcolonial*, in current usage, describes tendencies in cultural and institutional structures which foreground questions of race, sovereignty, and nationhood, with the colonial temporality of progress readable in terms of present identifications. So postcolonial situations are often post-colonial but enquiries which try to conflate the two, as in the historical investigation of whether Scotland has ever been treated as a colony, are often harmfully substituted for the positive move of using postcolonial qualities to develop political articulations, textual strategy" (qtd. in Bell 2004: 144). Commenting on Gardiner's perception of Scottish postcoloniality, Cairns Craig observes that such focus on "elements of Scotland's internal cultural situation" tends to overlook the fact of Scotland's real *post*-coloniality, namely its being historically "a *colonising* nation." He points out: "Concentration on the nation's internal hybridity emphasises what Scotland is assumed to have in common with the colonised of the English-speaking world – the interaction of local language and dialect with standard English, the interplay of local mythology and literary tradition with the

In his writing, Banks repeatedly showed his awareness of Scotland's being dominated by the institutional and cultural authority of England. Equally often, he attempted to challenge this authority either through explicit commentary or by adopting various novelistic techniques usually employed by writers from the formerly colonized Commonwealth countries. At the same time, Banks's fiction shows a marked development in the treatment of the Scottish postcolonial condition: from the bleakness following the failed devolution referendum to a more cheerful mood after the re-establishment of the Scottish Parliament in 1999.

Although Banks claimed it was not deliberate, many of his books, both mainstream and SF, are about identity: "There's often a character who is hiding their identity or who does not know all the facts about themselves" (Marshall 1998). Premeditated or not, the preoccupation of Banks's characters with identity and truth seems to be a manifestation of the "insistent Scottish identity-making" (Gifford 1996: 37), which proved especially poignant in the 1980s and 1990s. Many of Banks's characters, especially in his early novels, are either comatose or amnesiac, or have to live in ignorance of their past and real identity, which represents a more general trend in Scottish writing after the failure of the first devolution referendum. A feeling of national "concussion" led many Scottish writers to perceive Scotland, subordinate to Anglocentric British history and London's Conservative rule, as detached from its own past, incapacitated, and vegetating in a state of suspended animation. The political climate of disappointment and lethargy, as Cairns Craig postulates, spurred the appearance of numerous works in which the main characters suffer from a memory loss or lapse into unconsciousness, their oblivion being a metaphor of the predicament of the nation (2006: 125-6). The most prominent of those novels, which are sometimes recognized as a sub-genre of "coma fiction" (see Gardiner 2009: 186), is Gray's *Lanark*, published shortly after the referendum, whose eponymous character roams the dystopian city of Unthank unable to recall anything of his previous life as Duncan Thaw, a Glasgow artist. The same pattern of alternating narratives, one being the account of the character's real life and the other constituting an oneiric fantasy, appears

---

'standard' literature of the English cultural imperium – and represses the fact that it was Scottish writers such as Walter Scott from whom the colonised had to learn in order to acquire the imperial language and culture" (2004a: 237).

for example in Irvine Welsh's *The Marabou Stork Nightmares*, switching between the protagonist's life with his dysfunctional family in Leith, and his alternative comatose life as an adventurer in South Africa who traverses the wilderness in search of the Marabou stork.

Banks's third mainstream novel, *The Bridge*, is most representative of this trend. Its dominant narrative is focused on the life of an amnesiac patient, John Orr, who wakes to consciousness in the fantasy world of the gigantic Bridge. Parallel to it runs a realistic strand depicting the character's life in Edinburgh as Alexander Lennox, whose immersion in the self-aggrandizing fantasy of modern capitalism concludes with a car crash on the Forth Rail Bridge, which leaves him in a coma. Comatose Lennox, motionless and sustained by the machines, is a metaphor for the paralyzed and changeless condition of modern Scotland, where history is suspended into a "narrative without end, without purpose" (Craig 1999: 131) in a cycle of endless mechanical repetition epitomized in the structure of the Bridge.[2] "[C]ould death be the only way I might awake from this terrible, enchanted sleep?" (267) asks Orr towards the end of the novel, echoing Craig's claim that for the characters caught in "the hell of suspended history" death is the only means of escape (1999: 133).

While presenting typical features of the Scottish novel of the devolutionary period, Craig further mentions the narratives whose protagonists experience a breach in history. They either find themselves "in circumstances which negate [their] past identity," or they do not remember the cause of their present predicament:

> Not knowing where you are, not recognizing the place, not remembering the past, not knowing how you got here – the failed politics of the nation resonates at the personal level in lives that have lost the connection between the narrative of their past and the possible narratives of the future. It is a condition in which the requirements of the traditional novel seem impossible. Instead of being able to reveal the growing complexity and depth of a character's life, it is as though narrative progression is possible only at the cost of etiolation of personality. (2006: 126)

---

2   The novel, as Gavin Miller rightly observes, "with its endlessly repetitive symbolism" of the Forth Rail Bridge turns into "a meditation on a national symbol: a comatose man looking at a bridge rather than, as in Hugh Mac-Diarmid's long poem of 1926, a drunk man looking at a thistle" (2007a: 204).

Similar motifs can be traced already in Banks's first novel. When projected onto the Scottish national consciousness, Frank's insular isolation
(according to Duncan Petrie, a recurring emblematic feature in representations of Scotland [2004: 121]), in which he adopts the behavioural
model of aggressive misogynist masculinity after his femininity has been
pharmacologically put to sleep, becomes an illustration of the historical
lethargy of the country. The motif of amnesia as connected with the
question of history, both public and private, appears also in *Complicity*,
whose protagonist, Cameron Colley, has suppressed the memory of the
past which harbours a childhood tragedy. As a result, he lives in the
permanent "now," which is reflected in the persistent present tense of his
narration. The character's detachment from his own history and his imprisonment in the endless cycle of drug taking and game playing make
him an incarnation of the post-devolution consciousness, traumatized but
oblivious of the events which caused its current condition. Characters
struggling with the fragmentations of identity, displacement, seclusion,
and trauma people Banks's mainstream novels well into the 1990s, when
his fiction begins to show signs of a brighter outlook as if in anticipation
of the forthcoming historical changes.[3]

Although Banks's fiction is often regarded as part of the New Scottish Renaissance and its formal experiments used for the exploration of
Scottish identity (see March 2002: 3), the writer himself was rather cautious of such pigeonholing:

> About the Scottish literature thing. I'm always very wary about lumping
> people together because it so often doesn't work. I think maybe it used to
> when you had a café society and a group of chaps that used to get together

---

3   Discussing the creative response of contemporary Scottish writers to the con-
     dition of living in post-devolution Scotland, Berthold Schoene sees its utter
     manifestation in the writers' "cosmopolitanist effort to relate individuals, and
     induce them to relate to each other, across the restrictive parameters of sex,
     gender, class, race and nationality" in order to create "a strong sense of plane-
     tary commonality among people" (2007: 15). Similar motifs can be noticed in
     Banks's novels after 1999, e.g. *The Business, Dead Air*, and *The Steep Ap-
     proach to Garbadale*, whose characters cross geographical and ethnic bounda-
     ries on their path to self-discovery and a life within a heterogenic community.
     Although England remained a negative pole in Banks's private ideology and
     to a large extent in his fiction, his Scotlands do open up to a new life in the
     new globalized world.

for a few bowls of tobacco in their long-stemmed pipes to discuss issues of the day and to agree to write in a particular fashion, criticise each other and so on. I just don't think it works these days. But certainly there is an increasing awareness in the last ten years of the differences between Scotland and England, which does have a blanket effect on all writers working here. (Robertson 1989/90)

Certainly, Banks was aware of his domestic literary inspirations. He admitted that *The Bridge* was much indebted to Alasdair Gray's *Lanark*, which he considered "a landmark" and "the best Scottish novel of [the twentieth] century" (Dean). "I don't think *The Bridge* would be the way it is at all if it wasn't for *Lanark*," he declared elsewhere (Robertson 1989/90). At the same time, he claimed that he knew too little about Scottish literature to acknowledge any other particularly Scottish tradition or influence. "I'm certainly part of the English *language* tradition," he asserted, pointing to Joseph Heller's *Catch 22* and Hunter S. Thompson's *Fear and Loathing in Las Vegas* as his two most formative readings. His other influences included Günter Grass's *The Tin Drum* and, as Banks himself explained, "almost anything by Kafka," rather than "anything in Scottish literature apart from the single exception of *Lanark*" (Robertson 1989/90). Beside literature, both SF and mainstream, Banks's inspirations came from various other sources: film, television, and the radio of the 1950s and 1960s (Tallaron 1996: 143). Among his favourite authors he listed Jane Austen, Leo Tolstoy, Graham Greene, and Saul Bellow, alongside "loads of underrated science fiction authors" like M. John Harrison, John Sladeck, and Barrington J. Bayley (Wilson 1994).

Despite Banks's personal disclaimers, his fiction reverberates strongly with the legacy of the New Scottish Renaissance as well as more traditional and long-standing "Scottish obsessions" (Watson 2007: 255), elevated by the devolutionary writers to the status of fixed markers of Scotland's postcolonial consciousness. While discussing the cultural and linguistic distinctiveness of Scots within the Anglocentric history of British fiction, Cairns Craig points to three traditional "contradictions" inscribed in the Scottish novel which have been exploited by contemporary writers in their innovative novelistic styles: 1) "a conflict between the desire to maintain local realism and the attempt to shape the local in terms of some universal paradigm;" 2) a "dissociation of sensibility" reflective of the country's "divided history and culture," which involves "a lack of balance between emotion and reason, between heart and head," and results in a mixture of seemingly incompatible genres and styles within one work (being exemplary of the Caledonian antisyzygy); 3) the incoherence between the "English-writing narrator" and a group of "Scots-speaking characters," which leads to the emergence of the "uncertain narrative voice," either undermining or sentimentalizing the described Scottish community (2006: 127).[4]

As far as the question of local realism is concerned, it has already been asserted that Scotland with its rural and urban landscapes, social panorama, and pictures of everyday life is a regular feature of Banks's *oeuvre*. Alan MacGillivray thus comments on the ease with which Banks translates the social and topographical reality of his homeland into his fictional worlds:

> No one who reads the novels that are set wholly or partly in Scotland can doubt that here is a writer who is deeply involved with his country, who loves its landscapes and its cities, who feels strongly about the social and political state of Scotland, and sees it constantly as a valid society subjected to intrusive and unjustifiable pressures from outside. In all these novels Banks is accurate and vivid in his presentation of Scottish idiomatic speech from different classes and areas [. . .].
>
> The world of Banks's mainstream fiction, with the exceptions of *Walking on Glass* and *Canal Dreams*, is very definitely a Scottish world, drawing from the documentary realism of actual places, down to the level of real streets, pubs and natural features and from the generalised aspects of the Scottish scene, like the hills and lochs, beaches and lairds' houses, and the texture of life in Scotland in the seventies and eighties. (1996)

At the same time, the accuracy in conveying local realism through the minutiae of place, character, and speech is continually put in a wider perspective of history, literary tradition, and myth. Already in *The Wasp Factory*, Banks combines a story of a disturbed teenager killing animals and playing heroes on an island in the north of Scotland with a modern version of the Frankenstein myth and a motif of the savage from J. G. Frazer's *The Golden Bough* (cf. Sage 1996: 181). In *The Bridge*, the faithful presentation of Lennox's life in the Edinburgh of the 1970s and 1980s is intertwined with his life in the realm of dreams. In the oneiric

---

4   The three "contradictions" addressed by Craig appear in Francis Russell Hart's *The Scottish Novel* as apparent shortcomings of Scottish writing, which Hart calls "unsettled issues of Scottish culture" (1978: 407).

fantasy, the national symbol of the Forth Rail Bridge becomes a central point of the hero's Eliotesque journey across the mythic wasteland for a recovery of memory (Craig 2002: 73). Similarly, Isis Whit's journey from Scotland to London, rife with comic encounters with the inhabitants of contemporary Britain, at the same time explicitly alludes to Bunyan's *The Pilgrim's Progress*, Scott's *Waverley*, and to the myth of the Egyptian goddess Isis, which turns the heroine's quest into an archetypal Campbellian narrative. And the setting in *A Song of Stone*, despite its obvious correspondence to the Scottish landscape, is deliberately allegorized to make an impression that "[t]his could be any place or time" (1998: 272).

Banks's fiction is also representative of the second Scottish contradiction exploited by contemporary Scottish novelists (e.g. Alasdair Gray, Emma Tennant, A. L. Kennedy), namely a "dissociation of sensibility," whose first and most obvious trait, taking into consideration Banks's speculative acumen, is the blend of the mimetic and antimimetic elements, along the lines of G. Gregory Smith's concept of the Caledonian antisyzygy. *Walking on Glass*, for example, consists of three intertwining narratives representing three different genres and containing different degrees of "normalcy" of the fictional worlds: a popular romance, a schizophrenic account with elements of the mimetic and the fantastic, and a science fiction tale set on the dying Earth. *The Bridge* and *Complicity*, with their alternating narratives, shifting points of view, and exploration of fragmented identity, mix realistic accounts of contemporary life with surreal fantasy and the Gothic, echoing James Hogg's *The Private Memoirs and Confessions of a Justified Sinner* and R. L. Stevenson's *The Strange Case of Dr Jekyll and Mr Hyde*. Moreover, in his fiction Banks freely mingles high and low culture by fusing elaborate lofty diction and slang (e.g. *Whit*), or by combining popular formulas and genres like romance, thriller, or black comedy with myth or utopia (*Canal Dreams*, *The Business*, *The Wasp Factory*).

The third distinctive trait of cultural independence manifested by modern Scottish writers – and Banks among them – is the use of a Scottish demotic voice as the narrative centre of the novel. Pioneered by the New Renaissance novelist James Kelman in *The Busconductor Hines* and *A Disaffection*, the technique served as a means of emphasizing the conflict of standard English and Scottish vernacular "as the very identity of the characters" (Craig 2006: 132). The use of vernacular speech in narration became extremely popular and led to a crop of works written in the Scottish "street patois." Its most recognizable practitioner these days is probably Irvine Welsh, but it has also been used by Andrew Greig, James Robertson, Ian Rankin, and Christopher Brookmyre (Craig 2006: 133-4, cf. Bradford 2007: 164-5). Banks used phonetically transcribed Glaswegian dialect in *The Bridge* for the character of the Barbarian, who carries with him an obnoxious chimera-like creature called the Familiar, which speaks standard English. The uneasy relationship between the swordsman and his garrulous companion allowed Banks to explore the conflict of identity of the novel's main character, who is torn between his working-class roots and his studied upper-middle-class refinement.[5]

Interestingly, the three contradictions present in Banks's fiction, which are regarded as elements of a specifically Scottish tradition of the novel, and as an assertion of Scotland's cultural and linguistic difference within the allegedly homogenous British culture, are to a considerable extent convergent with the principal tenets of postmodernism. It has even led some critics to think of Scottish literature as inherently postmodern, using the term in retrospect with reference to the works of James Hogg, R. L. Stevenson, or J. M. Barrie (Craig 2006: 130-1; cf. Craig 2004b: 251). Addressing the postmodern quality of contemporary Scottish fiction, Randall Stevenson points to the literary tradition mentioned above as representative of "particular dispositions of Scottish imagination" to partake in "postmodern influences." "The irony of critics' under-use of postmodern analysis of Scottish literature," observes Stevenson, "is that it may be *more* appropriate to that literature than to

---

5 The use of vernacular speech in narration, which shifts gravity from the English centre to the Scottish peripheries, may be perceived in terms of the "decentering" quality of postmodernism, contesting such concepts as authority, unity, totalization, and homogeneity (see Hutcheon 1996: 57). The narrative accounts delivered from the perspective of cultural margins, in a narrative voice which defies the established versions of history or reality as well as the accepted aesthetic conventions, coincides with Lyotard's concept of *postmodern* as "incredulity toward metanarratives" and their implicit veracity and righteousness (1984: xxiv). Lyotard claims that "[w]e no longer have recourse to the grand narratives," seeing "the little narrative [*petit récit*] [as] the quintessential form of imaginative invention" (1984: 60).

many others" (2004: 221). Roel Daamen accordingly states that in contemporary Scottish writing "the aestheticism of postmodernism is not a
simple frivolity or cynicism, but rather an integral part of the world between tradition and innovation" (2006: 126).

The "universal paradigm" of the "local realism" in Scottish fiction
coincides with the claim of postmodernist fiction "to open itself up to
history, to the world" through a critical dialogue with "the textual past of
both the 'world' and literature" (Hutcheon 1996: 125). Intertextuality,
which, according to Linda Hutcheon, "situates the locus of textual meaning within the history of discourse itself" (126), is an important characteristic of Banks's literary technique. It involves imaginative and paro-
distic reworkings of ancient myths, subversive allusions to the Bible and
the Arthurian legends, with an extremely powerful symbolism of names,
as well as numerous, if frequently oblique or misleading, references to
works by Shakespeare, Eliot, Kafka, Peake, Borges, English and Scottish Romantics, Wells, Orwell, various science fiction writers, popular
music and cinema of the 1970s and 1980s, and many other sources (see
MacGillivray 1996, and MacGillivray 2001: 5).

The antisyzygical quality of Banks's writing, which involves the
combination of contradictory genres and styles, and especially the su-
prageneric cross-dressing of the mimetic and exomimetic (i.e. science
fiction)[6] elements, is yet another recognizable trait of postmodernist fiction. According to Brian McHale, postmodernist fiction and science fiction have been advancing along "parallel but independent tracks;" however, there has been a tendency between the two kinds of writing to influence each other (1987: 65-6). Discussing postmodernism's indebtedness to SF, McHale points to the motif of temporal and less frequently
spatial displacement, i.e. "projecting worlds of the future rather than
worlds in distant galaxies" (66). In *Walking on Glass*, Banks's most representative text in terms of the interconnectedness of postmodernism and
SF, the world of the Quis-and-Ajayi narrative involves both spatial distancing and temporal extrapolation, as well as the avowedly dystopian
colouring of postmodernist futures, visible in the war-torn universe and
the Kafkaesque imprisonment of the two characters in endless games on
a dying planet. On the other hand, the text reveals its indebtedness to the

---

6   In my use of the terms *mimetic* and *exomimetic* I rely on the definitions pro-
     pounded by Andrzej Zgorzelski in his book *Born of the Fantastic* (2004: 32).

poetics of postmodernism in its generic hybridity and its employment of multiple conflicting perspectives tied to the consciousnesses of the characters, whose epistemological limitations contribute to the unreliability of their respective narratives. Other postmodern traits of *Walking on Glass* (also exhibited by *The Bridge* and several later works) can be noticed in the novel's play with ontological levels and its metatextual awareness of its own constructedness (Craig 2006: 130; for stylistic features of Banks's postmodernism cf. Craig 2005: 230-1).[7]

The postmodernist discourse questioning certainty, continuity, and origin can also be partly responsible for Banks's preoccupation with the narrative (re)construction of history (both national and personal) and with the memory of the past which is either impossible to access or misinterpreted and thus forms an unreliable basis of the present. Some of his works dealing with history and memory have already been discussed as examples of the devolutionary novel. However, Banks's concern with the way history is experienced, remembered, and recounted goes beyond the Scottish context, as it reflects the same preoccupation among many British writers who explore the complex relationship between literature, history, and remembrance. The reliability of historical or any form of narrative; its dependence on the perspective of the writer/teller, which involves the possibility of creating multiple histories; the effect of history on the life of the individual; the influence of power relationships (gender, cultural, political) on historical accounts – these are all questions which Banks repeatedly addresses in his novels. This quality of his writing links him to such contemporary authors as Graham Swift, Ian McEwan, Martin Amis, Kazuo Ishiguro, Salman Rushdie, and, to a lesser extent, A. S. Byatt and Peter Ackroyd.

Banks's interest in history can be examined in terms of four major criteria proposed by David Malcolm with reference to contemporary

---

7   The postmodern literary game in *Walking on Glass*, which reflects the games played by and with the characters in their respective narratives, is but one example of the game-playing motif in Banks's novels. According to Cairns Craig, Banks's entire fiction represents the "transformation of the real into a game," which is identified by Lyotard as characteristic of postmodernism (2005: 231). However, in contrast to Lyotard's concept of reality being translated into a game, games in Banks's novels become reality (238). For a discussion of the game-playing motif in Banks's fiction see also Miller 2007b: 47-65.

British fiction, namely: "precise dating," "motifs of recall and [. . .] the narrative organization of recollection," "motifs of transience," and "an explicit presentation" of interconnectedness of public and private histories (2000: 33). These four factors foregrounding the historicity of the text are especially effective in Banks's novels when combined with the writer's employment of fairly traditional genre forms such as Bildungsroman, Künstlerroman, or the family saga, whose various combinations can be noticed, for example, in *The Crow Road*, *The Steep Approach to Garbadale*, *Espedair Street*, *Whit*, or *Canal Dreams*. It not only anchors Banks's works in a specific social-historical milieu (dates, places, important historical events) but also allows the author to present the characters' individual lives as connected with or resulting from the operation of greater historical forces, i.e. political, cultural, or economic phenomena. Furthermore, such a choice of genre enables Banks, first, to show history as a process by accentuating the passage of time in the life of several generations or in the character's life over several decades, and, second, to organize the acts of memory into the chain of flashbacks within the novel's present, which is a recognizable trait of his narrative technique.

At the same time, Banks's novels often reveal an almost postmodernist awareness of history and fiction being human creations (see Hutcheon 1996: 5), which makes the author and his characters investigate and challenge the reliability of narrative accounts and historical givens. Isis, the protagonist of *Whit*, discovers that the establishment of her religious community is a consequence of her grandfather's falsified account of his own past and prophetic visions, which became the foundations of the Luskentyrian doctrine contained in the holy book of *Orthography*. Similarly, Frances in *The Wasp Factory* discovers herself to be a victim of her father's mendacious account of past events, which gave rise to the girl's twisted worldview and her imprisonment on the island. By controlling the past, Angus Cauldhame, like Salvador Whit, influences other people's present, which, using Isis Whit's expression, has been "constructed on a base more dangerous and shifting than [. . .] sands" (1996: 423).

In his fiction, Banks is also preoccupied with the question of storytelling, out of which, predictably, arises the problem of narratorial bias and the partiality of narrative accounts (see Malcolm 2000: 182). It becomes particularly striking in the case of the character trio in *The Crow Road*. The father, Kenneth, teaches his son Prentice the history of the land and its peoples, explaining to the boy the mysteries of the world through stories of both realism and fantasy. He is also the first person to clarify to Prentice the difference between story and history, treating the first as invention and the second as an objective account of facts and events. Over the course of the novel, Prentice, a student of History at the University of Glasgow, is drawn into a single-handed investigation of the disappearance of his uncle Rory several years before. He eventually finds the clues to fill the blank pages of his family history in Rory's unfinished novel, whose plot is based on the presumed murder of Rory's sister, Fiona, by her aristocratic husband. Pondering over the reliability of Rory's account, Prentice admits: "Of course, all I had was Rory's fictionalized word for any of it" (2005: 414), and his friend Ashley ironizes: "Prentice, have you been reading crime novels instead of your history books?" (416). In the end, the story turns into history, as Rory's fictionalized revelations lead to at least partial explanation of the family secrets. However, the fact that Rory's novel has the same title as the one in which he is a character turns Banks's *The Crow Road* into a self-conscious meditation on the limits of the narrative and the textuality of the text itself.

According to Randall Stevenson, the origins of the self-questioning postmodern idiom which resulted, among other things, in the appearance of the self-conscious novel of history, can be found in the cataclysm of World War II, whose atrocities were exerting a long-lasting influence on the British literary imagination as late as the 1980s and 1990s (cf. Finney 2006: 19). Stevenson gives the examples of William Boyd, J. L. Carr, Maureen Duffy, Sebastian Faulks, and D. M. Thomas as novelists who explore the profound emotional impact of wartime experience – both World War II and the Great War – on human memory and morality (2006: 441-5). In doing so, the authors of the new historical novel use precise settings and atmosphere of the era and combine them with naturalistic descriptions of the horrors of the trenches (like Pat Barker in *Regeneration* and Sebastian Faulks in *Birdsong*), or the moral shock of the Holocaust (like Thomas in *The White Hotel*, McEwan in *The Black Dogs*, or Faulks in *Charlotte Gray*).

Although none of Banks's novels fictionalizes the hostilities of either of the two World Wars, the violence and cruelty of war, its lasting influence on human memory and geographical landscape, as well as its moral ramifications are a frequent subject of his fiction. Frank in *The Wasp Factory* builds his fantasy world on an island whose landscape still bears traces of World War II such as bunkers and unexploded German shells. Hisako in *Canal Dreams* is an heir of the culture which perished in the Hiroshima blast in 1945, and the memory of past violence constantly recurs and takes its toll on the heroine's life in the present. In *Complicity*, the characters live traumatized by more recent wars, the conflict in the Falklands and the first Gulf War, whose horrors are beyond their capacity of verbal description.

Cairns Craig argues that "war, real or imagined, is the background against which all of [Banks's] characters develop, attempting to understand the relationship between the virtues of peaceful civilization and the violence on which it seems to be based" (2002: 11). The author's exploration of the relationship between peace and violence and its moral implications, as well as his preoccupation with the perennial conflict between civilization and savagery simmering within the boundaries of human society make him an heir to a generation of post-war writers such as William Golding, Iris Murdoch, and Anthony Burgess, who were more concerned, as Stevenson puts it, with the "primal or 'Adamic' moral implications of recent history, rather than its actual events" (2006: 417). *Lord of the Flies* is noted as a major influence on *The Wasp Factory* (see Craig 2002: 10); however, the tradition of Golding's allegorical apocalyptic writing is perhaps best represented in *A Song of Stone*. Set in an unnamed country at an unspecified moment in history, the novel presents a society destroyed by a civil war which has regressed to primitive power relationships. The post-apocalyptic dystopia of *A Song of Stone*, in which the land is ransacked and the last traces of civilization succumb to the forces of barbarity, echoes the works of Angela Carter (e.g. *Heroes and Villains, The Passion of New Eve*) and Doris Lessing's *Memoirs of a Survivor*. Its inspirations can also be traced back to the post-apocalyptic science fiction which became especially popular in Britain after World War II and found its major representatives in such authors as John Wyndham, Brian Aldiss, and J. G. Ballard.

The post-war legacy in Banks's writing can also be seen in his extensive use of the Gothic convention, whose old "fears and dreams" were activated with a new force in the second half of the twentieth century by the horrors brought about by Hiroshima and the Holocaust (Stevenson 2006: 454). It is significant that one of the writers who influenced Banks most strongly is Mervyn Peake, the author of the *Gormenghast* trilogy, a gloomy neo-Gothic fantasy which appeared shortly after the war and might have been at least partly inspired by Peake's wartime experience and by his visit to Bergen-Belsen after the camp's liberation (cf. Stevenson 2006: 454). Peake's works seem to have been particularly influential in providing Banks with the imaginative vision of the castle as a habitable labyrinth which repeatedly appears in Banks's novels, e.g. *Walking on Glass*, *The Crow Road*, or *Espedair Street* (cf. Sage 1996: 22-3). Banks's fiction reveals many typical Gothic props: doubling narratives and doubles reminiscent of the divided self in the fictions of Stevenson and Hogg; gloomy landscapes and forlorn castles, with the typically national specificity of the isolated island locus and self-enforced seclusion; madness and savagery; occult rituals and supernatural powers; child and animal abuse; as well as the traditionally Gothic element of terror as filtered through the Scottish Calvinist consciousness (see Petrie 2004: 119-25 and Sage 1996: 20-37; cf. Punter 1999: 101-18, and Colebrook 2010: 1-6). All these have contributed to Iain Banks's appointment into the ranks of contemporary Scottish Gothic writers, alongside John Burnside, James Robertson, Elspeth Barker, John Herdman, and Alice Thompson, to name a few.

The use of the macabre and grotesque elements of the Gothic convention, which contemporary British writers, and Banks among them, often combine with such genres as the historical and crime novel, serves the purpose, as Suzanne Keen argues, of disclosing the sins of the past and bringing to the surface the memory of crimes against the conquered and the discriminated (2006: 178-9). In the case of Scottish literature, this retrospective orientation of the Gothic mode evokes, as Alan Bold claims, "a Grim Presence, the ghostly persistence of the frequently disastrous Scottish past" (qtd. in Punter 1999: 103). The combination of genuine and absolute Gothic terror and the motif of past traumas haunting the characters' present is perhaps most effectively employed in Banks's *Complicity*, with its alternating narratives of gruesome murders, repressed memories, and ritualistic revenge. A similar sinister equation can be found in *The Wasp Factory*, which dramatizes "both an individual tragedy and the tragedy of Scotland itself, imprisoned in a madhouse of militarism, racked by its own violence, and reduced to finding meanings in the rituals of its own torment," as Murray Pittock observes (2008: 117).

The question of war and violence in Banks's fiction is often explored through the prism of gender identity and sexual transgressions, which constitutes yet another of the author's main preoccupations. Many female characters in the Banksian universe take on characteristics traditionally associated with masculinity, which helps the author to foreground the connection between gender and power relationships (Craig 2002: 15):

> The wrecked landscapes that litter Banks's novels are the outcome of an ideology of power and oppression within which masculinity has been defined. For Banks, sexual transgression can be simply another form of the will to power, of the individual's assertion of himself – or herself – on the world, or it can be the opening of alternative forms of sexual identity that will help us escape the wreckage of the past. (Craig 2002: 18).

The assertion of one's own power through gender transgression can be seen in the character of the lieutenant in *A Song of Stone*, who adopts male behaviour and wears male clothes to secure the loyalty of her soldiers and follow her own private agenda in a world where the only law is survival. Kathryn in *The Business* realizes that her rise in the world of capitalism has been largely due to "the freedom always to behave selfishly, or always to do what a man would do in the circumstances" (2000: 389). On the other hand, Hisako Onoda in *Canal Dreams*, who is first submitted to male domination through gang rape, turns into a ruthless warrior and executes a bloody revenge on her tormentors, thereby exorcising the demon of the past which is her Hiroshima heritage. Similarly, Isis Whit, oppressed and manipulated by the male members of her family, resorts to scheming and lies, like her grandfather Salvador and her brother Allan, only to prevent their materialistic self-serving plans and restore balance to her endangered religious community.

"In Banks's novels," writes Craig, "gender is not a destiny but a social convention which can be transferred between the sexes" (2002: 16), so alongside androgynous femininity, the author also shows emasculated or failing masculinity. Abel, the protagonist of *A Song of Stone*, is gradually ousted from the positions of master of the castle and his lover's sexual partner by the female lieutenant. His execution, when he is tied to the great trophy gun named the Lieutenant's Prick in homage to the domineering woman, is an apt metaphor for the reconfigured gender relationships in the novel. In *Complicity*, Cameron's affair with Yvonne establishes the female lover as the dominant side of the relationship, and the journalist often finds himself on the receiving end of her violent fantasies. Similarly, Angus in *The Wasp Factory* falls prey to the determined and dominant womanhood of his wife Agnes, who leaves him burdened with her new-born illegitimate child and limping for the rest of his life. Moreover, Angus's son Eric reveals a traditionally female propensity for nurture and sensitivity to human suffering, while his daughter, Frances, believing herself to be a castrated boy, engages in a violent fantasy of compensatory masculinity, ruthlessly killing children and animals.

It is not surprising, therefore, that it is Banks's female characters – defying deep-rooted gender stereotypes – who become the hero(in)es of exotic and magical travel narratives as pilgrims, seafarers, and visitors to alien lands, a role which has been considered a traditionally male domain in literature. Isis, a member of a religious sect from the north of Scotland, embarks on a quest to London in search of her missing cousin Morag. Her journey south allows Banks to present the playful clash of the divine and the quotidian, as Gaia-Marie Isis Saraswati Minerva Mirza Whit of Luskentyre descends among the mortals and roams unholy lands like a goddess of ancient myths and a pícaro rolled into one. In *The Business*, on the other hand, Banks reworks the utopian motif of Shangri-La, having the protagonist, Kathryn Telman, an executive in the very material and materialist world of tough rules and big money, travel to Thulahn, an almost forgotten mythical kingdom in the Himalayas, to become its long-awaited queen. In *Canal Dreams*, Japanese cellist Hisako Onoda, the posthumous child of the soldier father and a member of a traumatized nation, goes on a sea voyage around the world which takes her to Panama. But it is also a journey through dreams and back into the past, in the course of which the heroine will come to fully acknowledge her previously rejected Japanese identity.

Banks's interest in travel narratives, combining elements of the heroic quest, religious pilgrimage, and a journey to imaginary lands, owes as much to Egyptian mythology, classical epics, and fairy tales as to the Anglo-Scottish literary tradition which goes back to More's *Utopia*, Bunyan's *The Pilgrim's Progress*, the travel writing of Defoe and Swift, Smollett's picaresque, Scott's border romances, R. L. Stevenson's novels of sea adventure, James Hilton's *Lost Horizon*, and George Mackay Brown's mythic Orcadian narratives. On the other hand, it can also be regarded as a reflection of a more recent trend in British writing whose authors imaginatively blend travel, holiday, and literature. This interest could already be noticed in Fowles's *The Magus* and Durrell's *The Alexandria Quartet*, but, as Randall Stevenson observes, it grew in importance by the end of the twentieth century alongside the phenomenon of new mass travel. The literature of the period saw a revival of the travelogue in the works of Bruce Chatwin, Hilary Mantel, Esther Freud, or Lisa St. Aubin de Terán, while remote places, history, and magic realism – present also in Banks's *The Business* and *Canal Dreams* – have been successfully intertwined in the novels of Louis de Bernières and Salman Rushdie (Stevenson 2006: 479-82, 496-7).

The form of a journey embarked on by a female character, which involves foreign or exotic locations and encounters with alien cultures through the mediation of dream, magic, and myth, gives Banks an opportunity to present the heroine's path to self-discovery, which often turns into a study of otherness. This kind of writing has a long tradition in English literature. It developed in response to the rise of the British Empire and its flourishing colonial power in the nineteenth and early twentieth centuries, and included such writers as Rudyard Kipling, Joseph Conrad, E. M. Forster, and Graham Greene (one of Banks's favourite writers). Colonization is also present in *Canal Dreams* and *The Business*, where it assumes, however, its twentieth-century facets of cultural and economic imperialism, i.e. Americanization linked with the hegemony of the English language and corporate multinational businesses.

In *Canal Dreams*, Hisako distances herself from her native Japanese culture and its violent past, and instead she builds her identity in relation to the Other of the English-speaking Western world with its classical music, literature, and codes of behaviour. However, the suppressed Same of her Japaneseness begins to resurface through dreams full of violence and national symbolism on a sea voyage to the mythical centre of the world. The violent encounter with the American agents leads to Hisako's ultimate rediscovery of her Japanese identity, which is emphasized by her final course towards the rising sun. In *The Business*, the heroine travels from the modern cosmopolitan world of big money and super-advanced communications technology to the impoverished mountainous kingdom of Thulahn in Asia. The encounter with the oriental Other, whose Buddhist cheerfulness and values of fellowship and moral integrity constitute a stark contrast to the acquisitive materialism and sustained progress of Kathryn's own world, makes the heroine redefine her life objectives. Banks's vision of Thulahn is to a large extent informed with the romantic image of the exotic East predominant in Western thought which was rather vocally criticized by Edward Said in his *Orientalism*. However, it may also be a conscious strategy on the writer's part, as it half-heartedly implies that a woman's only way of salvation in the male-oriented world is through an escape into a romanticized illusory world of utopia or a fairy tale.

***

These are the main recurring characteristics of Banks's fiction, his principal concerns and motifs, and some of the lines along which his mainstream novels can be placed in the context of contemporary British and, specifically, Scottish fiction. These traits, however, do not in themselves satisfy a critical appraisal of Banks's output, the sheer diversity of which, even if one dismisses the science fiction, is astounding.

This book, entitled *Mediating the World in the Novels of Iain Banks: The Paradigms of Fiction*, constitutes an attempt at developing a critical paradigm capable of uniting the extremely versatile mainstream production of this Scottish writer. Apart from the analyses of Banks's better known and artistically challenging texts like *The Wasp Factory* or *The Bridge*, which have been frequently discussed by scholars, critical attention is also given to novels which have been largely or altogether neglected in the academic studies of Banks's work, presumably because of their employment of popular genre pattern and the resultant lack of artistic complexity. The corpus for the book comprises all fifteen mainstream novels, from *The Wasp Factory* (1984), the first novel in the *oeuvre*, to *The Quarry* (2013), Banks's last work of the kind.

In order to give justice to the extremely eclectic novelistic production of Iain Banks, the analysis of his novels contained in the present
study employs diverse interpretative "tools," fusing elements of various
methodologies. The analytical basis is provided by the structural-
semiotic methodology of the Tartu-Moscow Semiotic School (Y. Lotman, B. Uspienski, W. Toporow), and especially the concept of the
semiosphere (*sensu* Lotman), defined as the space of signs oriented from
a particular perspective, with its internal division into the centre and the
periphery.[8] This method is supplemented by a mythographic approach
based on the studies of mythology and comparative religion of Sir James
George Frazer, Joseph Campbell, and Mircea Eliade, along with the psychological and gender specific theories of the heroic journey propounded
by Susan Lichtman and Carol Gilligan. In the case of Banks's postmodern texts, the structural-semiotic analysis has been additionally supplemented with relevant elements of the theories of Brian McHale, Hilary
P. Dannenberg, as well as Andrzej Zgorzelski's theory of supragenological types in literature.

---

8   The methodology was formulated in the following studies: Łotman, J. (1984).
     Struktura tekstu artystycznego. Warszawa: PIW, 298-403; Lotman, Y. (1990).
     Universe of the Mind: A Semiotic Theory of Culture. London, New York: I. B.
     Tauris & Co. Ltd. Publishers, 123-213; Łotman, J. (1977). "Zagadnienia prze-
     strzeni artystycznej w prozie Gogola." *Semiotyka kultury*. Ed. E. Janus, M. R.
     Mayenowa, S. Żółkiewski. Warszawa: PIW, 213-65. Moreover, the semiotic
     theses concerning the concepts of history and myth were expounded in:
     Uspienski, B. (1998). "Percepcja czasu jako problem semiotyczny," 19-51,
     and Łotman, J. and Uspienski, B. (1998). "Mit-imię-kultura," 63-80, pu-
     blished in *Historia i semiotyka*. Gdańsk: Słowo/Obraz terytoria. See also To-
     porow, W. (1977). "O kosmologicznych źródłach wczesnohistorycznych opi-
     sów" in E. Janus *et al.* (eds.), 103-46.

CHAPTER 1

Ab Ovo
The Wasp Factory as the Blueprint of Fictional Worlds

When *The Wasp Factory* appeared in 1984 under the imprint of Macmillan, it was after four years of its maturation period interrupted by occasional rejections from several publishing houses. Already at its appearance the novel generated a great deal of controversy, its reception ranging from utter delight to deep indignation. Hailed as "a minor masterpiece" (*Punch*) and "a truly remarkable novel" (*Daily Telegraph*), *The Wasp Factory* was praised for its "curdling power and originality" (*Cosmopolitan*), "control and assurance" (*The Financial Times*) as well as "brilliant dialogue," and "cruel humour" (*Irish Times*). At the same time the novel was condemned as "no masterpiece and one of the most disagreeable pieces of reading" (*Sunday Telegraph*), "just the lurid literary equivalent of a video nasty" (*Sunday Express*), and "a joke, meant to fool literary London into respect for rubbish" (*The Times*). "You can't laugh and throw up at the same time," went a line in *The Factory*'s review in *The Scotsman*, raising the importance of comic relief in disarming the charge of the book's sickening violence. This half-mocking observation seems to draw the very essence from the mass of the contradictory responses: either you like the book or you abhor it, there is no room for half measures.[1]

In spite of – or perhaps thanks to – the initial polemic, three decades after its first publication, *The Wasp Factory* still remains the most popu-

---

[1] The review quotes come from the inside covers from the 1994 Abacus edition of *The Wasp Factory*, which shows that the publishers acknowledged this controversial response to the novel.

lar among Iain Banks's novels, both mainstream and SF. It has been translated into more than twenty languages, including Hebrew, Japanese, and Chinese, it has gone through numerous re-editions as well as stage and radio adaptations, it gave its name to several bands and one record company, and it is now being taught at various university levels as part of the academic curriculum.[2] It is also the most frequently discussed work from Banks's entire *oeuvre*, inviting feminist and psychoanalytical interpretations (with a chief focus on gender construction, sexual transgression, and the question of family relations) as well as studies of the Scottish Gothic, as it features such elements of the stock Gothic repository as madness, revenge, violence, entrapment, family secrets, the presence of a doppelgänger, not to mention explicit allusions to Mary Shelley's *Frankenstein* (cf. Macdonald 2011: 37-41, Colebrook 2010: 217-26, and Davison 2009: 200-14).

The Wasp Factory tells the story of Frank Cauldhame, a sixteen-year-old boy who lives on a nameless island north of Inverness. The first-person narrative covers the sequence of twelve days in the present, when Frank is awaiting the arrival of his mad brother, Eric, recently escaped from a psychiatric hospital. At the same time, the protagonist's account allows numerous flashbacks, which give us an insight into his family's past and his own traumatic experience: at the age of three Frank was savaged by an old bulldog called Saul, which apparently led to the boy's emasculation. Attempting to come to terms and compensate for his embarrassing disability, Frank has murdered three children and turned the island into a gigantic training ground and a barbarian kingdom rolled into one, where he indulges in cruel warfare against birds, rabbits, gerbils, and other representatives of the insular fauna. The end of the novel, however, brings an (un)expected revelation: Frank turns out to be Frances, a girl who was made to believe she was a boy. As part of a scientific experiment conducted by her misogynist father, Frances has been regularly dosed with male hormones, all for the sake of eliminating any female influence on the island.

---

2   In 2007, *The Guardian* listed it among the 50 books which best defined their eras, as a representative of the 1980s, along with such books as *A Brief History of Time*, *Beloved*, and *Midnight's Children*. The history of the novel's writing, publication, and reception can be found in *The Banksoniain* 1: 7-8 and 14: 6-7.

It cannot be denied that Banks's first novel was significant for his career as a writer, not only because it initiated his unceasing popularity but also because it exerted an important influence on his opus ever since. Cairns Craig recognizes the founding role of *The Wasp Factory*, postulating that the work introduces several important issues explored by the author in his later novels, namely war and peace, sexual transgression, rules of the game, and genre subversions (2002: 10).[3] Craig's categorization reveals difficulties with dealing holistically with Banks's creative output, which, coming from an author who is "eclectic, protean, cross-generic" (Gifford 1996: 40), cannot be reduced to one common denominator. Banks's novels are typically discussed in terms of "themes" or "motifs," regardless of their class or category, as those can at least approximately function as a medium of critical unification of Banks's diverse production.[4] By the same token, most critical works, which are still few and far between, usually focus only on selected works, while avoiding more thorough approach. There exist only two works, both published over ten years ago, i.e. *Iain Banks's* Complicity. *A Reader's Guide* (2002) by Cairns Craig, and *Rewriting Scotland* (2002) by Cristie L. March, which offer a relatively comprehensive overview of Banks's mainstream novels. Moreover, as the authors of those works simultaneously set out to include Banks's SF novels in the corpus discussed, the analysis, though undoubtedly perspicacious, is inevitably rather perfunctory.

What, in my view, unites Iain Banks's varied *oeuvre* is the question of *mediation*, either experienced or effected by Banks's characters with reference to the world in which they function. Depending on the nature of mediation, whether it is external or internal to the character, we are able to distinguish its two major facets. One relates to the domain of that

---

3   Alan Riach, similarly, observes: "*The Wasp Factory* presents a handful of key images and ideas which Banks has elaborated and developed in his later fiction, but which underlie all of it" (1996: 69).

4   This can be noticed in Cristie L. March's discussion of Banks's fiction in terms of such dissimilar categories as "disrupting the genres and narrative manipulation," "linguistic manipulations and the realm of the fantastic," "technological ambiguities," or "modern traditions," to give just a few examples. Such an approach is dictated by the subject of March's work, in which Banks appears as a representative of certain trends in modern Scottish fiction and not as the sole focus of study.

which is socially, ideologically, and historically determined, and which is therefore conceived of as impersonal and objective. As such, it forms a foundation on which rests a sense of commonality among the members of a particular group, and which stipulates the rules of their interaction. The other aspect of mediation relates to that which is textually represented as being personal and subjective, and which may either conform to or resist the previously mentioned uniform social or historical perspective.

Used in the first sense, the term *mediation* corresponds with the understanding offered by the theories of culture according to which one cannot access and comprehend a non-representable – unmediated – world, the raw flesh of reality, otherwise than by means of language and various symbolic systems (i.e. mediations) such as religion, mythology, ideologies, and the like, which underlie cultural practice. The picture of the world, despite our illusion to the contrary, is never direct or immediate but it is always a product created through language and other sign systems operating within a particular culture in which a person is immersed and whose precepts and prejudices he or she shares. From the point of view of cultural semiotics, as Stuart Hall observes, the material world stands in opposition to the symbolic world of signs, responsible for the generation of meanings:

> [W]e must not confuse the material world, where things and people exist, and the symbolic practices and processes through which representation, meaning and language operate. Constructivists do not deny the existence of the material world. However, it is not the material world which conveys meaning: it is the language system or whatever system we are using to represent our concepts. [. . .] It is social actors who use the conceptual systems of their culture and the linguistic and other representational systems to construct meaning, to make the world meaningful and to communicate about that world meaningfully to others. (qtd. in Oswell 2006: 14)

This sense of mediation, which denotes the cultural mechanisms responsible for the world's representation, and thus also for our perception of the world, relies on the concept of *semiosis*, which can be defined as the cultural production and interpretation of signs. Semiosis involves the establishing of a model of reality which underlies a particular culture and influences all types of interaction – social, political, or artistic – within its limits. Such a world model is produced at the centre of the *semiosphere*, i.e. the semiotic space of a particular culture (*sensu* Yuri Lotman), and represents the ideal image of the culture in question, generated by the metalanguage of its self-description. According to Lotman, this idealized image, projected onto the whole semiotic space and dictating the norms (linguistic, political, social, moral, artistic, etc.) of the centre, is recognized by the contemporary people as "reality" (1990: 129). It thus represents the symbolic systems which shape (or mediate) the people's perception of the world. On the other hand, such an idealized image produced at the centre often contradicts the semiotic reality on the periphery of the semiotic space. The phenomena taking place on the periphery may appear culturally insignificant from the perspective of the metastructure, as they lie as if "outside the domain of [governing] semiotics" (129). However, the periphery often constitutes a transgressive space: it calls into question the apparent unity of a particular culture, as well as the validity of its mediation systems.

At the same time, semiosis presupposes our familiarity with the codes (media) by means of which reality is "written," so that we can read and interpret its various representations. According to Lotman, every semiotic act is an act of communication whose participants (an addresser and an addressee) must have some prior semiotic experience. They must be able to recognize the codes (or languages) operating in their culture and be familiar with the means by which the messages can be decoded – they must therefore be "'immersed in semiotic space'" (1990: 123). Moreover, a "presumption of semioticity" must be made on the part of the participants, namely the intuitive and conscious acceptance of "the possibility that structures may be significant" (128). Every act of semiotic communication (even thinking) is at the same time an act of translation, as a result of which a message in a foreign language is expressed in terms of our own. This signifies that every process of meaning attribution is simultaneously the process of meaning (re)creation, which implies a degree of automatization of semiosis on the one hand, and its epistemologically subjective or personalized (whether collective-*we* or individual-*I*) character on the other (127, 140).

Connected with the subjective (and communicative) nature of semiosis is another sense of *mediation*, which comes from the field of narratology, and which can be defined, in the simplest way, as the "process of transforming and transmitting the story in the discourse" (Hühn 2009: 1). Peter Hühn notices:

The basic constellation constituting a narrative can be described as a communicative act (narration) through which happenings – including existents
such as characters, places, circumstances, etc., within the storyworld (fictional or factual) – are *represented* and thus *mediated* through a given verbal, visual or audio-visual sign system. This representation is inevitably
shaped – in the selection, combination, perspectivization, interpretation,
evaluation of elements – by the agency producing it, ultimately the author
who, however, may delegate *mediation*, particularly in fictional narration,
to some intermediary agent or agents, typically a narrator (*narrator's
voice*) and, at a lower level, to one or more characters (*character's perspective*) located within the happenings (in verbal texts) and, according to
some theorists, to the recording apparatus and/or voice-over (in film).
(2009: 1, emphasis added)

In this respect, narration in the literary text is treated as an act of communication between the author/narrator/character and the reader, where
the signified – the various aspects of the fictional reality – finds its representation on the verbal level, through a choice of words linked in se-
quences, communicated from a particular standpoint and revealing personal bias, as it is filtered through the medium of the narrator's/character's mind.

This aspect of *mediation* takes us to the problem of the point of view
in the artistic text, which Lotman defines as the relation of the system to
its subject, i.e. a consciousness which is capable of generating such a
system (on the linguistic, ideological, or other levels), and which can be
reconstructed in the text. In its most general, as Lotman claims, the artistic model reconstructs the world-picture for a particular consciousness –
in other words, it models the relationship between the individual and the
world (Łotman 1984: 376). By comparison with a culture, the model of
reality which emerges from the text can be treated as a space of signs, a
semiosphere, oriented from the point of view of a particular consciousness, for example, the narrator or the dominant character(s), whose perception determines the language of spatial modelling and the axiology of
its binary categories such as same/other, familiar/unfamiliar,
safe/dangerous, orderly/chaotic, cultured/barbarous, and the like.

Lotman further postulates that the point of view becomes discernible
as an element of the artistic structure the moment it is changed for, and
thus juxtaposed against, another point of view within the narrative (376)
– a differently oriented semiosphere. Because, as Lotman notices elsewhere, the artistic text, by its very nature, models an infinite object (i.e.

reality) by limited textual means (300), quite often only one point of view in the text is presented *in extenso*, while others, more or less marginal but reconstructible, introduce tensions and clashes which help to foreground or verify the major perspective in the text. Such a collision of individual mediations of reality – different ways of its semioticization, and thus distinct world-pictures (or semiospheres) – is also a test of their respective validity, and it contributes to the overall meaning of the text. The "truth" is thus *negotiated* through the clash of two (or more) mediations, the term "negotiation" offering yet another sense of *mediation*, implying a neutral intercession which reconciles two conflicting sides and helps them reach a middle ground between the extremes.

In Banks's novels, one can find all the above-mentioned senses of mediation, which are not independent of each other but rather operate dialectically. His characters' perception of the world is often shaped (or even manipulated) by various symbolic systems, such as religion, social hierarchies, political ideologies, or deep-entrenched patterns of social behaviour, involving culturally established notions of class, gender, and family relationships. On the other hand, Banks's characters are always the centres of perception, and it is their perspective which is adopted whether they are the narrators of their own stories or focalizers. The acts of perception, (mis)interpretation, and verbalization of meanings as related to the outside world – i.e. the process of its semioticization – are delegated to the character and filtered through his or her subjective point of view, which orients and gives significance to the space of signs. Semiosis is therefore affected not only by the characters' immersion in a particular semiosphere, which determines particular modes of decoding on their part. It is also influenced by the characters' idiosyncratic position vis-à-vis the world, their affinity with the centre or with the periphery of the semiosphere, which makes them either endorse or question and redefine the world-picture mediated by the prevailing systems of thought, belief, or social milieu. In the end, in the case of Banks's characters, mediation is always tantamount to negotiation, as it involves a continuous interplay between the consensual external world and the characters' idiosyncratically mediated visions of reality, their own semiospheres.

The observable complexities in the characters' relationship with the world, as modelled by particular texts (see the reference to Lotman

1984: 376 above), make it possible to group the novels in question into four distinct types with different spatial dominants, each type being representative of a different case of world-modelling, in which the process of cultural or individual mediation takes place with relation to a distinct fictional world. The first model comprises those texts in which mediation involves the conflict between the private/subjective/inner space and the public/objective/external reality, while the characters are caught between the constantly shifting layers of the mimetic and non-mimetic. In the second model, the process of mediation is effected with reference to the broadly understood community and its historical narratives, which is here inextricably linked with the space of Scotland. The third model combines the poetics of myth with the space of the road which is subordinated to the outlook of travelling female protagonists. The last, fourth, model shows the characters' entrapment, both physical and psychological, and their worldmaking or escapist efforts within different manifestations of apocalyptic and post-apocalyptic space.[5] Interestingly, *The Wasp Factory* stands apart from the body of Banks's other works, not because it does not match the spatial models described above but because it contains them all. It fits into every category and at the same time it is too comprehensive to be included in one place and not elsewhere. Being the first and all-embracing work, *The Wasp Factory* constitutes a category *sui generis*, a point of departure for Banks's fiction, simultaneously distinct and present in all spatial models variously used and developed in his later novels. It can thus be considered the crucible of fictional worlds.

It does not mean, of course, that those later texts indiscriminately replicate the spatial paradigms established by the primary text. More accurately, those paradigms represent the four directions of world-modelling (i.e. four types of relationship between the individual and the world) outlined by the blueprint, although the world models are inevita-

---

5   It is not the inherent quality of a space *per se* but the way it functions with reference to the governing consciousness of the novel's universe that determines the former's allocation to a particular spatial dominant. This discrepancy between space as detached from the character and space as being contingent on the character is noticeable for example in Banks's literary representations of Scotland: on the one hand, Scotland provides a fertile ground for a family history and personal growth, on the other, it appears in the capacity of a post-apocalyptic wasteland.

bly prone to a certain degree of mutability in the course of the author's prolific and extremely "whimsical" literary production. However, before we proceed to the derivative literary universes, it is necessary to take a closer look at the parent universe, which spurred their existence, *The Wasp Factory* itself, and its quadruple spatial line-up.

1.1. Model ONE: Alternative Worlds[6]

In his seminal work *Scottish Literature: Character and Influence* (1919), which has long constituted the springboard for all later approaches to writing by Scots, G. Gregory Smith addresses the question of the "true Scottish note," i.e. the distinctive quality of Scottish literature which forms the basis of its national idiosyncrasy. This quality, according to Smith, reveals itself, as much in literature as in all forms of Scottish life

---

6   My understanding of the term "alternative" comes close to the one proposed by James Walters in his study *Alternative Worlds in Hollywood Cinema* (2008), according to which alternative worlds can be divided into the follow- ing three types: "(i) Imagined Worlds, where a character dreams or halluci- nates a world away from the world they inhabit, (ii) Potential Worlds, where a character visits an alternative version – or alternative versions – of the world they inhabit, and (iii) Other Worlds, where a character travels to a different world entirely from the world they inhabit" (10-11). The predominant catego- ry of alternative worlds in Banks's fiction corresponds to Walters's Imagined Worlds, as they appear in such mentally-generated manifestations as dreams, delusions, paranoia, as escapist, wish-fulfilment, compensatory fantasies, or as the worlds of fiction and imagination (*The Wasp Factory, Walking on Glass, The Bridge*). The Potential Worlds type finds its equivalent in the many worlds of *Transition*, with the characters' flitting between different versions of Earth in the multiverse. However, it is also present in *The Wasp Factory*, in Frank's mediation between the island and the mainland, which represent the violent microcosm of the equally violent greater world, and in Graham Park's temporary existence in a more romantic and idealized version of the hostile and degenerate world he knows from experience. The Earths of *Walking on Glass*, namely the dying planet of the third narrative and the London of the 1980s in the first and second narratives, can also be placed in this category. Last but not least, the Other Worlds type applies not only to Frank's physical transfer between the world of his creation, in which he is god and ruler, and the public semiosphere, in which officially he does not exist, but also to the fantastic transfers of Steven Grout and Quiss and Ajayi between ontologically disparate planets and dimensions.

and culture, in the combination of opposites, a phenomenon to which Smith applies the term *Caledonian antisyzygy*:[7]

> [It is] a reflection of the contrasts which the Scot shows at every turn, in his political and ecclesiastical history, in his polemical restlessness, in his adaptability, which is another way of saying that he has made allowance for new conditions, in his practical judgement which is the admission that two sides of the matter have been considered. If therefore Scottish history and life are, as an old northern writer said of something else, "varied with a clean contrair spirit," we need not be surprised to find that in his literature the Scot presents two aspects which appear contradictory. Oxymoron was ever the bravest figure, and we must not forget that disorderly order is order after all. (4-5)

The term, which nowadays serves as a handy tool for explaining "the occurrence of practically any kind of contradiction, incongruence or irreconcilability in Scottish literary representation," as Schoene-Harwood claims, was originally intended as a medium for describing the perennial duality of the realist and fantastic modes in Scottish fiction (1999: 133). The "'actuality,' 'grip of fact,' 'sense of detail,' 'realism'" (Smith 1919: 5) on the one hand, and "the confusion of the senses, [. . .] the fun of things thrown topsy-turvy, [. . .] the horns of elfland and the voices of the mountains" (19) on the other hand, are precisely what Smith identifies, rather poetically, as two contrary moods of "the Scottish Muse:"

> Does any other man combine so strangely the severe and tender in his character, or forgo the victory of the most relentless logic at the sudden bidding of sentiment or superstition? Does literature anywhere, of this small compass, show such a mixture of contraries as his in outlook, subject, and method; real life and romance, every day fact and the supernatural, things holy and things profane, gentle and simple, convention and "cantrip," thistles and thistledown? We see this constitutional liking for

---

7   In his article "Constructing the Contemporary Self: the Works of Iain Banks," Tim Middleton disambiguates the notion of anti-syzygy, providing evidence that it should rather be termed as syzygy: "*Syzygy* means the pairing and yoking together of opposites; but a pairing in which the two opposed terms or things retain distinctiveness; as in, the OED suggests, copulation. [. . .] Thus it concerns opposition and conjunction; difference and similarity brought together into a yoked unity but always remaining distinct. Antisyzygy must be the opposite of syzygy – meaning not yoked; not paired; not opposed; or perhaps meaning a yoking in which things actually do merge and meld; in which distinctiveness and identity are lost" (1995: 20).

contrasts [. . .] There is more in the Scottish antithesis of the real and the fantastic than is to be explained by the familiar rules of rhetoric. The sudden jostling of contraries seems to preclude any relationship by literary suggestion. The one invades the other without warning. They are 'polar twins' [. . .] of the Scottish Muse. (20)

What Smith (rather haplessly) calls "the antithesis of the real and the fantastic" (20), perhaps needs rephrasing into the less terminologically wobbly antithesis of the mimetic and antimimetic (*sensu* Zgorzelski 2004: 32), with their distinct mechanisms of world-modelling. Nevertheless, the implicit supragenological "mixture of contraries" invading each other "without warning" undoubtedly finds its manifestation in the construction of the world in *The Wasp Factory* and the other novels of the same model.[8]

---

8   The dichotomous quality of Frank Cauldhame's world has been emphasized in several critical works devoted to Banks's first mainstream novel. For example, Alan MacGillivray observes that the protagonist lives his life "wrapped up in a fantasy world of cruel war-games" created by himself in a "landscape inspired by action fantasies of the Sword and Sorcery genre," while parallel to it "there is the real world that he has to find a place within" (2001: 21-2). Victor Sage likewise draws attention to the imaginary quality of Frank's own world, which the latter is "compelled [. . .] to invent [. . .] from scratch," and which in the end takes the form of a barbarian microcosm, with Frank being at once a god and a warrior at the centre of his "little world of death and retribution" (1996: 25-6). For Berthold Schoene-Harwood, Frank forgoes "the real world" in order "to re-imagine it as a narcissistic reflection of who he would like to be;" therefore, the island he inhabits turns into "his self-aggrandizing fantasy" (2000: 110). Andrew M. Butler, on the other hand, postulates that Banks mixes "an apparently realistic account of a dysfunctional family with fantastical tales of members of that family all of which can be explained away as the flights of fantasy of Frank" (1999: 25), which points to the character's propensity for projecting figments of his wild imagination onto the phenomenological world of everyday life in Scotland. In the Preface to the 25th anniversary edition of *The Wasp Factory*, Banks discusses the influence which his earlier attempts at writing science fiction exerted on the novel's universe, which may cast additional light on the work's supragenological dichotomy: "In the end I went for something that kept me closer to my by-then comfort zone: a first-person narrative set on a remote Scottish nearly-island told by a normality-challenged teenager with severe violence issues allowed me to treat my story as something resembling science fiction. The island could be envisaged as a planet, Frank, the protagonist, almost as an alien. With an

The Wasp Factory presents the reader with two contiguous worlds governed by distinct organizing criteria, which in turn depend on Frank's position as a semioticizing consciousness with reference to each of those worlds. On one level, the locale for Frank's experiences is provided by the space of the Scottish Highlands, which constitute a part, even if peripheral, of the larger semiosphere of the British Isles. The trivia of everyday life mentioned in Frank's account reveal his familiarity with the British culture of the 1980s, whose manifestations can be noticed in the popularity of punk music, electronic games, ubiquitous BBC documentaries, or the programmes of John Peel, a well-known English DJ from BBC Radio 1. This mimetic picture of the dominant semiosphere, which emerges from Frank's narration, is pitted against an alternative world model of Frank's own devising – a macabre imaginary order, with himself standing at its centre, which materializes on a solitary island on the outskirts of the United Kingdom, and which subverts the ontological and axiological norms of the outside world.

The clash between the two world models, juxtaposed along the horizontal axis, is underscored by their physical separation. Between the mainland, which represents the dominant culture, and the island, which reveals Frank's subjective mediation, there is a clear topographical boundary – a narrow isthmus, which at high tide turns the island into a completely isolated enclave, enabling the teenager to pursue his violent fantasies in relative safety. At the same time, the island is permanently connected with the mainland by a bridge, where, as Frank himself admits, his kingdom practically ends (1994: 28), and which allows him and his father to communicate with the nearby town of Porteneil. However, the bridge also facilitates inland communication, and thus occasional visits from the outsiders, such as old Mrs Clamp, who does shopping and cooks for the Cauldhames, and the local policeman Diggs, who represents the moral and legal norms of the dominant semiosphere, and therefore poses a possible threat to the perpetuation of Frank's alternative vision.

The simultaneous connection and separation of the mainland and the island, which translates into their distinct organizations, while allowing a

---

internal grimace I gave in to the write-what-you-know school but torqued with a dose of Skiffy hyperbole, mining my own past for exaggerateable experiences" (2009b: x-xi).

degree of exchange between the two, calls to mind the concept of the boundary as understood by Lotman:

> One of the primary mechanisms of semiotic individuation is the boundary, and the boundary can be defined as the outer limit of a first-person form. This space is 'ours', 'my own', [. . .] 'cultured', 'safe', 'harmoniously organized', and so on. By contrast, 'their space' is 'other', 'hostile', 'dangerous', 'chaotic'.
>
> Every culture begins by dividing the world into 'its own' internal space and 'their' external space. [. . .] The boundary may separate the living from the dead, settled peoples from the nomadic ones, the town from the plains; it may be a state frontier, or a social, national, confessional, or any other kind of frontier. (1990: 131)

The same mechanism of binary categorization of space underlies Frank's attitude, which is revealed in his frequent comments on the danger, unpredictability, and limitlessness of the external world, as opposed to the safety and control which he is allowed within the limits of the island, which is communicated in the following passage:

> I like to get away from the island now and again. Not too far; I still like to be able to see it if possible, but it is good to remove oneself sometimes and get a sense of perspective from a little further away. Of course, I know how small a piece of land it is; I'm not a fool. I know the size of the planet and just how miniscule is that part of it I know. I've watched too much television and seen too many nature and travel programmes not to appreciate how limited my own knowledge is in terms of first-hand experience of other places; but I don't want to go further afield, I don't need to travel or see foreign climes or know different people. I know who I am and I know my limitations. I restrict my horizons for my own good reasons; fear – oh, yes, I admit it – and a need for reassurance and safety in a world which just so happened to treat me very cruelly at an age before I had any real chance of affecting it. (136)

If Frank's mind is a medium through which the model of reality is reconstructed and conveyed, the protagonist's emasculation, which he sees as a consequence of his childhood encounter with the vicious outside world, becomes the decisive factor influencing his division of the world into the internal space of the island, which is synonymous with his "I," and therefore defined as his own, safe, limited, and reassuring, and the external space of the mainland, which is different, distant, unlimited, hostile, and not his own. What is also significant, Frank seems to project a correspondence between his victimized body, whose integrity was once disturbed by external forces, and the space of the island, whose boundaries are occasionally breached by strangers, either people from the mainland or the forces of nature, both being representative of the open and limitless outside world.

As a result, in Frank's polarized imaginary, the island functions as a rampart to be protected against intrusion from outside by all possible means. The domain is guarded by the Sacrifice Poles (sticks with animal heads on top), which he regularly checks, equips with fresh carcasses, and anoints with his own blood and body substances. He treats them as his first line of defence, his "early-warning system and deterrent rolled into one; infected, potent things which looked out from the island, warding off" (10). Frank's belief in the effectiveness of the Poles may seem naïve and childish from the perspective of the mainland; however, within the laws governing his alternative private semiotic space, the Poles are supposed to frighten off any potential intruder, as they speak of the lethal power possessed by the one who set them there. At the same time, they represent Frank's psychological control of the island, as the boy maintains a peculiar telepathic communication with the Poles, scanning the perimeter of his dominion through their eyes. Being the "dead sentries" and the "extensions" of their master (20), responding to his mental call, the Poles also function as guardians of Frank's psychological landscape, which is projected onto the physical space of the island, whereby the boy and the land become one entity.

The centre of the insular semiosphere, which is oriented from the point of view of the governing consciousness, i.e. Frank, creates its own language of self-description, which, in consequence, mediates the alternative world model. The island comes to reflect Frank's inner space, ruled by gender prejudice and the complex of his own sexual incapacity, its order being based on the male fantasy of domination, which Frank executes through killing and revenge, for want of another outlet. He therefore becomes "a small image of the ruthless soldier-hero," "a fierce and noble presence in [his] lands, a crippled warrior, fallen prince" (183), doing rounds of the island armed to the teeth and ready to stand up against his enemies, of which the greatest ones are Women and the Sea: "Women because they are weak and stupid and live in the shadow of men and are nothing compared to them, and the Sea because it has always frustrated me, destroying what I have built, washing away what I have left, wiping clean the marks I have made" (43). Believing in his own causative power, which definitely surpasses the abilities of an average man, Frank treats himself as a formidable opponent to the powerful primordial element of water, regarding their respective influences on the world as comparable in their gravity. This delusional discourse, based on the categories of hostility, struggle for power, and self-isolation, can be read in Frank's angry remark after he finds a bottle washed ashore by the tide: "[The Sea] still tried me out now and again, though, and I was in no mood to allow even the slightest encroachment on my territory" (47).

While the borders of the insular realm are in need of constant vigilance and protection against the inimical forces from the outside world, the inner world of the Poles and the battlefield is completely subject to the whim of its only master, Frank. Every semiotic act performed within the boundaries of this world is meant to "boost [his] ego, restore [his] pride and give [him] pleasure" (63), which makes Frank at the same time the producer and interpreter of signs in the process of self-addressed semiosis. A similar mechanism can be observed with reference to the land. Turned into a map of Frank's personal experience, where every landmark corresponds to some important event in his life, the landscape undergoes a private semiosis, in which both the signs and their meanings are of Frank's own making, and where reality is mediated into its alternative by means of language, which is visible, for example, in the symbolical names. And so the Snake Park is where Frank put an adder into the prosthetic leg of his cousin Blyth, due to which the latter died; the Bomb Circle refers to the jagged rocks left on the beach after the explosion of the bomb which killed Frank's younger brother, Paul; and the Skull Grounds mark the area where Frank excavated the skull of Old Saul, to give but a few examples.

By the same token, like an epic hero or a medieval knight, Frank gives names to his weapons and tools (e.g. Stoutstroke to a shovel, the Black Destroyer to his favourite catapult, or Gravel to his bike), at the same time noting sourly that his father "doesn't attach the same importance to them" (16) as he does. This emphasizes the semiotic rift between the world of everyday experience and Frank's gory fantasy, whose codes may have much in common with those operating in the Sword and Sorcery novels, which Frank reads avidly. Similarly, the incongruity between the two orders, with their respective normative and "alternative" morality, emerges repetitively from Frank's own observations, for example, when he fumes inwardly addressing the question from his father about his son's weird activities: "Of course I was out killing things. How the hell am I supposed to get heads and bodies for the Poles and the Bunker if I don't kill things? There just aren't enough natural deaths. You can't explain that sort of thing to people though" (13). Another time, he observes resignedly that he will have to postpone a War on account of his brother's comeback, as it is not "a good idea to start another War only to have to abandon it in the middle of things and *start dealing with the real world*" (24, emphasis added), which stresses the incompatibility of the dominant and private semiospheres.

A similar mechanism of personal mediation of reality applies to the beliefs and rituals that Frank perpetuates in order to reaffirm his hold on the world of make-believe (cf. March 2002: 91), which can be noticed on the occasion of christening a new catapult. A tiny part of Frank, which adopts a rationalistic perspective of the dominant culture with its contempt for superstition, watches the ceremony "with some amusement" (63), noticing its absurdity. However, the rest of Frank, who interprets the world through the mediating systems of his alternative semiosphere (violent ideology, religion, the poetics of exomimetic genres), believes in the effectiveness of such semiotic practices. "It gave me power, it made me part of what I own and where I am. It makes me feel good" (63), he declares, emphasizing the importance of fantasy and magic as world-modelling factors on the island.

The boundary between the two semiospheres, however, is not only a medium of separation but also a place of increased semiotic dynamism.[9] Quoting Lotman:

---

9   The boundary between the mainland and the island is a space of tensions, a no
     man's land in which the laws of both semiospheres are frequently undermined
     or collide. One such place is the Rabbit Grounds, where Frank collects tro-
     phies for the Sacrifice Poles, which are not really on the island but are rather
     situated on the mainland, between the "large branch of the creek and the town
     dump" (27). The space between the two worlds is difficult to control, and the
     rabbits there are "cunning little bastards" (28), so Frank needs all the strength
     he can muster. There are things there which both surpass the imagination of
     Frank and contradict the laws of probability recognized in the public semio-
     sphere. This can be noticed in the scene in which Frank confronts a giant

The notion of boundary is an ambivalent one: it both separates and unites. It is always the boundary of something and so belongs to both frontier cultures, to both contiguous semiospheres. The boundary is bilingual and polylingual. The boundary is a mechanism for translating texts of an alien semiotics into 'our' language, it is the place where what is 'external' is transformed into what is 'internal', it is a filtering membrane which so transforms foreign texts that they become part of the semiosphere's internal semiotics while still retaining their own characteristics. (1990: 136-7)

Such a semiotic "translation" also takes place in *The Wasp Factory*. Frank is aware of the difference between the world projected by his own wild imagination and the outside ("real") world with its laws and codes of behaviour, because he is a boundary character who lives in both worlds, though on completely different terms. When leaving the island, he adjusts to the rules governing the public space: he doesn't "bother people" so that they don't bother him (13), even though they may perceive him as eccentric or slightly crazy. It becomes especially noticeable when Frank, who regularly kills animals on the island and has killed three kids of his family, pleads with his deranged brother, Eric, recently escaped from a mental institution in Glasgow, not to resort to his old crazy ways, i.e. burning dogs and scaring children, for which he was certified and committed. "Don't do anything to antagonize people, you know? People can be awful sensitive . . ." (18), he admonishes, which shows his awareness of the fact that the transgression of public norms and taboos, which can be accommodated within the limits of his kingdom, brings about punishment in the public semiosphere, where they underlie social intercourse. Moreover, because Frank was not registered at birth (at least not as a boy), he is situated outside the semiotics of the official culture – he has no identity within the public semiosphere other than the one devised by Angus, which presupposes a manipulation of signs but nonetheless conforms to the laws of the outside world. The people from Porteneil, with the sole exception of Jamie, consider Frank Angus Cauldhame's nephew, instead of son, and whenever Diggs the policeman appears on the island, Frank keeps a low profile so as not to get his father into trouble. At the same time, the "texts" from outside which enter Frank's private space are resemioticized in accordance with

---

buck, a formidable enemy: "It was crazy! This wasn't Africa! It was a rabbit, not a lion! What the hell was happening there?" (32).

the norms dictated by its semiotic centre. It is particularly striking in the case of various objects, purchased in Porteneil or found in the rubbish dump or as flotsam, which acquire a different function in Frank's alternative universe and become the weapons of war or instruments of torture. Shuttlecocks become missiles inside which guinea pigs and gerbils are hurled into the sea, weedkiller mixed with sugar turns into explosive, and plastic drawers for keeping screws, washers, nails and hooks become coffins, each holding the body of a dead wasp which had crawled through the Factory's treacherous corridors.

Frank's creation of an alternative universe with himself as the commanding consciousness calls to mind Cristopher Nash's observation about a category of alternative worlds in fiction which he labels "epistemological" systems, and whose traits are "determined by the horizons of perception of their inhabitants" (1987: 67). According to Nash, the texts which present the epistemological systems focus on the "thematic *topoi* associated with signs, manifestations, sensations and memory," which places the problem of world-creation "in the nature of observation and 'registration'" (69). In Frank's case, the projection of the alternative world is connected with, to use Nash's phrase, the "[d]efects in [his] ways of apprehending things" (69), his restricted horizons, which makes him misinterpret the signs given by his body and labour under the misconception of his own emasculation. Therefore, instead of seeing himself for what he is (i.e. a woman), Frank sees himself for what he is not (i.e. a man), ending up on the boundary between the sexes.

Frank's lack of knowledge (or perhaps memory) of the suppression of his female identity by Angus and its replacement with the false identity of the castrated boy leads to the protagonist's own projection of a number of pseudo-identities, which are meant to compensate for his alleged childhood loss and enable his self-expression as a male. He becomes a soldier, a prince, a demigod, and a demiurge, each of which involves the production of its own epistemological dimension – and so the space of the island is perceived by Frank as a war-torn battlefield, a kingdom, or a land of godlike creation and destruction. Considered from this perspective, the island is a metamorphic space which assumes the form of ever different alternative worlds, depending on the workings of the mediating consciousness. Frank's distorted mind "shapes" the environment provoking changes as much in the landscape as in the lives of those who step onto his territory, thereby making themselves subject to its governing laws.

Believing himself unable to create life, Frank precipitates death, which is "[his] own conception," and an attempt "to construct life" (183), and thus yet another element of his subjective creative vision, which prevails despite the fact that (or perhaps because) he knows he is committing acts considered criminal from the society's point of view. It starts in childhood with his first and premeditated murder of cousin Blyth, after the latter incinerates Frank and Eric's rabbits with a home-made flame-thrower. "I hadn't said anything to anybody," recounts the protagonist. "I was wise in my childishness even then, at the tender age of five, when most children are forever telling their parents and friends that they hate them and they wish they were dead. I kept quiet" (38). A similar situation takes place when Frank is contemplating the murder of his brother Paul, whom he considers Saul's incarnation, and the murder of his cousin Esmerelda, who had to be dispatched merely for statistical reasons: "It would be risky, so soon after Paul's death, but I had to do something to even up the balance. I could feel it in my guts, in my bones; I *had* to. [. . .] I had to get rid of *some* woman, tip the scales back in the other direction" (88). In the world mediated by Frank's warped and traumatized psyche, even death must be meted out fairly. Moreover, the murders are easily accommodated within his personal world-picture because the desire to kill comes from the very core of Frank's self.

The duplicity of behaviour, which makes Frank put his intellect at the disposal of his psychopathic sense of justice, allows him to play a game in which he subordinates the normative system of morality to his aberrant personal ideology. After committing the crimes, he puts on an act in compliance with the adults' expectations of him, like "the tortured self-blaming child" he pretends to be after Paul's death: "I even carried out a double-bluff of appearing slightly guilty *for the wrong reasons*, so that adults told me I shouldn't blame myself because I hadn't been able to warn Paul in time. I was brilliant" (88). However, it is after Es-merelda's murder that he takes his acting talent to extremes, feigning shock, stupor, self-flagellation, and even illness, which he later looks back on as "a wonderful, if demanding, week of fun acting" (95). Frank, therefore, uses the established pattern of representation, i.e. the signs of remorse compliant with the moral principles accepted in the public semiosphere, in defiance of their function, turning them into false signs in order to mislead the others, to entertain himself, and to hide his villainous agenda. As such, it can be seen as one more instance of the process of semiotic translation mentioned previously.

Ironically, Frank's subjectively mediated fantasy world, in which he is the centre of creative and military power, eventually turns out to be a direct consequence of a lie concocted by his scientist father, with Frank being merely a pawn in the other's game.[10] Taking advantage of Saul's attack on his three-year-old daughter, Frances, Angus, ignored and disrespected by his go-getting wife, Agnes, decided to put into practice his idea of a life without women (yet another alternative world in the novel), and raised Frances as Frank, dosing her regularly with male hormones.[11] From the lord of the island and a demigod meting out death and punishment, Frank changes into a puppet in someone else's theatre, an ignorant

---

10   And the father's lie has all the appearances of truth – Angus even keeps the fake pair of wax testicles in a jar in his study, just in case Frank should one day confront him about his/her accident.

11   Moreover, Frances's fabricated life seems to have been based on Angus's readings, Gore Vidal's *Myra Breckinridge* and Günter Grass's *The Tin Drum*, with Frances enacting to a considerable extent the lives of two literary characters. Vidal's novel, written in the form of a diary, which offers "a mirrored doubling" of Frank's/Frances's life (Butler 1999: 23), tells the story of a transsexual man Myron Breckinridge who undergoes hormone therapy and becomes a woman, Myra. After numerous excesses, some of them quite violent, in the body of a woman, Myra is transformed back into Myron when a car accident interrupts her regular hormone intake. The other novel, *The Tin Drum*, describes the vicissitudes of Oscar Matzerath, who stops growing at the age of three, which is also the age of Frank's presumed castration (let alone the name of their mothers – Agnes – both being unfaithful to their husbands). Oscar's unreliable account of his former life, developing against the background of war and violence, "allows Grass [. . .] to switch at will between realism and fantasy," leaving the reader with a feeling that Oscar may be delusional (Butler 1999: 23). The two novels, whose artistic universes generate the counterfeit dimension manipulated by Angus, within which his child struggles against her alleged disability, are among the few real presents from Angus to his daughter, as if the father was dropping occasional hints to Frank about her entanglement within the multi-layered fiction. However, Frank refuses to read them as a matter of principle, thereby postponing the moment of recognition of his/her real identity.

and helpless female victim in her father's manipulated version of reality, Angus's own mediated world. The order established by Frank, of the violent kingdom whose existence is validated by the decrees of the sinister oracle, all of a sudden becomes subordinated to the higher order of Angus's gender mystification.

Frank's predicament, which involves the protagonist's passage through several identities before the final and actual identity of a woman is bestowed on her, echoes Hilary P. Dannenberg's discussion of the temporal orchestration of the coincidence plot. *The Wasp Factory* can be considered an example of the past-world plotting, in which a trip back to the past of the narrative world (i.e. Angus's confession of his experiment), involves a revision of the ontological status of Frank's seemingly actual world – that of the castrated boy (see Dannenberg 2008: 50-2). Recognition, as Dannenberg postulates, "evokes an experience in which a character is, often traumatically, transferred from a world that he or she has hitherto considered to be actual and thrust into a new alien version of reality" (52). Like Oedipus, whose discovery of his true origin turns his entire world into a virtual construct, Frank, too, upon the recognition of his "original" sex, finds himself – or rather herself – in a new world, with a new identity. "But I *am* still me; I *am* the same person, with the same memories and the same deeds done, the same (small) achievements, the same (appalling) crimes to *my* name" (182), argues Frances while trying to come to terms with her present status. However, crossing the epistemological boundary between the complacent oblivion of Frank's barbarian fantasy and the disturbing awareness of Angus's scientific fabrication inevitably involves the character's redefinition – from the brave eunuch prince standing at the centre of his misogynist world to the disoriented princess who has suddenly found herself outside her kingdom's semiotic reality, and who must now domesticate the alien semiosphere she has always defied:

> Each of us, in our own personal Factory, may believe we have stumbled down one corridor, and that our fate is sealed and certain (dream or nightmare, humdrum or bizarre, good or bad), but a word, a glance, a slip – anything can change that, alter it entirely, and our marble hall becomes a gutter, or our rat-maze a golden path. [. . .] I thought one door had snicked shut behind me years ago; in fact I was still crawling about the face. *Now* the door closes, and my journey begins. (184)

1.2. Model TWO: Community Worlds

In his work *The Scottish Novel: From Smollett to Spark* (1978), Francis Russell Hart thus describes the concept of community as developed by Scottish writers:

> A noteworthy feature of Scottish fiction is the moral primacy of community, the faith (some would say Calvinist in genesis) that community is the ground of individual worth and a condition of salvation. From Galt to Duncan, it is implied that true community nurtures genuine individuality; from Lockhart, Alexander, and Gunn, a denial of community is a threat to personal integrity. Idolatrous selfhood destroys community; false community, in Spark's *Miss Brodie*, *Girls of Slender Means*, and other novels, fosters only a specious individual discipline or private morality. For Mac Colla's *Albannach*, the only fulfillment is through reassimilation into a traditional community. For Duncan, community is the terrifying fact of interconnectedness, without which one's identity is in doubt. For George Mackay Brown, Calvinism is the historical villain that has temporarily destroyed a communal life rooted in ritual and myth; for Gunn, egoistic rationality has had the same effect. (401-2)

According to Hart, the Scots' long-established attachment to close, small communities results in their distrust of history in its "public guise," as the latter constitutes "an arbitrary, external force that invades the close communities," leading to the collapse of their organic structure. The history regarded as "real" is "local and domestic," it is a source of true wisdom, morality and tradition, fostering personal relationships and a spirit of fellowship (401).[12] If true community is small, then its "close mentality" fears and consequently shrinks from the "cosmopolis, the housing estate, the city" (402). And when the imperial history takes the adventurer far from home, "the exhilaration of the fugitive [. . .] mingles strangely with the strong nostalgia of the homing instinct" (402).[13]

---

12 This discrepancy is probably contingent on Scotland's own turbulent history and the place it occupied for centuries as a part of the British Empire, at once partaking in the latter's official history and trying to maintain its own national integrity.

13 The Scots' affection for the community, in Hart's opinion, has deeply influenced the "characterology of Scottish fiction," in which the domestic configuration, i.e. the space of the family, is the provider of enduring patterns of relationships. The strong and practical matriarch as opposed to the fanatic or quixotic father is a recurring cluster on the family "home front." At the same

The Scottish communal ethos finds its way into the works of John Macmurray, a Scottish philosopher of the mid-twentieth century, who in his famous *Gifford Lectures* (1952-1954) argues that the basis of human societies can be found in the so-called "communal mode," which is itself dependent on heterocentricity. According to Macmurray, the Self is constructed only in relation to the Other, the latter being not an antithetical and antagonistic force but an element necessary for the Self's personal existence (1995: 17). As the Self becomes the Other for another Self while in relation, "the centre of reference for the agent, when he seeks to act rightly, is always the personal Other," claims Macmurray. "To act rightly is then to act for the sake of the Other and not of oneself" (1995: 122). Cairns Craig comments:

> Heterocentricity is, for Macmurray, twofold: it is the fundamental ontological condition of Self in its construction through Otherness, and, at a moral level, it is the condition in which we recognize and act, on a social and personal level, in full acknowledgement of this fundamental nature of our existence as selves, and therefore in awareness of the demands made on us to maintain the fundamentally communal structure of human life. (1999: 90)

In order to achieve a truly communal spirit, both the Self and the community have to overcome their fear of the Other because "fear inhibits action and destroys freedom" (Macmurray 1995: 159). In Macmurray's view, such an ideal community comprised of persons in relation who enjoy personal freedom, disinterested mutual care, and unconditional fearless love, is to be found in the primordial model of the family:

> The family is the original human community and the basis as well as the origin of all subsequent communities. It is therefore the norm of all community, so that any community is a brotherhood. [. . .] What is characteristic of the family is that it is neither established by force nor maintained by a sense of duty. It is established and maintained by natural affection; by a positive motive in its members. They care for one another sufficiently to have no need to fear one another. The normal positive motivation is usually sufficient to dominate the negative motives of self-interest and individualism. (1995: 156)

---

time, the discontinuity between the generations and hence the community itself is often underscored by the conflict between the son and the father who "fail[ed] as an ancestor [. . .] because he is foolish or fanatic" (1978: 403).

Approached from a semiotic perspective, community forms a space of signification oriented from the collective point of view, which presupposes that each individual "I" (the personal semiosphere of the Self) is in dialogue with the "you" (the personal semiosphere of the Other), both being part of the general "we," which stands at the centre and determines the language of semiotic self-description based on the notion of care and affection. As the Self is constituted through an awareness of and active relation with the Other, and not in opposition to it, the boundary between their respective private semiospheres becomes the place of increased activity – a dialogue, "a constant exchange," as Lotman puts it, "a search for a common language," which leads to the emergence of a "creolized" semiotic space, "a new semiosphere in which both parties are included as equals" (1990: 142), and share the same communal perspective.

When considered in the light of the above observations, the Cauldhame family is far from Macmurray's communal ideal, as it fosters neither care nor love, and seriously impedes its members' personal freedom and their mutual understanding. It comprises a number of detached selves – Angus, Frank, Eric, and Frank's estranged mother, Agnes – none of whom enters into dialogue with the Other, but rather lives in a world of their own, forwarding his or her Self(ish) worldview, their subjective mediation of reality. The dysfunctional quality seems to be manifest in the very surname, Cauldhame, which in Scottish English means "cold home," and is clearly representative of the lack of warmth and tenderness in their family relationships (Walker 1996: 344). Both Frank and Eric suffer from emotional coldness and rejection in childhood, which is a direct consequence of the adults' egoism and social incapacity – that is their inability to become persons in relation. The axis of the Cauldhame family is the father, obsessed with his scientific experiments and personal quirks, unable to maintain a lasting relationship with the women appearing in his life. The mother, on the other hand, is physically absent, but her haunting presence as a disruptive (not nurturing) force makes itself felt in the bodily and psychological wounds sustained by the other family members.

Because the element of the feminine, incarnate in his wives – the beloved dead Mary and the desired wayward Agnes, represents an uncontrollable and subversive force, "an alien world antithetical to [male] Self," using Craig's words (1999: 90), it produces fear in Angus, which makes the communication between the two impossible. Angus's fearful Self rejects the dialogue with the Other, closing himself instead in an ideal world determined by the language of patriarchy and gender prejudice. The female and the maternal become the domains of the excluded, non-existent in the semiotic reality created by Angus's misogynist Self.[14] His fear of the female Other and the desire to remove its influence from the island leads Angus to conduct his "little experiment" with Frances's sexuality: he forces upon his daughter a false male Self, affecting the way in which she semioticizes the surrounding world. Immersed in a version of reality of Angus's authorship, in which all signs are interpreted in accordance with the chauvinist ideology of the semiotic centre, which Frank endorses as naturally hers, the girl is brought up not in relation to but against her female identity, which thwarts the dialogue between Self and Other. As a result, she learns to treat women as "weak, stupid and [living] in the shadow of men" (43), perceiving the opposite (or in fact her own) sex in terms of gender stereotypes.

By disturbing the healthy development of Frances's female Self, the father has separated his daughter from the outside world, provoking her detachment from the community, which she threatens as a deranged castrate. "I represent a crime" (13), says Frank about her father's illegal concealment of his child's birth seventeen years ago. However, this short comment in its (un)intended double meaning may also refer to Frank's own criminal behaviour, which she ultimately considers to be the direct consequence of her father's ruthless manipulation of her sex:

> Perhaps it was because I thought I had had all that really mattered in the world, the whole reason – and means – for our continuance as a species, stolen from me before I even knew its value. Perhaps I murdered for revenge in each case, jealously exacting – through the only potency at my command – a toll from those who passed within my range; my peers who each would otherwise have grown into the one thing I could never become: an adult. (183)

---

14   The female influence is apparently connected with a woman's still active sexuality, because Angus seems to have nothing against Mrs Clamp, who does shopping for him and is a frequent guest on the island. It is confirmed by Frank, who says that Mrs Clamp is old and sexless, and therefore not her enemy in a way young and sexy women are.

As a result of the experiment, Frank becomes bound to the limits of the island and anonymous life, away from humanity in all possible meanings of the word. She hides in her secluded world, shying away from empathy and commitment, simply because her Self has been formed not in relation but in opposition to the communal Other.[15] Frank lives in fear of the Other, guarding the island through the Sacrifice Poles and the cache system of weapons and traps located round the island, and avoiding any meaningful contact with the outside world. Her identity is formed in relation with the inner space, the inside, which is spatialized into the island, as opposed to the communal mainland – "I'm *me* and here's *here*," she asserts (16, emphasis added). She is therefore an example of a divided self, which, as Craig would phrase it, has "taken itself *out* of dialogue" with the Other, and will not acknowledge their mutual dependence (1999: 112).[16]

"Believing in my great hurt, my literal cutting off from society's mainland, it seems to me that I took life in a sense too seriously, and the lives of others, for the same reason, too lightly," Frank confesses in the end. "The murders were my own conception; my sex. The Factory was my attempt to construct life, to replace the involvement which otherwise I did not want" (183). The character's isolation from the community and her focus on the detached egocentric existence, without any intention to go beyond her own Self and reach to the Other, i.e. to become an Agent, reflects Frank's rejection of heterocentricity, which, according to Macmurray, always leads to dualism in the perception of the world:

> This egocentricity creates a dualism [. . .]. For the relation to the Other constitutes both oneself and the other; the intention to maintain, in general,

---

15   At one point Frank confesses: "Not going to school, and having to pretend I didn't live on the island all the time, has meant that I didn't grow up with anybody of my own age" (51-2), which proves that Angus's single decision has caused his daughter's alienation on many levels.

16   Frank's self-focus and reliance on her individual point of view, much like her father's preoccupation with his scientific ideas and dehumanizing experiments, echoes Descartes's claim "Cogito ergo sum," which gives primacy to a reasoning consciousness, largely detached from the world of social relationships. As such Frank represents the egocentric stance which is rejected by Macmurray because it positions "the Self as an individual in isolation" (1969: 31), whereas the Self, rather than being a thinker, should be an agent in relation with other acting selves. See Craig 2004b: 269-72.

the relations that unite the members in a community is a necessary intention. [. . .] So for the negative modes of apperception the world divides into
two worlds; an actual world which does not answer to our demands, and
refuses to satisfy us, and another world, an ideal world which we can imagine, which does. Whether that gives rise to a contemplative or to a pragmatic mode of morality depends upon which of the two worlds is thought
as the *real* world, which, that is to say, is taken as being for the sake of the
other. Similarly, the self becomes two selves, for each of which one of these two worlds is 'the Other'. There is a spiritual life and a material self
with a bodily life. The positive apperception, through its heterocentricity,
escapes this dualism. (1995: 123)

By the same token, Frank's egocentricity, which develops as a result of
her stunted sexual development, leads to a dualism in the way she perceives and deals with reality.[17] Considering herself a flawed male, she
forsakes the outside world, in which, in her own view, she cannot find a
fulfilment which she could enjoy if she was "a tall slim man, strong and
determined and making his way in the world, assured and purposeful"
(48).[18] Instead, as Macmurray would put it, Frank "seek[s] to realize
[herself] in the private, isolated world of [her] own thoughts and feelings
and imaginings" (1995: 123-4). She focuses on her idealized insular mi-

---

17   The refusal of heterocentricity can be seen in Frank's confession that he often
      thinks of himself as a political unit, a country or a city, in which different ide-
      as clash as if they came from "lots of different people inside [his] brain." A
      part of him, claims Frank, has always felt guilty about killing the three chil-
      dren, the same part is also guilty about killing the rabbits. There is yet another
      part which is scornful of the naming ceremony, considering it a piece of
      mumbo-jumbo. However, Frank dismisses those "voices," likening them to
      "an opposition party in a parliament, or a critical press; acting as a conscience
      and a brake, but not in real power and unable to assume it" (62-3). The ideo-
      logical push and pull in Frank's mind seems to be reflective of the tension be-
      tween his violent egocentric Self and the communal Other, the latent aware-
      ness of which comes in the form of such feelings as remorse.
18   Interestingly enough, Frank's formative process seems to be effected in rela-
      tion to the spectacular progress of her elder brother on the mainland (Schoene-
      Harwood 1999: 137). "I had the Skull, I had the Factory, and I had a vicarious
      feeling of manly satisfaction in the brilliant performance of Eric on the outside
      as, for my part, I slowly made myself unchallenged lord of the island and the
      lands about it" (139), reveals Frank while describing her and Eric's separate
      ways of development.

croworld, the world of her violent imagination, which becomes a form of her self-expression.

In order to maintain her male integrity while thinking of herself as sexually disabled, Frank intensifies the semioticity of her masculine behaviour, for example, through the multiplication of symbolical acts and rituals: construction of weapons, warfare, giving idiosyncratic names to parts of the island, and resisting the presence of her arch-enemies – Women and the Sea. Simultaneously, she judges her own body, which only partly yields to the secret hormone therapy, according to the standards of the masculine ideal which she will never attain, and thus as faulty. "I want to look dark and menacing, the way I ought to look, the way I should look, the way I might have looked if I hadn't had my little accident," complains Frank, but instead, she is "too fat," "chubby," "[s]trong and fit but still too plump" (20), her secondary sexual features persistently surfacing despite the hormonal diet. She therefore experiences a hiatus between the unrelenting biological reality and the semiotic norms of the mediating system of patriarchal ideology, according to which each sex has not only clearly defined modes of behaviour based on submission and domination but also the prescribed types of appearance. "Looking at me, you'd never guess I'd killed three people. It isn't fair" (20), communicates the protagonist, pointing to the fact that her body fails as a sign of masculinity, even though her semiotic acts comply with the gender stereotypes she lives by.

While Angus separates Frances from her true identity by a cruel hoax, which results in his daughter's self-isolation and thus drastically limits her experience of life ("I've learned to live with my disability, and learned to live without other people" [13]), he also becomes her source of knowledge about the outside world, which the latter cannot empirically know – Angus, therefore, becomes her mediator, an imposing one. However, even in teaching Angus rejects dialogue with the Other, producing misleading or manipulative messages, thus impeding his communication with Frank, who reminisces: "For *years* I believed Pathos was one of the Three Musketeers, Fellatio was a character in *Hamlet*, Vitreous a town in China, and that the Irish peasants had to tread the peat to make Guinness" (14). No wonder, when Angus finally sends a meaningful message by giving Frank the books containing signals which may allow her to discover her true identity, Frank refuses to consider them, as a matter of principle. Moreover, the father imposes patterns of thought, Angus's knowledge being literally (and tyrannically) inscribed into the space of the house. All over the place, there are little stickers attached to various pieces of furniture, vessels, or even to the leaves of plants, giving appropriate measurements of the objects they are stuck to. Angus's obsession with the "height, length, breadth, area and volume of just about every part in the house" (11), all of them expressed in Imperial measurements, becomes in Frank's childhood a medium of control and subjugation in the father-son relationship:

> When I was a child I once went round the house tearing all the stickers off; I was belted and sent to my room for two days. Later my father decided it would be useful and character-forming for me to know all the measurements as well as he did, so I had to sit for hours with the Measurement Book (a huge loose-leaf thing with all the information on the little stickers carefully recorded according to room and category of object), or go round the house with a jotter, making my own notes. This was all in addition to the usual lessons my father gave me on mathematics and history and so on. It didn't leave much time for going out to play, and I resented it a great deal. (11-2)

The stickers, all the time attached to almost every object in their house, mediate everyday reality through numbers, remaining a sign, if only nominal, of the domination of Angus's world-picture despite his weakness epitomized in his limp and the growing strength of Frank (cf. Schoene-Harwood 1999: 141-2). Metaphorically, the imposition of Imperial measurements on the domestic space may imply the manipulation of the Scottish national consciousness, which operates within the version of reality mediated by the Anglocentric systems of signs. In the same way, Frank's childhood rebellion may be interpreted as an attempt of the Scottish mind to shake off the oppressive imperialist symbolism of the dominant English culture, which Frank, accustomed to its constant presence in his surroundings, only weakly resists as a teenager, suggesting she and Angus "should have gone metric years ago" (12).

The same function of the mediation system which distorts the reality lying beneath can be noticed in Angus and Frank's use of language. Representative of the cultural centre of the British Isles with its idealized norms which do not correspond to the semiotic practice of the Scottish peripheries, the English language contributes to Frank's further alienation from the local community. Just as the Imperial measurements used by the father are a sign of English idiosyncrasy in the perception of length, breadth, and weight, opposing the international metric system, Standard English and Received Pronunciation, which Angus teaches to his "son," underlines Frank's incongruity among her fellow countrymen. It can be noticed in Frank's disquisition of the Union Streets, when her language fails to enter into relation with the vernacular idiom of her audience – Jamie the dwarf and the girl met in the bar. It thus shows its individualist and impersonal nature, in contrast to the community-making Scottish dialect. The two Scots, who are unable to understand the contents of Frank's speech, related after all to their national history and the Act of Union of 1707, seem to talk over Frank's head while she is trying to "*communicate*" in her intoxicated state with the representatives of the Scottish community:

> The girl looked at Jamie. 'Dud he say sumhin er?'
> 'I thought he was just clearing his throat,' said Jamie.
> 'Ah thought he said sumhin aboot bananas.'
> '*Bananas*?' Jamie said incredulously, looking at the girl.
> 'Naw,' she said, looking at me and shaking her head. 'Right enough.'
> So much for communication, I thought. Obviously both so drunk they didn't even understand correctly spoken English. (81)

Because the history of the nation is related in the metalanguage of the British centre, Frank's account contradicts the very idea of the union, the political equivalent of Selves in relation. Instead it gives primacy to the English version of the historical event, which involves the appropriation of the past by the governing idiom, while virtually neglecting the participation of the Scottish Other.[19] A similar use of language as a mediation system occurs in the case of Angus's creation of his daughter's male Self, which is defined by the masculine version of her proper name – Francis Leslie, which obliterates the feminine Frances Lesley, along with everything the latter represent. Last but not least, it is also language which offers a means by which domestic history – a kind of history,

---

19   Frank's isolationist attitude, if considered in national terms, makes him a metaphor of the imagined community (*sensu* Benedict Anderson), ruled by one ideology operating on the principles of exclusion and hostility, limited to a particular space – a Self without any intention to communicate with other Selves and become shaped through dialogue with Otherness. On the concept of the nation as a Self in relation see Craig 2004a: 251.

which is, paradoxically, considered one of the foundations of Scottish communal identity (see Hart 1978: 401) – is recounted and committed to memory by Angus, who is a liar and misogynist. Frank's predicament calls to mind Richard Grusin's opinion about the levels of mediation: "The logic of remediation insists that there was never a past prior to mediation; all mediations are remediations, in that mediation of the real is always a mediation of another mediation" (qtd. in Erll and Rigney 2009: 4). On the basis of what Angus "has chosen to let slip" (104-5), Frank, who has no memory of what happened when she was three, semioticizes a version of the past in which her mother, Agnes, is the source of all evils. Frank comes to "hate her name, the idea of her" (66). Therefore the family history, or rather the father's historical account, instead of consolidating the ties between the family members, becomes the disruptive force. Unsurprisingly, towards the end of the novel, Frank begins to doubt her father's identity and the official version of past events: "Angus. Agnes. I only had his word for anything that happened" (173).[20]

The disturbed relationship between the Self and Other in the Cauldhame family translates into spatial dynamics, as the two inhabitants of the island split the family house into their respective spheres of influence, where the other party is not granted access. The first such example is Angus's study, containing the laboratory on which Frank launches repeated attacks whenever her father leaves the house.[21] Smelling of am-

---

20 As a result of Angus's lie concerning Frank's past, the protagonist, according to Carol Margaret Davison, "suffers, like Scotland in the 1980s, [. . .] from a deep lack of self-knowledge and self-respect," hating the most what she is, namely a woman. In Davison's opinion, *The Wasp Factory* can be read as a national allegory which "presents a psychological portrait [. . .] of a patriarchally obsessed Scotland" (2009: 204). Along with the idea of Agnes, Frank also hates and rejects her own "'maternal' side," changing into an "aggressive, militaristic machine," and comes to represent "an emasculated Scotland" after the Act of Union, willingly playing its role in the "British male militaristic establishment" (204).

21 The motifs of a laboratory and of an artificial creature which appear in the story of Angus's scientific experiment conducted on his own child (he fashions a girl into a boy with monstrous inclinations) clearly allude to the most famous literary example of man supplanting God in the act of creation, namely Mary Shelley's *Frankenstein* (cf. MacGillivray 2001: 29). The connection is signalled already by the protagonist's evocative name: Frank/Frances echoes "Frankenstein," the latter being a bit of a misnomer as it has been increas-

monia, cluttered with papers, bottles, test tubes, and pieces of chemical apparatus, it is reflective of the father's egocentric life, which involves the scientific manipulation of the Other and his refusal of dialogue in order to maintain, as Frank observes, "what he sees as the correct father-son relationship" (16). The other locus that Angus has in his exclusive power is the cellar housing bales of cordite, a smokeless propellant which the Cauldhames use as a firelighter. Frank, who makes his own explosives for combat with animals and dam mining, cannot lay his hands on the material because the basement is watched over and regularly inspected by Angus. The latter seems to be rather nervous about this "time bomb" in the bowels of the house, but he refuses to throw it away, which Frank interprets as his father's "own little superstition [. . .] about a link with the past, or an evil demon we have lurking, a symbol for all our family misdeeds; waiting, perhaps, one day, to surprise us" (53). At the end of the novel, Frank's crazy brother, Eric, tries to set fire to the cordite and blow the house up, which is only prevented by Frank himself. The lurking evil demon in the basement is thus representative of the secret festering in the bosom of the family, which in the end blows into the faces of both Angus and his abused daughter when Frank's hitherto suppressed femininity comes to light.

As for Frank, his exclusive domain is the loft, where he keeps the Wasp Factory, a supernatural authority validating the existence of his violent kingdom, which, being a projection of Frank's alienated non-dialogic Self, contradicts the very idea of community. The devious prophesying mechanism, made up of the face of a giant old clock and a system of twelve glass tunnels, each containing a different death trap for a wasp crawling in its entrails, serves Frank's egocentric behaviour and justifies the acts of cruelty and manipulation in his dealings with other people and the natural world. His father is excluded from the loft because of his physical disability, which allows Frank to pursue in secret

---

ingly applied both to the creator and the monster from Shelley's work. Moreover, the locus of the island in the North Sea which is Angus's home is deceptively similar to that of the desolate Orkney island where Victor Frankenstein worked on the female monster whom he finally destroyed in the making (see Shelley 1999: 125-6). Angus's study likewise is a reflection of Victor's laboratory, the two doing research in much the same field, which is underlined early in the novel by Frank's observation: "My father is a doctor of chemistry, or perhaps biochemistry – I'm not sure" (14). Cf. MacGillivray 2001: 29.

his weird anti-social practices and perpetuate the irrational ideology through which he approaches the life on the island (10). Moreover, as Carol Margaret Davison claims, the Factory becomes a significant element in the novel's reading as a national allegory

> serving as both a superb Gothic sign of *memento mori* and a rich, multifaceted and even paradoxical symbol that taps a vein deep in the Scottish psyche. It yokes together at least three distinct concepts: the idea of (factory) labour, Scotland's primary role within the British Union since its establishment; Calvinism, a superstitious religious philosophy that underscores the idea of choosing one's own fate; and revenge on the 'wasps' (white Anglo-Saxon Protestants) whose patriarchal and militaristic worldview [. . .] is seen to have infected Scotland. (2009: 203-4)

In this light, the opposition of the loft and the laboratory acquires an additional meaning. The former, being filled with the signs of the traumatized national psyche, represents the nation's entanglement in the rituals of violence resulting from the separation from its own history and the need to assert its compromised masculinity. The latter, being the place in which the alleged emasculation of the nation was concocted, embodies the ruthless power or English bulldogs (viz. Old Saul), over the superstitious and irrational Scottish "barbarians" (cf. Davison 2009: 203-4).[22]

---

22   The vertical division of the domestic space in *The Wasp Factory* calls to mind Gaston Bachelard's discussion of the space of the house in his *Poetics of Space* (1958). According to Bachelard, people think about the house either as having an upward dynamic, which "appeals to our consciousness of verticality," or they picture the house as "a concentrated being," appealing to "our consciousness of centrality" (Bachelard 1994: 17). Bachelard perceives verticality as determined by the dichotomy of the attic and the cellar, and he ascribes the two places the qualities of rationality and irrationality respectively (17-8). Bachelard's "psychology of the house" (17), dividing its space into the rational upper part and the irrational lower part, corresponds with the split between Frank's mind, tied to the loft, and his feminine lower body, metaphorically imprisoned in the cellar. Ironically, in *The Wasp Factory* the "irrational" cellar remains under the control of the rationalistic father. Angus uses scientific means (hormones) to suppress his daughter's womanhood and her reproductive ability, which are centred in her womb. Similarly, he resorts to scientific methods in order to control the conditions in the basement, where the cordite is stored, constantly checking the level of humidity and other factors. The loft, on the contrary, is the place where the scientist father has no access. It therefore becomes the space of irrationality, housing the divination device

The spheres of power described above are a testimony to the rift existing among the members of the Cauldhame family, who, instead of true affection and understanding, are bound by the uncomfortable secret and an ongoing tension sustained by some surreptitious rules of engagement. Mutual stealing up and subterfuge as well as blatant lies keep the father and "son" apart in their "respective citadels" (128), which can be treated as the spatial representation of their egos. The only genuine affection within the Cauldhame family – the bond of mutual brotherly love – exists between Eric and Frank. Amidst the Cauldhames' emotional wasteland, Frank's recollection of her childhood intimacy with Eric stands out as the solitary bright beacon, their brotherly rapport being free of the duplicitous calculation inscribed in Frank's attitude towards her younger brother, Paul. When Eric comes to the island for holidays, his sensitivity and unaffected ways temporarily restore the grim place to normalcy, turning it into a paradise of happiness and true communal spirit, based on love, empathy, and fellowship. Eric is also the only person whose suffering Frank feels acutely as if it was her own (137-8).

Before his nervous breakdown, Eric is a perfect example of a person in relation, his sensitivity to the feelings of others and his ability to interact successfully within the community being emphasized several times in his younger sibling's account. Even in the world of "fabulous opportunities and awful dangers" (138), which encourages egocentric attitudes, self-love, and thus self-alienation, Eric remains a representative of communal values, which he upholds with utter selflessness. "Eric wrote me letters telling me how he was getting on, he called up and spoke to me and my father, and he would make me laugh then on the phone, the way a clever adult can, even though you might not want to let them. He never let me feel that he had totally abandoned me or the island" (139), Frank reminisces wistfully. Moreover, the communal ethos can be noticed in Eric's disinterestedness and the fact that he is drawn more to the nurturant (conventionally regarded as being the domain of women) than purely scientific and ego-boosting (and thus stereotypically male and patriarchal) side of the medical profession (cf. Schoene-Harwood 1999: 138). He voluntarily takes night shifts in the university

---

of the Factory and providing room for Frank's weird religious rites and sacrifices.

hospital and tends to the crippled and deformed children, displaying patience and compassion despite his personal problems and pain.[23]

Eric's psychological disturbance results exactly from a confrontation between his caring disinterested self, for whom the medical profession is first and foremost concerned with healing people and easing their suffering,[24] and the heartless machinery of science and experiment, which treats people as guinea pigs, or sustains the lives of those who are "little else than exhibits to be shown to students by the doctors and consultants" (140). As such, it is a conflict between two distinct worldviews: one based on the idea of mutual affection, nurture, and empathy, and the other forwarding egocentrism, indifference, and private gain over another person's misfortune – in a word, a clash between Macmurray's community and society.[25] As a consequence, Eric becomes a divided self, unable to establish a meaningful contact with others and scaring those he used to protect. He is perceived by his younger sibling as "an amalgam of both his earlier self (but satanically reversed) and a more worldly-

---

23 Eric's purity of heart and innate goodness may destine him to be a Christ-like figure, as he suffers because of the sins (cruelty and indifference) committed by the world towards the weak and helpless. This correspondence is strengthened by the fact that Eric (meaning "always ruler"), is the son of Mary, whose name calls to mind the Virgin Mary, Mater Dolorosa. The etymology of Mary's name, whose possible connections are "sea," "bitterness," but also "love" or "beloved," contain potential references to the suffering of Mary Cauldhame, while also implying the great affection that Angus – God the Father on the island – had for his first wife. Cf. Mcleod and Freedman 1995: 71, 150.

24 As opposed to his brother and father, Eric represents the pragmatic mode of morality pursued by persons who are agents, and for whom the sense of personal unity, according to Macmurray, is "sought in the community of the 'You and I'," while "this community is not merely matter of fact, but also matter of intention" (1995: 27).

25 Eric's madness is put in the perspective of the tension between the communal and the societal in the conversation between Frank and Jamie, the latter pointing out that the maddest people are often the leaders of countries, religious groups, or armies. Frank contests this view, claiming that they must in fact be the only sane ones if they can manipulate others into working or dying for them, while the leaders themselves get all the riches and power. If the "survival of the nastiest," as Jamie puts it, is the Darwinian dynamic of the society, so is, by implication, the death of the most sensitive (112).

wise man, [. . .] a hologram, shattered; with the whole image contained within one spear-like shard, at once splinter and entirety" (139). Paradoxically, Frank's description of Eric fits her own shattered Self, victimized by Angus's experiment. Seen in this light, it is not surprising that Eric in his insanity turns against his father, as Angus represents the ruthless, self-gratifying, and patriarchal facet of science, whose perverse manipulation of his sister Eric may have suspected all along.

Eric's eventual homecoming takes place amidst destruction and chaos, as he sets fire to the surroundings of their family house. His abnormal behaviour, paradoxically, once again restores Frank's world to normal, even if it also means the disintegration of the younger sibling's carefully established imaginary order. Frank is reunited with her true Self, Frances, which entails personal freedom but also her vulnerability in the face of the outside world. Cradling Eric's troubled head in her lap, Frances contemplates her inevitable departure from the island, which used to be *his* kingdom but which now appears to have been *her* prison. "I can't stay here, and I'm frightened of everywhere else. But I suppose I'll have to go" (182), she thinks to herself, anticipating her journey away from an isolated ego towards a true selfhood within the community.

1.3. Model THREE: Mythical Worlds

In his *Autobiography* (1954), one of the most influential works of twentieth-century Scottish literature, a poet Edwin Muir makes a distinction between two concepts – the *story* and the *fable* – which represent the levels between which man's life is enacted. The *story*, which Muir calls "our outward life [that] goes on in its ordinary routine of eating, drinking, sleeping, working, and making money in order to beget sons and daughters who will do the same" (2000: 39), constitutes a temporally arranged, linear sequence, focused on the present and geared towards the future. The *fable*, on the other hand, is an ageless pattern, "some legendary drama which [. . .] has recurred a countless number of times in time" (105), and which provides a mythical foundation for the events of an individual *story*, for the life that is empirically lived from our beginning to our end. Muir asserts: "It is clear that no autobiography can begin with a man's birth, that we extend far beyond any boundary line which we can set for ourselves in the past or the future, and that the life of every man is an endlessly repeated performance of the life of man" (39).

Muir's differentiation between the sequential and progressive nature of the *story*, and the repetitive, cyclical pattern of the *fable*, which underlies and gives purpose to man's ordinary "conscious life" (39), whereby an individual workaday existence is placed within the universal spectrum of myth, echoes the earlier ritualistic approach of J. G. Frazer (himself a Scot) expounded in *The Golden Bough* (1890). Frazer, who studied the nature of the human mind which had developed through belief in magic and religious training, could not help but notice the patterns of thought and association revealing themselves habitually across cultures and epochs (Frazer 1994: xx). He came to the conclusion that there existed "a solid layer of savagery beneath the surface of society, [. . .] unaffected by the superficial changes of religion and culture," and that the rationality of modern society was repeatedly shaken by the deep-entrenched belief in magic and myth (Frazer 1994: 54-5). Frazer, who studied agrarian cultures centred around the cult of the dying and resurrected gods, scandalized the British public with his claim that the pagan calendar tradition was in fact an archaic equivalent of the New Testament motif of the Lamb of God and Christian mystery rituals (Meletinsky 2000: 20; Frazer 1994: xxv-vi). Although he removed the study of Christ's scapegoating from later editions of his work, by pointing to a similarity between many pagan customs and rituals and the principal tenets of the Christian religion, he revealed, as Craig notes, "the illusion of the security of [Western culture's] distance from the 'savage'" (1999: 162).

Frazer's model of society, in which the superstructures of history and rationality rest upon the bedrock of myth, magic, and sacrifice, finds its reflection in the barbarian order created by Frank on the island, complete with its own cosmology and religion, where the protagonist, like a savage from *The Golden Bough*, asserts his hold on the world through the repetition of the violent ritual (cf. Sage 1996: 25). The setting of a nameless island somewhere on the northern outskirts of Scotland enables Banks to present a place which is largely peripheral to the historically determined perspective of the United Kingdom and the greater world of citizenry and politics. Instead, we are faced with a self-contained world built around its own centre, and projecting its own temporal dimension –

being proof positive of Frazer's claim that the human mind is inherently programmed towards violence and superstition.

The model of the world represented by Frank's insular realm is concentric, all the zones from the peripheries to the middle being organized around the *axis mundi* of the Wasp Factory, an oracle sitting in the loft of the Cauldhames' family house. Occupying the highest place in the area – a perfect vantage point for the observation of the island – the Factory itself remains concealed, working its sinister auguries in obscurity, by the altar which stores "the souvenirs of [Frank's] life" (124). This location not only underscores the Factory's domination over the island as an omniscient and overseeing presence but also points to its occult nature, which can be penetrated only by the chosen. The loft housing the Factory becomes at once a reliquary of Frank's past experience and a temple of the vengeful power which holds sway over his present. The Factory constitutes the centre of Frank's personal religion of death and violence, a menacing supernatural authority of Frank's own devising which is mollified into prophesying by means of blood sacrifices.[26] It therefore represents the space of the sacred, and Frank, caught between the Factory and the altar, is both the (only) believer and the chief priest of the subversive creed, and at times also a God, who relishes in the suffering of an insignificant insect crawling through the Factory's many corridors.

Paradoxically, being Frank's own invention, the Factory influences his perception and interpretation of everyday events. "From the smaller to the greater, the patterns always hold true, and the Factory has taught me to watch out for them and respect them" (37), he explains, pointing to the Factory's function in the mediation of the ritualistic world-picture. Moreover, the Factory provides a pseudo-metaphysical underpinning to the order which Frank has established in his realm, as it sanctions his uncompromising violence to weaker beings with a similar kind of violence but effected through its own treacherous mechanism of divination:

---

26 The island in *The Wasp Factory* is reminiscent of the island in *Lord of the Flies*, both being inhabited by barbaric children killing other children and animals. The sinister oracle in the centre of Frank's realm (along with the Sacrifice Poles "crowned" with animal heads) finds its reflection in the disgusting occult centre with the impaled pig's head, representing the demoniac power of Beelzebub (cf. Schoene-Harwood 1999: 142). The motif of man acting as God and of the savagery which underlies civilization is also reminiscent of Joseph Conrad's *Heart of Darkness*.

All our lives are symbols. Everything we do is part of a pattern we have at least some say in. The strong make their own patterns and influence other people's, the weak have their courses mapped out for them. [. . .] The Wasp Factory is part of the pattern because it is part of life and – even more so – part of death. Like life it is complicated, so all the components are there. The reason it can answer questions is because every question is a start looking for an end, and the Factory is about the End – death, no less. (117-18)

The Factory, therefore, becomes the mythical paradigm whose deadly qualities manifest themselves in the entire realm, infecting it with the death and cruelty that prevail at the source. At the same time, all forms of Frank's aggression, e.g. wars, scuffles, or instances of destruction or revenge, are semiotic acts which reaffirm the abiding pattern and the rule of the centre, as violence turns into a form of ritual.[27]

By subjecting the island to the ever-repeated ritual of violence, the centre also mediates the cyclical temporal order of the mythical space, which finds its visual representation in the face of the old clock that forms a part of the Wasp Factory.[28] Built in 1864 (exactly one hundred years before Frank's birth), it used to hang over the door of the Royal Bank of Scotland in Porteneil measuring the passage of official linear

---

27   According to Toporow, the cosmological consciousness places the axis mundi at the centre of the horizontal plane, which connects man and earth with God and heaven. It usually marks the point in space and time where the act of Creation took place, and whatever was brought to life then can and should be recreated in a ritual – the profane continuity of the world and its time is stopped and what was in the beginning comes to life again. As such, the centre of the world corresponds with the centre of the sacred places: the cosmos, the country, the city, the temple, the altar, etc., while the main figure of the ritual is the king who assumes the archaic role of the chief priest, becoming a participant in the cosmological act (1977: 109-10).

28   The cyclicity of Frank's perception of time comes to the surface when he recalls the moment of excavating of Old Saul's skull. Frank regrets that it did not occur "a decade to the day" since the dog's death, as it would have meaningfully completed the cycle with the "old enemy" coming under its former victim's control (109). Also, Paul's death reasserts the enemy's downfall. The younger brother is born on the day of the bulldog's attack on Frank, for which the dog is shot by Angus. Frank interprets the event as the "biblical" rebirth of Saul as Paul, and thus Paul must die, being the next incarnation of the mythological "Castraitor."

time in the space of public life. As such, it was an important element of the social and economic progress of the country and thus part of its rationalistic historical worldview. Thrown away to the dump, it had its mechanism and hands removed, which left only the face with twelve Roman numerals and the hole in the middle, through which the wasps are let inside the bowels of the Factory. The twelve hours no longer show the progression of time but mark the entrances to twelve tunnels, each housing a different deathtrap awaiting a crawling insect. The clock, therefore, becomes a symbol of superstition, foregrounding the repetition of the merciless ritual.[29]

Frank, a sacerdotal lord of this world, belongs to its mythical order, as he remains outside the country's historical time and its official records. Not registered at birth, and thereby deprived of the status of a British citizen, he has no birth certificate, no National Insurance number, nothing that could testify to his being a member of society. Moreover, Frank literally embodies the repetitive yet changeless pattern of death which holds sway over his realm. Believing in his childhood castration, he feels keenly the injury – "that thing which I knew would keep me in my adolescent state for ever, would never let me grow up and be a real man, able to make my own way in the world" (139). Unfit for sex and procreation, his body remains frozen in time and barren. Thus, as a form of revenge, he lays waste the lands in his power. The character's life is marked by the recurrence of self-instigated hostilities, weapon production, and a daily reconnaissance of his domain, all this aimed at reasserting his hold on the island by causing the death of everything that lives. Myth, therefore, instead of its usual regenerative energy and vitality,

---

29   This calls to mind the difference between the perception of time by historical and cosmological consciousness as postulated by Uspienski. Whereas historical consciousness arranges events in a sequence of cause and consequence, and the significance of those events is determined from the perspective of the future, cosmological consciousness presupposes the correlation of events with some initial primordial state whose emanation is constantly felt. The events taking place as part of this primordial state form a text – understood by Uspienski as *myth* – which repeats itself continually in all the later events (Uspienski 1998: 35). In the case of Frank, such a primordial state which is referred to time and time again is the moment of his castration, which deprived him of his reproductive ability and thus turned the island into a barren wasteland.

provides only a cycle of aggression and temporal stasis, where the sole form of "development" is the multiplication of weapons and carcasses.

At the same time, the space of the island undergoes the process of mythologizing, as the crucial events in the life of Frank, who is both the soldier hero and the demiurge of the insular world, are immortalized in the names of its landmarks, e.g. the Bunker, the Skull Grounds, or the Snake Park. The stories behind the creation of the places make up Frank's personal mythology in which the world of the island, as Schoene-Harwood puts it, appears to have emerged "at his god-like command [. . .] out of [its] primordial formlessness" (1999: 140).[30] The same mythologizing process takes place in the case of Frank's weapons which are aptly named and undergo protective rituals before they can serve their master. Consecrated with Frank's blood and other bodily substances, the weapons are infused with the power of their maker, failing when his own power fails, and only Frank knows their real name:

> The catapult ought to be safe as long as nobody knew its name. That didn't help the Black Destroyer, certainly, but it died because I made a mistake, and my power is so strong that when it goes wrong, which is seldom but not never, even those things I have invested with great protective power become vulnerable. Again, in that head-state, I could feel anger that I could have made such a mistake, and a determination it wouldn't happen again. This was like a general who had lost a battle or some important territory being disciplined or shot. (64)

The faithful weapon and its master become one in a spiritual union of killing, the catapult responding to Frank's mood and thought, which affects its combat performance, as Frank observes: "The catapult is an Inside thing, requiring that you and it are one. If you're feeling bad, you'll miss; or, if you know you're doing something wrong, you'll miss, too" (27).

The protagonist's belief in his god-like power is made explicit through the greatness and grandeur of his chief "mythological" enemy,

---

30 Frank's mythology reflects Meletinsky's claim that the fundamental characteristic of myth is that it reduces the essence of objects to their genesis. To explain the structure of an object is to tell how it came into being; "to describe the surrounding world is the same as recounting the story of its creation" (2000: 159). Frank regularly updates the maps of his territory, putting down new names along with the descriptions of acts which contributed to the creation of a particular place (see 56).

the Sea, and their eternal struggle (43). More importantly, however, the sea is also an element which apart from its destructive power is also traditionally associated with life, sensuality, changeability, and fertility, namely those qualities which are denied to Frank and which stand in clear opposition to the subjective world of his masculine fantasy and its sterile values. Quite appropriately, in Frank's mind, the sea becomes associated with Women, his second greatest enemy. However, in contrast to the respectful hatred which Frank feels towards the sea, for the women he has only abhorrence and disdain. In this context, the sea's repeated attacks on Frank's domain can be interpreted in terms of his own repressed femininity, whose latent presence has continually challenged the painstakingly constructed but artificial image of Frank as a man. It is because of his resurfacing womanhood that Frank's build is more rounded than other men's and that he lacks hair on his face and chest. His female genitals make it impossible for him to urinate in a standing position and they also impede his sexual contacts with other women. At one point, Frank semi-consciously voices his predicament: "I realize that you can never win against the water; it will always triumph in the end, seeping and soaking and building up and undermining and overflowing. All you can really do is to construct something that will divert it or block its way for a while; persuade it to do something it doesn't really want to do" (25).

Therefore, by way of compensation, Frank pursues the most extreme version of masculinity, which thrives on aggression and misogyny, as he does not realize that he is a living contradiction of the gender stereotypes he preaches:

> It occurred to me then, as it has before, that that is what men are really *for*. Both sexes can do one thing specially well; women can give birth and men can kill. We – I consider myself an honorary man – are the harder sex. We strike out, push through, thrust and take. The fact that it is only an analogue of all this sexual terminology I am capable of does not discourage me. I can feel it in my bones, in my uncastrated genes. (118)

Frances's spiritual journey in search of her real female self calls to mind Joseph Campbell's seminal work *The Hero with a Thousand Faces*, in which the eternal human struggle for identity is discussed in terms of the hero myth, a pattern which underlies the narratives of all the stories ever told, and which can thus be labelled as the *monomyth*. When investigating the monomyth, Campbell relies on the Jungian theory of archetypes, i.e. images recurring in the dreams of all people and myths of all cultures, which Jung sees as the manifestations of the *collective unconscious* (see Campbell 2004: 16-8, and Jung 1991: 3-41). The point of departure for Campbell's understanding of the monomyth is Arnold van Gennep's theory of the rites of passage (Meletinsky 2000: 49), and more precisely, the formula of s*eparation – initiation – return*, from which he reconstructs the mythological biography of the hero, the deity, or the prophet (Campbell 2004: 28). In Frances's case, the separation stage involves a very literal separation of the character from her feminine side, with which she is finally reunited after years of trials and internal struggle.

Therefore in *The Wasp Factory* myth underlies the historical reality of Frank's life, her individual story, in two different ways. Firstly, it provides the already discussed organizing principle behind the construction and functioning of Frank's personally mediated insular world-picture. Secondly, it offers an ageless universal character to Frances's quest, which concludes with the character's liberation from the world of death and superstition, and her eventual departure for the outside world of life and rationality. In the first case, we deal with a peculiar version of the myth of creation reworked on two levels as a small-scale cosmogony and anthropogeny. In the second case, we are faced with the monomyth whose hero struggles against the obstacles put in his way by his manipulative father, only to receive a gift of self-knowledge and transform into a heroine. Consequently, the traditional pattern of the monomyth, apart from its usual motifs of trial and revelation, also involves a reinterpretation of the binary categories of masculinity and femininity.[31]

---

31   The limited space of the chapter makes it impossible to discuss at length the pattern of monomyth in the novel. It is, however, useful to review briefly the stages of Frank's quest. The Separation phase can, of course, be equated with Frank's "transformation" into a boy, which follows his threshold battle with a monster represented here by Old Saul. The character then enters "the Belly of the Whale," or "the Realm of Night," and appears as if she has died. This stage, i.e. Initiation, corresponds with Frank's immersion in the world of violence and superstition, as well as with her lack of knowledge of her female identity, which is kept in check by the hormonal therapy. It is accompanied by the motifs of divestiture and reinvestment, as Frank is stripped of her feminine traits, while her sex is socially reconstructed through male clothes and gender

In his skewed perspective, Frank comes to apply the traditional division into the internal (female) and external (male) space to the realities of the island and the world beyond respectively. His own alleged disability makes him only half-male and ties him "inevitably" to the space of the domestic (a traditionally female environment), where he engages in his own "microcosmic cultivation of a compensatory masculinity" (Schoene-Harwood 1999: 137).[32] In contrast, his elder brother, Eric, being a "real man," is consumed by the "outward urge" and leaves the island to study medicine in Glasgow (138). After a brief respite in the mythical paradise of boyish games and joys, Eric reaches his adolescence, which is tantamount to his masculine personality taking shape. His time in the world of childhood dreams is over and he is naturally drawn into the narrative of history: growth and maturation, pursuit of knowledge marked by tests and examinations, new friendships, loves, and shifting priorities. Thus, it is the "outside world with all its fabulous opportunities and awful dangers" (138) that becomes the arena in which

---

stereotypes concerning appearance and behaviour. She becomes free of her fear by excavating Saul's Skull and following the prophecies of the Wasp Factory, thereby achieving "a godlike stature" as the lord of the island. Later Frank receives "Supernatural Aid," which comes in the guise of Eric, a fearsome being, who brings chaos to the patriarchal order of the island and paves the way for Frank's confrontation and final "Atonement with the Father." Despite her reluctance to Return, Frank is finally reunited with her female self, becoming the Master of Two Worlds, as a male in the female body. In the end, the hero returns not to the island, which has become too limited for her, but to the greater world, which she has always avoided.

32   In fact, the world of the island becomes the testing ground for the traditional roles ascribed to both sexes, turning inside out all binary divisions into "typically male" or "typically female" and proving them to be arbitrary cultural constructs. After all, leaving aside Frank's own subversive case, his own mother and father are perfect examples of such arbitrariness. Agnes, admittedly, gives birth to two children, but she abandons them without remorse in pursuit of her own freedom and fulfilment, storming her way out of the island over the broken leg of her husband. She leaves her marital home, which is traditionally considered the wife's domain, while the husband remains behind to mind the household and take care of the child that his wayward wife has dropped at his doorstep like a cuckoo. Using Frank's own words, it is his mother who strikes out, pushes through, thrusts, and takes, and his father, biologically a man, who is at the receiving end of her uncompromising nature.

Eric plays out his masculine ideal of versatile development: on the one hand, he struggles for self-accomplishment, pursuing knowledge and career, on the other, he looks after the sick, being of service to those who need his help.

Paradoxically, both Frank and Eric follow the underlying mythical pattern of their lives, each of which corresponds with a distinct set of values concerning the cultural construction of masculinity. Whereas Frank's *fable* requires that he enact the role of a savage warrior from pagan myths taken to the extreme, Eric's heroic progress, involving courage but also compassion and self-sacrifice, has more to do with the archetypal pattern of romance. Eric's purity of heart, moral integrity, and his sense of responsibility for the weak and the helpless, remind us of the heroes of chivalric romances like Galahad or Percival, or the disinterested love and charity embodied in Jesus Christ and his followers, Christian saints and martyrs. This romantic aura accompanies Eric from birth: his mother dies in childbirth leaving her husband grief-stricken and her new-born son cursed for life with pain, both physical (migraines) and emotional (alienation from his father and hypersensitivity to the suffering of others). As a boy, Eric is Frank's personal hero, with whom the younger "brother" plays "brave soldiers" and when Eric displays his inclination for romantic heroism:

> Those were the only times he deliberately hurt me, when his stories required his own heroic death and I would take it all too seriously as he lay expiring on the grass or the sands, having just blown up the bridge or the dam or the enemy convoy and like as not saved me from death, too; I would choke back tears and punch him lightly as I tried to change the story myself and he refused, slipping away from me and dying; too often dying. (137)

Later Eric sets off from home to make a name for himself in the greater world, on which Frank comments as follows: "[H]e was doing what he had to do, just like the brave soldier who died for the cause" (138). Even Eric's eventual downfall can be accommodated within the romantic pattern which he unconsciously acts out. He suffers a severe mental disorder as a result of an unrequited love, recurring migraines, and a horror of his hospital practice when he notices that a child in his care has its brain eaten out by maggots. Frank, however, recounting his brother's experiences, blames his breakdown on Eric's alleged effeminacy: "Whatever it was that disintegrated in Eric then, it was a weakness, a fundamental

flaw that a real man should not have had. [. . .] That sensitivity, that desire not to hurt people, that delicate, mindful brilliance – these things
were his partly because he thought too much like a woman" (147-8).

What Frank takes for Eric's emasculation can in fact be interpreted
as the latter's inherently romantic propensity for emotionality, empathy,
and care – the qualities which, though compliant with particular semiotic
codes of human culture, are nonetheless frowned upon within the
boundaries of Frank's heroic paradigm, which espouses meek women
and hard men. Eric's breakdown, however, seems to result first and
foremost from the confrontation of the model of manly heroism with
other people's suffering, which cannot be alleviated despite his best efforts. "Something in him could not accept what had happened, could not
fit in what he had seen with the way he thought things ought to be"
(147), speculates Frank, but it is not the feminine weakness in Eric but
his weakness as a man, his admission of manly defeat and his heroic
stance turned obsolete that Eric's idealistic innocent nature cannot successfully internalize.[33] As a consequence, Frank's elder brother changes
from the hero of romance into his opposite, taking to the extreme "the
deformative potential inherent in the masculine ideal itself" (Schoene-
Harwood 1999: 139), to which Frank refers after his vision in the Bunker: "The conflagration in his head was just too strong for anybody sane
to cope with. It had a lunatic strength of total commitment about it
which only the profoundly mad are continually capable of, and the most
ferocious soldiers and most aggressive sportsmen able to emulate for a
while" (127).

Eric's madness, which results in the period of confinement to psychiatric hospital, marks the phase of descent to the lower world in romance (*sensu* Northrop Frye), which involves such themes as "a break in
consciousness," entrapment, incapacitation, and a change from the human into the subhuman (1976: 129), as Eric not only becomes a social
menace but also undergoes a degradation to a wild dog-eater. However,
his escape from the hospital and his steady advance on the island creates
a momentum which finds its finale in the explosion of truth and thus in

---

33   Schoene-Harwood postulates that Eric's violence is motivated by his "ina-
      dequacy, failure and incompetence as a 'real' man." Therefore "it is not the
      feminine that softens him [. . .] but the masculine that makes him harden be-
      yond the humanly bearable, to the point of cracking up" (1999: 139).

the shattering of Frank's mythical order. As such, it contributes both to Eric's own romantic ascent from the underworld and to saving a damsel in distress, as it effects Frank's monomythic return to normalcy. The forever adolescent, hampered by his sexual impotence, turns out to be a "normal female, capable of intercourse and giving birth" (182), the qualities whose absence became the foundation stone of Frank's murderous microworld. However, the collapse of the mythical order is underscored not only by the resuming of the historical time of Frank's thwarted development but also by the shift of the *axis mundi* of the young woman's world – from Frank's loft to her father's laboratory, where everything began. From a demigod and the controller of the Wasp Factory, the pivot around which Frank established his private universe, Frances comes to be merely a specimen subject to her father's experiment, a wasp in the greater machine of human life.

Deprived of the excuse of her own disability, Frances is shaken from the familiarity of the self-projected image and the ritual which has so far shaped her existence. The space of the island becomes alien because its male-oriented order does not allow for a woman within its borders, and the "outside world with all its fabulous opportunities" has also its "awful dangers" in store (138). "I don't know what I'm going to do. I can't stay here, and I'm frightened of everywhere else. But I suppose I'll have to go" (182), muses Frances while looking out to the sea and recognizing the need to live out her future as a woman. What starts as the hero's fantasy of violence and domination, realized within the familiar limits of his private microcosm, ends as the quest of the vulnerable heroine, who has to come to terms with her re-discovered self, and follow her female *fable* out in the limitless, alien, and unpredictable world. "*Now* the door closes," she says, "and my journey begins" (184).

1.4. Model FOUR: Apocalyptic Worlds

In his study entitled *After the End: Representations of Post-Apocalypse* (1999), James Berger proposes three meanings in which the word "apocalypse" can be understood. The first is the *eschaton*, or the "actual imagined end of the world" as presented in the biblical writings or envisioned by medieval millenarians, whose more up-to-date equivalent is provided by contemporary visions of nuclear or ecological cataclysms. The second sense, an *eschaton*, signifies an ending which resembles "the imagined final ending." In this category Berger lists the expulsion of Jews from Spain in 1492, the Holocaust, or the Hiroshima bombing, which function as "definitive historical divides, as ruptures, pivots, fulcrums separating what came before from what came after." In the third meaning, the concept refers to the very etymology of the word "apocalypse," and thus its interpretative, revelatory function. "The apocalypse, then," writes Berger, "is The End, or resembles the end, or explains the end" (1999: 27). It splits history into what was before and what will be after, and it brings things to a conclusion in a flash of revelation.[34]

The dualistic quality of apocalypse, as a catastrophe on the one hand and an epiphany on the other, finds its representation in the world of *The Wasp Factory* and in the life of its protagonist. In his analysis of the novel, Cairns Craig argues that Frank lives in the aftermath of both personal and historical cataclysm – his own castration and the apocalypse of World War II:

> Frank's personal world – he prepares heads for his "Sacrifice Poles" in the "Bunker" – is a grim mirror-image of the world that twentieth-century history has bequeathed to those born after Hitler's death in his Bunker, and Frank's campaign to make himself "unchallenged lord of the island and the lands about it" [. . .] both mimics the violence of the first half of the twentieth century and, at the same time, asserts "his" desire to escape from that world into one that is under his own control. (2002: 10)

Craig's observation, though accounting for the catastrophic side of apocalypse in Frank's life, does not account for the event's revelatory function, unless we assume, rather misguidedly, that such a revelation comes slightly postponed in the form of the protagonist's anti-social compensatory ideology. Rather, the true epiphany takes place as a consequence of another catastrophe – the rediscovery of Frank's female sex, which he interprets in terms of his own death: "now that my father's truth has murdered what I was" (182). Frank's life, therefore, seems to be lived between two disastrous events, two metaphorical murders committed first on *her* and later on *his* self. However, whereas the first catastrophe leaves in its wake only destruction and violence caused under the aegis of the false religion, the second results in the character's awakening and is followed by a promise of regeneration and hope.

---

34   The above passage appeared previously in Pisarska 2012a: 247.

Interestingly, the novel presents the reader with the motif of post-apocalypse within another post-apocalypse. The war-ridden lands in Frank's domain are overwritten on the geographical landscape which still bears potentially dangerous traces of the last major cataclysm. Among its remnants there is the Bunker, which is turned into a temple of Frank's violent religion, and unexploded German shells washed ashore by the sea, one of which causes the death of Frank's younger brother, Paul. Moreover, the island reverberates with echoes of the Cold War, which come in the form of fighter planes "violating" the island's airspace on their way from or to their naval bases in the North Sea. Cairns Craig comments that Scotland at the time "contained the largest concentration of war weaponry in the Free World," and served as "an armed arsenal, a front-line battleship of the Cold War, providing a European base for the U.S. nuclear threat to Russia" (2002: 13). He further observes that the Cauldhames' house may in fact represent the country itself, as it also "sits on" the arsenal of military explosives, left in the basement after World War II (13). Similarly, Frank's constant war on the local wildlife is reflective of the ongoing terror and hostility in the greater world, the private semiosphere on a periphery of the greater world containing in its microcosm the macrocosmic mechanisms of global space.[35]

The pre-apocalyptic era in Frank's life is less a matter of the boy's own memory and more a conglomerate of his father's scant retellings and Frank's own presuppositions. The preserved vision is that of a blessed paradisiacal time when he toddled around "the way any normal, healthy three-year-old boy does" (105), presumably happy that the sudden arrival of his pregnant mother distracted the adults enough to give him "more freedom to do as [he] liked about the house and the garden" (106). The supposed fierce assault of Old Saul followed by Frank's fear and suffering constitutes a caesura at which the years of Frank's life begin to elapse in the shadow of the catastrophe, which activates the boy's deleterious potential.

---

35   Marshall Walker postulates that Frank's insular world constitutes "a parable of the big world's perverse mumbo-jumbo: territorialism, the Dow-Jones index, the exclusive cabal, the nuclear deterrent" (343), while Victor Sage sees it as "a brilliant parody of the weird insularity and the warrior-culture atmosphere of the Falklands campaign" (1996: 27).

The island ruled by Frank slowly turns into the reflection of the land-scape of his traumatized psyche, marked by his own tragedy and the tragedies he caused to others while taking revenge for his own disability (hence the landmarks filling his insular domain, connected always with the instances of death and hostility). Frank's sexual incapacity in combination with his self-devised creed of bellicose masculinity makes him not only an impotent warrior but also a destructive vengeful god in whose world procreation is replaced by its opposite. The infertility of the god inevitably translates into the infertility of the space under his rule, and whatever is born and alive in it must yield to his pernicious influence. "Having no purpose in life or procreation, I invested all my worth in that grim opposite, and so found a negative and negation of the fecundity only others could lay claim to," admits Frank turned Frances. "The murders were my own conception; my sex. The Factory was my attempt to construct life" (183). And the life over which the Factory holds sway can only become a wasteland, as the highest authority in the space of the island, whose decrees determine the laws of Frank's private semio-sphere, has been itself patched up from the waste collected by him in the nearby garbage dump.

The motif of an infertile ruler inhabiting an equally barren kingdom echoes the story of the Fisher King, whose wound translates into the wound of his entire land. According to some versions of the legend, there are in fact two wounded Grail kings, the father, whose more serious wound ties him to the space of the castle – sometimes he suffers from the effects of old age, and not the wound, as Jessie L. Weston claims in her *From Ritual to Romance* (1920: 111), whereas his son, the Fisher King proper, is capable of leaving the place and engages in various activities, including fishing. Depending on a version of the legend, the king's wound which will not heal was received either in the leg or in the groin, which calls to mind the situation of the two "men" inhabiting the island in *The Wasp Factory*. Angus, the father, had his leg broken many years ago, which left him limping and largely confined to his laboratory, whereas Frank, allegedly deprived of his testicles, wanders about his lands committing acts of savagery on the local fauna. And the boy does consider himself a "eunuch," "a fierce and noble presence," "a crippled warrior" and a "fallen prince" (183),[36] stressing the relationship between his own royal impotence and the wasteland that is his realm (cf. Kincaid Speller 2000: 29).[37]

Mediated by Frank's traumatized psyche, the space of the island appears as a battlefield on which an ongoing war is waged against nature. The latter functions as the provider of dead bodies which can be dismembered, beheaded, and defiled in pseudo-religious rituals to serve as deterrents hoisted on the Sacrificial Poles. Nature is also subject to acts of violence and deliberate cruelty: bombs explode in the middle of pastures and rabbit grounds, which contradicts a conventional image of the bucolic Highland countryside (March 2002: 104). Last but not least, nature is used as weapon and turned perversely against its own kind, as in the case of the Killer, a live catapult made from a young pliable tree to

---

36   Maureen Kincaid Speller observes that the Fisher King as a fertility symbol is in fact the Winter King, which she considers meaningful in the light of the family surname "Cauldhame" (cold home), which also implies the lack of warmth and affection between the inhabitants of the house (2000: 29).

37   Weston claims that the Christian Grail legend is in fact a remnant of old fertility rituals, and the Fisher King represents an agrarian god whose temporary sickness, impotence, or death brought about war, drought, or infertility in the land. Jesus's cup from the Last Supper as well as the lance mentioned in the Grail story are, according to Weston, representative respectively of the female and male reproductive organs, the cup and the lance being used in pagan ceremonies connected with the god's death and resurrection (see Weston's discussion of the Fisher King 1920: 107-29). In the light of the above observations, Frank's Grail is his own female identity along with the restoration of the protagonist's reproductive powers, which will consequently effect the healing of the land of war and infertility. Moreover, considered from this perspective, Carl B. Yoke's discussion of the "end of the world" myth in the context of fertility myths, featuring Osiris, Tammuz, Adonis, Orpheus, Mithra, Attis, Persephone, and Dionysus, sounds even more convincing. According to Yoke, the re-creation myths and post-apocalyptic narratives involve the same pattern, which is, however, played out on a different scale: 1) the violent death of a young god, usually as a sacrifice/ the catastrophic death of a culture or civilization, and the symbolic death of the hero or his detachment from the community; 2) a journey through the underworld/ a journey through the wasteland; 3) a return to the upperworld, after ensuring the return of fertility/ the hero's discovery of a place of refuge, a remnant of civilization etc.; 4) the rebirth of nature and the world/ a promise of a new, better world. See Yoke 1987: 3-4.

hurl little rodents like missiles. Nature is battered and infested, and even sheep grazing in the meadows look to Frank at one point like swarming white maggots (150).

Within the space of the island the binary qualities of the four elements – creative and destructive – are visibly imbalanced, giving predominance to the latter. Water is used for flooding dams and cities built by Frank only to be destroyed. Even the sea brings only rubbish like plastic bottles, used plastic bags, and dead marine creatures, as if its regenerative power was opposed by the forces of destruction embodied by Frank. Air is used as a carrier of deadly Aerosols in the war against flying insects but also as the element carrying the war planes which disturb the solitude of the island. Moreover, it is the air which allows Frank to send stones and catapult helpless creatures as living bullets and which carries little Esmerelda off to the sea and certain death. Earth is treated as a battlefield steeped in blood of numerous innocent creatures, both humans and animals. In addition, it is the building material of Frank's outdoor scale models of human settlements whose only purpose is their eventual demise by flooding or blowing up. And fire is used mainly for its burning and explosive quality in the form of bombs and flame throwers. What is important, the destructive qualities of the four elements are also used as methods of deadly torment in the entrails of the Wasp Factory, whose sinister prophecies, after all, influence Frank's interpretation of the world. The traps encountered by crawling wasps involve various lethal manifestations of air, water, earth, and fire, for example: the airgun, the Boiling Pool, the Acid Pit, the Ice Chamber, the Volt Room, the Deadweight, molten wax, skewering pins propelled by rubber bands, carbon dioxide from a soda-syphon bulb, or the Fiery Lake with burning petrol (122). Last but not least, the elemental forces are also incarnated in the two siblings, Eric (who lives in the wake of his private apocalyptic event) and Frank, whose final confrontation results in the eruption of regenerative chaos on the island.

In Frank's musings about his crazy brother approaching the island, Eric is all the time associated with the element of fire, mostly due to his blood-curdling penchant for burning dogs. Eric's advent to the island takes place amid the scorching heat, which immediately turns the water in Frank's bottle stale (needless to mention a burnt dog which Frank kills out of mercy), as if foreshadowing the approaching apocalypse.

Brandishing a torch and an axe, Eric executes on the island a Day of Judgement, which looks like hell on earth, Eric's divine anger being aptly summarized by Angus's plea "Oh, my God, no" (175):

> I could see flames from every window, hear the wails of the tortured sheep all around the house. [. . .]
> Sheep were everywhere, fire was all about. The grass over the Skull Grounds was ablaze, flames leaped from the shed and the bushes and the plants and flowers in the garden, and dead, burning sheep lay in pools of livid fire while others ran and jumped about, moaning and howling in their guttural, broken voices. (175)

In his study of apocalyptic imagery, Northrop Frye postulates:

> The apocalyptic world, the heaven of religion, presents, in the first place, the categories of reality in the forms of human desire, as indicated by the forms they assume under the work of human civilization. The form imposed by human work and desire on the *vegetable* world, for instance, is that of the garden, the farm, the grove, or the park. The human form of the *animal* world is a world of domesticated animals, of which the sheep has a traditional priority in both Classical and Christian metaphor. The human form of the *mineral* world, the form into which human work transforms stone, is the city. The city, the garden, and the sheepfold are the organizing metaphors of the Bible and of most Christian symbolism, and they are brought into complete metaphorical identification in the book explicitly called the Apocalypse or Revelation [. . .]. (2000: 141)

According to Frye, the *divine* and *human* worlds share the tripartite imagery of the city, the garden, and the sheepfold, which the Bible brings to a singular pattern of One God, One Man, One Lamb, One Tree (of Life), One Building/Temple/Stone, all being united in the figure of Christ (141). In literature, however, the above categories are conveyed through the medium of metaphors, which can also be noticed in Frank's apocalyptic account. The unity of God finds its representation in the Trinity of the Cauldhames, God the Father (Angus), his son by Mary (Eric), who comes as the Avenger with his mind set on punishing the wrongs by fire, and Frank/Frances, the verbal presence in the novel, with and at the same time *without* a gendered body, which makes him an equivalent of the Holy Ghost in this family triad. The unity of Man, following Frye's conceptual framework, is played out in the case of Frank through the paradox of "two in one," a man and a woman in one flesh. By the same token, the pastoral imagery gives way to speculations about the nature of particular social groups or whole societies, which are trained into submission by their political or ideological "shepherds" (see 144), which, as it potentially addresses the question of the patriarchal conditioning of women, provides the underlying metaphor of Frank's own unrealized predicament.

It takes a Christ to free Frank of the burden of sin and resurrect her femininity. Eric, a once living incarnation of the evangelical love of one's neighbour, now "satanically reversed" into the killer of helpless lambs, an Antichrist effecting his Second Coming, issues a challenge to his father, who represents exactly that sin of the world which led Eric to his madness and committal and Frank to a life of prejudice and isolation. The father stands for the ruthless face of science which makes gods from scientists letting them pursue their experiments for their own gratification irrespective of the consequences, be it the suffering of deformed retarded children or their own manipulated daughters. It is no wonder that Angus reacts with an almost religious fright to his crazy son's arrival: after all, Eric's main target is the cellar of cordite, which metaphorically represents Frances's locked femininity, ready to explode and reduce to ashes Angus's methodically established world without women. However, Eric does not destroy the contents of the cellar, but forces its door open, releasing Frances's biology from the stocks in which it was put by their father. Significantly, it is the feminine element of water present in Frances which stops Eric from igniting the cordite and quenches his desire to burn.

Eric escapes beyond the outskirts of the garden while Frank remains within to confront his deceitful father about the truth. If formerly Frank was Adam of the blighted paradise, now he turns out to be Eve (cf. Sage 1996: 27), whose departure from the garden has been prevented by God the Father's concealment of the necessary knowledge. Therefore Eric's fire, apart from its destructive power, is also regenerative.[38] It triggers the purification of the familial space from lies and scientific madness,

---

38   The balance of the elements is restored in nature itself, there being "no storm, no thunder and lightning, just a wind out of the west sweeping all the cloud away out to sea, and worst of the heat with it" (180-1). And earth becomes a safe heaven where the angel of the domestic apocalypse is lulled to peaceful sleep on his sister's lap.

giving Frances a new lease of life with her body liberated of patriarchal invasion and her mind purged of the distorted worldview resulting from her father's cruel experiment. Thus, the apocalypse set in motion by Eric's arrival, while it puts an end to the old order, is also, necessarily, epiphanic in nature (Schoene-Harwood 1999: 147). "I'm a woman. Scarred thighs, outer labia a bit chewed up, and I'll never be attractive, but according to Dad a normal female, capable of intercourse and giving birth (I shiver at the thought of either)" (182), Frances reveals her newly-found identity. The revelation means the death of Frank and the birth of Frances. However, she frantically tries to connect her pre-apocalyptic life with her present condition: "But I *am* still me; I *am* the same person, with the same memories and the same deeds done, the same (small) achievements, the same (appalling) crimes to *my* name" (182). But her perspective is already of the survivor who found herself on the other side of a cataclysm: "Why? *How* could I have done those things?" (182), which allows her to look back on and put in the right perspective her compensatory murderous impulse in the past, which was a consequence of her belief in "a lie, a trick that should have been exposed" (183). The cataclysm is thus conducive to a new outlook: the crippled Adam of the insular paradise is gone, and what is left is a vulnerable Eve, an exile from the garden. Victor Sage offers a proper summary of Frances's final predicament in the great Factory of life: "This destiny machine is another citadel-like labyrinth. No one escapes choosing their own particular kind of un-freedom, but the historicism which Frank invents (called 'my experience') in order to justify his choices is revealed as a fiction. In knowing this, Frances is about to enter life and her own real (i.e. present) history at last" (28).

The model of Alternative Worlds established by the blueprint novel introduces several key elements which will appear in the three novels discussed in Chapter 2, *Walking on Glass*, *The Bridge*, and *Transition*. Among those we can list, for example: the dichotomy of mimesis and anti-mimesis in the character's "reading" of the world; the motif of entrapment in the structures, whether material or mental, which construct the picture of reality for the character while preventing their access to the unmediated *real*; the notion of the subjective/inner world as being the only available reality and the character's refuge; the collision of different world-pictures which leads to the emergence of the hierarchy (or heterarchy) of embedded worlds; or the existence of parallel realities between which the characters transition and transform, just as Frank Cauldhame crosses the boundary between his own world and the mainland, mediating between their distinct semiospheres.

The model of Community Worlds will be developed in the novels discussed in Chapter 3, namely *The Crow Road*, *The Steep Approach to Garbadale*, *Espedair Street*, and *Stonemouth*. In the novels following the community paradigm, whose generic form is the family saga set against the background of the Scottish Highlands, or a fictional autobiography structured around alienation and abandonment of the community, the characters relationship with the world involves a reconsideration of their sense of belonging, or attempts to determine their own provenance. Replete with the issues which traditionally haunt communities in Scottish literature: the disturbed relationship between father and son, religious conflicts, family secrets, as well as exile and homecoming, the novels show the characters' mediation between their freedom from community and their need of it, which invariably culminates in their reconciliation with the domestic environment. As they come to regard their relationship with others in line with Macmurray's claim that the community of *I* and *you* embodied in the family, village, or entire nation, is a matter of intention and agency, they also begin to notice the importance of the local narratives intertwined with the history of the country and the world.

The model of Mythical Worlds presents the character's immersion in the world of self-devised religion and ritualistic violence, organized around the mythical centre – the sinister Wasp Factory. In the other novels of this paradigm, *Whit*, *Canal Dreams*, and *The Business*, the process of world-mediation is presented from the perspective of female protagonists who, similarly to Frank Cauldhame, transcend the categories of masculinity and femininity. The clash between historical and cosmological consciousness, exemplified by the apparent rationality of the greater world of business, politics, and secular society, and the apparent irrationality, superstitiousness, and parochialism of closed communities; the pattern of the monomyth employed for the journeys of self-revelation made by the female characters, which always involve an encounter with the cultural or ethnic Other – all those characteristics can be spotted in Banks's later novels which will be the object of analysis in Chapter 4.

In the model of Apocalyptic Worlds, the characters are shown as witnesses and/or survivors of various historical catastrophes which bring to an end the old pre-apocalyptic order – emotional, moral, social, and political. The motif of the wasteland in its multifarious representations noted by the characters, which is connected with the (post-)apocalyptic imagery of the Fisher King, Judgement Day, and elemental destruction, will find their way into the three novels from Chapter 5 – *A Song of Stone, Complicity*, and *Dead Air* – which traces the model's inner dynamic with respect to the characters' relationship with the world they inhabit from disintegration and ruin towards regeneration and balance.

We will see the elements of the four models coming together again in Banks's last novel, *The Quarry*, analyzed as a Coda to the present book. In this text, the concept of alternative worlds is explored in connection with collective fantasies and wishful thinking by means of which individuals and groups distance themselves from unacceptable or incomprehensible reality. The character's transition between two distinct semiospheres – that of contemporary British society and that of cyberspace – entails a change of identity and a shift from the peripheries to the semiotic centre, which is, in turn, used by Banks to interrogate the themes of communality and exclusion. Focusing on the nuances of social interaction, the author highlights the power of language as both a community-building medium and a tool of manipulation in the relationship between appearance and reality. Although Scotland is absent from Banks's last novel, the theme of departure and homecoming is orchestrated in relation to the character's settlement in London with the surrogate mother, which is also tantamount to his re-engagement with the real world and gaining freedom within community. The mythical quest for identity, which depends on the reunion with the feminine and the maternal, coincides with the death of the father and the apocalyptic end of the old way of life. Although the old order is destroyed by the elements of fire and earth, the world continues, forever changing, while the past becomes an object of nostalgia.

CHAPTER 2

Alternative Worlds
Walking on Glass, *The Bridge*, and *Transition*

In the blueprint novel, *The Wasp Factory*, the protagonist sees himself as bestriding the boundary between two distinct worlds – the alien and dissatisfying world of the public semiosphere, which other people regard as reality, and his own imaginary kingdom, which for him possesses the status of actuality in relation to the secondary order of the so-called real world. In contrast to the world of the mainland, in which he is but a crippled teenager forced to conceal his existence, the parallel dimension of his masculine fantasy becomes the theatre of Frank's heroics and indubitable power, contesting the mimetic prison of his disability. The split of the character's world into the real and the imaginary, the phenomenal and the fantastic, which complies with G. Gregory Smith's postulate of the syzygetic nature of Scottish literature, is consequently followed and further developed by *The Factory*'s "alternative" offspring – *The Bridge*, *Walking on Glass*, and *Transition*.

All of the works mentioned above contain in their respective fictional universes both the worlds semioticized by the characters as so-called empirical reality (which is empirical for them, even if it seems surreal or fantastic to the reader), and the worlds in which the laws of mimesis, as recognized by the characters, are variously disturbed or undermined. The two types function side by side, either as parallel dimensions, between which the characters travel back and forth adjusting themselves to the laws governing each world (i.e. effecting a translation between distinct spaces of signs, or semiospheres), or as nested worlds, which occupy different levels in the metalepsis-stricken ontological hierarchy. In the latter case, the characters either strive to decode the "reality" mediated through an alien semiotic system, trying to establish their own uncertain status on the rickety existential ladder, or, conversely, they contest and resemioticize the world-picture mediated through the metalanguages of the semiotic centre (cultural norms, ideologies, systems of beliefs, and the like), shifting to the periphery and establishing their own semiotic spaces there – alternative world models, oriented from their subjective point of view and reflective of their intrinsic prejudices and desires. Whatever the condition of such an alternative world – whether it offers a "speculation about other possible models of reality either by way of dreamlike design or by means of rational extrapolation or analogy" (Zgorzelski 2004: 32), or whether it involves the (re)interpretation of the semiotic reality according to the rules of a game or a particular genre – the ever-present tension between such oppositional systems invariably testifies to the supragenological dichotomy inscribed in Smith's antisyzygy.

2.1 Language, Literature, and Multiple Reality in *Walking on Glass*[1]

"We can be sure of *nothing*" (1986: 228), says the seneschal of the castle in one of the component narratives in *Walking on Glass*. This sentence aptly summarizes the characters' helplessness in the face of the disquieting and unstable nature of their respective realities. But it also reflects the vulnerability of the reader when confronted with the hazy ontology and the heterarchy[2] of the novel's fictional worlds. Like the paranoid character Steven Grout, who keeps reading SF novels in search of the Key to the "greater reality," the reader, too, goes through the chapters, hoping to decipher the enigma of a novel which *Walking on Glass* is.[3] Thom Nairn thus describes Iain Banks's method:

---

1   The first draft of my analysis of this novel appeared in 2008 under the title "Worlds in a Loop: Iain Banks's *Walking on Glass*" in *Structure and Uncertainty*. Ed. L. Gruszewska Blaim, A. Blaim. (Lublin: Maria Curie-Skłodowska University Press).

2   The term proposed by Douglas Hofstadter which can be explained as "a multilevel structure in which there is no single 'highest level'. This means [. . .] that it is impossible to determine who is the author of whom, or, to put it slightly differently, which narrative level is hierarchically superior, which subordinate" (McHale 1987: 120).

3   Thom Nairn comments: "*Walking on Glass* begins to seem a palimpsest of never fully decipherable possibilities, as, in turn, the castle comes to seem a

Playing games [. . .] is Banks's stock in trade, and he plays them with characters and readers alike. [. . .] Loading his text with symbols, images, cross-references and tangled coincidences, Banks allows settings, events and characters to filter from one narrative to another, undermining our assumptions until we begin to lose track of which of these narratives can be accepted as the real one. (1993: 130)

Two words are crucial here: the "real" and the "game." For it is the "real," or rather the degree of the "normality of the fictional worlds" (Zgorzelski 2004: 20) in particular narratives, which is the object of query both on the part of the reader and the characters. And indeed it is game playing which is the tool of producing the query mentioned above. In *Walking on Glass* games are played by the characters with other characters and with the fabric of reality. But they are also played by the author himself with the structure of his novel, for Banks blurs the boundaries between the various universes projected in the work, and thereby makes a breach in their established laws by introducing into their own homogenous systems the elements belonging to other systems.

Walking on Glass, Iain Banks's second mainstream novel, is comprised of three seemingly unrelated narratives developed simultaneously through five successive parts and the sixth short section which constitutes a resolution. The first narrative, played out against the realistic background of contemporary London, recounts the story of Graham Park, an art student, who is hopelessly in love with seductive and enigmatic Sara ffitch. The second story features the character of Steven Grout, a misguided SF aficionado, who believes himself to be an interdimensional warrior trapped in the reality of the early 1980s. The third narrative, set on a dying planet in the distant future, presents two warriors from the opposite sides in the Therapeutic Wars, Quiss and Ajayi, punished with imprisonment in an enormous ramshackle castle, who are forced to play impossible games in order to solve a riddle and regain their freedom.

The three narratives, apart from featuring different characters and settings, at first glance can also be seen as representing three different layers of "normality," reflected in three different dominants of their fictional worlds. The first story, the most "realistic" one, occupies the mi-

---

palimpsest within a palimpsest, while we, like Grout, read the novel awaiting the click of revelation" (1993: 131).

metic pole on the representational axis, while the Quiss-and-Ajayi narrative, with its futuristic milieu of warring species and advanced technology, seems to be dominated by the exomimetic element – the poetics of science fiction. Between these, the Grout narrative functions as the intermediary, as the world of the normal and everyday affairs borders on and is sometimes taken over by the world of the supernatural or imaginary introduced in the form of the protagonist's hallucinations. It can thus be regarded as representative of the fantastic motif of "a world next door."[4]

Just as there are tensions in the Grout narrative between the SF "reality," whose carrier is the protagonist, and the mimetic fabric of the world of his imprisonment, there are also glimpses of contemporary reality registered by the characters within the boundaries of the third narrative, which may in fact be interpreted as the introduction of the fantastic element in the context of the rules established for the extrapolated world of the future. At the same time, contemporary London in the Grout narrative is obviously treated by the protagonist as a false construct, a forged representation, which prevents him from reaccessing his native dimension of "greater reality." What on the surface appears as the projection of the paranoid mind, when read in the context of the Quiss-and-Ajayi narrative acquires an unexpected veracity and undermines the mimetic fabric of London reality. Even the most realistic narrative of the three confronts two different orders when a manipulative game devised by one character causes a disruption of semiosis on the part of another character, who unawares begins to interpret the surrounding world through the prism of a simulacrum.

The narrative of Graham Park, which opens the series, develops in the space of contemporary London, whose geographical connection with the character's story is already signalled in the titles of its consecutive parts: Theobald's Road, Rosebery Avenue, Amwell Street, Penton Street, and Half Moon Crescent. The streets represent the successive stages of Graham's walk through the city to the apartment of his beloved Sara ffitch, while he is reminiscing about the events of the last six months which have led to their current relationship. Graham, however,

---

4   The term used by Brian McHale in his study of postmodernist fiction to describe the intrusion of the fantastic element into "the world of the normal and everyday" (1987: 71).

remains unaware of the fact that the mysterious Sara and her secret lover, Slater, who also happens to be Sara's brother, play games with reality and truth which have affected his perception of the surrounding world by trapping him in the mechanism of simulation.

The motif of the simulacrum[5] in the Graham narrative is heralded already in its first paragraphs when Slater, the mastermind behind the whole deception, tells Graham about his idea for a book. It is the story of a courtier who has an affair with a princess, and who finds it increasingly difficult to share his time between the love affair and his courtly duties. To remedy the situation, he has an android made who looks exactly like himself and can thus function as his stand-in at official meetings and celebrations, without rousing suspicions, while the courtier can pursue his relationship with the princess. After the real courtier dies in a too intense bedroom romp, the replica takes over and is considered by the princess a better lover than the original, while also effectively fulfilling all his courtly obligations (15). The simulated version, therefore, appears to be more effective and durable than its prototype, as it is based on the idealized image of the original, who after all no longer exists.

Graham Park, accordingly, is caught in the devious planes of the simulacrum of perceptible reality, where signs are deprived of referents. For the most part of the narrative Graham (as well as the reader) is tricked into believing in the mystification devised by Sara and Richard Slater, who defy the official world-picture built on the mediating systems of religion, morality, and law, within the framework of which a romance between siblings is condemned as a breach of the incest taboo. Instead, the sister and brother devise a culturally accepted romance between Sara and Graham, which is supposed to cover up the inconvenient truth about their incestuous relationship and prevent the scandal which would ruin the political career of their father, a Conservative MP running for re-election. Therefore they first invent new biographies for themselves and then fill their projected world with non-existent occur-

---

5   In simple terms, a *simulacrum* as defined by Baudrillard can be considered a copy without a model (i.e. a copy of a copy which is so far removed from the original that it can no longer be regarded as a copy). A simulacrum, therefore, is not based on the original (which may be flawed) but on the idealized version of the original. For an in-depth discussion of simulacra see Baudrillard 2001a: 169-87.

rences and figures (like Bob Stock, Sara's be-leathered, bike-riding lover and Graham's rival, who is impersonated once by Slater, another time by Sara herself). Slater assumes the role of a motley homosexual and Left-wing sympathizer who hopes to seduce his innocent friend Graham into bed and who at the same time stands by the other's side in the tribulations of love.[6] Sara, on the other hand, projects herself as a wayward but ultimately kind and generous divorcee at loggerheads with her parents. Seemingly traumatized by her marriage with a violent sewage-works manager, she appears to hesitate about the role which Graham should play in her life.

Under the influence of the inspired game of Sara and Slater, Graham, initially aloof and rather unromantically predisposed, comes to play the role of a romantic lover and apply the romantic touchstone to the elements of perceptible reality. Graham's romantic discourse, developing in response to the siblings' deceitful mediation of reality, can be noticed in the descriptions of his growing fascination with Sara. Already at their first meeting, "instantly, in less than the time it took her to walk from one side of the room to the other, he knew he loved her" (55). He experiences all the symptoms of love at first sight – he is shaking, his heart is beating too fast, her touch makes him tremble, and he is lost for words under her gaze. A moment later he is shattered to hear Sara being addressed as a Mrs, like a married woman, because "[f]or the merest instant, some final, irreducible unit of desire, he had glimpsed a feeling, an urge within himself he had not imagined himself capable of" (55).

The elements connected with formulaic romances multiply: the first hallucinogenic dance, helping the damsel in distress and their first tête-à-tête, a reference (if humorous) to champagne-tasting competitions from ladies' slippers (64), or the lover's angst and uncertainty in the face of finding the only love that matters, and finally the first kiss. Although Graham is aware of the fact that love at first sight is the stuff of fairy tales and pulp literature, he cannot help looking at his present situation through the prism of romance:

---

6   The constructedness of Slater's personality is signalled in his own description of himself as "the communal ranger, superhom, the pinko pimpernel, the man in the Fabergé mask" (156), which involves references to the heroes of popular literature and culture, all of whom had to conceal their true identity.

All his life he had not believed anything could be like this. You stopped
believing in father Christmas, tooth fairies, paternal omniscience . . . and in
the sort of over-the-top crazy heart-thudding happy-ever-after love they
told you was the ideal. Life was sex, infidelity, divorces. Infatuation, yes,
but love at first sight, smell, touch? For him? Where was that carefully nurtured fine cynicism now? (64)

Graham, therefore, begins to semioticize reality contrary to the codes
governing his private semiosphere, his new wish-fulfilment attitude having no support in his semiotic experience to date. And Sara incites his
romantic feelings by being "poorly," "a weepy female," "just nerves,"
and in need to be held close (66-7). Their first encounter is a landmark in
Graham's life: he starts imagining himself as the romantic hero whose
determination and love will lead to a happy-ever-after future for him and
the woman. The five-hour walk back home after seeing Sara off to her
flat seems to him an epic journey which he is going to retrace one day
for the sake of nostalgia when he and Sara are already married and settled.[7] Her address, Half Moon Crescent, becomes for him "a mantra, a
chant, a litany" (69), which emphasizes conventional love idolatry, taken
a step further when Graham begins to draw Sara's portraits.

Graham's love affects also his previous perception of the surrounding world, triggering the process of defamiliarization and resemioticization with reference to London's cityscape. Presented from the point of
view of a man in love, the familiar sights of bridges, blocks, and towers,
of bookshops, workshops, sandwich bars, and cafés seem "fresher,
brighter, more real," and only now can he see "all his quite normal, perfectly standard surroundings" in their genuine glory, feeling "so lucky,
so good, so in tune" (12). Graham, the former outsider, suddenly feels
himself part of the community space, "like some vital cell in the blood-

---

7   Graham's imagining of his future with Sara calls to mind the concept of tem-
     poral orchestration described by Hillary P. Dannenberg in her work *Coinci-
     dence and Counterfactuality*. "In a multiple-worlds analysis of plot," writes
     Dannenberg, "retrospection (analepsis) and anticipation (prolepsis) can thus
     involve a journey into the virtual past of the narrative world or the projection
     of a virtual future that is not part of the story at all" (2008: 50). Seen in this
     light, Graham's forward musings are a good example of the projection of
     "nonactual future events" generated by "specific erroneous knowledge" – he
     does not know the truth about his beloved and therefore lacks the awareness
     that his version of a happy future is impossible.

stream of the city" (49), his newly found sensitivity to the signs of the world around him underscoring the harmony between the private and public semiospheres.

The same convergence of the private and public worldviews takes place with reference to Londoners. A "country hick," as Graham calls himself, and the son of an overprotective mother, he kept up his guard, reading "a threat in everything the big city had to offer" (12). Now, London no longer appears to him a dangerous place full of suffering individuals, or a place filled with people ready to assault him or take advantage of his gullibility. Fortified by his love for Sara, by "the promise of the strength *she* might give him" (12), he is able to look at London's estranged inhabitants (like a young black man talking to himself, or an old man with a torn shoe) without his previous bias, but with courage and understanding. Having shifted from the peripheries to the centre of the public semiosphere, he can see beyond all social divides, adopting the unifying point of view of one urban community (13).

The London summer, "the season for painting and scaffolding" and "[g]etting things done after the winter cover-up" (61), which Graham registers all around the city during his walk to Sara's place, coincides with the man's sense of the new beginning and the explosion of hope for his and Sara's life together. Throughout the narrative the reader is induced to observe and assess the events from Graham's point of view, and we are not only drawn into his romantic love discourse but also come to explain the confusing nature of certain occurrences in compliance with Graham's unwavering trust in his beloved's truthfulness and good will.[8] Yet the dimension within which the hero operates after meeting Sara – his alternative world of togetherness and budding affection – is only a simulacrum, an idealized image of a real-life relationship between two people.

The play of simulacra is visible in the very name of the heroine, which ranges from Sarah Fitch (the version Graham scribbles unawares

---

8   Through the employment of the focalization technique, and, more specifically, the medium of the narrated monologue (for a discussion of the term see Cohn 1978: 99-140), the narrator can manipulate the reader into adopting without corrections the viewpoint of the character and thus to treat Graham's misguided beliefs as a projection of an actual present and future. Cf. Dannenberg 2008: 49-50.

while taking down her phone number), through Sara ffitch (the name she uses for the most of the narrative), to Sarah Simpson-Wallace (née Slater), which the reader learns in the end.[9] The multiplicity of the names, in line with the woman's inscrutable nature, implies the existence of multiple identities she adopts, and thus also the existence of multiple worlds she inhabits, depending on her various personalities. Such a dissociation of the woman's self makes it impossible to establish her genuine identity which could give Graham (and the reader) a sense of which Sara is the original one. The two little 'fs' in her surname seem to epitomize not only the enigmatic aspect of this character but, most of all, point to the fact that the woman Graham fell in love with is a construct, a wishful projection of his deep-seated desire for romance, unusual and old-fashioned in the same way as the surname beginning with two lower-case "f's."[10]

The truth is never revealed to Graham. The only thing close to the truth is thrown at him in the form of another mediation, as Sara "discloses" to Graham the sordid details of her relationship with Bob Stock (193-6). He realizes that he has been a pawn in her game, a decoy whose supposed task was to put the spies of Sara's ex-husband off the scent because he was an easy prey, as Sara says, "like the sort of guy I might be able to charm" (200). Graham, therefore, has been living in two incompatible worlds: one subjective, with himself as the creator and the romantic hero, and the other in which he has been cynically played upon by Sara and Bob Stock. Every meaningful event in Graham's acquaintance with Sara, and every instance of her unusual behaviour, which he previously interpreted in terms of his romantic outlook, are now explained in compliance with the gruesome and uncompromising alien "reality" lying behind Sara's mediation (see 195). As a result, everything which seemed touching and loveable about her turns into filth, eroding Graham's fantasy.

---

9   Interestingly, Sarah's real name, Simpson-Wallace, echoes the name of Wallis Simpson, the American socialite who married King Edward VIII of Great Britain. This allusion implicit in Sarah's name is a powerful signal that allegedly explaining her "real" identity the narrator in fact creates another simulacrum into which to draw the reader.

10   Sara(h)'s multiple identities within the London narrative are reminiscent of the question of the transworld identity and the related concept of characterological counterfactuals. See Dannenberg 2008: 119-20.

While discussing different uses of counterfactuals in the genres of narrative fiction, Hilary P. Dannenberg addresses the question of the realistic ontological hierarchy: "Realism is based on the premise that the text depicts a 'real' world, and therefore only a single world can be represented as actual. In this form, counterfactuals are always hypothetical worlds embedded within the real world, that is, they are the product of speculations made by narrators or characters" (2008: 120). In the light of the above observation, Graham's world of romantic fantasies turns out to be merely a counterfactual of the "real" disenchanted world of lies and consuming passion between Sara and Stock. Even more ironically, the latter can be considered a counterfactual to the factual world of the diseased incestuous relationship between Sara and her brother, Slater, the knowledge of which is denied Graham but not the reader.

Graham's staggering recognition of his own romantic vision being a lie is connected with the hero's simultaneous acknowledgement and adoption of the laws governing Sara's world, into which he has suddenly found himself transferred:

> He had forgotten it all, forgotten all he had ever felt for her. [. . .] She had changed all the rules, put the whole relationship that had existed between them into quite a different category. He stored the old self, the hurt young man for the moment, concentrated as best he could, while still reeling inside from the sheer force and extent of the change, on what was being said now, on this new set of rules, his role he was being forced into, [. . .] trying not to sound hurt, trying to play it the way she was. (196)

Graham is translated, as Cairns Craig puts it, "from one genre of fiction into another" which "does not place the emotional life of one, well-off Western youth at its center" (2002: 25). Sobering up from the dream he has been living, the duped lover fails to perform the Othello-like role, which Sara obviously fears after the whole revelation, because a *crime passionnel* committed on an unfaithful woman is not part of the convention played according to the "new set of rules."[11] His relationship with a

---

11   For a moment, Graham contemplates two counterfactual scenarios in response to Sara's confession, both equally romantic and speaking of his passion and broken heart. One is to throw himself out of the window, which he abandons almost immediately, as it would give Sara "another display of grief and petulance." The other option is to sexually assault her, to use "the age-old violence, the ancient cruelty," and then plead temporary jealous madness – "She led me on, Your Honour." In the end, he decides to give up all big gestures

simulated woman has turned out to be a simulacrum itself, just as the portraits of Sara are the copies of an ideal woman who has never existed. The breaking of the romantic convention goes hand in hand with Graham's abandonment of the language of romance, which accompanied him when he was still a character living in a love story. The first genuine comment Graham is capable of producing after a series of monosyllables and dull questions is the abusive "You bitch, [. . .] you fucking cow" (200), which can hardly be accommodated within romantic discourse. Significantly, Graham's transfer from the world of illusion into that of mundanity is accompanied by his changed perception of the city. Unlike the first part of the narrative, now the sights are reflective of his inner devastation, inviting the imagery connected with dirt, deformation, disease, ruin, misery, damage, and waste. His earlier trust in humanity is also gone, and he avoids people in the streets, which emphasizes the restitution of a dividing line between the safe confines of his private world and the threatening and corrupt influence of the outside world. Now he can finally see the sordidness and ordinariness of existence that the wishful thinking of the romantic convention excluded (see 238).

Paradoxically, Graham can also notice the superiority of his romantically mediated vision to the "sheer crawling awfulness of existence" (238). Even in suffering he considers the portraits the best works he has ever produced, just as the simulacrum evoked in him the best feelings he had ever experienced. He throws the drawings into the canal to lie beside a tattered porn magazine and a piece of animal carcass – "this was what it really meant," he wonders, "[s]ex and violence, writ small like all our standard fantasies." Thus, exposing the workings of simulation enables one to get at the truth, the raw and unmediated reality lying underneath, yet at the cost of "the sickening burden of a cheap and tumid revelation" (238).[12]

---

and hysterical reactions, and he just leaves Sara's flat with a thought that his "brains are in the right place after all" (202).

12   The passage echoes Slater's earlier remark that "[m]ost people's ultimate fantasies, their idealized desires, are built of clay" (157). What Slater means is that the production of glossy magazines requires kaolin, a kind of clay used in a mixture of morphine which blocks diarrhoea. However, the words can also be treated as a commentary on the role of the media, and specifically the press, in the process of shaping our perception of the world. Porn magazines distort our natural sexual drive into appreciation of illusion, drugging men,

Whereas Graham realizes that his life is a game played by others, Steven Grout sees his life as "the only real life in a vast game that everyone takes for reality" (Craig 2002: 21). Grout's perception of London as a mere cover for the unmediated (greater) reality beyond it, access to which he has been denied, can be noticed in the following passage:

> They wouldn't succeed that easily! They had surrounded him with horror and stupidity, with all the paraphernalia of this so-called-human excess, and they expected it to bring him down, to reduce him still further from the once proud state he had fallen from, but they would not succeed. They were trying to wear him down, but they would fail; he would find the Key, he would find the Way Out and escape from this . . . joke, this awful solitary confinement for Heroes; he would leave them all behind and take his rightful place in the greater reality again. (27)

As signalled in the above quotation, the Grout narrative presents a tension between two contrasting world-pictures: one based on the collective consensus that what is observed around stands for reality, and the other generated by a paranoid mind, whose construction of reality is deeply idiosyncratic. For the delusional character, who believes himself to be a warrior from another dimension, London is a prison full of lurking perils such as Microwave Guns, laser weapons (attached to the axles of vehicles passing Grout in the street), and the Tormentors punishing him with burning rays for some crimes past. Trying to ensure his own safety, Grout needs to stick to certain protective rituals, which are treated by him as rules of the game. His behaviour in this respect is registered as unusual by the characters for whom London represents empirical reality, e.g. Mr Smith (the Roadworking Operatives Supervisor and Grout's

---

like morphine, with erotic images which surpass and falsify reality. That much is communicated by Graham's thoughts concerning his unfulfilled desire for Sara: "He hated the idea of pornography, even soft pornography, but he had almost come round to the idea that it might be better to buy one of the glossy girlie and accept the inhuman, labial beauty of those seductive image-women; it would at least absolve the release of his sexuality from the responsibilities of the real world" (157). The role of the media in the construction of a particular world-picture, and thus in the mediation of their intended image of reality, is touched upon several times in the novel, with reference to newspapers shaping people's attitudes at the time of Thatcher's government, like *The Daily Telegraph* (96), *The Economist* (149), or *The Sun* (150-1). Cf. Leishman 2009: 227.

boss), Dan Ashton (a union representative), Grout's workmates, and other city inhabitants. What he sees as his own awareness of the ontological entanglement of the two worlds is perceived by others in terms of stress, exhaustion, eccentricity, escapism, or sheer madness.[13]

As a result, the boundary between Steven's inner world (whose semiotics is dependent either on Steven's paranoia or on his genuine belonging to an alien dimension) and the London world, instead of being the site of dialogue, becomes the epitome of resistance, hostility, and lack of communication, both worlds interpreting each other through the prism of their respective languages. Grout relieves frustration and anger about his entrapment by throwing rocks at windows of the companies he was sacked from, defacing buildings, scratching the officials' cars, and making hoax bomb phone calls. What from the perspective of the London dimension seems injurious or criminal, from the point of view of an alternative-reality Warrior is a way of "getting back at them," the Tormentors (77).

Steven believes that the Tormentors use various ploys in order to imprison him in their deceitful mediation. Among such tricks the most difficult to defy are obstructive clerks and institutions (e.g. the Social Security system), meant "to confuse, anger and demoralize him" (29), in this way preventing his return home, because he has to start the game over and over again. Moreover, the Tormentors use false representations in the form of maps in order to mislead him into believing that the only existing world is Earth: they show it as "a reasonable-looking planet," whereas "[a]ny idiot could see" that the layout of its continents is "too carefully arranged to be natural" (114). A similar falsification of reality can be found in newspaper articles, which Steven keeps in his Evidence Box as proof of the Tormentors' bluff – "fillers and funnies, supposedly True Stories which Steven could tell were complete nonsense" (113).

---

13 Examining the hierarchy of the narrative levels in the novel, Katherina Dodou notices: "[Steven's] entire narrative is situated 'in limbo' between the realism of the first narrative and the science fiction of the third narrative. Depending on whether it is read in closer relation to the first or third narrative, the Steven narrative elicits two very different interpretations: one abiding by the rules of logic and realism, rendering Steven paranoid, and one adhering to the laws of science fiction, consequently labelling Steven as a lapsed warrior of the Therapeutic Wars" (2006: 30).

The only way to survive in this alien world is to examine the Evidence provided by speculative fiction which, along with drinking, offers "avenues of escape:" drink allows him a temporary way out of "their fetid reality," and books are soothing and give him hope because one of them certainly contains the Key to his native dimension (30). If we reject Grout's paranoia, his choice of literature may in fact substantiate the assumption that Steven is a projection of the exomimetic universe of the third narrative within the boundaries of the mimetic world, and that nonmimetic literature simply is his element. Science fiction and fantasy genres determine Grout's interpretation of London reality, providing rules for linking signs to their meanings, but they also mediate between the world of his present predicament and the world of his apparent provenance.

The description of Steven's library, a maze of "tower-blocks of books, whole walls of them" (30), with only small corridors left for him to walk (at one point Grout comments on the innovative method of stacking the books up so as to prevent them from collapsing through sheer height – namely, by putting the books together like bricks in a wall), inevitably calls to mind an analogous description from the Quiss-and-Ajayi narrative, the image of the Castle of Bequest, which is apparently made of text:

> What strange architect had designed this place? Ajayi found herself wondering every so often. The castle, rising on a single outcrop of rock from the plain, was built very largely of books. The walls were mostly slate, apparently quite normal, grained rock produced by a perfectly standard process of alluvial deposition. But when you loosened one of the slate blocks from the castle walls – an easy job, as the castle was slowly crumbling away – and split it open, on every surface so exposed a series of cut or engraved figures was revealed, arranged in lines and columns, complete with word and line breaks and what looked like punctuation. Quiss had demolished a significant part of the castle when he first discovered this, unwilling to believe that the stones, every one of them, all the tens of thousands cubic metres the castle must be composed of, all the kilotonnes of rock really were saturated, filled full of hidden, indecipherable lettering. (38-9)

Can the castle of Quiss and Ajayi be composed of Steven's books? Can the macrocosm of the prisonlike edifice on some forgotten planet constitute a mere reflection of the microcosm of his library? If this were the case, the entire universe of the third narrative would turn out to rest on the same mediating system, i.e. literature, which underpins the criteria of cognition and interpretation in Grout's private delusional world. The characters from the castle would then acquire a doubly literary status – being read about both by the reader of extratextual reality and by Steven Grout, who is a literary character himself. Moreover, assuming that Steven Grout is indeed "one of the mightiest warlords in the history of existence" (23), fallen from grace, or rather out of the futuristic universe of the third narrative, he may remember the torment of game playing to which he was once subjected, like Quiss and Ajayi. Therefore he continues playing games in the reality of contemporary London to ease himself out of imprisonment in both dimensions.

There may be a consistent rationale behind such an assumption, especially if we recall the predicament of the former prisoners of the castle who failed to escape and who in its infinite dungeons, with their heads stuck inside the glass ceiling, dream of the past while inhabiting the minds of human beings from before billions of years. If the seneschal is right about the extent of power that the mind-controllers can exercise over the lives of people from the distant past, even the characters from the "realistic" plane of contemporary London, i.e. Graham, Sara, or Slater, are only puppets operated by the free will and subjective visions of the agents from the future, the London world being indeed only a mediation, not the real thing. And Steven Grout, who is the only person capable of noticing the flashes of the greater reality, the Leaks, as he calls them, may in fact be such a mind-controlling agent with an increased awareness and a drive to escape.

In this light, the scene in which the red crow shows Quiss round the basement with dreamers acquires an additional meaning. Asked about the name of the old man who has spent ages switched to the glass ceiling, the crow answers: "Name's . . . Godot? Goriot? Gerrut?; something like that. The records aren't perfect, you know. An odd case . . ." (227). Leaving aside the first two names, Godot and Goriot, which sound highly allusive in the context of Banks's novel, which interrogates on various levels the interrelationship of life and literature, the third name mentioned by the crow, Gerrut, may in fact be Grout. While walking in the hospital gardens, Grout, amnesiac after a traffic accident, can hear the crows calling his name "Ger-out" – or perhaps "Get out," which may indicate Grout's imprisonment in an alien dimension. But it may also be the distant call of the notorious red crow, which pesters Quiss and Ajayi with its spiteful comments about their playing skills. As a result, the crows that Steven hears calling his name in the hospital gardens may be much more than a simple analogy, and become proof of the supragenological fusion between the two narratives, highlighting Grout's position on the boundary between their respective fictional worlds (cf. Dodou 2006: 31).[14]

However, even within the third narrative, which complies with the laws of the tertiary order of the fantastic, i.e. speculative/science fiction, there occurs a collision of two distinct orders. The world of ancient past epitomized in the castle, with its surreal and hardly comprehensible *modus operandi*, constitutes an alien element in the technologically oriented exomimetic world of Quiss and Ajayi, contradicting the characters' experience. The warriors find the principles operating in the castle bewildering and strange. First of all, there is no conventional way of getting to or leaving the place. The prisoners just appear there unexpectedly in an unknown way, like Ajayi, who arrived "seemingly deposited on one of the castle's flat, rubble-strewn roofs one night" (38). The prisoners are given substitute corporeal frames – Quiss and Ajayi have to en-

---

14   Seen from this perspective, the name Hotblack Desiato which troubles Steven Grout with its mysterious relationship to the latter's life, acutely mirrors the heterarchy of the novel. Hotblack Desiato is the name of a real estate agency in Islington (the quarter where Sara ffitch lives), whose name was borrowed by Douglas Adams for the character of a rock musician from the "biggest," "richest," and "loudest" band in history called Disaster Area (1995: 220-1) who appears in *The Hitch Hiker's Guide to the Galaxy*. The allusion to Adams is explained as late as Part Five, when Graham Park ponders over the name while browsing through Sara ffitch's edition of *The Restaurant at the End of the Universe* and remembers that in the book Hotblack Desiato has to spend a year dead "for tax reasons" (189). As we read in Adams, though Desiato's body is inert and connected to a "death-support system" (246-7), he can communicate "supernaturally" (242). Steven can obviously be seen as an individual who has to do time vegetating in the castle's basement while being psychically alive and constantly aware of his predicament in an alien dimension. Moreover, considering the possibility that Steven may in fact be a literary character from an SF novel (lapsed from the universe made of books in the third narrative), his transfer between dimensions will amount to his becoming a person in a quasi-extratextual world, which is a prison when compared to the greater reality of literature mediated by the author's imagination.

dure their imprisonment in the bodies of decrepit old people. Furthermore, the castle is not only constructed of layers of books but its topography is continually changing, which makes it impossible for the characters to become familiar with the maze of rooms and corridors. Apart from the bizarre inhabitants of the castle, the seneschal and his dwarfish scullions, Quiss and Ajayi are also plagued by talking rooks and crows which imitate the voices of their respective rivals, unfaithful lovers, or hated superiors. Finally, the games they have to play, whose names sound familiar at first glance, have to be played according to entirely different rules, and those, in turn, have to be inferred by trial and error.

Another extraordinary and problematic thing about the castle is time. There is no day and night there, only one flat monotone light, which makes it difficult to keep a tally of passing days. Moreover, the castle clocks, described by the characters as "immovable, and erratic too," (41) seem to live their own lives following the principles of the inverse square law, i.e. the time goes quicker or slower, depending on the castle's whim, the closer you get to the clock, which removes any possibility of accelerating the arduous game sessions and shortening the sentence. If all this were not enough, the castle is the place where two different temporal orders coincide – through the mind-controllers, the castle allows the world of the future to filter into the world of the past, and the boundary between them is formed by the glass ceiling with a sort of animal on top which translates the controllers' thoughts through time. As such, the castle can be perceived as the space of mediation between the fictional universes of the first and third narratives.

At first, the world of Quiss and Ajayi seemingly exists in isolation from the "earthly" referent depicted in the Graham narrative, the castle's "Subject world." However, the counterreality haunts their narrative in the form of a disturbing ellipsis, as the name *Earth* has been removed from every book in the castle, and the characters are unable to fill in this gap otherwise than with the name *Dirt* extorted by Quiss from one of the castle attendants. Moreover, the confrontation of the two worlds within the single narrative structure is signalled by the names of the games played by the characters, e.g. chess, dominoes, scrabble, or a form of bridge called tunnel. Another injection of the authorial reality, and thus a confrontation of the two perspectives, can be seen in the dialogue between Quiss and one of the scullions when the two are watching the operation of a *number-cruncher*. Asked by Quiss about the material from which the crushed numbers are made, the creature answers the bewildered warrior that it is "Plaster of Salt Lake City," which is "like Plaster of Paris, except duller" (173). Needless to explain that in Quiss's semiotic universe there is nothing like Plaster of Salt Lake City or Paris. Last but not least, further signals of the earthly reality are provided in the form of the castle's "original tongues," like Chinese or English, which Ajayi learns in order to be able to read "all the classics of the un-named planet's past" (175), or in the form of names of literary and legendary characters, and authors.[15]

As in the case of Grout, for whom literature, having a mediating function between worlds, is expected to produce a means of liberation,

---

15   The scattered bits of the Earth's reality gesturing to the comparison and confrontation of the two visions of the universe can be interpreted in terms of Zgorzelski's study of equivalents in nonmimetic fiction. Zgorzelski argues that the pattern of narration in those genres where the fantastic constitutes a basic constructional principle (i.e. the utopia, the gothic novel, the fantastic novel of adventure, etc.) presents two distinct worlds within the same structure (text). First, the mimetic order is presented, then the elements occur which break the laws of the former system and introduce a new world model governed by different laws. As a consequence, the comparison and confrontation of the two models takes place within the single text. "As this pattern of narration continues to be reproduced in the development of many genres [. . .]," postulates Zgorzelski, "its semantic dynamics decrease and the genre structure becomes progressively more automatised. As a result of this process and in reaction to it, one type of fictional reality, the mimetic model, becomes more and more restricted, until in some works it appears as a rudimentary signal of the former system, that is, its equivalent" (2004: 45). Among such equivalents Zgorzelski enumerates: the title (e.g. Orwell's *Nineteenth Eighty-Four*), characters' language (which does not differ from the model of the ethnic language in phenomenal reality), or, for instance, maintaining the continuity of space (so as to include the planet Earth or other constituents of the Solar system) in the expanding universe (45-54). The factors mentioned above can be considered examples of "an anticipatory preparation for the reader to meet a certain type of literature" (47). Therefore the crow's final revelation of the castle's whereabouts as well as the juxtaposition of the mimetic world of past human experience with the exomimetic nature of the protagonists' universe, can be perceived as an example of the so-called "retrogressive execution of the fantastic" (Zgorzelski 2004: 56-8), which brings about the confrontation of two distinct alternative world models.

for Ajayi, too, the books which form the castle – namely the literature of the Earth – become a means of connection with another dimension, i.e. humankind's past, offering Ajayi a way out of her physical confinement. In order to interpret the incomprehensible systems of signs found in the castle's building material, which would amount to understanding the alternative "reality" encrypted in the castle walls, Ajayi needs to possess the knowledge of the code in which this reality was "written" in the first place. Eventually, she learns such a code, or rather a series of different codes decipherable by means of other codes, e.g. English through Chinese, and then the entire Indo-European system through English. Language(s) thus allow(s) the reader an insight into the model(s) of reality created by the literary imagination, which marks Ajayi's shift from obscurity to cognition: "The castle was no longer the prison it had seemed before; it was a library, a museum of literature, of literacy, of language" (175).[16] In this way, the castle of books becomes a universe of alternative worlds accessible to those who know the Key to their respective realities. This universe of human imagination and language, like the multiverse of Banks's later novel, *Transition*, is steadily expanding with every book read by Ajayi.

At one point, Quiss observes with anger that in Ajayi's case "the appearance [is] taking over the reality" (130), which seems to pertain as much to her changed attitude towards the games they have to play – she behaves as if "motions and apparent choices mattered" (130) – as to her immersion in the world of language and literature, which changes her perception of the surrounding reality.[17] The castle, bizarre and maze-

---

16   Therefore the names given to the castle – the Castle of Bequest (Ajayi) and the Castle Doors (Quiss) – seems to match perfectly the characters' respective perception of the edifice's role. For Ajayi the castle truly contains the Earth's bequest to its future generations in the form of the literary works which are the castle's building blocks. For Quiss, the castle functions as the door to the world of humankind's past, represented by the dungeons with the mind-controllers.

17   Quiss's comment calls to mind Lyotard's opinion that what we call reality is nothing else but a sequence of "*language games*," which points to language as the main mediating system in our perception and interpretation (or maybe even production) of the real (1984: 10). The Lyotardian concept of reality being a game seems especially pertinent in the case of the two characters trapped in the castle made of language (represented in writing), and where games are a

like, suddenly becomes "transparent" (174), and Ajayi becomes more and more oblivious of her punishment and physical limitations. Her avidity for reading, during which she (re)lives the lives of various literary characters in a number of alternative worlds of fiction, is in fact similar to the situation of the controllers from the castle dungeons, who become engrossed in lives not their own. Depending on whether we accept the seneschal's warning that "the ceiling-ports allow full control of the primitives' minds" (228), or whether we subscribe to the red crow's opinion that the controllers are mere zombies delusional about their real influence on the minds they inhabit, we are faced with two possible interpretations of the narrative's self-reflexive message.

In the former case, which can be compared to the relationship between the author and his/her creations, the characters of the fictional world and the narratives of their lives are completely subordinated to the author's/controller's will. "Everything can be altered. Every mind contains its own universe" (228), reveals the seneschal, which takes us back to the problem of the semioticizing consciousness in a text to which/whom the author delegates the act of mediation. Thus, the author acts and speaks through his/her characters just as the controllers think and act through the people of the past, who in turn are deluded that their existence is of their own making (cf. Craig 2002: 23). On the other hand, mind-control can also work in the opposite direction. The connection to the primitive's mind, the seneschal asserts, is "too beguiling," as it offers "every form of human excitement" (228), which points to literature's ability to dramatize human experience, which readers often find far more engaging than their own lives. As a result, their reality becomes "just a grey dream" (228) compared to the alternative reality of fiction, as they

---

medium of reaccessing the real (cf. Craig 2005: 231). Even more significantly, the representation of the real through various language games is underscored by the textualization of reality in the third narrative, as the construction of the (fictional) world of Quiss and Ajayi apparently depends on the imitation of the fictional universes of Kafka's *The Trial* and *The Castle*, Peake's *Gormenghast*, and Borges's "The Library of Babel." As such, it echoes Linda Hutcheon's opinion that "[f]iction does not mirror reality; nor does it reproduce it. [. . .] Instead, fiction is offered as another discourses by which we construct our versions of reality, and both the construction and the need for it are what are foregrounded in the postmodernist novel" (1996: 40). Cf. Leishman 2009: 223.

mediate between the two, seeking Interest and avoiding Banality (see 38).

If we, however, agree with the red crow that the controllers are mere parasites who, contrary to the seneschal's opinion and their own delusion, are not responsible for the workings of the minds they haunt, the predicament of the millions of unfortunates in the universal basement round the planet resembles the predicament of literary characters. According to the crow, "[t]hey experience what others have experienced, they even have the illusion of altering the past" (225). However, they are only apparently endowed with free will and the ability to make choices as if they were real people. Fed by the castle (or maybe castles) made of books, they remain in their "own little world" (226) – a literary text, which always models a picture of reality for a given consciousness. Their existence, like all literature's, is therefore contingent on the medium of both the authors' and the readers' minds – when they are written and every time they are read about.

If we accept the possibility that Quiss and Ajayi are two literary characters trapped within the "reality" of the author's imagination, Ajayi escapes her predicament by becoming a reader and participating in the process of communication across the ages. Having learnt the code through which to (re)construct and explore the literary universe, Ajayi is in control of the previously unpredictable reality. Towards the end of the novel, she stumbles upon a book without a title page whose first line is actually the same as the opening sentence of the Graham narrative in *Walking on Glass*, and in the course of reading is bound to produce the answer to the riddle.[18] Last but not least, the disruption in the ontological hierarchy the moment the entire text of *Walking on Glass* becomes subordinated to the third narrative as a novel within a novel may actually point to the fact that a sense of freedom and ontological superiority on the part of the "real" people in extratextual reality is a mere illusion. Reality is a text in which we play out the narratives of our lives according to rules familiar only to our "authors" – just as the lives of twentieth-

---

18   Ajayi, as can be expected, will also read about Grout, who in the last part of his narrative stumbles upon a discarded matchbox offering the answer to the question the two warriors have been trying to answer: "Q: What happens when an unstoppable force meets an immovable object? A: The unstoppable force stops, the immovable object moves" (217).

century inhabitants of Earth are presumably lived out and controlled by the warriors stuck into the glass ceiling (cf. Craig 2002: 23). In this way, the third narrative also becomes an allegory of man's predicament in the universe of representations, and of the limits of its understanding and control.[19]

2.2. Into the Subconscious: The Dream Worlds of *The Bridge*[20]

"Perhaps the dream is a bridge. [. . .] Perhaps the bridge is a dream" (1987: 27), reflects Dr Joyce, one of the characters in *The Bridge*, while trying to convince his amnesiac patient John Orr of the significance of dreaming. The psychoanalyst's observation offers a pertinent commentary on the complexity of the novel's fictional universe, simultaneously addressing the character's mediation between its various ontological levels. On the one hand, Dr Joyce refers to the oneiric quality of the world in which the conversation takes place because the Bridge is a projection of the comatose mind of a patient who escapes from his waking life into a self-projected dream fantasy. On the other hand, by toying with the concept of the dream as a bridge, the statement points to the act of dreaming as a passage to another ontological dimension and implies the existence of a world "on the other side." Therefore Dr Joyce's words underscore the combined role of the bridge and the dream in the process of world mediation in the novel. The bridge is invariably the symbol of transition between two different orders (mimetic and antimimetic, conscious and unconscious, etc.), while the dream, being a representation of the character's inner fears and desires, mediates the hidden reality,

---

19 Dodou postulates that the Quiss and Ajayi narrative, much in the vein of the Renaissance allegories, functions as a "'fictional reality' within the realistic 'reality' of the novel, which helps explain the realistic Graham narrative" (2006: 37, note 11). Dodou concludes that seen from this perspective, the entire *Walking on Glass* can be perceived as "an allegory of the real world" (38, note 11).

20 The extended version of this analysis appeared under the title "Living a Dream within a Dream: Iain Banks's *The Bridge*" in Pisarska K. and A. S. Kowalczyk. (eds). *The Lives of Texts: Exploring the Metaphor* (Newcastle upon Tyne: Cambridge Scholars Publishing, 83-113). Parts of the essay mentioned above are published with the permission of Cambridge Scholars Publishing.

which can be accessed only by retreating into the space of the subconscious.[21]

The Bridge is Banks's third published work and also his personal favourite, being "the best of the bunch in terms of the actual craft of the novel," as he admits in a 1992 interview for The Times Literary Supplement (qtd. in Middleton 1995: 21). Inspired on the one hand by the technical artistry and political perspicacity of Alasdair Gray's influential postmodernist novel Lanark, The Bridge can also boast numerous other antecedents in Scottish literature and beyond, among which the most significant are those works where the seemingly dominant mimetic plane is constantly disrupted by the intrusion of antimimetic elements, and where "imagination is used to heighten realism into surrealism and fantasy" (MacGillivray 2001: 4).[22] Like Banks's earlier novel, Walking on Glass, The Bridge also makes use of several intertwining narratives, each being set in a different world governed by distinct principles, but which inform one another by means of various correspondences till their common resolution in a single narrative strand. Unlike Walking on

---

21   The dream therefore becomes a major structural device contributing to the emergence of a number of alternative realities – a hierarchy of worlds within worlds. For a discussion of the Chinese-box structure of The Bridge see Pisarska 2012b: 83-113.

22   Banks's novel shows an affinity with the subgenre of oneiric, i.e. man-in-a-coma or delirium fictions, initiated by Gray's 1982 Janine (1984) (Miller 2007a: 204), as well as with the entrapment fictions of Kafka and Peake (Binns 1991: 11). Moreover, the novel's structure of two alternating narratives, which will become a distinctive feature of Banks's later fiction, is an unambiguous homage paid to the doppelgänger pattern employed by R. L. Stevenson in his Dr Jekyll and Mr Hyde and by James Hogg's in The Private Memoirs and Confessions of a Justified Sinner (Watson 2007: 253). There are also recognizable references to the "stream of consciousness" novels of Joyce, to Claude Chabrol's 1971 film The Butcher, and last but not least, to the Orpheus myth (Middleton 1995: 23). To that one could also add Marcel Carné's 1951 film Juliette ou La clef des songes (Juliette, or Key of Dreams), and the tradition of Orwell's and Huxley's anti-utopian writing. However, as Alan MacGillivray notes, "[t]he range of cultural, literary and psychological reference on all levels of the story is very wide, making The Bridge a very difficult yet rich book to read; a full set of accompanying notes would be required for the serious reader who wishes to pick up all the possibilities of the text as they are presented" (2001: 5).

Glass, however, all the narratives of *The Bridge* possess the same protagonist, who projects different alternative worlds and flits between his different and only seemingly disconnected incarnations in search of a more assertive self and the roots he left behind (cf. Gifford 1996: 41).

The Bridge is composed of three narratives, enclosing one another in a structure of embedded worlds. The first narrative presents the story of a Scottish engineer, Alexander Lennox, whose professional career and personal vicissitudes are shown against the background of the social and political changes taking place in Britain in the 1970s and 1980s. The second narrative, which develops in parallel, is set in the surreal world of the Bridge, a massive habitable structure, avowedly imitating the real Forth Railway Bridge on the Firth of Forth river.[23] This world has been generated in the comatose mind of Lennox, who lies unconscious in a hospital after a car accident, while his dream alter ego, John Orr, afflicted with memory loss, tries to unravel the mystery of the Bridge and the lands beyond it.[24] The third narrative recounts the heroic exploits of a brutish warrior who speaks the Glaswegian dialect and carries on his shoulder a talking creature called the Familiar. The Barbarian's travels through realms of fantasy, fairy tale, and myth are dreamt by John Orr, while the warrior turns out to be yet another dream incarnation of Lennox (cf. MacGillivray 2001: 4).[25]

---

23   Ronald Binns argues that the novel's division into parts corresponds to the structure of the Forth Rail Bridge with its three main sections, two linking sections, and viaducts on either side (1991: 11). Thus, the real bridge in Scotland, the fictional Bridge of Lennox's dreams, and Banks's novel itself, represent the facets of the same pervasive metaphor.

24   I deliberately capitalize the word "bridge" whenever I refer to the city-state from Lennox's fantasy, even though it is not capitalized in the Orr narrative. To my mind, the Bridge represents a world in its own right, which should be distinguished from other uses of the "bridge" in the novel.

25   Lennox-Orr-Barbarian can be regarded as an example of the transworld identity (for further details see Dannenberg 2008: 118-22), but also of the notion of "the fragmentation of personality" which John Kuehl sees as a medium of character presentation in contemporary antirealist writing (1989: 6-14). The embedded narratives mirroring some of the aspects of the narratives of the higher order, along with the similarity between the characters at various levels, give *The Bridge* a structure of *en abyme* (see McHale 1987: 124-8).

As shown above, *The Bridge*'s fictional universe can be described as Orr's dreams within Lennox's dream of Orr's life on the Bridge within Lennox's biographical narrative of his life in Edinburgh, which, surprisingly, turns out to be a dream in its own right:

> I know one thing [. . .]. The choice is not between dream and reality; it is between two different dreams.
>   One is my own; the bridge and all I made of it. The other is our collective dream, our corporate imagery. We live the dream; call it American, call it Western, call it Northern or call it just that of all we humans, all life. I was part of one dream, for good or ill, and it was half nightmare and I almost let it kill me, but it hasn't. Yet, anyway. (281)

The dreamlike, idealized character of Edinburgh is signalled in the first instalment of the Edinburgh narrative, which begins with Lennox's arrival to study Geology at the local university, an opportunity he welcomes with inexpressible joy. The "old Edwin's town" seems like a dream come true and a paradise; it is "another country to him, a new and wonderful place; Eden ascendant, Eden before the fall" (100), which offers a young student freedom, happiness, and creative energy. Edinburgh, with its beauty and historical grandeur, stands in sharp contrast with Lennox's home, Glasgow, characterized by industrial cityscape and working-class lifestyle, best represented by his father, "a Labour man" who "lived for football and pay day" (99). Lennox's geographical transition between the two cities is thus representative of a more personal transition, namely the character's mediation between his proletarian roots, of which he grows "a little ashamed" (99), and a more affluent life of the upper-middle class. The character's shifting loyalties find their reflection in his contrasting attitudes towards the two cities. While completely taken by Edinburgh and its possibilities, Lennox looks back on Glasgow as a place dying a slow death of suffocation – "silting up with cheap fat, starved of energy, clogging and clotting and thickening and threatened" (101).

Drifting away from his family and city of origin, Alex becomes immersed in the social life of Edinburgh, with which he becomes acquainted through Andrea Cramond, the love of his life. Alex and Andrea are complete opposites, like Glasgow and Edinburgh, he being a poor boy of limited means and with a complex of his lowly background, and she a rich "Edinburgh girl" who has "a Lotus Elan, a four-roomed flat, two hundred records, and seemingly inexhaustible supplies of money, charm,

Red Leb and sexual energy" (102). As can be expected, in the company of Andrea's family and her affluent school friends Alex is all the time aware of the differences between their respective statuses, feeling embarrassed of his alleged social inferiority, even his west-coast accent. Consequently, he begins "to change, trying to find a middle-ground between all the different things he wanted to be" (103), which amounts to a resemioticization of his identity according to the norms dictated by the social élite of Edinburgh.

Edinburgh, therefore, becomes a scene of Lennox's ideological "makeover," which goes against the grain of his socialist sympathies and youthful idealism, and marks the subordination of his private semiosphere to the codes of the public space. Apart from his already mentioned snobbery, which makes him distance himself from his "humiliating" Glaswegian provenance in speech and behaviour, Alex also gives up Geology for a more profitable degree course in Engineering Design. His desire "to do something which would be of real use to the world" (104) means sacrificing his personal interests for the sake of utility and self-gratification, the values advocated by the ideology of late capitalism and the economic policy of the New Right, which mediate the image of British culture at the time, influencing all areas of social life.

Moreover, Alex's belief in his self-invented Unified Field Theory of consciousness, which involves the rationalization of feelings and emotions, not only makes it difficult for him to understand another person's point of view, but also becomes a medium of his self-deception. For Alex, the machine and its power, represented by the train engine he saw in childhood, constitute an ideal of creativity, the epitome of "all that could be done with work and sense and matter" (108), and, paradoxically, this rationalistic technocratic attitude comes to encompass social life and human relationships. Reason and rationality make Alex suppress his natural yearnings, forsaking togetherness, trust, love, and communal values. Out of logic and counter to his professed anti-Thatcherism, he takes full advantage of the economic opportunities created by the Conservative government, aspiring to riches and success. The same logic and rationality make him tolerate Andrea's sexual flings and her long-standing relationship with a Frenchman called Gustave, despite his deep-entrenched longing for romanticism which results from his traditional upbringing. As a consequence, he gradually adjusts his own expectations (of love, marriage, and sexual exclusiveness) to Andrea's lifestyle (Lyall 1993: 50), letting himself become a victim of emotional exploitation. In time, however, Alex begins to notice the falsehood of the capitalist culture of success in which he has immersed himself, its painted façade concealing the ugly and diseased reality lying beneath. There are moments of uncomfortable acuteness of perception on Lennox's part when he realizes his slavish devotion to capitalism and his role of a turncoat who has forsaken the values he once cherished, which highlights the simmering tension between his latent socialist outlook and the one mediated by capitalist hierarchies and ideologies:

> Nothing seemed to work quite perfectly. The car had annoying rattles, the house CD player had an intermittent fault, the camera had to be replaced and most of the records he bought seemed to have scratches on them; his dishwasher kept flooding the kitchen. He found himself becoming short-tempered with people, and traffic jams infuriated him; a sort of pervasive impatience seemed to fill him, and a callousness he could not evade. He gave money to Live Aid all right, but his first thought when he heard of the Band Aid record had been about the revolutionary adage which compared giving to charity under capitalism to putting a Band-aid on a cancer. [. . .] What, in the end, am I really doing? he asked himself. Just another fucking brick in the wall, just another cog in a machine, if a little better oiled than most. I make money for oil companies and their shareholders and for governments that spend it on weapons that can kill us all a thousand times over instead of just five hundred; I don't even operate at the level of an ordinary decent worker, like my dad did; I'm a fucking *boss*, I *employ*, I have a real drive and initiative (or I used to); I actually make it all run just that little better than it might if I wasn't here. (248-9)

When commenting on the catastrophe of Lennox's life, Thom Nairn observes that as Alex's "uncertainty and instability grow increasingly visible, some kind of impending crash is clearly signalled, and duly takes place within sight" of the Forth Rail Bridge (1993: 133). It is the last thing he sees from the parallel Forth Road Bridge before the crash when he is driving from Dunfermline to Edinburgh (i.e. from the Kingdom of Fife to the City) to talk to Andrea about his feelings for her and the future of their relationship, whose open nature has become too difficult to bear. His car accident, therefore, as Cristie L. March postulates, becomes a "symbolic resistance to his former lifestyle" (2002: 94), the crash being a collision as much with the self as the bridge (Nairn 1993: 133).

The accident on the Forth Road Bridge initiates Lennox's passage into the realm of the subconscious, the stage of transition being underscored by his chaotic first-person account in the novel's opening section,
Coma. The frenzy of Lennox's internal monologue comprises the impressions from the crash scene, e.g. the police cars, his own hemorrhage,
the blood colour of the bridge, or the hazy recollections of the minutes
preceding the accident. Exclamations alternate with questions, italics
with block capitals, standard English with Scottish dialect, the main text
of immediate report with inward musings and reminiscences put in pa-
rentheses and square brackets. The speaker, who with growing anxiety
admits to having forgotten his name, begins to experience hallucinations
in which the dominant and all-obliterating colour is white – white
screen, white noise, or white pain – which is frequently used (e.g. in cinema) as a representation of retreating consciousness. The scene is also
the point of divergence between distinct narrative levels, as the all-
embracing whiteness subsides and gives way to a perplexing duality of
vision:

> I lie on a flat plain, surrounded by tall mountains (or maybe on a bed), sur-
> rounded by . . . machines? People? Either; both (Like, man, in the *really*
> wide view, they're the same. Far out.) Who cares? Do I care? Shit, maybe
> I'm already dead. Maybe there's life after life . . . hmm. Maybe all the rest
> was a dream (yeah, sure), and I wake up to ('Thedarkstation') – what was
> that?
>   Did you hear that? Did *I* hear that?
>   *The dark station*. There it is again. A noise like a train whistle; some-
> thing about to depart. Something about to begin, or end, or both. Some-
> thing that is THEDARKSTATION me. Or not (me no know. Me new here.
> No ask me.)
>   *The dark station*.
>   Oh, all right . . . (12)

Coma, therefore, not only introduces the dimension of the character's
dream(s), the passage between which is highlighted by the train imagery,
but it also emphasizes the mirroring quality between Lennox's and Orr's
narratives, turning the two characters into each other's doubles (see
Pisarska 2012b: 90), indicating the subconscious provenance of the
Bridge world and its central character, John Orr.

The limits of the comatose brain become a private space in which
Lennox finally finds his own voice (the first-person narration of the in-

troductory passages of Triassic and Eocene, as well as the present-tense sections narrated by Orr on the Bridge) as opposed to the biographical story of his Edinburgh life, in which he is a focalizer in someone else's narration. In this light, the third-person narration of the Edinburgh narrative metaphorically highlights Lennox's alienation from himself and the subordination of his private semiosphere to the external social and political outlook of the mediating centre of British culture. Interestingly, Lennox speaking in a coma underlines his detachment from the Standard English narrator of the Edinburgh parts, as he ineffectively tries to control the commencement of the biographical narrative with the power of the Scottish vernacular:

> – O hek gang, look, you don't want to listen to my problems (and I *certainly* don't want to listen to yours) so howsa bout I introduce my fren here; old pala mine, fren frum waybak, wontchya ta giv him
> *Ghost capital –*
> steady boy. Like I was saying, me an this guy go waybak, an I wantcher to give him a real
> *Ghost capital. Real city of –*
> OK OK on ye go fur fuksake
>
>   . . . basturt. (98)

A similar tension between the two narrators – the impersonal narrator mediating Lennox's thoughts and speech in the Edinburgh narrative, and the garrulous Lennox in a coma – takes place in Eocene (185). Such a split between the two identities, the Lennox in a coma and the Edinburgh Lennox, which symbolically represents the separation of the (active) mind from the (inactive) body, is thus underscored by the change of the point of view (the first-person vs. the third-person) and tense of the narration (present vs. past). As a consequence, the Lennox in a coma and the Edinburgh Lennox seem to occupy two different levels in the hierarchy of beings, the former holding a mediating position between the latter and the realm of dreams (i.e. Orr's life on the Bridge).

Ironically, Lennox, dreaming or not, still remains a character in the fictional world of the Edinburgh narrative, his current state of "disembodied" consciousness being a direct consequence of his drunken drive in the waking life, described in his biographical story. The connection (or rather disconnection) between the character-focalizer and the character-narrator is implied by the sequencing of their respective narratives: the third-person Edinburgh passages follow those narrated by the Lennox in a coma within the same sections – Triassic and Eocene.[26] In contrast, Orr's narrative always develops in Meta-sections (Metaphormosis, Metamorpheus, and Metamorphosis), whose names, as Middleton observes, "carry the implication of crossing over and transition" (1995: 22), and as such foreground the process of the character's mediation between the novel's dream worlds.

Because of its far earlier commencement than that of the Edinburgh narrative, the Orr narrative initially offers the only version of quasi-phenomenal reality. Already in the first Orr-related section, the protagonist reveals himself to be an amnesiac, undergoing dream therapy. It may deceive the reader easily into treating this section as a continuation of the preceding Coma, John Orr being (quite appropriately) taken for the anonymous victim of the described car accident. Further credibility to the narrative's mimeticism is provided by Orr's description of the circumstances of his appearance on the Bridge and the reasons for his amnesia, which correspond with the chaotic account in the preceding Coma, whose speaker raves about the bridge, the accident, the "circle of pain on chest" (12), and the inability to recall his own name. It is as late as Triassic that the mimetic yardstick of the Edinburgh narrative is introduced in its own right and like a rear-view mirror reflects back on and calls into question the reliability of the Bridge world, on which Craig comments:

> In Banks's third serious novel, *The Bridge*, the relationship between what is presumed to be "reality" and what "fiction" is explored from the opposite perspective. In this case, the novel constructs an alternative world, the world of the Bridge, which we take to be real, but real only in the sense that fantasy asks us to suspend our disbelief and accept as real a world which does not correspond to the actualities of our own. This fantasy world, however, turns out to be the allegoric dreamworld of a man in a coma, a refracted version of the actualities of his life and of the world in which he has lived. We learn, in the course of the novel, to interpret the allegory and to see through it the real nature of a life which, told simply in itself, would have revealed almost nothing of the depths of the character's existence because they are depths of which he is not himself aware. (2002: 24)

---

26 On the importance of the intermediary narratorial dimension of Lennox in a coma see Pisarska 2012b: 92.

Lennox's biographical narrative functions therefore as the literal plane to the "dream vision" of his life as John Orr. The realm of the mysterious, as postulated by Lotman, is thus duly transferred to the internal space, i.e. Lennox's comatose mind, which expands into a strange quasi-mimetic universe housing the enormous multi-level structure of the Bridge, situated on the way between the equally unknown extremes of the City and the Kingdom.[27]

Due to its massive proportions, the Bridge provides space for various human activities. Intersected horizontally by railway tracks, tram lines, tunnels, and numerous decks crammed with various types of architecture, and vertically by lift shafts, chimneys, and aerials, the Bridge constitutes a habitable maze which is perhaps not entirely impossible as an architectonic enterprise but definitely extraordinary and far from the protagonist's experience. John Orr is an outsider to the Bridge and although he adapts himself quite successfully to its laws, he also feels acutely the lack of memories concerning his previous life and place of origin (even his name, John Orr, was given to him by the hospital personnel). This ambiguous status makes it even more important for him to explore the nature of the extraordinary edifice. Such knowledge could consequently lead Orr to the discovery of his own past and provenance, which presumably lie somewhere beyond the Bridge. Therefore he tries to gather every piece of evidence concerning the lands at its either end:

> Coffee is brought. I have never seen a coffee plant on the bridge. My lamb's kidneys must come from somewhere, but where? On the bridge we talk of down- and up-river, and of Citywards and Kingdomwards; there must be land (would a bridge make sense without it?) but how far away?
> I did all the research I could, given the limitations of both language and access which the organization of the bridge's facilities impose on the amateur investigator, but for all my months of work, I came no closer to discovering the nature or location of either the City or the Kingdom. They remain enigmatic, placeless. (45)

The Bridge, being Lennox's creation and a refuge from his disappointing waking life, is supposed to keep his dream alter ego within its confines,

---

27 Lotman thus describes the change in the understanding of the dream over time: "The dream-prediction (a window into the mysterious future) gave way to the notion of the dream as a way into the self. In order that the function of the dream could change, it was necessary to change the location of the mysterious space. From the external it became internal" (2009: 144).

preventing Orr from regaining his memory and waking Lennox up from his fantasy. Thus, although evidently open to rail traffic and trade, the Bridge is also closed in the most obstructive, or even totalitarian, way, blocking not only the exchange of ideas between its inhabitants concerning the lands beyond it but also preventing the influx of "intruders" from outside. Orr's inquisitive urge is continually dampened or called into question by the local people he meets in this world: Mr Brooke, an engineer, for whom the Bridge is the only point of reference and the islands supporting its pillars are the only subject of exploration, or Abberlaine Arrol, for whom both the City and the Kingdom "exist somewhere" (118) but remain obscure and not really of interest. In fact, the locals seem to take the Bridge for granted, being used to its gigantic proportions, geographical indeterminacy, and its general *modus operandi* of a self-regulating system, having no need to interrogate its rationale or look beyond it. Moreover, Orr's own mobility is limited by the hospital wrist band, which identifies him as a patient and allows gratuitous passage "between two tram termini only; a range of a dozen bridge sections and about the same number of miles in each direction," which, despite being quite generous, is "a restriction, nevertheless" (46). Last but not least, Orr is stopped in his search by the local authorities, who not only withhold the information concerning the Bridge but apparently also try to keep at bay all signs of the regions lying beyond it, as seems to be the case with the barrage balloons put along the Bridge, which are meant to prevent the flight of alien planes (122). Paradoxically, the Bridge itself, following some peculiar dream logic, seems to thwart Orr's attempts to probe deeper into its tissue. It becomes strangely obvious in Lennox's search for the Third City Records and Materials Library, so far "missing presumed lost forever" (32), which becomes a metaphor of Lennox's lost memory. Due to its volatile topography, in which corridors, passages, and lifts are shifted or go missing overnight, or because of the acts of inexplicable self-sabotage and violence (fires, impending accidents), the Bridge is impossible to map and therefore very difficult to explore.

As stated before, Orr's ineffective attempts to recover his memories can only be blamed on Lennox's reluctance to re-emerge from the world of his oneiric fantasies, which he misguidedly regards as being under his own control in contrast to his life in Edinburgh. Remaining in a coma, Lennox is free; although his body is incapacitated and manhandled by the hospital stuff, his mind is independent of all influences, it is "in charge, in command, invulnerable" (183).[28] The split of the character's world between the "corporate" waking nightmare and his own wish-fulfilment dream of the Bridge proves that Lennox is able to discriminate between the two orders; however, he opts for the latter because it affords him safe confines and control over his own creation. Lennox's deliberate clinging to his inner world of dreams when he is finally the pivot of Andrea's life and not her plaything (she has been watching over him instead of taking care of his French rival, Gustave, who suffers from MS) becomes obvious at the end of the novel in the section Coda, when he is already awake but still refusing to open his eyes to the outside world (279).

Lennox's retreat into the refuge of the Bridge world, whose design recreates on a larger scale that of the Forth Rail Bridge, appears quite logical in view of the fact that the Forth Bridge functions as a recurring landmark in Lennox's life, appearing at the moments of change and transition in the character's life, and being as much a personal as a national symbol (cf. Pisarska 2012b: 97). Moreover, the Bridge world complies with Alex's nostalgia for the past, before technological progress forever changed the traditional railroad, at the same time spatializing in its retro-structure his suppressed longing for romance (190). One can hear "the continual hisses and clanks, grindings and gratings, klaxons and whistles of the trains on the deck," while "great pulsing clouds of white steam roll around the street and upwards" (37). The same romanticizing of the past is noticeable in the overall ambience of the upper-class sections of the Bridge, of which grand lifts fitted with rugs, chandeliers, brasswork, mahogany, and sepia photographs are but one example.

The alternative world mediated by Lennox's comatose mind allows the protagonist, at least initially, to enjoy an extremely pleasurable life. Orr's story begins at the very top of the social ladder and also at the top of the Bridge, as he occupies the apartments close to its summit. Thus,

---

28 As such, Lennox's escapism complies with Freud's ideas concerning the mechanism of *psychical repression* (called by Freud the "ostrich policy"), which is governed by the Pleasure Principle and leads to the subconscious avoidance of the memory of everything that once caused distress and "unpleasure" (Freud 2010: 596).

the spatial relationship of "up" and "down" perspective translates into the Bridge's social stratification – the privileged castes inhabit its upper decks, while the lower decks are a "natural" habitat of menial workers and the proletariat. Hospital financing allows Orr to lead an equally luxurious lifestyle: to dine in elegant restaurants and clubs, to visit art galleries, where he buys paintings and sculptures, and to become involved in different sorts of leisure activities, which to a large extent resembles Lennox's consumerist way of life. Yet another aspect of Alex's enviable dream life is the gentlemanly poise and exquisite appearance of his dream counterpart (43), as opposed to Lennox's ordinary looks and "a bald patch on his head [. . .] the size of a bath plug-hole" (249). No wonder that Orr unwittingly torpedoes Dr Joyce's attempts to make him regain his memory. At first, he concocts false dreams or conceals the true ones, and finally, he refuses to be put under hypnosis because all that might shake Lennox, the instigator of the dream world, out of the pleasant and self-flattering oblivion into which he put himself after the accident.

Orr's narrative replays in reverse Lennox's social advancement and moral downfall, his awakening memory working like a photographic negative for Lennox's progressive amnesia of his proletarian past. As a perfect representative of the Bridge's élite, Orr often manifests a sense of superiority towards the lower classes (see 41-2), his inherent snobbery being reflective of Alex's separation from his working-class background. Orr's aloofness from the caste of workers is aggravated by his lack of understanding of their speech (49). Strangely enough, whereas everybody else on the Bridge speaks at least one other language connected with their work or official position, Orr can speak only the Bridge's official, ceremonial tongue, i.e. the language of the Staff and Administrators. This monolingualism constitutes an explicit reference to Lennox's success in dropping his Glaswegian accent, which initially marked him out among Andrea's affluent Edinburgh friends. Another pointer to the biographical narrative is provided by Orr's friendships on the Bridge – formed almost exclusively with engineers – whose implicit social prejudice and self-seeking character become manifest after Orr's degradation, when he is instantaneously excluded from their circle.

The Bridge world generated by Lennox's mind is an interesting case of semiotic determinism: the individuals are recognized and limited by their social function which is communicated by the type of attire they wear. "[Clothes] are, after all, a language; they do not so much say things about us, they are what is said" (41), asserts Orr, which ironically foreshadows his own painful experience of the Bridge's social discrimination when the fantasy eventually turns against its own demiurge. Transferred from the upper deck to Level U7, inhabited by workers, and forced to wear overalls, he is perceived in terms of his present clothes even by the people who used to know him as a privileged patient of Dr Joyce. The recognition of Orr as standing lower in the hierarchy is connected with the change of attitude towards him: indifference to his predicament or downright disrespect and violence replace the formerly manifested attentiveness and deference.

The fantasy of Lennox's alternative world begins to erode, first, by forcing Orr down the social ladder, and second, by allowing the intrusion of the memory of the car crash and the pain connected with his relationship with Andrea/Abberlaine.[29] More significantly, the comfortable oblivion of the Bridge is increasingly undermined by Orr's dreams, the most disturbing of which is the recurring dream of the barbarian warrior, who represents in an exaggerated manner Lennox's Glasgow provenance.[30] Wandering through the worlds of fairy tales and Greek myths, fighting wicked magicians and imaginary monsters, the warrior recounts his hack-and-slash adventures in phonetically rendered Scottish dialect, as a result of which the storehouse of folk and mythical lore is filtered through and questioned by the swordsman's practical Glaswegian consciousness. Alongside run the passages spoken in standard English by the Familiar, a talkative chimera-like creature perched on the Barbarian's shoulder, which benefits from the latter's strength and fearlessness, at the same time deriding him for his apparent brainlessness and crudity. The repartee between angry Scots and denigrating standard English is also an apt illustration of Lennox's mental "state of the Union" (Nairn

---

29   On the function of Abberlaine Arrol as Andrea's Bridge alter ego see Pisarska 2012b: 99-101.

30   In this way, Lennox's fantasy of the Bridge comes to epitomize Freud's idea of the return of the repressed, as a result of which "the very thing which has been chosen as a means of repression, [. . .] becomes the carrier of the thing recurring; in and behind the agencies of repression the material repressed finally asserts itself victoriously" (1917, Part II, sec. I, para 49). For details see Pisarska 2012b: 100-1.

1993: 133). It represents Lennox's mediation between his "embarrassing" Glaswegian roots and his later education and trained refinement, at
the same time providing a metaphor of Scotland's relationship with the
patronizing Anglocentric superstructure.

If Orr stands for everything Lennox would like to be, the Barbarian
represents what is latent in him, offering a somewhat aggressive interro-
gation of Lennox's confusing and masochistic feelings for Andrea. In
the first instalment of the dream, the warrior escapes with his life from a
confrontation with the evil queen (Andrea's obvious Sword and Sorcery
incarnation),[31] and quenches his unsatisfied desire for gold by performing a multiple rape on a group of mutilated women (much to Orr's revul-
sion). The ghastly act of violence inverts the pattern of abuse which repeats itself in Lennox's life – through his dream alter ego, Alex becomes
the abuser, realizing the masculine fantasy of domination. The second
stage of the warrior's quest describes his descent into the Underworld
and through direct allusions invites comparison with the Orpheus myth
(cf. Middleton 1995: 23-4). The swordsman becomes an unconscious
carrier of parody by defying the perennial paradigms of several Greek
myths. Challenging ancient mythology, one of the mediating systems of
European culture, the barbarian turns inside out the archetypes which
hold sway over the collective imaginary, proving not only his own re-
sourcefulness and stamina but also revealing, with a truly postmodernist
élan, the flimsiness of established and apparently unquestionable grand
narratives.

Orr's passage through the lands beyond the Bridge, which comprises
most of the section Metamorphosis, on the one hand reflects in a distorted mirror Lennox's life after graduation from university as described in
the preceding Eocene, and on the other, brings him closer to the awakening, which he instinctively voices: "Cities and Kingdoms and Bridges
and Towers; I'm sure I'm heading for them all" (210). Orr's journey is

---

31   The connection Lennox – Barbarian is made obvious in "Eocene," when Len-
      nox's comatose self launches into the following jeremiad: "And what a filthy
      trick, what a typically dirty piece of underhand undercover underclothed mis-
      understanding by the evil queen herself. How could she stoop so low? (Well,
      yer jurst bends over like this—) Rousing the goddamn barbarians against me;
      ha! Was that the best she could think of?" (183). The passage not only estab-
      lishes an association between Andrea and the evil queen, but also links Len-
      nox's refined speech with the Glasgow slang used by the warrior.

gathering momentum, its speed being underscored by the titles of the subchapters – Oligocene, Miocene, Pliocene, Quaternary – named after the most recent geological epochs. The world seen through the train window changes in landscape, the Bridge gives way to mountains, plains and tundra, and Lennox's wish-fulfilment dream turns progressively into a nightmare. Thom Nairn postulates that "as the Bridge world crumbles, its superior surreality begins to concede to the real scenario of contemporary Edinburgh," and so "[t]angents converge eerily but convincingly, worlds come closer, overlaps grow more distinct" (1993: 133). Indeed, because in Metamorphosis the Edinburgh narrative develops practically hand in hand with Orr's narrative, the analogies between the two become more evident and easier to notice.

The further Orr gets from the Bridge, the more chaotic, unstable, and dangerous becomes the space through which he travels, while the fantasy becomes uncontrollable and begins to repeat the horrors of Lennox's waking life. After a series of trials and vicissitudes which apparently correspond to Lennox's professional development and his alienation from the space of origin (Orr's stay in the Republic or his imprisonment in the underground compound [215-20]), Orr continues his train journey working as a waiter to some elderly bureaucrats speaking an almost incomprehensible language. The lands watched by Orr through the window are shaken by war and volcanic eruptions, the prevailing chaos and destruction standing in visible contrast to the almost totalitarian order and tight security of the Bridge. The train with the officials (who apparently represent the post-war consensus in British politics) is eventually destroyed by the forces of the Field Marshal (which is, presumably, Banks's satire on Margaret Thatcher and her election victory), a sadist figure who treats men like pigs and pigs like men, and perpetrates heinous war crimes on soldiers and civilians alike.

The escalation of the hostilities in Orr's narrative runs parallel to Lennox's reports of contemporary tragedies, political upheavals, and acts of military violence, i.e. the failure of the devolution referendum, Lennon's assassination, Israel's attack on southern Lebanon, the Falklands War, and the militaristic ambitions of Reagan's administration endorsed by the British government of the time. Orr's degradation is taken to the extreme when he is forced to wear a woman's dress and sodomize the Marshal with a rifle barrel when the latter is raping a pig. His initial fearful surrender to the Marshal's power and his eventual killing of the brute and escape from his quarters represent Lennox's reaction to Thatcher's policy in the Edinburgh narrative – first obeisance and then violent rejection of his degrading servile attitude, which finds its ultimate manifestation in the crash on the Forth Rail Bridge.

Lennox's impending awakening and thus also his transition between the two worlds are heralded by the repeated glimpses of the Edinburgh world on the level of Orr's narrative which take the form of dreams about Lennox's life, with the haunting image of the Forth Rail Bridge (212). However, before he has a chance "to wake up into another existence, a different life; just a nice clean hospital bed" (267), he must return to the Bridge, the place of mediation between his two parallel lives. The ruined and forlorn structure to which he returns, standing in the middle of the golden echoing desert, is far from the vibrant metal colossus presented in Metaphormosis and Metamorpheus, and as such it becomes a fitting metaphor for Lennox's shattered self, exhausted by painful and corrupting experiences, and stranded, partly of its own accord, in the white refuge of sleep. "Its feet still stand, its bones still rise, but its linking arms, its connections – they have gone" (270), muses Orr in the cooling shadow of the Bridge's towering girders, duly voicing Lennox's disconnection from the fabric of his waking life.

Orr's narrative voice gradually loses its distinctiveness, as the narrator suddenly finds himself not *outside* but *inside* the Bridge, in bed, surrounded by machines and connected to drips. The images of the hospital room alternate with the fading images of the Bridge, as the narrator registers the presence of the characters from Orr's narrative (Dr Joyce and Abberlaine Arrol), while mingling elements of the two stories (272). The next section is narrated by what sounds like the garrulous Lennox in a coma, his style deprived of Orr's conspicuous dignity and refinement but rife with jargon and swear words, which points to the approaching fusion of the two identities, and the character's transition from the world of dreams into the world of contemporary Scotland. The passages offer a reversal of the situation from Coma: Orr/Lennox still cannot recall his own name, but he can hear first sounds of the outside world, and the blankness gives way to the images taking shape behind his closed eyelids.

The beginning of Coda, the last section of the novel, brings the dialogue between what can be considered two sides of Lennox, the one who
wants to hide from the real world in the security of the Bridge and the
other, who is apparently responsible for the already initiated process of
awakening. The latter turns out to have been also responsible for the
drunken accident seven months before, which therefore indicates not only the character's return to the level of the Edinburgh narrative but also
his return to and eventual resuming of the suspended biography, which
underscores the circular movement of the narrative. From this moment
onwards the narration is continued consistently in the present tense, from
the first-person perspective, which indicates the unification of the narratorial voice preceded by the unification of Lennox's multiple identities
from all levels. Last but not least, Coda is also the point of unification of
Lennox's mind with his inert machine-supported body.

Paradoxically, Lennox reawakens not to reality but to another dream,
or rather nightmare from which he quite violently opted out by crashing
his car on the bridge – that of "Thatcher's Britain and Reagan's world
[and of] all the usual bullshit" (280). Alex's participation in the corporate dream eventually brings him back to where he started, his abandoned hometown, Glasgow (ironically, he was moved to the Southern
General Hospital from the Royal Infirmary in Edinburgh). It marks his
physical return to the space of origin and presumably implies his greater
awareness of the dangers posed by his complicity in the capitalist illusion that the contemporary world has become. He is again on the bridge,
his life torn between his former economic pursuits and his social as well
as moral obligations, but he has returned a changed man. As Douglas
Gifford observes, his laconic answer to Andrea after he wakes up
("Welcome back" – "Oh Yeah?"), "indicates Alex's cautious optimism:
life is worth living in Scotland, but only on one's own more confident
terms" (1996: 41).

To sum up, on the thematic level, the parallel, convergent alternative
lives of Lennox/Orr/Barbarian are texts which comment on and interpret
one another, foregrounding the novel's preoccupation with the issues of
Scottish identity within Thatcherite Britain. Descending to the deepest
recesses of his subconscious, Lennox retrieves those elements of his
Scottish self which have been lost to him through repression and denial,
and thus returns to his waking life as one of the few awakened among

the millions of dreamers of the collective dream. The "quality bridge" of Lennox's oneiric fantasy, which eventually turns into its own ghost in the middle of the desert, may, in fact, be symbolical not only of Lennox's individual predicament but also of the situation of all Scottish people. This connection becomes especially striking if we consider the dependence of Banks's Bridge imagery on the real Forth Rail Bridge, whose recurrent presence in the novel makes the latter, as Gavin Miller observes, "a meditation on a national symbol" (2007a: 204), and, by implication, on the condition of Scotland. Therefore, with its initial luxury and final devastation, the Bridge seems to function as a subconscious (or mythic) reminder of what has been suffered both by Lennox and the whole nation as a result of the Conservative policy – a crisis of identity, the loss of the communitarian spirit, and the nationwide amnesia of (and thus separation from) one's social and moral heritage. At the same time, Banks apparently suggests, Scotland resembles its major engineering achievement – the Forth Rail Bridge, which is cyclically repainted, bit by bit, and remains, as Lennox aptly phrases it, "an everlasting bridge, a never-quite-the-same bridge, its vast and ruddy frame forever sloughing off and being replaced, like a snake constantly shedding, a metamorphosing insect which is its own cocoon and always changing" (281), which emphasizes the nation's capacity for rebirth and endurance.

2.3. Across the Multiverse: The Many Worlds of *Transition*

The theme of mediation as explored in the context of alternative realities is also present in Banks's 2009 novel, *Transition*, whose fictional universe of infinite parallel realities is indebted to the many-worlds interpretation of quantum mechanics.[32] Set in the period marked by three wa-

---

32   As opposed to the British edition, in the United States the novel appeared under the name Iain M. Banks. This evidently points to its speculative character, which made the publisher acknowledge it as part of the author's science fiction opus. Banks, however, seems to have treated it as a mainstream novel and his attempt to write something comparable to *The Bridge* (Walker 2009). In his review of *Transition* James Walton explains Banks's intention concerning the genre of the novel: "Faced with the complaint that too wide a gap has opened up between his mainstream novels and his science fiction (published under Iain M. Banks), he's not only admitted that this is probably true, he's even promised to correct the problem in the way the critics have recommended: by putting some of the fantastical elements back into the mainstream work

tershed events, i.e. the Fall of the Berlin Wall (1989), the Al-Qaeda attacks on the WTC (2001), and the onset of the 2008 financial crisis, the novel presents several intertwined narratives featuring distinct homodiegetic narrators or focalizing characters whose lives turn out to be connected, in one way or another, with the activity of an elusive organization – the Concern. Based on the planet Calbefraques, one of the many versions of Earth, the Concern (also called L'Expédience), sends out its agents called transitionaries to parallel worlds, where they interfere with the course of events in order to push the said world onto an alternative historical path envisaged as desirable by the Concern.

The idea of transition to multiple alternative dimensions is related to the concept of mediation in its several meanings. To begin with, transition presupposes "flitting," i.e. crossing the boundary between two distinct time-space realities, which can be effected by the Concern agents under the influence of septus, a special substance which induces a state of "waking dream" (2009c: 14) – a mediating mental condition necessary for an interdimensional jump. The ormolu pill, containing the drug, as the transitionary Temudjin Oh observes, has the power of "flicking one into another soul and another world" (73), thus functioning as the catalyst for a transfer of the agent's mind from his/her own body into the body of an inhabitant of the target world, temporarily displacing the latter's personality. As a result, the body of the host becomes a medium through which the agent can act and thus accomplish his or her mission: it allows them to "fit in" a particular social and political context by complying with the codes of an alternative semiosphere in appearance and behaviour.[33] Transition can therefore be understood in terms of semiotic translation across the interdimensional boundary.

---

again. *Transition* certainly proves that he wasn't lying" (2009). Because *Transition* was clearly meant as part of Banks's literary fiction, I am including its analysis in my book.

33   This physical adjustment is shown as significant for a transitionary's own safety and his/her mission when Temudjin flits to a Judeo-Islamic version of Earth where Christians are terrorists. Reassured that he does not resemble a Christian terrorist, Tem adds: "I look bland. But bland is good, bland is safe, bland blends: perfect cover" (15). The same concern with "fitting in naturally" is voiced by Patient 8262, a former transitionary and one of the novel's narrators, who is currently hiding (presumably from the Concern trackers) in a hos-

While retaining his agent awareness, the transitionary is always affected by the physiological and temperamental peculiarity of the "host" body, which points to a dialogic nature of the process. At the same time, the choice of the target person seems to be at least partly determined by the traveller's unconscious preferences or even gender, which is communicated in the following passage:

> Plainly, I inherit something of the character of the person whose being I usurp. That must be where the OCD [i.e. Obsessive Compulsive Disorder] comes from, and one's sexual inclination, as does the taste for, variously, coffee, tea, chocolate, spiced milk, hard liquor, bland or spicy food, or prunes. I have found myself, over the years, surveying the reality I find myself in with the eyes of somebody who is plainly a general medical practitioner, a surgeon, a landscape designer, a mathematician, a structural engineer, a livestock breeder, a litigation lawyer, an insurance assessor, an hotelier and a psychiatrist. I seem to be at home amongst the professions. [. . .]
>   On the other hand, I have never been a woman, which is slightly odd and even a little disappointing. Obviously there are limits. (72)[34]

Although involving a shift between physical realities, transition appears to be first and foremost a mental process, which requires the agent's use of his or her entrenched and thus familiar conceptual models for the sake of visualization of a particular target world. Pondering over the fate of the transitionaries who are reported missing in action, Temudjin Oh remarks: "*When we flit we go to where we imagine*, and if – distracted, disoriented – we imagine something too far away from what we know and where we wish to go, we may end up somewhere it is somehow impossible to imagine one's way back from" (87, emphasis added).[35] At

---

pital in one of the parallel realities: "[E]thnicity, physiognomy, skin colour, language, skills – all must be taken into account" (12).

34   Temudjin's incarnations in the various many worlds are accompanied by his many names – Temudjin Oh, Mr Marquand Ys, Snr Marquan Dise, Dr Marquand Esmere, M. Marquan Demesere, Mark Cavan, or Aiman Q'ands. Although the names appear different, they "tend to gyrate round a certain sets of sounds, clustering about a limited repertoire of phonemes" (50), which points to Oh's use of familiar patterns in his mediation of alternative identities. At the same time, he never knows in advance what his name is going to be.

35   A similar point is made by Patient 8262, who comments on his pursuers' knowledge of him and his way of thinking, which makes it easy for them to determine his flitting destination (13).

the same time, while the transitionary's mind flits between the many worlds of the multiverse, his or her version remains on Calbefraques, sustaining life functions and basic social interaction. However, the intellectual capacity and motor activity of "this residual self" are limited, its state close to stupor or vegetation (see 83), which emphasizes the importance of the individual mind in controlling the corporeal frames not only in target realities but also on the home planet.

Calbefraques, the version of Earth from which the Concern operates, holds an exceptional position among the infinitudes of worlds in the multiverse:

Calbefraques was the ultimate Open world, the mirror image of one of the numberless perfectly Closed Earths where nobody knew about the many worlds; a place where possibly every single adult soul who walked its surface knew that it was merely one world within an infinitude of worlds, and a nexus at that, a stepping-off point for as much of that infinitude as it was possible to imagine.

And a world, an Earth that was close to unique. Logically there had to be other versions of this Earth that were close to the Calbefraques that we knew; but we seemed to be unable to access them. It was as though by being the place that could act as a gateway to any other version of Earth, Calbefraques has somehow outpaced all the other versions of itself that could have existed. It seemed that in the same way that the true consciousness of a transitioner could only be in one world at a time, there could only be one world that was perfectly Open, and that world, that unique Earth was this one, called Calbefraques. (212-13)

As stated above, taking the idea of Openness to the extreme, the planet constitutes the place of mediation – the causal link and the centre – in the interdimensional communication, being at the same time the closest to the universal earthly prototype which repeats itself in the multitudes of worlds, called meta-Earths. As such, Calbefraques is quite appropriately perceived by Patient 8262 as a "greater reality" to the dull Closed versions of Earth represented by the world which has become his prison (344). Functioning as the pivot of the meta-universe, allowing travel to its parallel worlds while being itself unparalleled, Calbefraques represents the "root reality" for transitionaries like Oh (84), the world from the perspective of which every other reality may appear secondary.

Aware of the existence of the many worlds and possessed of the power to visit and influence them, the Concern acts from the position of singularity resultant from the uniqueness of its planet, perceiving the other meta-Earths and their respective histories in accordance with its own sense of what is right, necessary, or beneficial. First, the Concern agents and scientists rely on a set of binary categories, e.g. plausible/implausible, hermetic/connected, banal/bizarre, kind/cruel, by means of which the alternative worlds can be "judged, evaluated and ranked" from the perspective of the ultimate Open world (the patient, for example, makes clear that the reader's version of Earth is plausible, hermetic, banal, and cruel) (58). Second, in its activities, the organization focuses on the places which reveal a degree of instability, "spinning, wobbling plates [. . .] where it feels that matters could go either way," towards the restoration of balance or a complete catastrophe, depending on the actions undertaken or not by the transitionaries from Calbefraques (89). The possibility of two alternative futures is best encapsulated in Temudjin's report of his chase in one of the many worlds after two young Maghrebis who intended to rape and mutilate a girl from their neighbourhood:

> All gallant stuff, and she would allegedly turn into either a cowed, failed little thing who'd jump with her baby from the roof of this very block before she was twenty, or a noted authority on psycho-semantics – whatever that was – at the universities of Trier and Cairo, according to whether the mooted violation took place or not. (277)

Depending on the gravity and development of the pivotal situation in an alternative world, the transitionary may act as a murderer or avenger, or, quite conversely, as "a positive angel, a good fairy, an imp of the benign" (84), preventing crimes and accidents, improving people's fortunes, and creating other beneficial circumstances influencing their future.

The many-worlds interpretation, which on the higher level underpins the construction of the novel's multidimensional setting, on a deeper level foregrounds the theme of individual mediation, which is reflected in the novel's structure of several narratives, dominated by different centres of perception, and thus presenting the reader with distinct and often colliding alternative world-pictures. Especially significant in this context is the dichotomy of Open vs. Closed worlds, and the related question of awareness and the lack of it, which is played out as much on the (mac-ro)cosmic scale of the quantum universe as on the smaller scale of inter-personal and social relationships.

Talking about Open and Closed worlds, Patient 8262 defines the former as those in which most people are "Aware" of the existence of the many worlds and of the possibility of flitting between them, and the latter as those in which the people have no knowledge of the parallel realities, let alone of the fact that they are connected (179). Consequently, Open worlds recognize their place within a web of connections, within "a multitude of worlds, forever exponentially and explosively multiplying through time" (82), while Closed worlds perceive themselves as "singular, settled and linear" (82), functioning as their own frames of reference. The discrepancy in the open vs. closed perception calls to mind a conversation between Mrs Mulverhill, a teacher at the Concern's University of Practical Talents, and Temudjin Oh, which casts light on the combined meaning of individual consciousness, human interaction, and mediation:

> She said, "No, I see consciousness as a matter of focus. It's like a magnifying glass concentrating light ray on a point on a surface until it bursts into flame – the flame being consciousness. It is the focusing of reality that creates that self-awareness." [. . .]
> "There is no intelligence without context [. . .]. Just as a magnifying glass effectively casts a partial shadow around the point of its focus – the debt required to produce the concentration elsewhere – so meaning is sucked out of our surroundings, concentrated in ourselves, in our minds."
> [. . .]
> "I'd have said," (I said, instead) "that we give, even . . . Even that we radiate, emanate meaning. We ascribe context to external things. Without us they exist, I suppose –
> "Do they?" she murmured.
> "– but we give them names and we see the systems and processes that link them. We contextualize them within their setting. We make them more real by knowing what they mean and represent." (29)

As can be inferred from the above passage, Mrs Mulverhill believes that the person's awareness of him/herself and their position in the world results from their immersion in the outside reality, a particular semiotic space which mediates patterns of signification for our individual perception. Without the larger context, the awareness of what surrounds us, no conscious existence ("intelligence") or self-awareness are possible. Whatever our minds consider meaningful is only so with reference to our semiotic experience and the yardstick of the external world. On the other hand, nothing really signifies unless it is translated and (re)constructed – viz. semioticized and channelled – through the medium of our minds. Therefore what we call the world or reality exists only in the form of our mental concepts. Temudjin, however, ventures the opinion that "external things" (or reality) do exist outside human perception but that they become tangible and comprehensible to us only when mediated by the sign systems such as natural language or the meta-language of science. In effect, reality, though existing in its own right, is real only when placed within the bounds of our own semiotics, being described, ordered, and contextualized in terms of the codes and categories devised by our consciousness, either collective or personal.

At the same time, in order to see things as they truly are, one should go beyond his or her familiar context because self-focus can limit perception to the point of obliteration of meaning, which is implied by Temudjin's thoughts following his conversation with Mrs Mulverhill: "I recalled that the eyes only see by moving; we can fasten our gaze on something and stare intently at it only because our eyes are consumed with dozens of tiny involuntary movements each second. Hold something perfectly and genuinely still in our field of vision and that very fixity makes it disappear" (30).[36] The above observation pertains as much to the idea of Closed and Open worlds, the former operating within their immediate limited context and the latter being able to transcend it to the effect of (self-)awareness, as to groups of people and individuals, and their (in)ability to notice that the existence and meaning of their Self is

---

36   Wandering through the city of Venice on the reader's Earth, Temudjin remarks on our world's corruption, greed and selfishness, insisting on the fact that despite it being the reader's world, the Transitionary, as an outsider to it, knows it far better than its inhabitants (274). A similar look from outside our own context occurs when the transitionary discusses our Earth in the context of other "limited company worlds." As Temudjin knows, such worlds develop fastest; however, the price which is paid by society is too high (301). Ironically, he makes this observation waiting in Venice for Adrian Cubbish, a City trader and the devoted apostle of late capitalism (and the novel's another narrator), which produces an interesting clash of perspectives. It also defamiliarizes the reality the reader takes for granted, allowing us to take a step back and adopt the position of an outsider judging ourselves.

defined only in relation with the Other, the many worlds of nations, communities, and particular human beings.[37]

The awareness of and responsibility to the Other are the principles which seemingly lie at the core of the Concern's activity, its agents being "fixers" who improve histories going or already gone awry in other realities. This moral duty on the individual and collective levels is voiced by Mrs Mulverhill as follows:

> "There is a grain to the fabric of space-time [. . .]. A scale on which there is no further divisible smoothness, only individual, irreducible quanta where reality itself seethes with a continual effervescence of sub-microscopic creation and destruction. I believe there to be a similarly irreducible texture to morality, a scale beyond which it is senseless to proceed. Infinity goes in only one direction; outward, into more inhabited worlds, more shared realities. In the other direction, on a reducing scale, once you reach the level of an individual consciousness – for all practical purposes, a single human being – you can usefully reduce no further. It is at that level that significance lies. If you so something to benefit one person, that is an absolute gain, and its relative insignificance in the wider scheme is irrelevant. Benefit two people without concomitant harm to others – or a village, tribe, city, class, nation, society or civilization – and the benefits are scalable, arithmetic. There is no excuse beyond fatalistic self-indulgence and sheer laziness for doing nothing." (126)

Mrs Mulverhill's claims can be read in connection with Patient 8262's account of the Philosophy class devoted to solipsism which he attended at the UPT as part of his transitionary training. Described by the tutor as "the default state of humanity," solipsism makes us believe that "we personally, our own individual consciousness, [is] the only thing that really exist[s] and that nothing else matter[s]" (241). Consequently, all the external things which we call reality are a projection of the person's own

---

The web of interrelationships and mutual dependence among individuals and groups is best encapsulated by Patient 8262, who describes our way in life as subject to Brownian motion, as a result of which our private worlds, like particles, collide with and are influenced by the alternative worlds of other people, in which accident and free will operate in equal measure. As a result, we not only live in parallel dimensions of the multiverse but also in the many worlds of the future, the shape of which depends as much on our own choices as the activity of others: "We live in infinity of infinities, and we reshape our lives with every passing thought and each unconscious action, threading an ever-changing course through the myriad possibilities of existence" (57-8).

mind, while the Self becomes the only point of reference. In the end, such an excess of subjectivity and a feeling of the singular righteousness and superiority of one's own perception may lead to a denial or even active resistance to what others consider to be "objective truth." Such self-absorption and egotism is especially dangerous when revealed by the people in a position of power, which Mrs Mulverhill detects in the behaviour of the Concern's self-proclaimed leader and her own chief-enemy, Madame d'Ortolan: "She has self-belief raised almost to solipsistic levels. [. . .] And that self-belief, it makes her think that she can do no wrong just because she is who she is" (332).

Being the case of solipsistic self-righteousness, Madame d'Ortolan is also, quite predictably, a model example of the greed for power and political superiority. In her figure, Banks presents a combination of unquestionable authority, manipulative streak, and a fear of the Other and the unknown. A crypto-racist with a "fanaticism for neatness" (332), she opposes the idea that the mankind of the multiverse could come in contact with alien civilizations, and she persecutes those who welcome this possibility.[38] On top of this, the transition drug, septus, which gives the Concern access to the parallel realities, constitutes a weapon ensuring its domination. Therefore those who can flit without the Concern-rationed ormolu pill, like Temudjin Oh, must be eliminated as a threat to the organization's economic and military security. Madame d'Ortolan's criminal methods to prevent humanity's encounter with beings from outside its anthropomorphic context,[39] endorsed by her cronies from the Central Council, who want to perpetuate their power (and life), are best summa-

---

38   One of her victims – kidnapped by Madame's agents – becomes a film director known in his various many-worlds personalities as Miguel Esteban/ Mike Esteros/ Michel Sanrois/ Mickey Sants, who tries to convince film producers that they should finance his film about finding aliens (327).

39   In answer to Temudjin's opinion that there are no aliens in the multiverse, just humans, Mrs Mulverhill mentions the "problem of unenvisionability" discussed by transitioneering specialists, which amounts to the fact that transitionaries either do not want to imagine a world with aliens or they are prevented from doing so by a "deliberate quarantine, systematic enclosure, some vast cover-up" (325), apparently effected by Madame d'Ortolan and her Concern supporters. In this light, the transitionaries who can flit without septus are even more dangerous because their imagination concerning the parallel realities cannot be controlled, which may result in a close encounter.

rized by Mrs. Mulverhill: "Under her, if they haven't already, they'll come to countenance anything to avoid what she sees as contamination. Anything. Encouraging world wars, genocide, global warming; anything at all to disrupt the slow progress towards the unknown" (337).

The Concern's activity, which starts as scientific research with the policy of limited interference, comes to follow the pattern of expansionist imperialism, in which the author presumably allegorizes similar processes taking place in the history of our own world (one of the many worlds of the multiverse):

> "Unless we have been lied to even more comprehensively than even I suspect, the Concern has existed for a thousand years. In that time, certainly for the first eight centuries, it spent its time investigating the many worlds, researching the properties of septus and the abilities it confers upon people trained to take it, and theorizing regarding the metaphysical laws governing the many worlds and the composition of whatever context they might be said to exist within. Until about two hundred years ago, interventions were rare, much argued and agonized over, heavily monitored and subject to extensive subsequent analysis."
>
> "So what happened two hundred years ago?"
>
> "Madame d'Ortolan happened [. . .]. She discovered how a transitioner could take somebody else with them between the realities and that opened up a whole new set of opportunities for l'Expédience; the number of worlds investigated soared. Then when she was on the Central Council she pushed for a far more aggressive policy of interference and a still wider spread of influence." (329)

From this perspective, septus represents any means which guarantees political superiority – military, economic, or political – and ensures the control and exploitation of others. Making the state, group, or individual who use it both secure in their power and fearful of losing it, it breeds hostility and watchfulness, and thus further increases self-absorption.

In the end, *Transition* appears to be much more than a book to be read between JFK and Heathrow (see Ness 2009). By giving the narrative form to the scientific concept of quantum universes, and combining it with topical political and economic references, Banks interrogates such diverse issues as individual perception, the relationship between Self and Other, the struggle for power and domination, and the importance and limits of freedom. Defamiliarizing our own political and social reality by providing visions of Earth which are similar yet different, and making our world one of the many worlds (and far from the pivotal one), the novel addresses our own solipsism and self-importance, on the anthropological and universal levels.

***

The three novels discussed in this chapter present the reader with a spectrum of alternative worlds which variously develop the paradigm established by the blueprint novel. The alternative worlds of *Walking on Glass* on the one hand, take the form of a projection effected by characters within the boundaries of the quasi-empirical model (i.e. the simulated version of reality devised by Sara and Slater, or the counterfactual romantic model of reality whose author and main hero is Graham Park), and are accepted by their creators as the supreme orders of reality. On the other hand, the alternative worlds realize a hierarchy of different ontological levels, with the characters being carriers of metalepsis and pivots of mediation between different supragenological types (Steven Grout, Quiss, and Ajayi). Ultimately, the characters' relationship with the world of increased textualization, dictated by generic conventions and intertexts, comes to reflect the Lyotardian postulate that we are all entangled in "language games." In the world in which "the appearance is taking over the reality," the concept of truth is not synonymous with our discovery of the *real* but rather with "the construction of the world according to the rules of a particular game" (Craig 2004b: 260) – here, a literary one. As reality becomes a text, the relationship between the multiple reality of *Walking on Glass* takes the form of a Moebius strip. The order which at first glance occupied the most "realistic" level, in the end becomes subordinated to the principles of the least "realistic" universe, which itself, upon closer examination, fails as the superior level. The novel, therefore, through the heterarchy of its worlds in a loop, offers a commentary on the relationship between life and literature and the freedom or the lack thereof of the authors, readers, and literary characters.

In the second novel discussed in this chapter, *The Bridge*, the main character's mediation of his alternative world takes the form of a dream fantasy realized on several narrative levels. In his comatose mind, Lennox creates the retro world of the Bridge, "a vast alternative reality to the messy, restricted reality of his own past life and relationships" (Rennison 2005: 20). The character descends inwardly to the deepest levels of his subconscious, the subliminal space of genuine reality, which gives meaning to his waking life and allows his transformation. Ultimately, the narrative structure of the novel resembles a spiral: it descends in a Dantesque manner when the successive ontological levels unfold before the reader's eyes, and ascends when they close up on one another like a concertinaed paper, heading for the unification of the character's three distinct dream incarnations. Like every spiral, this one also presupposes the circular movement at each level, which is duly represented in the inherent horizontal dynamics of all the component narratives. The same pattern of "withdrawal" and "reengagement" (see Brewster 2006: 182-3) is reiterated in the structural return of the overall text, as the novel leads us from Lennox's coma through various multi-dimensional re-runs of his past experiences only to bring us all the way back to its own starting point, where we become witnesses to the character's awakening.

In the last novel discussed in the chapter, *Transition*, the theme of mediation combined with the theory of the many worlds finds its formal representation in the multiple narratives recounted by different centres of perception. While underscoring the distinctiveness of personalities and outlooks, the technique of the many narratorial worlds seems to serve, first and foremost, the purpose of foregrounding mankind's similarity across parallel dimensions, showing instances of love and compassion, but also of abuse, torture, terrorism, exploitation, and suffering, as present in various parallel realities. Moreover, by toying with the concept that different versions of us inhabit parallel realities and have more or less similar pursuits, Banks undermines our delusion of singularity and uniqueness, at the same time implying that the idea of humanity transcends that of individuality, and that in the many worlds of the multiverse everyone is simultaneously same and other. The act of transition, which allows one person to go beyond his/her immediate bodily and psychic limitations, and thereby feel for and through the other in an act of intentional benevolence, echoes Macmurray's idea of persons as agents in relation, which is prerequisite for the idea of community. As such, *Transition* stands on the border between two models of fictional worlds, alternative and communal, epitomizing in its transitional worldview the very notion of mediation.

CHAPTER 3

Community Worlds
The Crow Road, The Steep Approach to Garbadale, Espedair Street, and *Stonemouth*

In *The Wasp Factory*, Frances Cauldhame becomes a victim of her father's scientific experiment, as a result of which she grows up believing she is male. The father's manipulated version of domestic history, in which Frank suffered emasculation at the age of three, conditions his daughter's gender identity to the point of disturbance. The character's separation from her own past translates into Frank's detachment from her female self, which combined with the complex of flawed masculinity, consequently gives rise to a life of seclusion and egocentricity, her "literal cutting off" from community (183). It is only after her father's revelation of the truth that she is ready to acknowledge the fact that an individual existence can be made truly meaningful only within the larger context of human interrelationships. The protagonist's anticipated departure from the island which has been her home signals a possibility of a shift of Frances's perspective from egocentric to heterocentric, and thus also the possibility of her reintegration into the community of Selves in relation, a dynamic which Banks fully explores in his later novels – *The Crow Road, Espedair Street, The Steep Approach to Garbadale*, and *Stonemouth*.

Although the return to the fellowship and mutual affection of communal existence motivates many characters in Banks's novels, the four texts selected for discussion in the present chapter display two important common features: first, they all deal with the concept of community as related to the space of the family; secondly, they all highlight and variously develop the motif of the community's immersion within the larger communal domain, the nation, which is Scotland. Thus, community is ascribed an intermediary role in the relationship between the individual and the land. A formative influence exerted on the character through a tangled web of biological, social, and psychological relationships played

and replayed over the decades of the family's private history is here enhanced by the effects of the characters' rootedness in Scottish landscape,
history, and tradition. As a result, the characters' desires and conflicts
are both dramatized within and go beyond the family environment, the
tension between resistance and identification being projected from the
space of home into the space of the nation. It is through constant mediation and interaction between the domestic and the public, between individual fantasy and national imagination, that the characters' private
worlds, conflicted and unbalanced, undergo a process of reordering. In
the novels discussed in this chapter, family romance, which according to
Christine van Boheemen, projects "the relationship to origin as the journey of a return home" (1987: 5), comes to encompass both the family
and the country, due to which the characters' identities are
(re)constituted through the recognition of private and public origins.[1]

3.1. The Wor(l)ds of Magic, Memory, and Truth in *The Crow Road*

"I reflected it had always seemed to be death that drew me back to Gallanach" (2005: 3), notes Prentice McHoan, the protagonist of *The Crow
Road*, as early as the second sentence of the novel, after he has been
summoned from Glasgow to attend the funeral of the McHoan materfa-
milias, Grandma Margot. The above observation points to death as being
inextricably linked with the recurring motif of the character's homecoming, and thus it sets death as the driving force behind the dynamics of
Prentice's quest to find his own place within the context of the family
and the country. On the one hand, the deaths and subsequent funerals of
Prentice's various friends and relatives inevitably involve a physical
movement to the heartland, into the space of the community with its in-

---

1   Significantly, all the novels discussed in this chapter have as their titles the
     names of places which combine references to the national and the communal.
     On the one hand, they all denote some tangible elements in the urban or rural
     Scottish landscape: Crow Road and Espedair Street are real streets in Glasgow
     and Paisley respectively, Garbadale is a fictional estate in the Highlands, and
     Stonemouth – a fictional town near Aberdeen. On the other hand, all the
     names are connected with the communal life and personal or domestic history
     which needs to be revisited or (re)discovered, and hence they doubly presup-
     pose the characters' return to the space of home.

ner dependencies and conflicts. On the other hand, two particular deaths function as major catalysts for the protagonist's re-identification with the space of home, giving rise to important self-discoveries on Prentice's part.

Kenneth's death effects Prentice's physical return to his father's house, and thus helps the son to come back to the fold and get his turbulent life in order. More importantly, however, it provokes Prentice's return to the space of memories linked with Kenneth and his teachings, and, as a result, fosters the son's understanding and acceptance of his father's life philosophy based on the importance of family connections and biological continuity, as woven into the history of the land.[2] In addition, Prentice's return home spurs anew the boy's investigation of his uncle's unfinished novel, which casts some light on the mystery of Rory's disappearance eight years before, thanks to which young McHoan finally discovers an important part of his family's past. Prentice's own world is therefore (re)constructed as a response to the private worlds of his father and uncle, which will be fully explored in the course of the present analysis.

The scarcity of information concerning the protagonist's development outside the family circle (e.g. his school years or details of his university experience), makes the family environment almost the sole focus of the novel, and consequently underscores its major formative influence (MacGillivray 2001: 34). Frequent flashbacks to Prentice's childhood and adolescence describe the protagonist's growth in a vibrant community of closer and more distant relatives, related by blood or marriage, and brought together by the confines of their geographical residence. The life of the McHoans and the families of the Urvills and the Watts, to whom they are related, is set in the area of Argyll, in which there are three principal locations tied to the fortunes of each line. The first place is the fictional town of Gallanach, which is the home of the working-class Watts living in a council estate, but also the site of the Gallanach Glass Works, the main local employer, owned by the Urvills. The Urvills, in turn, who are local aristocracy of Norman descent, first inhabit a country mansion beyond the northwest limits of Gallanach and later the

---

2   Dorothy McMillan observes that *The Crow Road* is "Banks's first attempt to grapple with the idea of the nation, an idea which in any case rises predictably out of the family" (1995: 89).

old medieval Gaineamh Castle, restored and modernized by Fergus Urvill, which allows a perfect vista of Gallanach and the surrounding area.
The last family place is the real village of Lochgair on the Shore of Loch
Fyne, the home of the middle-class McHoans, who have been for many
years involved in the management of the Gallanach Glass Works and in
the local system of education.[3]

The residential topography is reflective of the social position and the
distribution of wealth among the three branches, which are predictably
responsible for such differences as political views, domestic life matters,
or even the level of education and idiom. However, the proximity of
their residences and the communal ties that have bound them for generations make the three families mingle together. The children of the
McHoans, Urvills, and Watts acquire the "generic and roughly affec-
tionate" name of the Rabble (119), i.e. the group to whom Kenneth tells
his stories on family Sundays, the term nullifying all differences in the
equally egalitarian environment. The community, therefore, can be perceived as a superior semiosphere containing within its confines the respective semiospheres of the three families. Its apparent heterogeneity
(social, ideological, topographical, etc.) is brought into unity by the dynamics of communal life and the space of common consciousness projected by Kenneth the story-teller.[4]

---

3   For a detailed discussion of the geography and genealogy of *The Crow Road*
     see MacGillivray 2001: 17. Cf. Petrie 2004: 123.
4   In the case of the three families, the Urvills, McHoans, and Watts, the bounda-
     ries are connected to their differing social status (upper, middle, and working
     class), places of residence (the castle, country house, council estate), and ide-
     ology and language as well. The social macrocosm of the world of the adults
     with its boundaries is visible on the small scale in the world of the children
     whom Kenneth often takes on trips in the Scottish countryside. And so the
     Urvill twins, Helen and Diana, daughters of Fergus and Fiona, are nicely and
     tastefully dressed, their hair well-groomed, and their language always correct.
     They are also aware of the fact that they are Tories. In contrast, the young
     Watts, Darren, Dean, and Ashley, are coarse in all respects, be it dress, man-
     ner, or speech (and victims of domestic violence at that). In his early teens,
     Prentice starts noticing these differences, becoming a snob for a time, as he
     grows ashamed of the working-class Scots because his beautiful Urvill cous-
     ins do not speak it while "those coarse Watt children" do (106).

The constant mediation across the boundaries separating the three subsets of the communal semiosphere translates into a web of various internal relationships and dependencies, many of them perceived in terms of family tradition, which include loves, friendships, intermarriages, choice of profession, and the like. The bonds of friendship and common experience among the children from Prentice's generation continue through adolescence to adulthood, maintained and nurtured through regular private meetings and social occasions (pub crawls, parties thrown by the Urvill twins in the castle observatory, Hogmanay celebrations, etc.). It is within this familial community that the young McHoan establishes his closest friendships and loyalties, and where he also finds his love. The only person from outside this circle is Gavin, Prentice's roommate from Glasgow, but even he is usually mentioned with relation to Prentice's meetings with his kith and kin, such as aunt Janice Rae, Rory's former girlfriend (who later becomes Gavin's girlfriend), Ashley Watt, or Prentice's brother Lewis (cf. MacGillivray 2001: 50-1).

This "contained quality of the emotional and sexual relationships" (MacGillivray 2001: 50), is contrasted with the outward movement of various characters from Kenneth's and Prentice's generations who distance themselves physically or psychologically from the space of their community in order to look for new opportunities and experience away from their Scottish home. In the light of those individual pursuits among his elders and peers, Prentice comes across as the only one whose purpose in life is as yet undetermined. He feels no drive to seek his fortune away from the heartland, but instead revolves around the Scottish base of Gallanach and Lochgair in a holding pattern of his own. He is always easily summoned to the family environment, visiting his grandmother, meeting his mother, or rubbing shoulders with his local mates (MacGillivray 2001: 50).

The only place Prentice tends to avoid is the house of his father, with whom he remains in a religious conflict, which introduces a breach in the otherwise unifying space of the community. Grief-stricken after the tragic death of his friend Darren Watt, Prentice wants to believe that there is "something out there, just to witness, just to *know*" (217), which would make death less random and meaningless. Kenneth, on the other hand, is an atheist and rationalist who dismisses the existence of God or any supernatural consciousness bearing witness to human existence. For

Kenneth, death is the end, but people are allowed to continue in their children, their works and the memories of others. Whereas Kenneth's focus is on the individual (and secular) interpretation of reality, Prentice reveals a need to rely on religion, which would give meaning to the otherwise incomprehensible mystery of death. The reconciliation between the two distinct worldviews – Prentice's "need for meaning, for faith" (217), and Kenneth's view that "all the gods are false" (314) – seems impossible, and it is not only due to their inherent ideological incongruity. "There's almost nothing either of us can say that can't be taken the wrong way with a bit of imagination" (168), states Prentice, thereby pointing to an almost Lockean condition between himself and his father, whose private ideas and associations make them live in their private worlds, unable to interpret correctly one another's words and actions, or accept a different point of view. The father's and son's respective obsessions with Reason and Faith impede successful communication.

While drifting away from Kenneth and his house of rationalism, Prentice is accepted into the house of his uncle Hamish, which constitutes the epicentre of a bizarre religious cult with a single follower. Hamish perceives and interprets the surrounding reality through the prism of an adulterated Christianity combined with his personal theology of anti-creates, which is based on the conviction that what you did to other people during your life returns to you soon after you are dead. Though taking advantage of Hamish's hospitality, Prentice cannot help noticing that his uncle's heresy "sounds like something dreamt up by a vindictive bureaucrat on acid while closely inspecting something Hieronymus Bosch painted on one of his bleak but imaginative days" (176). It proves that Prentice's position is one of mediation between his father's atheist humanism, advocating man's individuality and freedom from superstition, which alienates him from his own son, and Hamish's vindictive Christianity (apparently rooted in Scottish Calvinism), which remains peripheral even in Hamish's own home, being taken for what it is – a harmless eccentricity – by his wife and daughter.

Grandma McHoan, whom Prentice recollects during her funeral, regards the father-son conflict as the most natural thing in the family dynamics: it restores the balance shaken over the generations by introducing an opposing force, an antithetical world-picture. Margot perceives such clashes in terms of historical necessity, which she corroborates with the wisdom of seventy-two years of experience: "Things can get imbalanced in families, over the generations. Sometimes a new one has to . . . adjust things." (11). What seems to be more important than ideological divisions and conflicting outlooks on life between the family members is the deep, almost primeval bond that unites them despite their apparent differences, something that goes beyond the notion of the family as provider of room and board, which Margot addresses in her short question, "'D'you feel for this family, Prentice?'" (11). What the grandmother seems to imply is a sense of loyalty and fellowship, and the meaning one attaches to their origin – not only biological but also spiritual identification with the space of provenance. Margot's question calls to mind Macmurray's concept of community as based on agency and intention, in which the relation between members is by nature heterocentric, and each of them "thinks and feels for the other, and not for himself" (1995: 158).

In Grandma Margot's case, this identification acquires yet another dimension: her sense of belonging and responsibility for the McHoans finds its equivalent in the very physical sense of the goings-on of her loved ones. She literally *feels* for her family by means of moles all over her body, which represent particular family members and itch her whenever someone is talking about her or something remarkable is happening to the person. The locations of the moles correspond to the qualities of their objects of reference, and so Prentice's father, Kenneth, has his mole on the left arm (obviously indicative of his leftist views), uncle Hamish on a knee (which seems only fair when one considers his religious zeal), and uncle Rory on the right wrist (which may in fact emphasize Rory's writing ambitions). Rory's mole has not been itching for the last eight years, since the day he went missing, which is proof enough to the mother that her son must be dead. Margot's body, therefore, becomes the family map in compliance with her theory of the generation pivots, i.e. members of the family around whom everybody else revolves, and among whom she also lists herself. What is significant, Prentice's mole is situated on Margot's abdomen and she calls it pivotal, as if in anticipation of his future central position in the family, and foreseeing the potential of his first-person narrative for summing up and consolidating two other discourses present in the novel: Rory's narrative of the family truth and Kenneth's tale of the nation.[5]

Rory and Kenneth, who play a significant role in the process of Prentice's development and self-discovery, represent two models of individual growth, the former taking place in opposition to and the latter with relation to the community. Rory distances himself from his family, home, and land in his early youth, his sense of alienation and incompatibility growing more and more acute because of the changes taking place in the lives of his elder siblings, Kenneth, Hamish, and Fiona. Being the youngest child in the family, Rory feels himself to be on the margin of the family life: "It was horrible being this age when nobody else was; they were all either adults or children" (196). At the same time, he detests the communal customs and Scottish traditions, just as he dislikes the suffocating provincial atmosphere of Gallanach, which he mulls over during Hamish's wedding reception:

> Music played behind Rory. He balanced the empty whisky glass on the window-sill and gave his nose a last wipe, pocketing his hanky. He supposed he'd better go back into the ballroom. Ballroom; he hated the word. He hated the music they were playing – Highland stuff, mostly – he hated being here in this dull, wet town, with these dull people listening to their dull music at their dull wedding. They should be playing the Beatles or the Rolling Stones, and they shouldn't be getting married in the first place – modern people didn't. [. . .] Rory could hear the stamping, slapping feet

---

5   *The Crow Road*, therefore, seems to be constructed along two parallel temporal axes. The short axis, as Christine Bridgwood defines it in her study of the family saga in Colleen McCullough's *The Thorn Birds* (1977), is "a dramatic structure of various episodes, incidents and climaxes which revolve around and are supported by concepts of progress" and individual experience (1986: 177), and which can be briefly summarized as the life histories of particular characters. The short axis is therefore contiguous with each of the three main narratives depicting the lives of Kenneth, Rory, and Prentice. The extended axis, on the other hand, "works to defuse this structure of individual drama, experience and change by overlaying it with a discourse of the 'long view' which speaks in favour of tradition, the family, the heritage, the dynasty" (177). In the case of *The Crow Road*, the long-term perspective is based on the concept of the life cycle, and thus creates an imaginative space in which the domestic history can be informed and absorbed by the history of the nation.

move in time to the fiddles and accordions as they played a jig. People
were clapping, shouting out. God, it was all so provincial. (194)

Identifying himself with the modern, London-based culture, which opposes the more conservative codes of the communal semiosphere, Rory
perceives the merits of his community (i.e. tradition and a sense of belonging) as drawbacks, seeing it as a construct which limits people by its
parochialism and ties them down by its various commitments. Rory, in
contrast, yearns for the outside world of cosmopolitanism and unrestrict-
ed travel. Already in childhood, when he is neglected by his grown-up
siblings, Rory creates his own private world, exotic and remote from the
all too familiar Scottishness, fantasizing he is "a lion lying tawny and
sated under the African sun, or a sleep-eyed tiger basking on some rock
high over a wide Indian plain" (47). In his early twenties, Rory leaves
Scotland for London, and from there he goes on a World Trip, venturing
as far as India, which becomes the subject of his best-selling travelogue.
He is a poetic reporter of his immediate experience in the alien country,
whose exotic space undergoes a translation into verbal images, thus being creatively transformed by the power of Rory's word and imagination:

> He went with his eyes open, and, not having taken a camera, just tried to
> record everything on the pages of those cheap exercise books, straining to
> make it real for himself, as though he could not believe he had seen and
> heard and experienced what he had until it was fixed somewhere other than
> in his stunned brain, and so he could describe walking to the Taj Mahal –
> ho-hum, thinks the reader, immediately in the realm of the tacky postcard –
> and still give you a wholly fresh impression of the exact scale and actual
> *presence* of that white tomb; delicate but powerful, compact and yet
> boundlessly imposing.
>   Epic grace. With those two words he encapsulated it, and you knew
> exactly what he meant. (77)

The language of literature, therefore, functions as a tool of mediation.
First, it gives verbal representation to acts of individual perception, and
second, it creates the image of perceivable reality for the readers who are
themselves denied the experience of direct observation. Moreover, when
transfused and reconstructed through his Western mind, the space of
Rory's peregrinations at once retains its oriental strangeness and becomes familiarized. As he is "looking and listening and questioning and
arguing and reeling with it all, making crazed comparisons with Britain

and Scotland" (76), he mediates between two distinct semiospheres, his mind becoming a place of semiotic dialogue.

For Rory, a change of place means a change of thinking and believing, which he admits in a conversation with young Prentice during a holiday spent on the Hebrides (189). A removal from the familiarity of home into an unknown and distant part of the world, where you feel like a complete stranger, "*lumbering and self-conscious,*" among the expanses of otherness, is eventually tantamount to establishing a meaningful relationship with one's inner self, this "different, echoing place inside" (203). What is implied here is the perspective of an outsider which one develops in relation to their space of origin, our "first world," and which enables us to cross not only the physical boundaries of the country but also the social and mental limits it imposes on us. At one point, while standing on the sea shore, Prentice recalls the figure of Rory, who in his nephew's eyes, comes to represent the link between the Scotland-based relatives and "the rest of the globe," being their "wanderer on the planet" (75), and thus extending the space of home into far-distant corners of the world.[6]

Paradoxically, the world-travelling raconteur becomes the domestic historian who in his "serious" comeback work attempts to bear testimony to the murder, cloaked as a road accident, committed on his sister Fiona by her jealous aristocratic husband, Fergus. The secret of it remains hidden in the folder containing the papers and other materials for his *magnum opus* titled *CR* (*Crow Road*). The unravelling of the family secrets "buried" in Rory's papers falls to Prentice, whose predicament as a seeker trying to determine his place in the world makes him a perfect vehicle for the detective plot of the novel. In his search for the truth behind Rory's disappearance, Prentice is forced to cross the boundary between the world of the living and the world of the dead, which is underlined by the title of Rory's work. The phrase "that's him away the crow

---

6   It is worth noting that Rory holds the status of a half-imaginary figure in the peculiar family game in which his living relatives make up "stories, conjectures, lies and hopes" (12) about him and his whereabouts, not really accepting the fact he can be "away the crow road" (i.e. dead). Death being difficult to internalize and the truth unknown, they give rise to family fictions. The reality is thus mediated though the individual imagination and verbal accounts, Rory becoming a character in the family lore.

road" is a euphemistic adage used among the McHoans to say that someone is dead, which may as well apply to the character of Fiona as to Rory's own death at the hands of Fergus. The fact that the novel in which Prentice is the principal narrator is also titled *The Crow Road* points to his own metaphorical journey "away the crow road," not only for the sake of Rory but also for the sake of his own belated reconciliation with his father and his memory.

During his investigation, Prentice becomes increasingly immersed in his uncle's private world of thoughts and sensibilities, which he reconstructs from Rory's poems, notes concerning *The Crow Road*, diary entries, his own and other people's memories, but also by copying Rory's routes and emotional entanglements. For a while, Prentice becomes involved with Rory's last girlfriend, Aunt Janice Rae, whose address is Crow Road in Glasgow. On the first night they spend together, Janice recites to Prentice the lines of Rory's poem which she used to listen to every time she and Rory made love. Not surprisingly, Aunt Janice calls Prentice by his uncle's name while wishing him a good night. On another occasion, the woman wistfully observes that the nephew happens to sound just like his missing uncle, which further emphasizes the affinity between Prentice and Rory, and, in a sense, between their worlds. Interestingly, having accidentally lost his uncle's papers by leaving them on a train (along with a white Moebius scarf, a gift from his dead friend, Darren), Prentice becomes haunted by the mystery contained in Rory's work and he feels a suffocating grip of the past on his present which cannot be released: "Even now, months later, I had dreams about reading a book that ended half-way through, or watching a film which ended abruptly, screen whiting-out . . . usually I woke breathless, imagining there was a scarf – shining white silk looped in a half twist – tightening round my neck" (262).

Prentice's entry into Rory's world means also an entry into the world of artistic creation, in which the nephew is made privy to his uncle's deliberations on the form of his watershed work (a novel, a film, an epic poem, a concept album) and its subject matter:

> This work, *Crow Road*, would be Serious. It would be about Life and Death and Treachery and Betrayal and Love and Death and Imperialism and Colonialism and Capitalism. It would be about Scotland, (or India, or an 'Erehwon???') and the Working Class and Exploitation and Action, and there would be characters in the work who would represent all of these

things, and the working out of the story *would itself prove the Subjectivity of Truth.* (173)

Rory's critical inspirations (nomen omen *Death of the Author* by Barthes) appear next to his own ideas concerning the work's style, location notes for a film and the choice of the cast, a list of contemporary bands potentially interested in doing the *CR* album, and several poems reworked for that purpose into songs. Rory's creative ideas are interspersed with "doodles, mazes and uninspired drawings of faces" (174), which only emphasizes his indecision about the type of art which suits him best. The uncle's indecision about a mode of artistic expression may point to the fact that Rory was truly a "glorified hack" (141), as he once called himself in a conversation with Kenneth, rather than a real artist.

Prentice's exploration of Rory's personal world, which could give the boy a clue as to where *The Crow Road* can be found, involves not only the ordering of the material scattered on a mixture of loose-leaf papers but, most of all, grappling with the language in which it was written – Rory's indelible mark of authorship. The nephew has to reconstruct the text by interpreting his uncle's idiosyncratic and almost incomprehensible code of mental shortcuts – initials, acronyms, and compressions, which Prentice calls "chaotic witnesses of a past that [he] could not comprehend" (383). If the road to finding Rory's work is difficult, even more difficult is the deciphering of its contents: stored on old floppy disks, too large to be inserted into modern drives, and written in an unauthorized program on a rare and failure-prone Apple clone machine made in Hong Kong. The literal decryption of the family history is only possible thanks to a specialist from the other side of the world – an academic from the University of Denver, Colorado. The past, therefore, constitutes a space of signs, whose encoded languages must be decoded by another generation, while the medium (computer software and hardware) becomes part of the communication act which takes place "vertically," in time.

The family drama of Fiona and Fergus as described by Rory is conveyed through the guise of belle lettres and appears in the body of Banks's *Crow Road* in the form of italicized sections, which additionally enhances the account's fictionalized character. In his imaginative rendition of the family past, Rory adopts free indirect discourse while presenting the dilemmas of his own character and those of his sister and brother-in-law. The artistic status of Rory's narrative inevitably leaves the question of authenticity of facts open and nagging, of which Prentice is all the time aware, commenting on his own quixotism: "I kept coming back to the distinct possibility that maybe I was making something out of nothing, treating our recent, local history like some past age, and looking too assiduously, too imaginatively for links and patterns and connections, and so turning myself into some sort of small-scale conspiracy theorist" (402). Although ready to believe that his uncle's unfinished book recounts the truth of what happened, he is also aware that it is marked by the subjectivity of Rory's imagination, his prejudices and artistic choices, and thus it cannot serve as evidence for a crime, as it would indeed "prove the Subjectivity of Truth."

Shortly before Prentice reads the printouts of Rory's novel, he recalls their walk together in the hills when Rory told him about the vibrations he once had thought he produced in the TV picture using the power of the mind: "So the screen looked funny, *but only to me*, that was the point. And it made sense that the further away you were from the screen – as long as you could still make it out, of course – the more pronounced the effect would appear" (399). Rory's words may refer as well to his knowledge of the family drama involving Fiona and Fergus, which was imperceptible to the members of the community, but which was noticed by him, an outsider and a traveller to distant lands, who could actually see the wood for the trees. "Things in your head can be real" (411), says Rory on the same occasion, pointing to the shaping force of an individual consciousness with relation to the outside world. In the end, also the product of Rory's "fertile imagination," his own creative vision of the McHoans' past, finds a confirmation in reality, when Fergus Urvill, if posthumously and in the manner understood only by Prentice, confesses his two crimes, one committed on his unfaithful wife, the other – on her inquisitive brother. Yet the confession becomes part of another *Crow Road*, which makes the quest for truth and facts never-ending.

The mediating power of the word, individual perspective, and imagination proves even more striking in the case of Kenneth McHoan with respect to the space of the community and the country. All his life Kenneth reveals an incredible attachment to the land he was born to and its peoples, his development from boyhood to adulthood simultaneously documenting the evolution of his national consciousness from the impe-

rial citizen to the Scottish nationalist. The former can be noticed in various flashbacks to the time of his boyhood, when he played with Fergus
Urvill and Lachlan Watt and was often a witness to the class-conscious
tension between the two. The elegant luxury of the Urvill household
with spacious rooms and Persian carpets stands in sharp contrast with
the destitution and violence of the house of the Watts, of which Lachy
seems to be painfully aware. His crude manners and shabby hand-me-
down clothes of the working-class kid make his presence in the Urvills'
mansion distinctly incongruous. Understandably, he vents his anger and
frustration in the form of taunts and jibes directed at his richer mate and
the signs of his privileged position, to which Fergus responds with
equally spiteful comments and physical aggression:

> Lachy picked up some lead soldiers from a couple of trays ranked full of
> them, then stood inspecting some maps on the wall, of Scotland, the British
> Isles, Europe and The World. 'They red bits aw ours, are they?' [. . .]
> 'Well, I don't know about "*ours*", but they belong to Britain.'
> 'Well,' Lachy said indignantly. 'Ah'm British, am ah no?'
> 'Hmm. I suppose so,' Fergus conceded. 'But I don't see how you can
> call it yours; you don't even own your own house.'
> 'So whit?' Lachy said angrily.
> 'Yes, but, Fergus,' Kenneth said. 'It is the British Empire and we're all
> British, and when we're older we can vote for MPs to go to parliament, and
> they're in power, not the King; that's what the Magna Carta says; and we
> elect them, don't we? So it is our Empire, really, isn't it? I mean when you
> think about it.'
> Kenneth walked into the middle of the room, smiling at the other two
> boys. (148-50)

Kenneth makes an attempt to reconcile the two boys by appealing to
their sense of Britishness, which is here perceived as the common denominator and thus as the ultimate criterion of equality. For Kenneth, the
all-encompassing concept of the British Empire nullifies the social differences existing in their immediate environment, where one father is the
owner of the factory and the other a worker in this factory. In the British
Empire, as the young McHoan understands it, political power is given to
all citizens, which supposedly entails their equality and makes them
beneficiaries of the same system of privileges. By verbalizing the ideal
of Britishness, Kenneth creates a space of the nation as an imagined political community, whose limits are marked by the "red bits" on the map,

whose sovereignty is manifested in the empowerment of its citizens, and which, as Benedict Anderson notives, "regardless of the actual inequality and exploitation [. . .] is always conceived as a deep, horizontal comradeship" (2006: 7).

Kenneth's disquisition on their common status as imperial citizens reveals an awareness that by its immersion within the British Empire, the space of Argyll and in fact of all of Scotland expands beyond its organic territory. At the time of the boys' conversation (i.e. several months after the end of World War II), the Empire is still geographically vast, its boundaries extending to the farthest parts of the globe and encompassing many ethnic groups, cultures, and languages under one dominant colonial authority with the centre in London. Therefore Scotland, being an integral part of the imperial body, both contributes to its worldwide greatness and shares in its history.[7] Still, such an immersion in the tentacular imperial space is double-edged, and the above-quoted passage from the novel perfectly reflects Scotland's ambiguous place within the boundaries of the Empire. The order in which Lachy studies the maps hanging in Fergus's room, i.e. first, Scotland, then the British Isles, Europe, and The World, implies the possibility of both the central and peripheral position of their homeland. When studied backwards, Scotland, the most northernmost part of the British Isles, may in fact appear as the least im-

---

7   This calls to mind Cairns Craig's observation concerning the concept of the nation as developed by Ernest Renan in 1882: "Renan, at the height of imperialism, refuses to limit the nation to its territory: its spiritual principle can be everywhere and anywhere, can belong to anyone who chooses its ancestors as their ancestors. The nature of the nation has been deeply intertwined, in the period of the growth of nationalism, with the fact of Empire, and in Renan's historicist constructions the notion refuses to be contained by national space. It is built not upon the bounded territory of its own origin but on the ground of the many territories where its flag is planted, for the imperial nation acknowledges no boundaries to its national significance: its history may derive from a particular plot of ground but that history pours outward upon the empty and not-so-empty places of the earth as the nation becomes an extended assertion of its own refusal to be bounded by anything but global space" (1999: 236). In "What is a Nation?" Renan calls a nation "a large-scale solidarity, constituted by the feeling of the sacrifices that one has made in the past and of those that one is prepared to make in the future." A nation "presupposes a past; it is summarized, however, in the present by a tangible fact, namely, consent, the clearly expressed desire to continue a common life" (2009: 19).

portant part of the world, the space off the beaten track, somewhere on
the margin of the global map. When one adopts this approach, it is possible to see the space of Scotland as yet another manifestation of English
colonialism, whose bitter metaphor is provided by the uneasy friendship
between Fergus and Lachy.

In this trio Kenneth functions as a boundary character and mediator,
his middle-class position allowing him to avoid open conflicts with the
two boys and see "both points of view" (85). His intermediary position
between Fergus and Lachy translates, on the one hand, into his awareness of the progression of imperial history (represented here by the
whole generations of his family's relations with the Urvills) and, on the
other hand, into his deep sense of belonging to the ancient space of the
northern peripheries. Already in his boyhood Kenneth can feel a profound unity with the land, which can be noticed in the scene in which
young Urvills, Watts, and McHoans play hide and seek in the ruins of
Gaineamh Castle, where he hides on the ledge of a high window and is
struck by a sudden revelation:

> I love this here, he thought to himself. I don't care if there is a war on and
> Fergus's uncle got killed in North Africa, and Wullie Watt got killed in the
> North Atlantic and Lachy gets hit by his dad and we might have to move to
> another house because Mr Urvill wants ours back and I don't understand
> trigonometry and the Germans do invade us; I love this. If I died right now
> I wouldn't care; wouldn't care at all. (88)

Being a part of the British Empire, Scotland is involved in the global
conflict which, using Cairns Craig's phrase, disrupts the single national
identity of Scots "by the multiple spaces into which the nation has entered, the plethora of other narratives with which it is entwined" (1999:
237). To Kenneth, however, those other spaces, tied to the progress of
imperial history and epitomized by the battlefields of the war, seem to be
equally irrelevant as the bustle of the ordinary life, as he finds himself
caught within a space outside of time and history.

Gaineamh Castle is important for this early epiphany and the development of Kenneth's imagination as a story-teller, being the focal point
of the countryside and the beginning place of Scottish statehood. It
stands on the side of the hill in the very "epicentre" of the ancient Scottish kingdom of Dalriada, not far from the millennium-old Celtic hillfort
of Dunnad, where the Dalriadic kings were once inaugurated. Kenneth

has never been inside the old edifice before but he knows that "you could just see it from the house, if you knew what you were looking for, and you could see it quite well if you used dad's binoculars" (86). The castle, on the other hand, allows a view from above, as it forms an eyrie from which man's sight can reach as far as the sea beyond Gallanach, the mountains in the north and the forested hills in the south, which allows the observer a holistic view of the land to its very limits in one panoramic sweep.

Whereas initially Kenneth's outlook was that of below, from the house window, now it is the one from above, which lays the land open to his eyes. This relationship brings to mind what Craig calls "the double perspective – within history, without history – which is driven by the spatial conjunction, and cultural and historical disjunction, of Lowland and Highland space, of national and imperial narratives" (1999: 239). Inside the castle Kenneth experiences the touch of eternity: for a while, the imperial history of conflict and combat becomes unimportant, the linear progression of time is suspended and the vastness of the world is reduced to the space enclosed within those "rough, uneven stones" (85). The castle and by projection all Scotland concentrated around its ancient hub become "the 'otherside' to history [. . .] where history's grand narratives are reflected in absurd miniature, where history abuts on the eternity which is its negation" (Craig 1999: 240).

Years later the ancient castle is restored and modernized by Fergus, who turns it into his family residence, and Kenneth cannot help the feeling of resentment directed "at the Urvills in general and Fergus in particular, for having [. . .] stolen part of his memories from him" (91). This unverbalized conflict has its roots in the fundamental difference of attitudes towards the space within which each of them functions. Whereas Kenneth belongs to the land, acknowledging his own subordinate and transient status within its vastness and permanence, Fergus makes the land belong to him, duly appropriating and branding every inch of it with the mark of his ownership. The singularity of experience that affected Kenneth in childhood, allowing him to become immersed in the almost mythic dimension of the Scottish "otherworld," seems to be now irretrievably lost. The castle is shaken out of eternity into modernity, being plastered, painted, panelled, varnished, and cluttered with the signs of Fergus's wealth and power, and thus turned into an emblem of his sybaritic lifestyle and a testament to the achievements of his Norman family (ironically epitomized by the badly-done modern stained-glass window presenting several centuries of the Urvills' history).

If Fergus follows the example of his conquering ancestry and models the space of the community and the country by very concrete efforts in order to bring it closer to his personal vision, Kenneth, like his brother Rory, creates and recreates the surrounding world, using the medium of words and imagination. It is only natural that Kenneth, whose sensibility already in childhood enabled him to see the layer of the mythic underneath the events of everyday life, himself becomes a myth-maker and a story-teller. In numerous countryside lessons, he acquaints the Watt, Urvill, and McHoan children with the elements of the surrounding reality through fairy tales of his own making. Kenneth puts an additional, wondrous, film onto the seemingly familiar and ordinary environment, thanks to which weather phenomena, water and rock forms, buildings, streets, or even guide posts begin to reveal an extraordinary occult significance. He creates an island ruled by magic, where time passes more slowly and where to believe is to see (25). Kenneth's mythmaking quality is discernible in one of the earliest memories that Prentice has of his father, namely in Kenneth's account of mythosaurs, gigantic (and completely fabulous) animals that lived in the far-distant past, through which he explains the origin of cairns, geological formations in the shape of piles of stones which are scattered over the Scottish landscape. In his interpretation, cairns were apparently huge rocks swallowed by mythosaurs to grind the food inside their stomachs, and they were left over the ground after the animals died and decayed (30-1). Kenneth unites the seemingly irreconcilable dimensions of historical science and myth: by referring to the realm of the mythic, he constructs meanings behind various manifestations of reality, turning them into representations of the past which lies outside historical records and human experience (cf. Craig 2002: 37).

Despite or perhaps thanks to his story-telling acumen, Kenneth is also the first to point out to Prentice the difference between the real and the imaginary, which in turn translates into the opposition between history and story. Significantly, in Kenneth's view, "real" things are too random, too "messy" to communicate or teach anything, because they simply "happen." It is invented stories which most effectively explain the mystery of the world, but which, at the same time, are always coloured by an individual imagination, having "different endings according to who you listen to" (239). In this way, Kenneth makes his son aware of the fact that imagination can shape reality, and its power can influence not only the external world but also other people's inner worlds:

> 'Because the only place anything is ever real is inside your head, Prentice. And the mythosaurs exist inside your head, now.'
> 'Does it, dad?'
> 'Yes, it used to exist in my head but now it exists in your head too, and the others.'
> 'So, is God in Mrs McBeath's head, then?'
> 'Yes, that's right. He's an idea in her head. Like Father Christmas and the Tooth Fairy.' He looked down at the child. 'Did you like the story about the mythosaur and the cairns?'
> 'Was it just a story then, dad?'
> 'Of course it was, Prentice.' He frowned. 'What did you think it was?'
> 'I don't know, dad. History?'
> 'Histoire, seulement. [. . .] No, it was just a story.' (32)

Like a born enchanter, relying on the magic of geology, physics, and chemistry, Kenneth offers his sons an insight into the nature of things. The father, by being Prentice's first teacher, becomes a symbolical source of the word and language, through which his son's perception of the world is shaped and conditioned. It begins on the very fundamental level of grammar, when Kenneth corrects Prentice's childlike errors in forming negatives and in adjective gradation, in order to shift later to the level of concepts and definitions. Recalling the occasions on which his father taught them the names of insular plants, Prentice compares the long lists of such plant names as marsh samphire, procumbent pearlwort, autumnal hawkbit, or germander speedwell to a delightful litany (322).[8] The knowledge of names, indeed, gives Kenneth almost biblical power over the world, which he imparts to his sons as the religion of natural science, and thus enables them to claim their native land as their own.

---

8   The role of Kenneth as the source of the word and the impact of his inner world on the space of the community can be noticed in various phrases repeated by his family, e.g. "Better lionised than mauled" (141), which are credited back to him though he himself does not remember saying them in the first place.

Last but not least, by spinning tales about former inhabitants of Scotland and the signs they left behind, the father makes his sons conscious of being heirs to the millennia-old legacy of human endeavour – "the Bronze Age and Iron Age people, the Vikings and the Picts, Romans and Celts and Scots and Angles and Saxons who had all found their way to this oceanically marginal little corner of northern Europe" (322) – the only immortality man is ever granted, woven into the shape of the land.[9] Kenneth, therefore, makes possible the communication across epochs and whole millennia of culture, the addressees of the message from the national past being his own children. Through Kenneth's mediation, Prentice is made aware of the fact that the past is connected with the present; without the former the latter remains incomprehensible, or at least devoid of meaning. And that the history of the land encompasses and makes possible the domestic narrative:

> The car engine made a steady growling noise, and I remember thinking it was funny that those long-dead plants had been turned into the petrol that made the car growl. I chose to forget the absence of reptiles in those carboniferous forests, and imagined that they had been populated by great dinosaurs, and that they too had fallen into the ooze, and made up part of the oil, and that the noise the car made was like the angry, bellowing growls they would have made while they were alive, as though their last dying breath, their last sound on this planet, had been saved all these millions and millions of years, to be exhaled along a little road on a little island, pushing the McHoan family north, one summer, on our holidays. (308)

By journeying back to the times when his world was a fairy tale brought to life by the word of the father, the son effects a symbolical reconciliation with Kenneth, who, although dead, will be forever present in Prentice's heart and mind thanks to a magic that is memory. Recalling his

---

9 In this light, the only completed artistic work of Prentice's dead friend, Darren, becomes part of the landscape too. The huge concrete block put on a small beach with a combination of pipes and metal doors in its belly unites in its austerity man's creative skills and innovative ideas and the primordial power of the ocean, whose waves, when caught inside the pipe-system, produce wailing sounds and impressive spouts as if from "some stranded cubist whale" (301). It is yet another example of the imaginative projection of an individual vision onto the external space, no wonder Block One is a place where Prentice succumbs to recollections, as it is a testament to his friend's life as much as to his father's life wisdom.

father's teachings about their national heritage being the combined product of various geological and biological forces as well as human thought, Prentice is finally able to understand Kenneth's dismissal of religious eschatology and accept his view that mankind perpetuates itself in the ever-repeating cycle of death and regeneration, in the dialogue of men across time, rather than in an afterlife devised by a religious system. "We continue in our children, in our works and in the memories of others; we continue in our dust and ash" (484), Prentice repeats after Kenneth towards the end of the novel.

This time Prentice has another death to mourn, that of his Uncle Rory, whose family legend has come to an end at the bottom of Loch Coille Bahrr, providing an apt conclusion to his novel, *The Crow Road.* Now wrapped in his father's old coat and holding in his hands the glass paperweight with which Fergus killed Rory, Prentice becomes the point of convergence, the pivot, in which Kenneth's and Rory's narratives find their common dénouement. Thrown into the grey waves north of the Butt of Lewis, the instrument of crime becomes symbolical of the story of Rory's own life, which duly sinks into the ancient expanses beyond the Scottish Highlands, becoming part of the eternal cycle, which swallows individual existence.

Life itself brings another confirmation of Kenneth's philosophy – his death is immediately followed by the news of the conception of Lewis and Verity's child, which, ironically, is broken to Prentice when the two brothers are in the process of digging their father's grave. The wheel of the family history has therefore come full circle. Named after his late grandfather, the baby is the proof incarnate of the fundamental truth voiced by Kenneth and finally acknowledged by Prentice that death is change, leads to "new chances, new vacancies, new niches and opportunities," and it is not all loss (484). The novel starts with a funeral but ends with a baptism, with the proud godfather, Prentice, standing on the battlements of Gaineamh Castle at the very core of the Argyll landscape, and cradling little Kenneth in his arms as his own father must have once cradled him. This last joyful scene, when the baby's head is anointed with a drop of ancient whisky, *uisge beatha,* the "water of life" for Scots, is the point when the history of the family is once again entwined with that of the nation, when the past connects with the present, and which, with Prentice's loving thoughts reaching to Ashley on the other side of the Atlantic, brings a promise of an equally joyful future.

3.2. Gardens of Love and Communities of the Heart in *The Steep Approach to Garbadale*

The Steep Approach to Garbadale (2007) is yet another of Banks's novels in which the character's identity and his place in the world are mediated through his uneasy relationship with the clan and the homeland. Frequently inviting comparisons with *The Crow Road*, *The Steep Approach* runs the gamut of familiar motifs, which though far better orchestrated in its acclaimed predecessor, contribute to the emergence of the Bildung narrative developing against the background of the Scottish family saga. We again deal with the protagonist's rebellion, this time not against his atheist father but against his economically oriented clan, the mighty Wopulds, with the intimidating and uncompromising figure of the grandmother Winifred in charge of the century-old family firm. As in the case of *The Crow Road*, *The Steep Approach* also sports a terrible secret festering in the bosom of the family, as the quest of the novel's protagonist, Alban McGill, is tied to the mystery of his mother's suicide over thirty years before. Its final unravelling, which brings Alban back to the family heartland, proves fundamental not only for the resolution of Alban's emotional conflicts but also, more importantly, for the discovery of his true origin.

The action of the novel begins when Fielding Wopuld, Vice-President of the family firm Wopuld Games Ltd., producer of the game *Empire!*, comes to Perth in Scotland in search of his long-estranged cousin Alban, the company's former manager, who left his post and discontinued relations with the family to become a simple woodcutter. Fielding's visit north is more than a courtesy call: he wants to solicit Alban's help to protect the family business against a takeover by Spraint Corp, an American giant in the games market, which will soon be the topic of the shareholders meeting at Garbadale House, the Wopulds' estate in the Highlands. The occasion, as well as the ensuing celebration of Grandmother Win's eightieth birthday, will also provide the last opportunity for the entire family to see the place before it is put up for sale.

Cousin Fielding represents a community to which Alban had been tied since birth by bonds of blood and upbringing. This community was abandoned by Alban for another community. Among Alban's friends from the woodcutting business and his drinking companions from the Perth council estate, belonging is a matter of personal choice rather than necessity – it is a community of intention and agency, in line with Macmurray's ideal (see Macmurray 1995: 27). In contrast, Alban's attitude towards the community of kinship is one of escapism. He deliberately distances himself from home and the life he used to lead in order to create an enclave of personal freedom beyond the reach of the clan:

'Once upon a time I felt . . . constrained, all tied up by this family. I had this idiot idea that if I could get away for a year and a day, I'd be free of it somehow, or at least able to accept it on . . . On mutually agreeable terms.' He glances at his cousin. 'You know? Like in the days of serfdom? If a serf could escape his master for a year and a day without being caught, he was a free man. [. . .] Stupid idea, anyway. Glorified gap year. But anyway. After I came back, after I took up my supposedly rightful place in the company, and then got fed up with that, that was when I knew I had to get out, and decided – realised – a year and a day wouldn't be enough, that it would never have been enough. Not with this family.' (2007: 22-3)

Alban's relationship with the clan is a combination of sympathy and resistance, in which his "childish love for them all, for the institution the family as a whole represented" (110) is pitted against his distaste for the Wopulds' self-interest and financial predation. The exemplary specimen of those characteristics is Grandmother Winifred, who now by proxy invites her stray grandson to take part in the family gathering and her birthday party. To Alban, Winifred has grown into a symbol of corporate greed and fierce capitalism, to which the entire family has succumbed in one way or another, drifting away from the communal ideal of fellowship and selflessness (see Macmurray 1995: 157). Win's adoption of the ethos of capitalism is revealed in her memorable (and apparently slip-of-the-tongue) toast "To trade fairs, not fair trade" (279), raised to celebrate the first deal with Spraint Corp, to which her grandson strongly objected. This association is playfully underscored (which seems to be a glimpse of Banks's own dislike of Conservative governments) by Alban's memory of Win's Thatcherite hair, twinsets, and very English voice, which strikes him as peculiar in light of her twenty-year residence in Scotland.[10]

What is interesting, in Alban's view, the family as a community would benefit from the disposal of the firm which bears their name. Their financial and psychological association with the company, which is primarily oriented at economic expansion and money-earning, is responsible for greed, excess of ambition, and disappearance of genuine affection among the Wopulds, turning the original community into an organization defined in relation to their common purpose – much like Macmurray's society (see 1995: 157).[11] Alban reveals his awareness of this social-communal ambiguity in the shareholders' meeting at Garbadale, presenting the company's sale as a chance for the Wopulds' self-revelation and a test for their communal strength:

---

10   The character of Thatcher-like Winifred and the case of the takeover of the Wopuld Group by Spraint Corp give Iain Banks an opportunity to voice through Alban's mouth his own distrust of the US foreign policy and the British government's "servile" attitude towards their powerful ally. For Alban the correlation between Spraint Corp and America is obvious: the predatory American corporation is a microcosmic reflection of the country it takes its origin from, and the latter's expansionism. Spraint Corp are the co-owner of the Wopuld Group, which is one of their more profitable assets but over which they have rather limited control, being in possession of only one-fourth of the shares. Here the Wopuld company seems to be a metaphor of the country, which should be protected against imperialism in any form, "whether it's military or cultural" (352). Alban's comment reverberates with Tom Nairn's claim that Britain's relationship to the United States "has fossilized into a form of self-colonization" (Nairn 2004: 27), which turns Scotland into a country doubly colonized.

11   Macmurray explains the difference between community and society in the following way: "Any community of persons, as distinct from a mere society, is a group of individuals united in a common life, the motivation of which is positive. Like a society, a community is a group which acts together; but unlike a mere society its members are in communion with one another; they constitute a fellowship. A society whose members act together without forming a fellowship can only be constituted by a common purpose. They cooperate to achieve a purpose which each of them, in his own interest, desires to achieve, and which can only be achieved by co-operation. The relations of its members are functional; each plays his allotted part in the achievement of the common end" (1995: 157).

[A]t least we'll have the chance to discover what we're really like as a group of people tied together by blood, rather than by blood and money. Maybe we'll discover things about ourselves that we wouldn't have discovered otherwise. Maybe we'll discover things about ourselves that we wouldn't have wanted to discover, but – as a rule – I think it's always better to know the truth. (352)

Alban is torn between his love for the family as a community and hate for it as a corporation, in which the communal codes blur with the corporate ones, and in which his relatives, cousins and uncles, appear in the capacity of junior and senior executives. For Fielding, in contrast, blood and business relationships can be rhymed in a perfect amalgam of double-knit loyalty. The family, after all, is the provider of wealth and security, and Fielding himself has no qualms about taking advantage of both. Therefore it is this contiguous solidarity with the family and firm that Fielding appeals to when trying to persuade his cousin to accompany him to Garbadale: "This is our firm, our family, Al. It's our name on the board. It's what we've done for four generations. It's what we do, it's what we *are*" (24). In Fielding's view, the Wopulds' professional activity is what defines them also on the communal level, and selling their firm to Spraint Corp is like selling their name and themselves – it will entail the loss of identity, due to which the Wopulds will end up as yet another rich but nameless and rootless family. Fielding perceives the potential takeover in terms of tearing the family away from its heritage, and, consciously or not, he pinpoints the very nature of this complex interdependence. For, paradoxically, it is the board game *Empire!* that has ensured the Wopulds' unity as a clan, and to which their identity has been bound for one hundred and fifteen years. After all, they are "those Wopulds, the games family, the people with their names plastered all over the board of *Empire!*" (1), and the fortunes of the game have determined the fortunes of the family.[12]

---

12   Fielding and Alban represent the ambiguity implicit in the attitude of the Scottish people, who found themselves benefiting from the free-market economy promoted by the Conservative British governments but who at the same time observed the need to defend the community against the self-gratifying rampant capitalism. Alban's name is significant here, Alba meaning Scotland in Gaelic, which emphasizes the character's affinity with Scotland and his defensive stance as far as the latter's communal ethos is concerned.

The beginnings of the game and the family with its present status go back to the Victorian era and to British imperial conquests, which *Empire!* initially represented in its graphic design:

> Henry Wopuld was a clerk with a farming supplies company based in Bristol when he dreamt up *Empire!* in 1880-81. It was the heyday of the British Empire; the map of the world had turned or was turning pink and red or whatever hue map-makers chose to illustrate the holdings of the first Empire in history on which the sun never set, because it encompassed the globe itself. Civilisation, Christianity and trade were being taken to those inhabiting the furthest corners of the world whether they thought they wanted it or not, and in a sense all *Empire!* did was epitomise this, allowing the Victorian middle class – along with the more aspirational denizens of the lower orders – to fight and trade and preach and bluff their way to world domination from the comfort of their own homes. A claimed educational aspect to the game – in the fields of both geography and morality – helped it appeal to all ages and classes, and earn the praise of school boards and parish councils alike. (129)

Consequently, the rise of the family is closely connected with the rise of the British Empire, within which the Wopulds function as law-abiding citizens, exploiting London's colonial policy for their particular interests. It is worth noting that the fortune made from the original game allows Old Henry, the founder of the dynasty and its riches, to settle his family in Somerset in south-western England (he buys Garbadale only later as a hunting estate), which seems to reaffirm not only his mercantile outlook but, most of all, the family's immersion in the official culture of the United Kingdom.

As can be deduced from the above passage, the Wopulds' success but also their metamorphosis into a corporation can be attributed to one man, Henry, whose invention tied the family forever to business and made them continually preoccupied with the topicality of their product. In time, the Wopuld company opens itself up to new possibilities, trying to colonize overseas markets – the game undergoes numerous transformations to cater for various tastes, becoming a medium of representation of the changing political and social conditions. And so there is *Liberty!* suited to the US market, *Morning Crescent* based on the map of the London underground, a more purely trade-based game called *High Seas!*, *Speculate!* based on stocks and shares, *Commonwealth* reflecting "the changed political realities of the planet," until the electronic version of *Empire!*

> proved popular, then very popular. Then wildly popular. More PC and games-console versions followed, gradually creating a uniquely smooth spectrum of gaming potential to suit virtually all tastes, from those who aspired to the most calm, cerebral, turn-based experience – more akin to chess than anything else – to users who just wanted to wade straight into the most gore-spattered slice- or shoot-them-up, jerking round floors and couches, teeth grinding, eyes wide, face contorted, sweat beading. (130-1)

The spread of the company's product from its British heartland to other parts of the globe goes hand in hand with the emergence of various foreign branches of the Wopuld Group. It consequently involves a multidirectional migration and settlement of the family members outside the limits of the UK, and hence to the establishment of the American, Australian, and other offshoots of the Wopuld clan. (The extent of this dispersion becomes obvious during Alban's round-the-world journey, when the travelling youth makes stops at the places of his various relatives scattered through all continents.) It can be observed, therefore, that both the company and the family have transformed from national to multinational.

Alban's life develops between two major places within the territory of Great Britain, which at the same time represent the island's two geographical extremes: Garbadale in the Scottish Highlands and Lydcombe in Somerset. The location of the estates, Garbadale in the north-west and Lydcombe in the south-west, translates into their diametrically different character in terms of appearance as well as purpose. Garbadale is referred to by Alban as "one of those vast huntin', shootin' 'n' fishin' estates in the far north" (2), which emphasizes its gloomily recreational character connected with man's most primitive urges to kill for sport or diversion. The house, later humorously described as a "monstrous pile" (258) by Alban's girlfriend, Verushka, is a four-storey mansion in Scottish Baronial style, with sombre grey walls and numerous turrets, which makes it look like a Gothic castle, and initially it was also given the name Garbadale Castle. The estate, although tended by workers and supervised by estate managers, yields to their influence only partially, revealing signs of natural processes which cannot be harnessed by human effort and technology. The gardens surrounding the house are seen by Al as "rhododendron-choked," the grounds as "water-logged," and beyond

Garbadale's residential bounds there is only "the rocky desolation of the steep slopes" (36) and the moors.[13]

The old house is often exposed to raging storms of lashing rain, sleet, and a high wind howling around it, but it defies the power of the elements with the ancient sturdiness of its masonry and the comforts of its interior. It becomes a witness to the eternal fight between the forces of nature, whose primordial spectacle Alban has a chance to observe in all its terrifying beauty from the window on one of his infrequent visits: "It was like the most fabulous elemental battle between air, water and gravity and he recalls standing at the window in the drawing room, watching this chaos with a feeling of almost sexual excitement" (263). By experiencing the intensity of the natural phenomena, Alban becomes infected with some primeval passions that can be held in check and hushed away only by withdrawing to the safe space of the ordinary and the civilized enclosed inside Garbadale House. But the passion of the storm is perpetuated in all members of the family whose lives have been in any way connected with the area. It simmers underneath the Wopulds' impeccable manners and calculated self-control and reveals itself in their uncompromising nature and business predation, best represented by Grandma Win.

Even as a grown man Alban feels strange uneasiness at the very mention of Garbadale and everything it represents (94). Alban's resistant

---

13   The gloom of the house, the stubborn ground, the moors and hills beyond its limits, and the battle of elements which the old manor withstands, along with its externalizing quality inevitably bring to mind Wuthering Heights. In contrast, Lydcombe, with its ordered parks, manicured gardens, and omnipresent light, connotes the flimsy elegance of Thrushcross Grange. The Victorian walled garden, which Alban tends and explores as a boy, may have been inspired by Frances Hodgson Burnett's The Secret Garden and its theme of growth and regeneration. The allusiveness of the two manors can be read in the context of the stereotypical representation of Scotland as England's polar opposite, its "repressed other" (see Bell 2004: 72). According to such binarism, as Beveridge and Turnbull observe, Scotland is "dark," "backward," "fanatical," "barbaric," "intemperate," or "unruly," whereas England, by comparison, is "enlightened," "advanced," "reasonable," "moderate," and "orderly" (qtd. in Bell 2004: 72). Significantly, Garbadale is associated in Alban's mind with the death of his psychologically disturbed mother, the memory of whom he has repressed but which returns only as a nightmare.

attitude towards the northern house of the Wopuld family seems to be connected primarily with the death of his mother, Irene, who drowned herself in a nearby loch when her son was only two years old. The loss of his mother translates into the loss of connection with the place, and thus alienation from the familiar space. While he abhors Garbadale, Lydcombe in Somerset on the north edge of Exmoor National Park, where Alban and his father move after Irene's death, comes to constitute a real home to him, the first and only space he knows as a child and within the boundaries of which he establishes his personal world. With its Victorian country manor, walled garden, ruins of an ancient abbey, sunny weather, friendly neighbourhood, and fertile ground Lydcombe functions as a complete antithesis of Garbadale. Unlike the northern estate, whose premises are a constant battlefield between man and nature, and where the house is open to raging elements, Lydcombe consists of several safety buffers which protect Alban while fostering his curiosity at the same time – the zones of lawns, gardens, and orchards smoothly ushering him into the wilder regions of the countryside:

At first he only felt comfortable on the lawns and terraces around the house, usually staying close to his dad as he sat on his little stool before his easel, painting, but after a while he started to make friends with the Victorian walled garden, and later began to play inside the old apple orchard within the ruins of the ancient abbey. The orchard had gone to pasture and was used to help feed the estate's few sheep and goats, which were more pets than anything else. Later still, expanding what he was starting to think of now as his domain, he began venturing out beyond these concentricities of safety and security and familiarity into the further meadows, copses, fields and woods of the estate. Then, one bright day, he rambled as far as the river with its banks strewn with wild flowers and bushes and, on that day of wanton exploratory zeal, even went on and out past that, across the broad, sluggish ford to the dunes and beach beyond, out to the margin of the land where the rollers boomed and the hills of Wales shimmered in the blue distance. (34-5)

This slow but methodical exploration of Lydcombe and the adjoining grounds becomes symbolical of Alban's growth into boyhood. The lush vastness of the estate, with animals bred but never killed (in contrast to Garbadale's hunting purpose), provides an almost paradisiacal space, which he can roam like his exclusive territory in the vein of the prelapsarian Adam. "He felt he was special, somehow secretly in charge of it all. It was his" (35), thinks Alban about his position in Lydcombe, and the statement holds a lot of truth when we consider Alban's childhood fascination with horticulture, which makes him spend hours around Lydcombe's old gardener helping the latter tend the garden. In time the boy starts charting his domain, drawing up maps of the place, giving names to its various parts and features and "invoking his own lore" (36), mediating the outside world through the languages of his private semiosphere. It is not surprising, therefore, that when his father takes him and his new family to London, Alban feels "betrayed, exiled, cast out" (37), his position at the centre of Lydcombe's space shifting to one beyond its borders, while his familiarity with it turns into detachment. It is now "the place to go on holiday to" rather than "to go on holiday from," a "destination, temporary and somehow conditional" (37), and on the occasional visits to his one-time home, he can notice various changes obliterating the remnants of his former residence.

Quite naturally, Lydcombe, which is shaped according to the character's creative vision, also becomes the setting of his youthful romance with cousin Sophie, the stage for their sexual initiation and its ensuing discovery by Grandmother Winifred and Uncle James, Sophie's father. If Alban is like Adam, then Sophie is his Eve, his "girl in the garden" (110), tempting him innocently with the power of her blooming femininity. The two project their private world away from prying eyes; within its boundaries they engage in a relationship which is at once forbidden, because they are too young and related, and for Alban – sacred. The line "Cuz, cuz, sweet cuz," which he associates with her, becomes "like a precious incantation for him, a sort of mantra" (63). His infatuation with his cousin is described in religious terms, as an act of receiving Holy Communion or venerating a holy relic, in which Sophie is the altar bread and the relic at the same time, and his own desire provides both a monstrance and reliquary (63), a proper imagery type for describing a love budding in a Garden of Eden.

"In a way, none of this is real" (156), says Alban to Sophie in a moment of portentous perspicacity, and the comment, which refers to the garden of Lydcombe, eventually proves to be a glum prophecy about their own relationship. It turns out that the gardens of the southern estate were created with the rock, soil, and plants brought by sea from Garbadale by Henry Wopuld, the "great, mythical great-grandfather" (156) and founder of the dynasty. Garbadale, therefore, assumes the quality of a mythical prototype which gave life to Lydcombe's present beauty, while Lydcombe itself turns into a false Eden which can only produce diseased fruit. Despite its favourable climate and its appealing man-made order, it takes its origin from the sinister northern fountainhead, being the latter's reflection if not in appearance then in spirit, and allowing itself to be penetrated by the same serpent that infected the mythical centre. Unbeknownst to Alban, his love for Sophie carries the danger of the same degeneration that brought him into the world. Alban is the fruit of the forbidden affair between siblings, Irene and her brother Blake, which led the former to depression and suicide, and the latter to compulsory banishment from home. As in the case of their biblical predecessors, tasting the forbidden fruit (i.e. committing an incest taboo, which undermines the community's foundations) results in the expulsion of the lovers from the Garden, aggravated here also by their forced separation: Alban is made to return to Richmond whereas Sophie is sent to Spain.

To Alban, Lydcombe is lost forever, he can neither return there nor communicate with its inhabitants. However, he continues to pursue his romantic fantasy now turned melodramatic, living in the self-instigated world of torment, writing letters and hundreds of poems for his beloved, which sentences him to many years of suffering and hopeless pining for the lost happiness. Despite the passing time, he harbours inside himself the picture of Sophie "as the same girl she had always been, but stopped, frozen, paused, something caught in amber or carbonite [. . .] but still staying the same person, ready to resume her life, their life, the instant whatever spell had been cast over them could be broken" (248). Love unfulfilled becomes the prism for Alban's adulation of Sophie, which eventually proves false and delusional. Only years afterwards is he able to put his teenage romance in the right perspective, which leads him to the conclusion that his love for his cousin was a false religion born in a false paradise out of his own need to believe in something better than himself. It became an idol in his otherwise atheist and secularist outlook (359). Significantly, his affection for Verushka Graef, a Glasgow mathematician of Czech origin, bears similar marks of veneration, functioning as "a kind of rival religion in his head; a new, shining, more effective, more earthy and hip cult compared to the ancient adoration of Sophie" (360). This proves that Alban lives in the world of self-constructed representations, in which a simulacrum tends to replace the prototype, obliterating reality for the sake of idealistic mediation.

By the same token, the language of blighted romance underpins his hatred for Winifred, who separated the young lovers, Alban's self-pitying infatuation with Sophie preventing any inquiry on his part into Winifred's reasons. As can be expected, the truth behind his grandmother's cruel determination to keep him and Sophie apart is not to be found in Lydcombe. It can only be learnt at the source, by returning to the *locus classicus*, Garbadale. Winifred's revelation of Alban's incestuous provenance triggers a process of resemioticization on his part. As a result, both his mother's suicide and his grandmother's actions find a rational explanation, simultaneously leading to a redefinition of his own place on the family canvas. The family romance has run its course, culminating in Alban's acceptance of who he really is and where his loyalties lie, namely with the Wopulds, now doubly his kin and clan.

The protagonist's visit to Garbadale, therefore, entails his re-identification with the community, with which he turns out to be inseparably connected by bonds of kinship and love. The last sections of the novel bring news of McGill's blooming relationship with Verushka, and their plans to settle down together within the circle of their family and friends. Moreover, Alban decides to allocate the money he inherited after the suicidal death of his biological father, Blake, to creating a centre in the Highlands for disadvantaged city kids. The money made by Blake, an uncompromising business magnate from Hong Kong and an exile from his native land, are in the end put to a good and noble purpose for the benefit of the Scottish community. With this remarkable gesture of selflessness and care, a manifestation of pragmatic morality typical of selves as agents, Alban, twice a Wopuld, finds his way back from the indifference and corruption of society to the heart of a truly communal spirit.[14]

---

14   The news of Alban's altruism is here accompanied by that of Tango, his friend from the Perth council estate, who narrates the last chapter. Tango decides to settle down with Big Mifty, a woman with bad experiences and another social outcast, and becomes the devoted foster father to the latter's children. The inclusiveness of the novel's ending, which brings together the rich and the poor, the Scots and the outsiders (i.e. Verushka), may reflect the post-devolution cosmopolitanism of Scottish literature (Schoene 2007: 15). At the same time, Alban's acceptance of his origin – involving incest and bastardy – may be

3.3. The Land of Music and the Music of Homeland in *Espedair Street*

The motif of the character's disappointment with society and his eventual return to communal values is further explored in *Espedair Street* (1987), the fictional autobiography of the Scottish rock-star Danny Weir, whose character was apparently modelled on Marillion's lead singer Fish (see Rosenthal 1999). Danny Weir's life narrative seems to break down into two main stages. The first one, related to his development as an artist and to the rise of his band, Frozen Gold, in the rock'n'roll business, is characterized by Danny's movement outwards from the space of home in the physical and spiritual sense. The second stage shows the protagonist's gradual movement homewards, which marks his return not only to Scotland but also to the past and the roots, which he has abandoned in pursuit of fame and self-gratification. Danny's life quest, therefore, takes the form of a circle, in which true fulfilment and harmony can be achieved only by humbly going back to where he began.

Danny's movement away from the space of origin is spurred by a combination of social factors, religious inadequacy, and personal ambition, which constitutes a fitting departure point for the Bildung narrative. Within this framework, Danny's family setting functions as the negative pole in the process of the protagonist's growth and maturation. The nest, out of which he gladly flew at the age of sixteen, is situated in Ferguslie Park in the suburbs of Paisley, which he sees as the "roughest area" of the city, "a wasteland of bad architecture and 'problem' families." "It was a toss-up which were the most broken; the families or the houses" (2003: 21), observes Danny when recalling occasional visits to his mother's.

The Ferguslie Park from the protagonist's memories is a space of ongoing devastation: the streets are full of glass from the ground-floor

---

seen as a manifestation of yet another characteristic of the post-devolution Scottish novel, of which Craig writes: "In this most recent wave of Scottish fiction, the recovery of creativity is made possible by the acceptance of illegitimate or adopted identity: recollecting of the nation's impurity is the beginning of recovery from the nation's amnesia" (2006: 138). Such an interpretation seems even more convincing when we consider Alban's amnesia of his mother and the nightmare of her suicide from which he finally recovers, but also the protagonist's very name, which can be translated into "Scot."

windows ("Ferguslie's equivalent of a gravel drive"), which are instead fitted with hardboard panelling, and the "only thing holding up the walls [is] the graffiti" (21). The district overflows with rubbish: sodden chip pokes, half-burned sheets of hardboard, aluminum take-away containers, as well as empty bottles of wine and drained cans of lager left after nightly binges, "as though people put out wine bottles instead of milk bottles, waiting for a morning delivery that never came" (21). Moreover, one can hear shouts coming from flats which are signs of the family quarrels; the noise, however, is usually drowned out by television watched by indifferent neighbours. The violence at home mirrors that in the streets, where local gangs keep wrecking cars, smashing holes in walls, defacing buildings with graffiti and the bodies of their rivals with gashes (21). The district, therefore, forms a multi-faceted aggregate of various social pathologies, blending architectural ugliness, social squalor, domestic violence, alcohol abuse, and rampant crime.

"Ferguslie Park lay in a triangle of land formed by three railway lines, so no matter what direction you approached it from, it was always on the wrong side of the tracks" (21), remarks Danny alluding not only to the place's penury and degradation (which are implied by the ambiguity of the phrase) but also to its confined character. The overwhelming sordidness, which seems to be contained within the limits of the area, is also the main and ever present element of its reality, trapping the inhabitants in the grubby mundanity with an almost deterministic force. Consequently, the desire to get away from it becomes Danny's major drive in life: "I wanted out of this. I wanted away" (23).

Significantly, Danny's family home, instead of being a zone of safety and comfort, constitutes a small-scale projection of the repulsive quarter. Being an epitome of poverty, physical and psychological oppression, and general unhappiness, all the more acute because of its personal impact on the protagonist, Danny's home only exacerbates his need to escape. "[T]he place depressed me," confesses Danny when trying to explain the briefness of his visit paid to his mother, the love for whom is not enough to "outweigh the bad memories" evoked by the place (21). A large part of such unpleasant recollections concerns Danny's violent drunkard father, who interrupted the boy's fifth birthday party and beat his wife senseless in front of the terrified kids, preventing Danny from blowing out the candles. The drunken fit of aggression traumatized the boy to such an extent that for some time he stopped using the number five in speech and writing (157-8). Thus, domestic violence, which is an emanation of the degraded social space, affects Danny's inner world and its semioticization mechanisms.

Another trauma from the past is connected with the concept of guilt as developed in Catholicism, which was instilled in him by the priests, teachers and, most of all, by his deeply religious mother, which emphasizes the interference of the public space into the space of the domestic. Feeling guilty is the first thing Danny was ever aware of, his most formative experience and, in its unnaturalness, the most natural thing in the world. As such it becomes the dour legacy and, in his own musical nomenclature, "the constant bass line" (19) to his life of escapism. It is a testimony of the ever-present tension between the outside world and Danny's private worldview, which contests the public institutions of the church, the school, and the university, along with censorious conventional morality (20). The fact that "a full time job" is, according to the priests, the only way to "save [Danny] from eternal damnation" (20), whereas his dream is to become a rock star, further underscores the discrepancy between the duty-obsessed, castigatory outlook of his religious community and his personal world-picture, structured around the values of individual freedom and self-fulfilment.

During Danny's occasional visits to Ferguslie, his mother always addresses this deeply entrenched sense of guilt, trying to persuade him to go to church, to confession, or at least to see the priest for a talk, while the son dodges the subject by enquiring about her own well-being and that of the siblings. The mother, therefore, becomes a mouthpiece of institutional constraints, based on fear and subordination to an external authority, which she attempts to impose on her son. The family flat becomes a place of failed communi(cati)on between Self and Other, a space in which Danny's and his mother's respective messages fall on deaf ears. The two family members use different codes, corresponding with their oppositional world-pictures, due to which instead of talking "together" (i.e. forming a semiotic dialogue), they talk "apart" (22). The oppressive atmosphere of the family home, with its revolting smell of cheap cooking, cigarettes, and above all, emotional pressure and mutual disappointment makes Danny feel "inadequate and hopeless and nervously out of place" (22) to the point of suffocation. When he finally gets away, even the smell of urine in the street comes as a relief, and he feels as if he has started breathing again.

Considered from this perspective, Danny's interest in writing songs, which follows the convention of Künstlerroman, appears to be one of the earliest methods of distancing himself from the surrounding reality and its manifold ugliness. He escapes into his private world filled with sounds, not only thinking up the tunes to convey what he wants to say but also devising at the age of eight a complicated and deeply idiosyncratic code – a system of musical notation, which becomes his pride and "a sort of personal institution" (24). Danny's private language of mediation, understood only by himself, emphasizes a one-sided character of communication, as the messages can be decoded and encoded only by Danny, making him both the addresser and the addressee in the communication act. His eventual adoption of the traditional musical system eight years later, and the resulting transfer of the songs "into the real world" (25) to be played and sung by Frozen Gold, represents Danny's shift across the boundary of his internal semiotics and the ensuing dialogue with the external semiosphere, which provides a tangible escape route from the confinement of his original community.

All of a sudden, Danny's music, which has so far existed only in its creator's inner world, finds its external emanation when arranged and interpreted vocally and instrumentally by the singer, Christine Brice. Its materialized force of words "belted [. . .] out through the chords" summons up visual images in Danny's head of "machine guns firing through propellers; American marines at the Edinburgh Tattoo, marching past each other twirling flashing bayonettes inches from their noses; a perfect tennis rally; Jimmy Johnstone taking on four defenders and scoring" (78). The composer's fantasy, translated into the languages of the public space (words and notes), surpasses his original vision, yet it sounds "right," affecting Danny in a new unexpected way. "I was close to tears by the end, not because of the lyrics but because it was there, it was real; it had been inside me and now it was born" (79), admits Danny, which underlies the fact that his music becomes a semiotic act when performed in compliance with the rules of external semiotics recognized by other people. Moreover, it provokes an emotional response in himself and the rest of the band, turning into the language of artistic communication, while his songs become texts in this language. Last but not least, music ensures a very literal dialogue between Self and Other. "[S]omebody else thought it was beautiful too; she must have, to have sung it like that . . ." (79), observes Danny, his words foregrounding the dialogic influence of art, which leads to the acceptance of an ugly boy from a council estate among his attractive and well-off peers.

Danny's first encounter with Dave Balfour and Christine Brice, the rich and beautiful frontmen of the band, strikes him with a realization of his own inadequacy and a well-known feeling of guilt, this time about his incongruity in the vicinity of the well-matched couple. Danny and the beautiful pair represent two opposite poles in every respect but their devotion to music. Interestingly, Danny, who describes himself as "*imposingly* bad-looking" (37), comes to perceive his appearance as indicative of his native environment and its squalid conditions, as if the ugliness of the Paisley suburb maliciously materialized in his own physiognomy. This nagging self-consciousness makes Danny project an almost scholastic discrepancy between himself and the two: he is "a monster, a mutant [and] a gangling ape" in comparison with the "Adonis" (33) and "Greek god" (28) of Dave and the "blonde angel" (35) of Christine.[15]

Later, Danny's apparently hideous and fear-inspiring looks mark him out to become an icon of youthful defiance, "a sort of anti-hero figure" (162), whose posters fans put up on their bedroom walls to shock their conservative parents. As such, he comes to represent a transgressive element filtering into the socially recognized institutions and hierarchies. His body, which is an independent copy of the space of provenance, undergoes an additional and deliberate modelling (through hairdos and mirror shades) to highlight Weir's innate ugliness, which opposes social concepts of harmony and order. In this way, he turns into an epitome of subversion, "something menacing but contained" (162), like Ferguslie Park itself, dreadful yet limited by the triangle of railway tracks. His newly acquired status finds its confirmation in the nickname Weird (i.e. Weir, D[anny]), which points as much to his peculiar (and unsightly) image as opposed to the glamour of the leading duo, as to his shying away from the worldly attention he could never handle (114).

---

15 Danny's perception of himself as a monster metaphorically represents what Craig calls self-hatred on the part of Scotland, which emerged as an apparent consequence of the nation's acceptance of its own cultural inadequacy and parochialism as opposed to England and its dominant culture (Bell 2004: 80-1).

Danny's deliberate *emploi*, intended as a means to capitalize on his objective ugliness, can be interpreted as his further escape from himself and his true identity. In the band's pursuit of success and Danny's growing importance as a song-writer, his real name, Danny Weir, gradually stops appearing in the song credits and becomes marginal for the sake of numerous playful pseudonyms like Justin O'More, Oliver Sutton, Alan Sundry, Patrick Thistle, and Gerald Hlasgow, by which he becomes a mystification. However, while teasing the record company and testing the intelligence of his fans, he sometimes loses himself in his own in-jokes and puns that rely on the Scottish dialect but which turn out to be comprehensible only to himself. Though he wants to come across as a "nonchalant, debonair and sophisticated man of the world" (143), he ends up embarrassed by his own parochialism:

> I hadn't realised how much of my speech marked me down as from north of the border; not just the obvious accent, but the words and phrases I used, too. I didn't know people in London didn't say 'neither it is' or 'back the way' or 'see what like it is' or 'see the likes of me?'; I didn't know English people didn't call shopping 'messages', or little fingers 'pinkies'; and I didn't realise that knowing all those other words would, to some people, make me seem ignorant. (144)

Among game playing and false identities, Danny's music remains the only world where "a misfit" like he, who would "never really be comfortable anywhere," truly belongs (13). In the interview with Jasper Rees for *The Independent*, Banks revealed that with *Espedair Street* he wanted to write "a fantasy novel set in reality" (1998). If this was indeed the author's intention, then the fantasy element in the novel seems to be best employed in the space of music which informs Danny's autobiographical narrative. Each of the band's albums – *Frozen Gold and Liquid Ice*, *All Wine Tastes Sour*, *Gauche*, *Night Shines Darkly*, *MIRV*, *Nifedge*, *And So The Spell Is Ended* – becomes a separate story drawing the audience into its distinct universe, rendered imaginatively through the medium of sounds and lyrics. Moreover, through the band, Danny's music truly brings an element of another, higher order into everyday reality, which is particularly striking in live performances:

> It was light and shade again, the sheer contrast of the mundane and the fabulous; the dull grey weight of the endless workaday days, and the bright, startling burst of light in the darkness, as though the five or more of us on stage before those thousands, even tens of thousands, were a concen-

tration of excitement, glamour, life; the very pinpoint place where all those ordinary lives somehow focused, and ignited. (280)

In concerts, the emanation of Danny's talent – his inner world – becomes "materialized" on stage through singing and playing, creating an ocean of sounds drowning all the listeners and giving the musician total control over the world. The stage becomes the space of synaesthesia, music being intertwined and communicated through other media employed in the show – visualized in the play of light, colour, lasers, and the smoke curtain. Projected onto the outside world, the music created by Danny changes people and affects their lives: Christine, singing his erotic song, is transformed from a neighbourhood girl into a vamp, and years later both she and Dave lose their lives as a result of music turned into a stage act.[16]

The development of Danny as a composer is highlighted by the changed climate of his successive albums, which reflects the broadening of the band's artistic horizons and going beyond familiar artistic solutions. They start with slightly rugged and raw but energetic first records, which reveal his and the band's artistic roughness, lyrical naivety, and youthful spirit. Then they break with the familiar formula and structure and move to the "vastly complicated, symphonic, lyricless" *Nifedge*. Thus, the unassuming vibrancy of rock'n'roll and folk tunes gives way to the intricately woven canvas of progressive rock epic. With the "muscle-bound, over-developed, strangled" platinum album *And So The Spell Is Ended*, Danny becomes aware that music is starting to elude them. The "contrived" songs with "tourniquets" become testimony to the decadent pursuits of the band members, who are more preoccupied with the "beguiling mathematical filigree of production and mixing possibilities" (288-9) than with tunes. But Danny's music also becomes a touchstone of the progressing dissipation of the character's inner space in the all-engulfing world of international fame. It gets increasingly externalized and exploited in tours, shows, and exhaustive recordings, leaving Danny stranded in an empty life.

Danny's work on the successive albums and the band's concert tours takes him further and further from Paisley and Scotland, first to London

---

16 Dave suffers fatal electrocution as a result of the smoke curtain, and Christine is assassinated by a religious fanatic after she has staged her own crucifixion. Both the curtain and the crucifixion are Danny's ideas for a show.

and other parts of the United Kingdom (e.g. Wales and Cornwall), then to Scandinavia, continental Europe, the Caribbean, and the United States, with infrequent and rather noncommittal visits home. At a certain point, he and the other members of Frozen Gold move out of the UK for tax reasons, and their addresses become as virtual as the credits of the song-writers mentioned on their album covers. "I think, technically, we lived in LA for the second half of the seventies. But it might have been the Cayman Islands" (179), comments Danny while recounting the band's rise to fame, and their loyalties influenced by economic factors more than anything else. Moving physically in international space, inside Danny carries the same complexes and habits which he imbibed in childhood. Despite his life in the limelight and his growing wealth, he remains in many respects the same boy from a poor quarter who was deprived of various comforts when growing up; thus, he does not attach much value to them (10). Even years after the band's break-up, when he lives as a recluse in Glasgow, Danny still hates telephones and television. He prefers local bars with cheap food like pie, beans, and chips to elegant dishes in five-star hotels, admitting to himself that he has "never shaken off the tastes of [his] childhood" (57).

In his pursuit of fame and fortune, Danny loosens or severs the bonds not only with particular places but also with his former mates. Among those the most significant turns out to be his teenage relationship with Jean Webb, resident of the eponymous Espedair Street. In Danny's memories, the figure of Jean is linked with his first sexual experiments but also with his physical and, worse still, emotional clumsiness, which eventually contributed to their drifting apart. Jean remains calm and understanding, not only about his awkward behaviour but, especially, about his dreams of being rich and famous, which Danny keeps harping on. Ironically, in Danny's mind, Jean becomes associated with the space of origin, functioning as a touchstone of his ambiguous attitude towards his hometown – he wonders whether she will restrict his freedom or will rather be a safe haven, "somebody to come home to" (63). Initially, his dream to get away encompasses also his girlfriend's future, as he promises Jean at one of their dates that he will "take her away from all this [to] London, Paris, New York, Munich . . ." (63), letting her believe in the possibility of their life together. In the end, he leaves her behind like the rest of his uncomfortable past, letting her "slip away" (65), as he later wistfully observes.

The further Danny moves from the space of home, the more tied to it Jean becomes, giving up her plans of going to the arts college, working as a secretary with the gas board, and settling down with her husband, Gerald. In the hustle of his spectacular musical career, as Danny remarks offhandedly, he has rarely spared Jean Webb a thought. Ironically, his drift away from the community is marked by his growing loneliness and the general disenchantment with the rock culture lifestyle, which he and his bandmates find incompatible with their personal dreams and desires, looking for more and more extreme activities to hush the overwhelming disappointment (March 2002: 102). Each of them becomes increasingly involved in a folly of his own – a unique space of eccentricity which alienates them from the rest of the band and represents their individual attempts to give meaning to the life they live in the unstable and inchoate world of show business.

Only Mickey Watson, the drummer, avoids the identity problems and frustration experienced by the others, paradoxically thanks to his rootedness in the stable and ordinary existence within the community and his space of origin, among persons in relation, which he keeps separate from his professional life. "To him, despite all the money and fripperies, it was still a job" (183), observes Danny. The others, in contrast, put on masks in order to live up to the audience's perception of them as idols, adopting false identities, which alienate them both from their past lives and their real selves:

> We took it seriously, in our own ways. We worked at being Rock Stars; not musicians, not even Personalities or ordinary Stars, but Rock Stars. It was a way of life, like a religion, like becoming a totally different person. We *believed*; we had an obligation to our public to behave like Rock Stars, offstage as well as on, and we did our best, dammit. (184)

A life like Mickey's, ordered and meaningful because lived for and with others, away from recording studios, concert tours, glamorous parties, and the anonymity of hotel rooms, eludes Danny. The pace of changes in the lives of those he left in Scotland, marked by deaths, births, and marriages, makes him realize his own age but also his existential futility. The recognition of this dawns on him during a solitary walk on the Greek island of Naxos, bringing thoughts of Jean Webb, whose life progresses somewhere back home with her husband and a baby daughter. "It was as though she was somebody I should have known fully, perfectly, and then parted from, older, wiser, still good friends . . . instead, somehow, we had never got that far" (236), he ponders nostalgically. In its unfulfilled potential of a life of simplicity, togetherness, and love, which he could have lived by Jean's side, the past becomes separated from the present, just as Danny becomes disconnected from his Scottish roots. His subsequent relationships with women are superficial and devoid of genuine affection on both sides. "Anthea, Rebecca, Sian, Sally, Sally-Ann, Cindy, Jas, Naomi . . ." (163), Weir reels off, reminiscing and reviewing the emotional wasteland of his rock star life.

Dave Balfour's tragic death at a concert in Atlanta and the following split-up of Frozen Gold can be seen as the turning point in Danny's life, marking his withdrawal from the international scene and his gradual return to the space of Scotland and the community. Just as in his early youth he tried to disconnect himself from Ferguslie and its deprivation by fleeing from Scotland to become the citizen of the world, so now he finds anchorage in Glasgow, escaping from his rock and roll past and stardom into the life of an anonymous recluse. His direction, therefore, is homewards as much as inwards, as Danny isolates himself from the outside world physically, taking residence in the solitude of St Jute's church, and mentally, seeking refuge in the recesses of the mind, reliving old memories and retracing his footsteps in search of something that could give meaning to his life.

St Jute's seems a suitable dwelling for someone who used to be known as Weird and has been plagued by Guilt with a capital G for his entire life. The building is a testimony to madness and a symbol of heresy, having roots in a great fortune and a terrible personal loss. Built in the second half of the nineteenth century by a jute merchant, Ambrose Wykes, it was initially a temple devoted to the worship of his wife and baby son, both of whom had died in a train crash. Bought by Danny in 1982, it allowed the protagonist, distraught after Davey's death and disillusioned with his own life in the limelight, to "make [his] own retreat from the world at large" (48). Ironically, Danny has swapped his rootless life of meaningless relationships, lived in hotel rooms and company-owned villas, for the anonymity and seclusion of the strange Glasgow fortress, and Danny thus comments on the compatibility of the edifice and himself: "So I became a hermit crab instead, and look at the big shell I found! [. . .] St Jute's and I are suited" (170).

St Jute's, which came to be called Wykes's folly, has been turned by Danny into an emblem of his own "folly." With a storehouse of the COMCON products (household appliances, vehicles, crates of vodka), the building constitutes an enclave if not of communal values then at least communist goods, as if in rejection of the self-serving capitalism to which its owner once actively contributed. Most of all, however, it is a citadel allowing its only inhabitant to shut out the outside world at will. The massive doors and barred windows fitted by the folly's original owner have been complemented with CCTV guarding all entrances, which enables the monitoring and selection of guests. These are few and far between, as Danny is fiercely protective of his privacy. The people who visit him most often are local inhabitants of rather ill repute, whom he calls accomplices (not friends), like the one-time docker McCann, the adolescent solvent abuser Wee Tommy, and the prostitute Betty. Naturally, none of them knows Danny's true identity. Trying to keep a low profile, he passes himself for the folly's caretaker, Jimmy Hay (an alias alluding to a Scottish footballer from the beginning of the twentieth century), not the famous rock star who actually owns the place, which in effect takes the strain out of their interaction.

Closing himself in his private world within the folly's walls, Danny at the same time blocks all channels of communication with the outside world. For a large part of the year he remains unaware of what happens domestically and globally, as he avoids newspapers, television and radio. "[T]hey could start the next world war and I wouldn't know anything about it until the streets filled with people pushing carts and prams and sticking tape over their windows . . ." (59), he admits, although every several months he indulges in one-week-long Information Binges when he reads, watches, and listens to everything he can. Moreover, there are no telephones in St Jute's, important mail gets delivered to his lawyers, who for their part spread rumours and fuel legends concerning Weir's whereabouts, while any personal mail and contact are simply pointless. The same escapist policy applies to Danny's music; despite having an entire recording studio in the basement, he generally shuns composing and comes up with new works only occasionally, and when he does, he never listens to them. "Haven't been able to stand my own stuff since the band broke up, not once it's out there, public, no longer mine" (48-9), he confesses, and we cannot help but wonder at the change which has taken place in him since that evening in Davey's garage when Christine sang his songs for the first time, reducing Danny to tears.

Paradoxically, the glamour of the greater world, which once penetrated into Danny's inner self and lured him out of Paisley and Scotland, has in the meantime filtered into the country, altering its former face. The past and tradition meet the future and innovation, as the cityscape of Glasgow starts filling with modern buildings, like the Britoil office complex with its "glossy, tinted mirror-shade façade" (57), opposite the neo-Gothic silhouette of St Jute's. The Britoil building was raised where there used to be only a hole in the ground, so in a way it has disturbed the natural organization of space, to which the inhabitants were accustomed for about a century, and which is here metaphorically conveyed by the folly's distorted reflection in the building's glassy surface. When in response to McCann's remark about the monstrosity of the Britoil complex Danny calls him "a reactionary old bastard" (58), the latter vehemently denies the epithet. While Danny has been adjusting to the conditions of the international scene, Scotland has itself undergone numerous changes under international influences. However, just as there appeared a voice of resistance in Weir against the disintegrating force of a worldly life without roots, affection, and meaning, a similar resistance seems to be voiced for the country by such Scottish McCanns, for whom there is "nothing reactionary about tryin tae maintain yer heritage, even if it is a hole in the ground" (58).

The changes brought by globalization have not missed Danny's hometown either, which he registers with a mixture of elation and bitterness. Paisley looks the same yet somehow different, newer and brighter, with more cars, fewer people, and some higher buildings around. Even Espedair Street, where Jean Webb used to live, is changed, to Danny's disappointment. Rebuilt and reorganized, it gives the impression of being "more mixed up and unsure of itself," just like Danny after his prolonged period of dislocation (333). The new pizza place seems out of place to Danny, "something bright and plasticky from another age, another planet" (334), and the street on the whole looks strangely unfamiliar. Only the Waterloo Bar, where he once sat with Jean before setting off to become a star, seems to have remained the same over the years, which can function as a metaphor of the continuity implicit in their youthful relationship and point to the permanence and power of Jean's love.

Weir's visit to Espedair Street immediately follows his trip to the Highlands, during which he plans to commit suicide. The idea of suicide comes to him after he learns that Christine Brice has been killed by a religious fanatic because she staged her own crucifixion in concerts while touring with her new band in America. Danny, being the mastermind behind the crucifixion idea, cannot help regarding Christine as the last victim of his youthful desire to do something "more *impressive*, more *memorable*" (308). He holds himself responsible for the tragedies that happened to her and Dave (the latter died of electrocution at the age of twenty-five in the stage act of the Great Contra-Flow Smoke Curtain devised by Weir), encapsulating his pernicious influence in imagery which echoes *Macbeth*, the biblical annihilation of Sodom and Gomorrah, as well as Judas's betrayal – "I was the ghost at the feast, the angel of destruction, the kiss of extinction" (308). To Danny, the rise to stardom which took him out of Paisley, which was supposedly his natural element, was like an attempt to change his own destiny: "I could create grace, I could *compose* grace, even if I couldn't be graceful myself" (308). In his twisted fatalism he assumes that it was Christine and Dave who had to pay dearly for his aspirations to fame, individuation, and self-aggrandizement. Paradoxically, the death trip to the Highlands marks the protagonist's return to life. It is here in a dark hotel room that he can hear his old songs made real and alive again by the voices of his dead friends, Davey and Christine, who, like ghosts of the halcyon past, call him to live on, despite the pain, disillusionment, and remorse. The message in the language of his own music, sent across time, elicits Danny's response in tears. Finally able to grieve for the dead, he wakes up the next morning with a newly-found strength and perseverance to remain among the living.

The account of Danny's return to life in the hotel room is immediately followed in his narration by the flashback of his visit to Espedair Street seven years before and the conversation he had with Jean's invalid mother. The visit helped Danny at the time to find peace and consolation in his grief for Davey Balfour and the band's break-up. Danny thus describes his ensuing change of spirit:

> I left the flat depressed but, as I walked down Espedair Street, back into town under a glorious sunset of red and gold, slowly a feeling of contentment, intensifying almost to elation, filled me. I couldn't say why; it felt like more than having gone through a period of mourning and come out the other side, and more than just having reassessed my own woes and decided they were slight compared to what some people had to bear; it felt like faith, like revelation: that things went on, that life ground on regardless, and mindless, and produced pain and pleasure and hope and fear and joy and despair [. . .]. [U]nder that startlingly gaudy sky [. . .] I walked, and felt I could be happy again. (326-7)

The two instances of Danny's "resurrection" call to mind the motif of temporary death as a way of the hero's transferring from one state into the other, which Lotman calls "the single mythological invariant of 'life-death-resurrection (renewal)'," which, in more abstract terms, involves "entry into a closed space" and then "emergence from it" (1990: 160). Considered from this perspective, both the hotel in the Scottish Highlands, where Danny spends the night of musical recollections, and Espedair Street function as the spaces of regenerative force spurring the character on his way back to love, commitment, and internal harmony.

It is Danny's second "sentimental journey" to Espedair Street, undertaken after his reconciliation with the memory of Dave and Christine, which gives him hope for happiness, as he learns from Jean's brother Gerald that Jean is divorced and might be ready for a new relationship. This makes Danny begin another journey to the Scottish Highlands, this time, embarked on in an attempt to win back the love of a woman he abandoned, and to return to the joys and sorrows of the simple life he once rejected for the sake of money and fame (March 2002: 102). Last but not least, under the influence of the once familiar neighbourhood, Danny comes up with the first new song in many years, which is the product of his newly found life energy, and which best communicates the street's redemptive quality: "It's the wrong side of the wrong side of the tracks/ The dead end just off Lonely Street/ It's where you go, after Desperation Row/ Espedair Street" (333).

In the song, the name Espedair Street turns into a metaphor for "an amalgam of places and feelings and times" (345). It denotes a locus which cannot be found on a map other than Danny's own mindscape – it comes to encompass a space of memories like the objective correlative of his heart. Music, therefore, becomes a means of synthesis for the character's past and present, but also a medium of Danny's reintegration into community. While in childhood music made him escape from the jarring world of the family into the inner harmony of sounds, in youth, it took him away beyond the community's reach. Now, through the sounds and words conveying the image of the street, music turns into a medium due to which the space of home is translated back into the heart of its long-estranged son. This time Danny abandons everything he achieved in the whole wide world, leaving to himself the only thing that has always been part of him, his talent to write songs. He goes north to the village of Arisaig and turns at Jean's doorstep empty-handed, like the Danny he used to be, but finally knowing who he is and what kind of life he desires most.

3.4. Big Movies and Private Narratives in *Stonemouth*

As in its 1992 predecessor, *The Crow Road*, *Stonemouth* (2012) explores the theme of mediation in relation to the notion of community, the past, and the relativity of truth in historical accounts. Just like Prentice, whose visits to Gallanach have always been triggered by the funerals of family members, the protagonist of *Stonemouth*, Stewart Gilmour, returns to his hometown after five years of "exile" in order to participate in the funeral of Old Joe, the paterfamilias of the Murstons, a local gangster family. Stewart used to be engaged to the Murstons' daughter, Ellie, on whom he cheated a week before their wedding. Summoned back to his hometown on Joe's specific request, Stewart puts his life at risk, as the Murstons have not forgiven him for his "sin(s)" (2012: 5).

Stewart's "sin," committed against his beloved, is also a "sin" in a more general sense, as it amounts to his transgression of such values as fidelity, trust, loyalty, affection, and mutual respect, which underlie the life of the family and community. As Ellie's fiancé, Stewart had been given "the title of an honorary Murston" (234); therefore, his disloyalty towards Ellie is tantamount to betrayal of the clan. It causes havoc in its internal dynamics and disturbs the balance in the functioning of the family, leading, like a bad omen, to other misfortunes: Stewart's forced departure from Stonemouth, his solitude and loveless relationships, as well as Ellie's rushed marriage with Ryan MacAvett, her miscarriage and eventual divorce.

The community of Stonemouth constitutes Stewart's formative environment, in which his outlook on life and identity are shaped through his relations with friends, girlfriends, relatives, and neighbours. However, apart from fostering his development and providing support, the community shows cracks in its surface, as it is being eaten away by an inner disease. The town is ruled by two gangster families, the Murstons and the MacAvetts, who ensure the town's peace and order, "preserving professional, commercial, middle-class values and generally maintaining Stonemouth as a safe place to raise your children and do business" (185). At the same time, they subordinate the place to their business objectives, namely drug trafficking, or they can murder a person "with relative impunity," as the police turn a blind eye to their business, intimidated like the rest of the populace (186).

The uneasy balance of the town community matches the disintegration of the communal on the level of the Murston family, who are in control of the area. Due to their family business, the bond of blood is (un)naturally strengthened by common interest and vice-versa, which turns the family into a company, inciting ambition and a desire for domination. These are all the more dangerous because they may result in the struggle against or betrayal of one's own kin. The business-related tensions come to the surface in the disagreement between Murdo and Don, evidently caused by the son's aspirations to leadership, as well as in Callum's on-the-side negotiations with a Glasgow gang to take over the Murston's trafficking routes, which presumably results in Callum's death at the hands of his own brothers.

Interestingly, the distortions within the community – murders and betrayals – are brought to light by media like film and photography. The novel is replete with mentions of cameras, movies, or CCTV, which record the images of hidden or otherwise unregistered reality, in its most gruesome or unpleasant aspects. It is the monitoring system on the road bridge over the Firth of Stoun which records the moment of Callum's "jump" to his death into the river. The tape, which disappears from the security files, is later repeatedly watched by his father, Don (at least, according to Callum's sister Grier). The same is true for photos, the most drastic example being Lauren and Drew's wedding, at which Stewart's sex with Jel is immortalized by one of the instamatic cameras given out for fun to all children, which blights Stewart and Ellie's relationship. The photos which have brought Stewart's infidelity to everyone's attention are posted on the Internet and years later mediate the image of the past. However, apart from being an embarrassing reminder of his stupidity, upon examination the pictures also reveal their own artifice, speaking of how they were taken in the first place. The evidence which Stewart collects studying the medium convinces him that the photos were not taken by a child but by an adult, and with deliberation (299). This contradicts the collective memory of the event, pointing to an intentional falsification of the past, a fact which is signalled by Jel ("It wasn't just my idea, Stu" [137]), as well as by Katy Linton, one of the kids at the wedding, whose camera was used for taking the incriminating pictures.

The media, therefore, not only convey the uncomfortable truth people want to conceal but they also uncover the evil streak and ill intentions behind the community façade. The evidence points to Grier, Ellie's younger sister, as the person behind the ill-fated photo shoot. This seems plausible, considering Grier's evident propensity for dabbling in representations, which goes beyond her job as a trainee photographer and her appearance in a few music videos. "Grier was always a great mimic, always quoting lines from film and TV, and adopting different accents" (95), notes Stewart upon their meeting. As a fourteen-year-old, disgruntled with Don's refusal to buy her a horse, she came up with the terrifying idea of planting tulip bulbs on the main lawn of the Murstons' house so that in spring they would form a severed horse's head – "a combination of a *Godfather* reference and guerrilla horticulture" (261), Stewart comments, showing how Grier's vengeful side is expressed through representations. Last but not least, Grier's playing with reality is reflected in her fake stories, one of which, told to the heartbroken Ellie, concerns Grier's stay at Stewart's in London and his alleged nocturnal advances.

Grier's manipulation of facts on the verbal level points to another form of mediation effected within the community, namely how stories and verbal accounts convey, modify, or falsify history, revealing the teller's bias, bad memory, or deliberate manipulation. Listening to the "recited, edited, rosified highlights of Joe's life" (275) at the funeral, Stewart cannot help feeling embarrassed, as much for the posthumous glorification of the gang's founder as for the religious, "fantasy-and-superstition" mediation of human mortality (275). A similar distortion of the family history occurs at the funeral reception when Murdo Murston retells the story of the practical joke his grandfather played on one of his drinking mates, which originally did not involve Joe but one of his uncles. Listening to Murdo's version of the story Stewart muses inwardly: "It irks me that history's being rewritten like this, but if I say something now I'll just look like the bad guy" (291). "In the end, after all, what does it really matter?" he asks himself and almost immediately concludes that defending the truth "always matters" (291).

However, despite all the evidence he has collected, Stewart is never allowed to get at one important truth concerning the authorship of the unfortunate pictures. When he confronts Grier about her apparent agency and reasons, she accuses him of fantasizing and throws at him a series of plausible explanations of his past humiliation: her own jealousy of Ellie, Ellie's intention to test his fidelity, Don's dissatisfaction with his prospective son-in-law, who wanted to be an artist, and thus had better be removed "from the picture." "Maybe you should think of all that, if we're entertaining all the possibilities, even the crazy ones" (330), she sums up. Grier's disquisition, which shows how reality can be (mis)represented and (mis)interpreted, points to our entanglement in a series of mediations, authored by others and enacted by us, which recalls Stewart's own idea of lives being like narratives:

> I suspect we all sort of secretly think our lives are like these very long movies, with ourselves as the principal characters, obviously. Only very occasionally does it occur to any one of us that all these supporting actors, cameo turns, bit players and extras around us might actually be in some sense real, just as real as we are, and that they might think that the Big Movie is really all about *them*, not us; that each one of them has their own film unreeling inside their own head and we are just part of the supporting cast in their story.
>
> Maybe that's what we feel when we meet somebody we have to acknowledge is more famous or more charismatic or more important than we are ourselves. The trick is to know when to go with the other player's plot line, when to abandon your own script – or your own thoughts for what to improvise next – and adopt that of the cast member who seems to have the ear or the pen or the keyboard of the writer/director. (239-40)

The above passage points to a person's perception of his/her respective history, in which they are the axis of the world and the pivot of the plot, treating other people's worldviews as marginal or subordinated to the semioticizing centre of their own consciousness, the movie imagery underscoring the workings of the ego which sees reality as a script written for its own sake. However, as the passage implies, there are many different ways of experiencing and making sense of the world, many distinct individual self-focused perspectives, and there is, in addition to that, a sense of possible hierarchy. Somebody else's story may be more important than ours and eventually obliterate our sense of self – of being someone with a narrative/perspective/life worth living in and for itself. It is also worth emphasizing the conditional aspect, which amounts to a wisdom of a sort: knowing *when* to accept or acknowledge, and even adopt, someone else's narrative as our own; to recognize the point or situation at which it makes sense to sacrifice ourselves for others or a larger other.

The need to recognize that our lives are not lived in detachment from others but in connection and through the other necessarily means stepping over the boundary of one's ego, and thus also over the confines of one's solipsistic narrative, in order to connect consciously with other narratives. What reverberates with Macmurray's philosophy of community as formed by persons in relation, finds its verbalization at various points in the novel, one of which comes with Alan Linton's talk about the dialogic character of our relationships on various levels of social life:

> 'We all start out as idealists. I certainly did. I hope I still am, deep down. But idealism meets the real world sooner or later, and then you just have to [compromise].' [. . .] 'Marriage is about compromising,' [. . .] '[f]amilies are about compromising, being anything other than a hermit is about compromising. Parliamentary democracy certainly is.' [. . .] 'Nothing but.' [. . .] 'You either learn to compromise or you resign yourself to shouting from the sidelines for the rest of your life.' [. . .] 'Or you arrange to become a dictator. There's always that, I suppose.' [. . .] 'Not a great set of choices, really, but that's the price we pay for living together. And it's that or solitude.' (193)

What Alan calls compromise involves the abolition of our deep-rooted conviction that other people are like us – one of the major mistakes in our perception of reality, as Joe once told Stewart (292). Therefore idealism, which means promoting one's own outlook on things, must yield to mediation – the bringing together of two distinct visions, two individual world-pictures, and working out common ground, a common semiotic space in which the two languages come into dialogue, fostering togetherness rather than hostility and solitude.

The categories of dialogue and agency in relation, as opposed to solipsism and failed communication, are orchestrated through the dynamics of the characters' relationship with the space of the community, which is played out between the binary categories of inside/outside, internal/external, and explored on various levels of signification. One example of such a dichotomy is the characters' inward and outward movement in geographical terms. Despite her plans to move away from home to some "warm place" (249), after her university years Ellie ends up living not far away from the Toun, working part-time in charity rehabilitation centres for drug users, thus remedying the evil to which her drug-trafficking family has also contributed. Having attended the University of Sheffield, Jel returns to Stonemouth and becomes involved with Stewart's childhood friend, Phelpie, who now works for her father, Mike Mac. Also Fergus, Stewart's best friend, although "fantasis[ing] about the heady delights of the central belt – the dreaming spires of Edinburgh, the urban chic of downtown Glasgow" (41), lives in Dundee but is a frequent visitor to Stonemouth, whose barmen know his name and drinking preferences. The Stonemouth community is therefore a source of stability and permanence resulting from family ties and long-standing personal engagements. It is, as Fergus observes, "the land that time forgot" (41), which is a playful reference to the title of Edgar Rice Burroughs's novel about a lost prehistoric world. The unchanging quality of the place is also noticed by Stewart, who watches the people sitting in the pub:

> I recognize most of them. So many people doing the same things they were when I left, hanging out in the same places, saying the same things, having the same arguments. It feels comfortable, reassuring, just being able to step back into our old shared life so easily, but at the same time a bit terrifying, and a touch sad.
>
> They are happy. *Are* they happy? Let's assume they're fairly happy. So, that's all right. Nothing wrong with that. Life is patterns. Old man Murston said that, I think, on one of our hill walks: Jo the Obi. Nothing wrong with people having patterns to their lives, some stability, some set of grooves they can settle into, if that's what they want. Don't get the existential horrors just because some people like staying where they were

raised, marrying the bod next door and getting a job that means they'll never win *X Factor*. Good luck to them having steady paid employment these days. (48-9)

Stewart's cautious belief in the locals' happiness is one of the outsider who has always been consumed with an outward urge, his outlook going beyond the immediate space of his hometown or even Scotland. Already in his teens, he dreamt of the international scene: he wanted to become a great artist, "a cross between Charles Rennie Mackintosh, Jef Koons and Andy Warhol," gaining the recognition of the artistic world and entire humankind, while the stage for his creative pursuits was to be provided by London or New York (84). Although his artistic ambitions have not been fulfilled, Stewart has indeed become a citizen of the world. He travels around the globe, realizing commissions in countries as far away from home as India or China, remarking in his conversation with Ellie that he is "[s]till based in London, though you'd struggle to tell that from my credit card receipts" (245).

The outward drive in the topographical sense matches a similar tendency on a more personal level, namely Stewart's dissociation from his real self. His "exile" from the community necessarily means "making a new life" for himself, which involves not only career pursuits but also forgetting or repressing everything which would remind him of old Stewart, including his friends and town, as the space of home is inevitably connected with the past and its mistakes. He tries to transform into a different person, disconnected from the one he used to be, in order "to forge a *Stewart Gilmour:* 2.0, a newer, better me who'd never behave like a fool again" (238). Moreover, his relationships are based on business interest, money, ambition, and self-aggrandizement, being deprived of a closer bond or intimacy. Such a detachment from the emotional and the personal on Stewart's part is metaphorically reflected by his profession:

'I point lights at buildings. I'm an exterior decorator fussing over the phallic substitutes of rich boys. I window dress the grotesque status symbols of a kleptocratic worldwide plutocracy, the undeserving elite of the far-too-impressed-with-themselves über rich. It's exciting, it's rewarding, it's well paid and it takes me all over the world, and so long as I don't actually think about it I have a great time.' (315)

The above passage reflects ironically on the very first words spoken by Stewart the narrator, who stands on the misty road bridge before entering Stonemouth: "Clarity. That would have been good" (3). Pointing lights at buildings (outwards), he never points it inwards, lacking or avoiding clarity of who he is and what he really wants from life. It is only after his reunion with Ellie, his love from when he lived in/with the community, that he recognizes his lost wholeness: "I think back to the last time I felt . . . connected with myself, all of a piece, and I think of you, I think of when we were together" (316). Stewart's confession is a statement of the communal dynamics in which the Self as Agent realizes its selfhood only through its relation with the Other. In Macmurray's view: "Persons [. . .] are constituted by their mutual relation to one another. 'I' exists only as one element in the complex 'You and I'" (1995: 24). Considered from this perspective, Stewart represents a Self which has taken itself out of dialogue with the Other, becoming an isolated observer of life and a cog in the society's machine, fulfilling fantasies of solipsistic minds and massaging his own ego with financial rewards.

However, in the end Ellie and Stewart decide to go back together, with a promise of becoming a family one day. Stewart thus returns both to his old friends and to the woman he once lost, and through them his bond with the community undergoes restitution. His reintegration into the communal relationship fosters the character's return to his real dreams and desires – Stewart intends to leave the company, which has allowed him to live a comfortable yet solitary life. Instead, he resumes his idea of becoming "a struggling artist," earning his livelihood from what he really loves. The space of the personal is therefore rediscovered and understood as a result of the reestablishment of the active relation with the Other. Unlike in the other novels of the Community Model, in *Stonemouth* neither the hometown nor Scotland are seen as the characters' final destination, as Ellie and Stewart decide to leave the Toun for somewhere "warm and sunny," which would not, however, be like Stewart's life to date "all over the world" (352). In the end, community is not (at least, not *only*) where you were born and grew up, Banks seems to tell the reader, but remains in the people with whom you are related by bonds of mutual love, care, and respect wherever the Big Movie of your life will take you. "Whatever we do, we'll be okay; we'll always survive," concludes Stewart, which refers as much to his union with Ellie as to his other relationships. "We'd always be okay as individuals but together we'll be brilliant, unbeatable" (352).

***

All the novels discussed in this chapter link the space of community with that of the family or neighbourhood, which are always contained within the larger space of the nation. As a result, the character's personal or domestic history is frequently informed by public history, the intertwining of the two historical perspectives being achieved by the use of such traditional genres as the family saga, autobiography, Bildungsroman, or Künstlerroman. Their conventions involve the character(s) rootedness in a particular landscape or social milieu, which allows the author to explore the development of the individual against the background of social and generational changes.

The families depicted in the first three novels are always in some sense dysfunctional from the point of view of the central consciousness, which makes impossible the desired communion of the Self and Other. Prentice from *The Crow Road* remains in conflict with his father Kenneth, whose atheist and rationalist outlook on life offers the son neither explanation nor consolation after the deaths of his closest relatives and friends. Alban from *The Steep Approach* perceives the Wopuld clan and its leader, Grandma Win, as epitomes of rapacious capitalism, abandoning the corporation-like ranks of the family in exchange for a communal life among social outcasts in Perth. For Danny Weir in *Espedair Street*, the family is inextricably linked with his mother's extreme Catholicism (whose punitive and restrictive outlook seriously impedes communication between the two), his father's violence, and the poverty of the council estate in Paisley, which provoke his escape from home. Although Stewart's immediate family in *Stonemouth* is the source of love and support, his observations are principally tied to the Murston clan, a drug-dealing family gang comprising his fiancée's relatives, which at once protects and causes disintegration within the community space.

The characters of *The Crow Road*, as much as they are influenced by their family environment and rootedness in the Scottish landscape, are also shown as mediating the picture of the family and the country through words and imagination. As a boy, Kenneth creates a space of political and social compromise by verbalizing the dream of the British

Empire as an epitome of equality and fraternity. As an adult, he creates a similar space of common consciousness when by means of fairy tales and etiological legends of his own devising he explains to the children the origin of the Scottish landscape and their own place in the history of the land. His creative word, therefore, shapes not only the physical space but also the psychological space of the younger generation. The imaginative (re)construction of space takes place also in the case of Uncle Rory, who leaves Scotland and becomes a lonely traveller in an alien culture. In his travelogue, Rory, the mediator between his family and the greater world, creates an imaginative space of his peregrinations, fictionalizing the experience of the Other just as his brother presents and elucidates the familiar though his stories. In the end, Rory, who has been avoiding his return home, becomes the domestic historian, creating his own written account of his sister's death, thereby explaining the secret of the family just as Kenneth explains the secrets of the land.

Prentice, the main character of *The Crow Road*, constructs his personal world within the community and the country in relation to the word of his father and his uncle. Kenneth's death, which brings Prentice back into the family, activates the memory of his father's tales and countryside lessons, which makes the youth acknowledge his own connection with the land and its peoples, and his own and the family's place in the great cycle of death and rebirth. Simultaneously, Prentice's search for Rory's missing novel, *The Crow Road*, involves the nephew's immersion in Rory's personal world and the past, in which the signs must be read to ensure continuity with the present. In this way, Prentice becomes the pivot uniting in his first-person account two parallel mediations of history – Kenneth's national and Rory's domestic narratives, creating his own space of the word and imagination as a rightful heir of the two story-tellers.

In *The Steep Approach*, Alban's constant search for his own place within the family is reflected in his attitude towards the two major spaces of residence of the Wopuld clan, which predictably translates into the character's mediation between the Scottish North and the English South, with their mutually exclusive axiology. Avoiding the sullen and windy Garbadale in the Scottish Highlands, Alban turns to Lydcombe, whose space he personalizes through gardening: he cultivates the land, grows plants, explores the magic of hortilore, and draws the maps of his dominion. The paradisiacal atmosphere of Lydcombe fosters Alban's immersion in his private world of love for Cousin Sophie, while their fractured romance affects his future relationships with women and contributes to his uneasy relationship with the family.

Alban's return to the Wopulds after years of voluntary separation also involves his return to Garbadale, where the family narrative concealing the secret of his mother's death comes to a resolution and allows Alban to put to rights his disturbed loyalties and troubled identity. It is also the moment of resolution of the Wopulds' corporate past, as their company and thus their flagship product, the game *Empire!* is sold to an American competitor. The Wopuld family, renouncing their "imperial" history and their role as a money-making institution, remains, on a deeper level, a metaphor for Scotland, which discards its "imperial" dependence on its past and present colonizers (England and America), going back to the communal ethos which has always shaped its national consciousness.

In *Espedair Street*, the character's relationship with the internal and external world is developed through the medium of music. Since childhood, Danny lives in the space of sounds, by means of which he communicates his thoughts and emotions. Danny's idiosyncratic system of musical notation allows him to make music that is exclusively his and is understood and decipherable only by the creator of the code. In this way, the boy projects an enclave of personalized space within the external world of the dysfunctional home and bleak neighbourhood, music being a medium of escape inside himself. In youth, Danny's music becomes translated into the international system of notation, thanks to which it can be taken beyond the limits of the personal space and Ferguslie, and provides a means for the character's drift away from the local environment to the international scene.

The space of music in the novel seems to pervade all the other spaces inhabited or created by Danny. A perennial outcast, unable to form successful emotional relationships or find a geographical anchor and stability, he is at home only in the space of music, getting control over the listeners and the world through the hypnotic effect of sound and concert shows. Music in *Espedair Street* comes to reflect Danny's development as an artist (Künstlerroman), but also the dynamics between the communal and the societal. In the end, reborn and inspired by the space of home and the street connected with Danny's adolescent love, music also effects the character's reintegration in the community and his return to a life of simple values and tradition.

In *Stonemouth*, the structuring of the community space reflects the polarization in the distribution of power between two gangster families, which translates into the corruption of the communal ethos by elements of corporate ethics based on profit and exploitation. The hidden or uncomfortable reality simmering behind the deceptive front mediated by community values (love, friendship, or mutual care) is registered and made noticeable by technological devices (CCTV and cameras). At the same time, the representation shows signs of "contamination," making it possible to detect the circumstances of its creation and the creator's bias. This, in turn, foregrounds the role of individual consciousness in the (re)construction of the image of reality – the community present and past, which are mediated and remediated through visual media, memory, or imagination, resulting in a series of parallel narratives. In the end, a successful personal relation is invariably connected with the notion of dialogue (compromise), which involves mediation between two oppositional world-pictures to the effect of creating a space of mutual understanding, presupposing individuality on the one hand and communion on the other.

CHAPTER 4

Mythical Worlds
Whit, Canal Dreams, and *The Business*

Looking back on her past life and considering her uncertain future, the protagonist of *The Wasp Factory* reveals an awareness of her former imprisonment in the "crippled" male body, which led to her confinement in the ritualistic order of her insular world. Her life lived between the moment of her "castration" and the discovery of her real sex follows the traditional Campbellian pattern of *separation – initiation – return*, culminating in the revelatory confrontation between the father and the daughter. The protagonist's victory against her father's manipulation marks at once her death and her regeneration, as the male hero dies and is simultaneously reborn as the heroine. In the end, Frank's liberation involves a change in her perception of the world. Her imminent departure from the island indicates her return to the outside world of historical time and progression, from which she was once separated and which she has so far considered an exclusively male domain.

Following the example of the blueprint novel, in *Whit, Canal Dreams*, and *The Business,* space is semioticized exclusively from the perspective of female characters who embark on and variously realize the monomythic journey, traditionally associated with male heroes.[1] This inevitably involves a clash between conventional notions of femininity and the androgynous quality of the three characters, who take up

---

1   Although Campbell's *The Hero with a Thousand Faces* focuses primarily on the quests of male heroes, the pattern of the hero journey has been successfully applied to the vicissitudes of female characters in literature. Campbell himself observes at one point that the hero is "the man *or woman* who has been able to battle past his personal and local historical limitations" (2004: 17, emphasis added). However, he persistently uses the pronouns "he" or "his," which may explain frequent accusations of his study being phallocentric.

the roles of the pilgrim, the warrior, and the saviour, questioning the division male/female, and striving for the central role in the narrative. In contrast to the male characters described in Chapter 3, whose identity is found or determined with relation to the domestic amalgam of the family, community, and Scotland, in the novels of the Mythical Model the character's sense of self and her particular worldview is established or reaffirmed with relation to an alien culture or as a result of her encounter with an ethnic Other. Whether it is a pilgrimage of an Egyptian deity, a journey through dreams informed with national lore and images of violence, or a passage through fundamental archetypes of womanhood, the characters retrace the mythical pattern of their *fables*, which helps them to better understand their life *stories*, reevaluating and giving meaning to those stories in ways which provide them with a sense of accomplishment and renewal.

4.1. Into the Unholy Lands: the Pilgrimage of a Goddess in *Whit*[2]

In his study *The Hero Journey in Literature: Parables of Poesis* (1997), Evans Lansing Smith observes:

> The circular structure of the hero journey is well known: it involves three stages (separation, initiation, and return), with threshold crossings and guardians, helpers, trials, and ordeals, all leading to a transformation of the consciousness of the hero, heroine, and the society they live in. [. . .] The key stage of the adventure is the initiation, during which two things typically occur: revelation and transformation. Something fundamental about the world, the society, and the self is typically revealed at the climax of the journey, with the resulting transformation of the world, the community, and the self. (xv-vi)

The above description of the monomyth points to several issues which are important for the discussion of mediation in the semiotic context: crossing, consciousness, and transformation. The hero journey makes possible the juxtaposition of two distinct semiotic spaces, as shown from the perspective of the semioticizing consciousness. The hero thus crosses the boundary which separates his/her native space, a particular semiosphere with its proper mediation systems which structure his/her

---

2   Parts of this analysis appeared in my earlier publication, "A Heroine's Quest for Self: the Poetics of Monomyth in Iain Banks's *Whit*," 2007: 79-100.

worldview, and enters the space outside, characterized by a different semiotic organization. The convergence of two distinct world-pictures produces tensions, which trigger the dialogue mechanism, effecting the process of resemioticization on the part of the orienting consciousness. This leads to the emergence of a new semiosphere, a transformed world-picture, in which the languages of both semiospheres are mutually included and restructured, and the truth is negotiated between the two extremes (cf. Lotman 1990: 142).

The plot of *Whit*, which shows the protagonist's adventures against the background of contemporary Britain, conforms to the semiotic dynamic of the monomyth.[3] The heroine, Isis Whit, a member of an isolated community in the north of Scotland, the Luskentyrian Sect of the Select of God, is entrusted with an important mission. She must venture into the land of the Unsaved – the outside world of sin and apostasy – and track down a stray sheep, her cousin Morag, who decided to sever all ties with the order and turned her back on the Luskentyrian faith. Before she accomplishes this task and restores balance to the community, Isis has to go through numerous trials in the land of the Unsaved but also face a conspiracy and temporary excommunication from the Luskentyrians. This changes the heroine's perception of both her native space and her own place in it, and eventually leads to a feminist redefinition of its originally patriarchal order.

Before the hero of the monomyth has a chance to prove his/her quality, s/he is usually introduced in his/her ordinary world, his/her native element, which mediates his/her picture of reality, and which stands in sharp contrast with the alien world s/he is going to enter. The picture of Isis's native space, which emerges from her first-person account, is that of topographical and ideological isolation. Occupying a secluded patch of land in northern Scotland, almost entirely encircled by the natural boundary of a coiling river, High Easter Offerance is accessible to visitors only on foot and only from the south across a bow-arched iron

---

3   Stephen R. Jones discusses the way in which Banks creates and manipulates a traditional quest narrative by means of employing "particular narrative techniques," such as "flashbacks, foreshadowing, and foregrounding." Relying on the narrative theories of W. Labov and V. Propp, Jones demonstrates how Iain Banks creates "a reading experience that mirrors Isis Whit's experience of constantly changing truths" (2004: 373).

bridge, once strong but now thoroughly rotten (1995: 5). Little creature comforts, austerity of life, and deliberate inconvenience are the principles of Luskentyrianism; therefore, computers, telephones, TV, and hi-tech equipment are banned, and the faithful wear second-hand clothes, sleep in hammocks, and sit on hard surfaces (see 53-4). Based on agriculture and fishing, the least contaminated ways of earning a living (49), High Easter Offerance is at first glance a primitive Arcadia, established according to a pastoral pattern and functioning in cyclical time. The life of the Community, attached to the land they farm, is determined by seasonal changes and festivals, among which the quadrennial Festival of Love is of paramount importance. Held in the late spring before a leap year, its participants being sexually mature, it is a celebration of fertility and a manifestation of the Luskentyrian doctrine – the Festival fosters the conception of a Leapyearian (a child born on 29 February), and consequently underscores the cyclical renewal of the world.[4]

The Luskentyrian religion is said to be a fruit of revelation of Isis's grandfather Salvador, the sect's Founder, who became the medium through which God has been speaking to the people. Its provenance is thus inherently patriarchal, although in Luskentyrianism God is without gender, being "both and neither male and female, and everything else as well" (52). The centre of the order can be found in the apartments of the prophet – his room with an enormous bed and the Cogitarium, a lounge where he gives in to meditations and where he supplements his *Orthography*, the holy scripture of Luskentyrianism. Even the most important ritual, which ensures the perpetuation of the Community, has its source in Salvador's perception of his own role and the Community's future:

> Grandfather thought up the Festival of Love in 1955. It occurred to him that it might not be wise to rely entirely on providence to provide Leapyearians, who were now seen very much as prophets and potential Messiahs. [. . .] Our Founder therefore decreed that the end of May before a leap year should be the time for a Festival; a Festival of Love in all its

---

4   The Community's holiday, therefore, reflects Toporow's observation that in a ritual which repeats the cosmogony the profane continuity of time is broken, time stops, and there appears what was in the beginning – the structure of a festival re-enacts the moment when Cosmos emerges out of Chaos (1977: 110). The Festival of Love gives rise to what Mircea Eliade calls "the regeneration of the world and life through repetition of the cosmogony" (Eliade 1954: 62).

forms, including the holy communing of souls through the blessed glory of
sexual congress. (201)

At one point Isis reveals: "my Grandfather knew [. . .] that he was the
One; the Enlightened, the OverSeer, to whom God had given the task of
establishing an Order which would disseminate the Truth of Their message on earth" (69). And, as can be expected, it is the events from the
life of Salvador, the mouthpiece of God, which have given rise to most
of the principles of Luskentyrianism. Among these we can find such articles as the sacredness of hammocks (being the first sleeping place of
Salvador and his two wives at Luskentyre, the sect's original establishment, from which they were exiled [111-12]); a ban on entering all retail
shops (as Asni and Zhobelia were rejected by their family of retailers
after their marriage to Salvador [172]); the so-called reverse-buttoning
ritual (started because Salvador was embarrassed by the mismatched
buttons on his shirt [121]), or singing in tongues, which is connected
with Salvador's "first and most glorious vision" (48).

The above observations call to mind Uspienski's ideas concerning
the cosmological consciousness, in which all events repeat a certain primordial state with which the past, present, and future are connected in
equal measure (1998: 43). The repetition of such a primordial state takes
the form of a ritual, which reaffirms the hold of the centre (here, the divine prototype of Luskentyre) and regenerates the community by effecting their symbolic return to the source. By the same token, the holy book
of the *Orthography*, because produced by the Founder as a result of his
divine visions, which have always been "believed in, trusted and celebrated" (19), is the source of answers to all queries and constitutes the
foundation on which depends the order's interpretation of the world.

Similarly, the religious and mythological naming practiced among
the Luskentyrians is a manifestation of the cosmological consciousness,
which is saturated with various religious/mythological connotations (see
Uspienski 1998: 39) and projects the qualities of a deity onto the person
having the same name. Though paradoxical in its nature, the juxtaposition of her two names defines Isis and her status in the Community. The
name Gaia-Marie clearly refers to the Greek and Christian heritage: the
first goddess, the earth incarnate, and the epitome of the Creation and
fertility, and the Virgin Mary, the mother of the Messiah. Though still
intact at the age of nineteen, as an Elect of God and a Leapyearian, Isis

feels pressured by the other Luskentyrians, and most of all by Salvador, to take an active part in the forthcoming Festival of Love, and to conceive another Leapyearian, who would become a future leader of the Sect.

However, it is with her Egyptian namesake, Isis, that she reveals the closest affinity.[5] One common feature is the moment of their respective births, which enhances their unusual or godlike status. The Egyptian Isis was born during the days that belonged to no month – one seventy-second part of the moon's light which was won by the god of wisdom, Thoth, from the moon in a game of draughts.[6] Isis Whit was born on 29 February, the day which occurs every four years, and as such can be regarded as existing outside regular time. For this reason, she is considered an Elect of God and holds a special place in the Community: she is expected to succeed Salvador as the Luskentyrians' spiritual guide. Moreover, like the Egyptian Isis, the goddess of Nature and rebirth, Isis Whit can bring creatures back to life and is a healer among her people (cf. Witt 1997: 25-35).[7]

---

5   Interestingly, as Frazer informs us, Isis's epithets and hieroglyphs were so numerous that she was often called "the many-named," "the thousand-named," and, in Greek inscriptions, "the myriad-named," which constitutes an important analogy to Isis Whit's multiple names and their relevant qualities (1994: 387).

6   Quoted after the White Goddess website: <http://www.thewhitegoddess.co.uk/the_goddess/isis_-_goddess_of_the_throne.asp>.

7   The goddess Isis's journey in Egyptian mythology seems to constitute the fable to Isis Whit's story in the novel, offering an archetypal dimension through which to read the character's quest. The goddess takes a trip down the Nile to Phoenicia to retrieve the coffin with the body of her murdered husband and is then able to dispose of the usurper Seth. Isis Whit, by the same token, continues her peregrinations till she finds her cousin, and they both eventually defeat Isis's brother, Allan, by exposing his attempts to deprive Isis of her leadership (it is not without significance that Isis Whit begins her journey to Babylondon by boat). After she has prevented Allan's back-door scheming (and consequently a schism in High Easter Offerance) and has been recognized as a leader of the Luskentyrians, Isis can feel the same flow of energy as the one she felt years before while resuscitating the fox (454). Yet this time it is the Community and the faith which have been given another lease of life. The motif of healing and restoration, therefore, acquires here a double significance.

Beyond the boundaries of the religious community, where the ultimate points of reference are Divine Providence and the teachings contained in the *Orthography*, and where simplicity is an article of Faith,
there lies the "greater world" of luxury, technology, and official culture.
Although public authorities and institutions do not interfere with their
way of life, the Select of God still have to comply with a few regulations
of the governing culture, one of them being the education of their children. The Gerhardt Academy, where young believers are sent to receive
formal schooling, lies at the boundary between the two semiospheres,
fostering the meeting, exchange, and occasional tensions between the
two distinct modes of thinking. The Academy constitutes the first important testing ground for the young Orderites in their confrontation with
the temptations lurking on the other side, such as goods in shops and
technology (82), whose allure Isis acknowledges even as an adult, pointing to their ability to "distract a person; beguile them, fill their head up
with clutter and an obsession with fripperies, drowning out the thin, quiet voice [. . .] of God" (34-5). However, the Luskentyrian way of life also filters into the external semiosphere, affecting its inhabitants' perception of the world. Although behind the times as concerns creature comforts and scientific innovations, the children from the Community are far
better informed (if usually only theoretically) about sex and drugs than
their Unsaved peers. In this way, as Isis observes, "[they] can give as
good as [they] get when it comes to peer-impressing" (84).

The tensions between the mythico-religious orientation of Isis's native space and the secular semiosphere of the dominant culture become
even more foregrounded the moment Isis accepts her "call to adventure"
(i.e. is persuaded by the Community to go in search of Morag), and
crosses the "first threshold," fully entering the road of trials (cf. Campbell 2004: 71, 89). Once Isis gets into the boat to Edinburgh, the spiritual
dimension of her quest comes to the fore, as she repeatedly perceives her
own journey in terms of the holy mission "of restoring Morag's faith"
(50), which must be made "with sanctity" corresponding with its purpose. The axiological conflict between High Easter Offerance and the
outside world comes to the surface on the level of names given by Isis to
the inhabitants of each space. Taken out of her native element, the Premises of the Just (or, in other words, "the Enlightened, the Sane, the Pre-
ferred, the Acute, the Chosen, the Refined, the Engraced, the Clear, the

Commissioned, the Active, the Dawned and the Awoken"), the pilgrim travels into the Cities of the Plain – the heathen territory inhabited by the Unsaved (also known as "the Wretched, the Insane, the Norms, the Obtuse, the Reject, the Clinker, the Chaff, the Cluttered, the Rank, the Passives, the Benighted and the Asleep") (81).

Isis's perception of her native space as righteous and the alien space as sinful calls to mind Lotman's observations concerning the medieval understanding of geographical space as ethically informed and divided into holy and impure lands. From the point of view of medieval society (but also from the perspective of all militant religious and ideological groups over the centuries), whose self-definition was linked to the notion of the elect, the spatial opposition "own/other" was often synonymous with the categories of "rightful/sinful" and "good/bad" (Lotman 1990: 174-5). Seen in this light, Isis leaves her own, holy, land – the enclave of the Select of God – in order to travel to the other, impure, land of Babylondon, whose locality is explicitly fused with its (im)moral value, in line with the medieval notion that "places have a moral significance and morals have a localized significance" (Lotman 1990: 172). Furthermore, because countries in the Middle Ages were categorized as holy or pagan, a geographical journey "meant moving in the vertical scale of religious and moral values, the top of the scale being heaven and the bottom hell" (171). In Isis's case, the vertical movement is underscored by her geographical descent southwards to the city of corruption, and by her transfer from the plane of the sacred to the space of the profane.[8]

The heroine's crossing of the boundary between the closed familiar space of the Offerance and the limitless outside world results in a feeling of uneasiness and incongruity, which is visible after she comes to Edinburgh. As can be expected, Isis rouses interest and provokes unpleasant comments from passers-by, but it is the very size and commotion of the city, its "strident clutter" (81), which make her uncomfortable. A similar feeling of immersion in the nameless gigantic mass washes over her in the streets of London:

> I looked around. Such crowds of people! I was conscious of the complete reversal of the situation one experienced living in the Community, where for days, weeks, and even in certain cases months at a time one would

---

8   For more information about the medieval fusion of morality/religion and topographical coordinates see also Guriewicz 1976: 77-81.

know, and know fairly well, every single person one came into contact with; to see a stranger was an event. Here the opposite was the case; one assumed that everybody one bumped into was a stranger, and meeting a familiar face was generally a cause for joy and celebration. (122)

The two spaces, therefore, are built in Isis's perception around mutually exclusive values, High Easter Offerance being invariably superior to the profane Cities of the Plain.

There seems to exist an interesting paradox implicit in the Luskentyrians', and, consequently, also in Isis's worldview. The sect constitutes a small and rather closed community. However, their all-inclusive faith, fusing elements of various religions and mythological systems (Christianity, Islam, Hinduism, Buddhism, legends of ancient Egypt, Greece, Scandinavia, etc.), opens the consciousness of this tiny isolated community to the vast expanses of myth. Isis's quest, therefore, develops on two planes: the empirical/secular/earthly plane of contemporary Britain and the mythological/religious/heavenly plane created by her sectarian consciousness. It is at once the journey of a person and a goddess – Gaia-Marie Isis Saraswati Minerva Mirza Whit[9] – who leaves

---

9   Equally important as Isis's affinity with the Egyptian goddess is her connection with her other namesakes, i.e. Saraswati, the Hindu goddess of wisdom and arts, and Minerva, the Roman goddess of war and peace, who was also the goddess of wisdom and arts, and patron of craftsmen, teachers, and (as Minerva Medica) doctors (Jordan 2004: 199-200, 291-2; Lurkar 2004: 126). Isis is a rational, level-headed person; although she is a faithful believer, her devotion is far from blind fundamentalism displayed by many members of the Sect. It is not surprising, therefore, that she is considered an arbiter in numerous issues, e.g. the controversies of the Luskentyrian doctrine, such as the dispute on the body and the soul between brothers Elias and Herb (11). Moreover, she is a gifted musician (even though she does not play the lute, like Saraswati, but the organ). Eventually, being not only closest to Morag but also the most constant in her beliefs and the most persuasive, she is sent among the Benighted as the only one capable of reasoning with and saving her cousin. Last but not least, her reluctance to become the mother of a Leapyearyan at the approching Festival of Love is also meaningful and further underscores her affinity with the virginal Minerva, who is associated with logos (she sprung out from Jupiter's head) and power, instead of motherhood and fertility. The title Mirza (Persian prince or chief) seems to refer to Isis's exceptional position and her belonging to the family of the Prophet and the Sect's leader (Kopaliński 2003: 775). All the mythological names are paradoxically under-

her heavenly abode and descends among the humans projecting onto the geographically restricted world of the everyday and the mundane her subjective and yet mythologically comprehensive world-picture.

A deity among humanity and the only righteous among the Unsaved, Isis filters and adjusts the geographical space she passes through to her sectarian consciousness, applying the principles of the Luskentyrian doctrine to her quest and reading the outside world through the mediating systems of her native semiosphere. Subordinated to Isis's religious outlook, which divides the world into the righteous and the corrupt, into the holy lands and the heathen lands, the space of her peregrinations undergoes allegorization. Its particular points of departure and destination (Edinburgh, London, La Mancha in Essex, etc.) become isolated and axiologically charged, and the continuity of this discrete space is ensured by the road itself. Typical for an allegory is also the image of man as torn between various temptations (of the devil, the world, and the flesh) but also aided by the divine Grace. This, in turn, stresses the problem of the character's moral choice, which predictably finds its manifestation in his/her choice of the road. The opposition of the right/wrong, given/found, difficult/easy path, which the allegorical character usually faces (cf. Abramowska 1978: 135-9), can also be observed in the manner of Isis's pilgrimage:

> The fact that I am not taking a train or a bus or even hitch-hiking to Edinburgh but instead am floating and paddling down this virtually untravelled stretch of twisty, muddy old river with the full intention of walking round half the city when I get there is because to do so is important for the holiness of my mission; to travel so is to sanctify the act of journeying itself and correspondingly increase my chances of success when I arrive at my eventual destination because I am travelling in the uncluttered sight of God, with a soul as uncontaminated by the fuss of Unsaved life as possible. (55)

As the sacred journey should be arduous and complicated, Isis chooses the most out-of-the-way routes and means of transport, in compliance with the tenets of the Luskentyrian faith, i.e. the Principle of Indirectness or Interstitiality, which says that the less ordinary one's existence is and the more extraordinary the byways of life, the more likely a person is to

---

mined by the surname, Whit, which means "the least bit" or "an iota," downsizing the grandiloquent naming to more human proportions.

receive God's message (55). She gets deliberately lost and has to find her way in the maze of Edinburgh, whose "erratic" centre, "convoluted and full of different levels and strange steep passageways," lends itself to journeying "with sanctity" (80). For a while, Isis ponders over the method of Back Bussing, which allows the Luskentyrians to travel without paying but takes a lot of time (see 99), or simply taking a London-bound train and avoiding the guards. However, both methods seem to her "insufficiently holy." "[M]y mission was so important I had to be rigorous in my piety," asserts the heroine, "and there was something too beguilingly easy about simply avoiding paying my fare on an ordinary passenger train" (84). In the end, she stows away on a freight train, which she "catches" while hiding in the bushes by an unused platform.

The further Isis gets from High Easter Offerance and its religious/moral centre, the closer she moves to the other extreme on the axiological axis, namely the Kingdom of the Wicked – Babylondon – the centre of the unholy space, which induces transformation even in once devoted Luskentyrians. Crossing the physical boundary amounts in such a case to crossing the moral boundary, which happens, for example, with brother Zebediah, a Luskentyrian missionary in London, who has slipped from the ways of the Order into the lifestyle of the Unsaved. Zeb and his flatmates, Dec, Wince, Boz, and Scarpa, indulge in binge drinking, adultery, and drug abuse, thus subscribing to the principles which, in Isis's view, govern the semiotics of Babylondon, at the same time opposing her own religious world-picture. The men mock Isis's faith and try to lure her into tasting the forbidden pleasures, e.g. Boz offers Isis marijuana, while Dec's amorous nocturnal advances are prevented only by the collapsing ceiling. Isis considers herself "the ambassador for [her] Faith amongst these people" (113), so she proselytizes her hosts through tales of her life at High Easter Offerance, the Community's history, Revealed truths, commandments, and rituals, which provokes peals of laughter and general hilarity. Isis is aware of the fact that she plays the holy fool among her company, from whose perspective religious piety is nothing short of madness. However, she counts it as no disgrace to the Order, admitting with a truly evangelical determination: "There are more ways than one in which to spread the good word!" (113).

Isis's touchstone for examining the outside world is her faith. It is not surprising, therefore, that alongside the story proper, she also presents the story of her Grandfather Salvador, and the history of their reli-gious establishment, intertwined with numerous passages devoted to the explanation of the Luskentyrian doctrine. Such digressions often func-tion either as a commentary on her own quest or as an ideological yard-stick for highlighting the follies of the Benighted in contrast to the sanity of her own people. This tension between the two types of perception, and the subordination of the outside world to Isis's sectarian conscious-ness come to light when she learns that in the Royal Festival Hall no-body has ever heard about Morag Whit, a world-famous baryton soloist:

> In such a situation the average person might start to doubt their sanity. However, Luskentyrians have it drummed into them from a very early age that it is the outside world, the world of the billions of Blands, that is obvi-ously, demonstratably, utterly and (in the short term) irredeemably insane, while they themselves have had the immense good luck (or karma, if you like, there's a fine and still debatable theological point at issue here) to be born into the one True Church with a decent grasp of reality and a plausi-ble explanation for everything. (131-2)

Isis's faith, however inspirational and edifying, not only alienates her from modern society but also makes her seem deranged in the latter's eyes.[10] It is out of her adherence to the Luskentyrian principles that she fights dogs, fascists, and police officers with the same determination as Don Quixote, who, following the chivalric code, stands his ground against flocks of sheep, obstructive inn-keepers, and windmills as if they were enemy armies or giants (La Mancha, the name of the mansion in Essex where Morag can supposedly be found, is not insignificant here, and brings into focus Isis's "quixotism"). The apogee of the tension be-tween her religious outlook and that of the Unsaved occurs on the way to Somerset, when Isis, travelling in the company of a motley hippie gang, is detained by the police as a consequence of her fierce objection to be-ing turned back from her course. Witnessing the destruction of the pre-

---

10　The clash between the dominant Luskentyrian perception and everyday reality can be noticed in Isis's conversation with the schoolchildren in Edinburgh. Her appearance, dignified language, and multiple names result in the chil-dren's opinion of her as "a Loony" (81) and provoke general laughter. In spite of that, Isis blesses the children thinking to herself "how misguided it is to be-lieve that the greater world is somehow ultimately cosmopolitan and tolerant" (82).

cious salve *zhlonjiz*, she puts up a fight and starts hurling abuse at the policemen, unaware of how nonsensical her revelations seem to them:

> 'Heresy! Impiety! Desecration! May God have mercy on your Unsaved souls, you wretches!
>
> 'This could be something, too,' the desecrator said, rubbing the dust between his fingers.
>
> 'Are you people *listening?*' I shouted. 'I am the Elect of God, you buffoons!'
>
> 'Put her in the wagon,' the sergeant said, nodding his head. 'Sounds like she might have escaped from somewhere.'
>
> 'What? How *dare* you!'
>
> 'And get this stuff bagged for checking out,' the sergeant said, tapping the vial of hearth ash and turning over the limp kit-bag with his foot as he turned away.
>
> 'Let me go! I am an officer of the True Church! I am the Elect of God! I am on a sacred mission! You heathens! By God, you will answer to a higher court than you have ever glimpsed for this insult, you ruffians! Let me go!' (195)

Again two semiotic orders collide, one ruled by God's law and the other by human law. From the perspective of the former, the actions of the guardians of peace and social stability, which stand at the centre of the British semiosphere, are interpreted through the semiotic codes of Luskentyrianism, as profanation and sin. From the point of view of the external space, the actions of Isis, though justified by the principles of her faith, go against the accepted norms of behaviour, and are seen as transgressive and indicative of mental imbalance.

Isis's adherence to her faith, as well as her total obedience to the teachings and authority of Salvador, are confronted by Grandmother Yolanda. Like the Great Goddess of the monomyth, Yolanda not only rescues Isis from arrest but she also addresses Isis's unverbalized anxieties about her obligations, which involve religious leadership on the one hand and motherhood on the other. Yolanda is the first to point out to the heroine the grim reality of power relationships behind the seemingly egalitarian arrangement of High Easter Offerance. She brings to the surface the hypocrisy of Salvador, who tries to force Isis into accepting her reproductive duties at the Festival of Love, regardless of his granddaughter's wishes, in order to ensure the perpetuation of his own custom and to strengthen his own position in the Community (223). Thus, the boisterous Texan, whom Isis sees as an embodiment of freedom and female power (she was Isis's teacher in the art of self-defence), challenges the patriarchal underpinnings of Isis's worldview from outside, urging Isis to protect her integrity as an individual and control her typically female self-sacrificial inclinations (237).

Isis's subjection to patriarchal authority, which results in her inability to voice her desires as an individual, is emphasized by the titles of books which she takes on her mission along with other indispensable objects, i.e. Salvador's *Orthography*, Bunyan's *The Pilgrim's Progress*, Scott's *Waverley*, Milton's *Paradise Lost*, and Maunder's *The Treasury of Knowledge*. The choice of the works she obviously considers her spiritual guides points to the fact that the heroine moves within a world "written" by men; therefore, she is forced to speak their language literally and metaphorically. The importance of the religious works of Bunyan and Milton, as well as Salvador's *Orthography*, for Isis's perception of the world needs no explanation. Moreover, her lofty style and sermonizing diction may owe a lot to the authors mentioned above; though beautiful and refined, Isis's language is also completely out of place in the Great Britain of the 1990s. The reference to Samuel Maunder's dictionary from the nineteenth century is especially pertinent here, as it may actually hint at both Isis's dated language and her subjection to equally dated representations of power relationships.[11] The reference to Scott's *Waverley*, apart from the motif of the journey north (here reversed into Isis's journey south), adds gravity to the conflict of two models of femininity, between which Isis also has to mediate, as *Waverley* shows the triumph of sweet and submissive Rose Bradwardine over passionate and self-assertive Flora McIvor in their fight for Waverley's heart.[12]

Yolanda's sinister prophecies concerning men and power come true upon their arrival at High Easter Offerance. Instead of love, support, and esteem, Isis meets with hostility, suspicion, and isolation (300). From the position at the centre of her native semiosphere, she is relegated to

---

11   Stephen R. Jones claims that the inclusion of Maunder's dictionary in Isis's kitbag represents "an adherence to old knowledge and a reluctance to embrace technological progress" (2004: 383).

12   According to Jones, the presence of Walter Scott's novel among Isis's literary inspirations implies the parallel between Waverley's attraction to the Jacobites and a danger of Isis being "distracted form her goal by the Un-saved" (2004: 383). The feminist overtone, however, seems to go unnoticed in Jones's study.

the margins as a transgressor of the law, facing unfounded accusations of stealing *zhlonjiz*, the community's sacrament. The Holy Isis from nine days before finds herself in the position of an apostate, a liar, and a thief; however, her own perception of the order also undergoes a significant change. An attempted rape by Salvador, who uses his authority to commit incest with his own granddaughter, and Allan's treachery to deprive Isis of the Community's leadership, which she discovers by chance, turns upside down the axiology of the space of Luskentyrians. Its former values of truth, faith, simplicity of life, and communality are now manipulated in accordance with patriarchal prejudices. The *Orthography* has gone through numerous amendments, one of them being the principle of primogeniture in the choice of leaders suggested by Allan. Moreover, Allan not only secretly uses technological equipment to plot against Isis, but he also plans to turn Luskentyrianism into a profitable proselytizing business, which runs counter to its original spiritual and non-commercial purpose. Thu, the space occupied by the sect now possesses the characteristics of the Impure Lands, as it has been poisoned by male jealousy and corruption.

Paradoxically, in order to clear her name and save the Community from sin, Isis is forced to adopt the methods which lie beyond the semiotics of her own space. She realizes that in order to fight the two men, who abuse the Holy Book for their particular interests at the expense of the moral well-being of the order, she has to resort to illicit means which will hopefully be justified by the glorious end.[13] And it is not the outside world but the space of the closed community that Isis sets out to affect by adopting the ways of the world, on which she reflects with frustration and penitence:

> I reviewed my actions so far. To date, I had stolen, lied, deceived, dissembled and burgled, I had used the weakness of a relative to winkle information out of him, I had scarcely talked to my God for two weeks and I had used the works of the Unsaved almost as they did themselves, telephoning, travelling by car and bus and plane, entering retail premises and

---

13   It is significant that shortly before Isis is attacked by Salvador and learns about Allan's plotting she reads the original version of the *Orthography* (one which has not gone through the amendments suggested to Salvador by Allan), and then she reads a few favourite passages from Machiavelli's *The Prince* (265). Her later actions show that in order to save the purity of Luskentyrianism she must use the impure methods.

spending an entire evening enjoying a large proportion of all the exorbi-
tantly hedonistic delights one of the world's largest cities could provide,
though admittedly this last sin had been while in the company of a forceful
and determinedly sensualistic relative from an alien culture where the pursuit of fun, profit and self-fulfilment was regarded practically as a commandment. (368)

Isis's frustration, which arises from her sense of departure from the
symbolic system of her native semiosphere, with which she still identifies, is deepened by the discovery of her Grandfather's ignoble past, and
thus the lie which underlies Luskentyrianism. In her quest, Isis reaches
the "innermost cave" (see Campbell 2004: 159-78), i.e. the Mitchell Library in Glasgow, and after a long and arduous search she comes across
an incriminating newspaper record. She learns that Salvador's real name
is Moray Black, that he absconded from the British Army with a bagful
of money from the Royal Scottish Linen Bank, and that the ship on
board of which he tried to escape to America, the *SS Salvador*, was
shipwrecked near the shores of the Outer Hebrides. To her despair, Isis
realizes her provenance, on the one hand, from a "thief, and a liar as well
as a potential rapist," and on the other hand, from a long ancient line of
Asian women "visionaries, faith healers and mediums" (423), like her
grandmother Aasni and great-aunt Zhobelia, Salvador's wives, who
found him unconscious on the beach and allowed him to appropriate
Zhobelia's prophetic visions so that he could become the guru of his
sect.

Isis's own identity becomes a space in which collide the oppositional
semiotic categories of that which is human and degrading against that
which is mystic and uplifting, and thus she brings together two conflicting semiospheres, "the warring forces in [her] soul [. . .] so evenly
matched and so precisely targeted upon their opposite" (429). Isis becomes a boundary character, both an insider and an outsider, her perspective allowing her to notice the discrepancy between the symbolic
system of Salvador's authority, in which he is the moral centre and the
mouthpiece of God, and the unmediated reality, in which Moray Black is
a "common thief on the run after an act of violence" (424), parasitizing
on the seer's Gift of his wife Zhobelia. Paradoxically, this dual perspective, apart from bringing confusion, is also the source of power, which
strikes Isis with forceful immediacy. She sees herself as Samson in the
temple, who can now shake the philistine foundations of Luskentyri-

anism, restoring the female agency to the centre of the Community, and saving what is good and righteous in their common faith, the reconciliation of old beliefs and new leadership finding its expression in Salvador's and Isis's final handshake. The heroine is at last vocal about her own desires, so she refuses to take part in the Festival, and her newly found voice of the Other (female and Asian) allows her to solve the conflict with Salvador, at the same time becoming his equal. The original version of the *Orthography*, inspired by Zhobelia's visions, is restored along with Isis as the leader, and the patriarchal order of the Community, based on falsehood and appropriation of power, is overthrown to give way to the leadership based on merit and Truth.

Isis discards her biological function, and instead of a child, she gives birth to her own scripture, in which she encloses not only the wealth of her experience, but through which she can also become a prophetess of her own doctrine. "I have a story to tell you" (454), says Isis to the congregation in the last sentence of the novel, which turns her pilgrimage, a *story*, into a new exemplar, a *fable*, through which true faith and knowledge can find their way into the hearts of her people. Isis's spiritual rebirth, therefore, affects the model of the world she inherits, as her word is placed in the centre, which used to be occupied by her Grandfather's false word (ironically subverting his role of the Saviour – "the way, the truth, and the life" [*John* 14:6] – implied by the name Salvador). It clearly demonstrates that in the world "written" by men, Isis has eventually found her own voice and inspiration to fill the pages of life (and literature) with her own writing. In this way, the Campbellian monomyth acquires a definite feminist twist.

4.2. A Female Samurai's Journey to the Centre in *Canal Dreams*.

The fire was complete; it had covered all there was within its scope to cover (the water pulsed around her, and she guessed a tank on *Le Cercle* had blown, or some of the armaments still left on the husk of the soldiers' Gemini had exploded), and when the encircling arms of the blaze had joined, and the whole brown coin of oil was alight, there was no airspace left in or near its centre to feed and fire there, and all there was was the oxygen at the limit of the slick, round the circumference . . . so of course only the fringes burned; only the edge of the great circle could combust into the

clear, isthmian air of Panama; a kilometre-wide ring of fire, enfolding and
enclosing a dark and lifeless heart. (1989: 197-8)

The above passage from the finale of *Canal Dreams* is remarkable for its
significance and compelling force. Through the arresting imagery of circles and circumferences, it renders an act of destruction and violence effected by the female protagonist, which is supposed to mirror an even
greater act of destruction and violence from the past. The passage, therefore, serves as an apt introduction to the present discussion, as *Canal
Dreams* presents the reader with the cyclical model of the hero journey
whose organizing principle is the ever-recurring ritual of violence.

    Canal Dreams presents the life story of a Japanese woman, Hisako
Onoda, who is at the same time a famous Westernized cellist and a posthumous child to the father who died of cancer from the Hiroshima blast.
Caught between the cosmopolitan world of art, which represents the values of beauty and peace, and "the metastising shadow of death" (186),
which is her tragic and violent Japanese heritage, the protagonist keeps
circling in the geographical, historical, and mental space in order to
complete the identity quest inscribed in her fate. Hisako's inner disturbance and her ambiguous status between the two cultures find their reflection in the novel's two alternating narratives. The first, using the conventions of Bildungs- and Künstlerroman, goes back to Hisako's past and
allows us to witness the formative events of her childhood, adolescence,
and adulthood. The second narrative, written in the convention of the
political thriller and moving forward in the novel's present, depicts
Hisako's sea voyage at the age of forty-four, and her ordeal and near
death during the hostilities over the Panama Canal. The employment of
the two alternating narratives foregrounds the two-dimensionality of the
single monomythic pattern. Played out on the spatial and spiritual levels
(geographical and identity quest), the formula *separation – initiation –
return* invariably underlies the heroine's relationship with Japan.[14]

    Hisako's heroic journey takes place between two distinct semio-
spheres: the protagonist's native, Japanese, culture, and the culture of the
West, which appears here in such semiotic representations as classical
music, the English language, and Anglo-Saxon literature. Hisako's affinity with the metastructure of her native semiosphere, responsible for her

---

14   Parts of this analysis appeared previously in my essay "Music as a Colonizing
     Other in Iain Banks's *Canal Dreams*," 2012b: 201-20.

cultural self-definition, is gradually weakened as she grows up and develops. Instead, her cultural identity is (re)constructed in connection with the metalanguage of the semiotic Other, which not only determines her position on the boundary between the two cultures but also offers her a medium of self-expression, i.e. music, which models her inner world.

Initially, music and English are a form of escapism, as they give the character access to the world of peace and beauty, in contrast to the dreary reality of post-war Japan with its economic shortages and the school in which she suffers prejudice on account of her learning problems and, most of all, her different appearance. Hisako looks like one of the Ainu, indigenous inhabitants of Japan, not like the Yamato Japanese, who conquered all the Japanese islands and established their own culture in place of the already existing one. The girl's deep black hair, bushy eyebrows, and deep-set eyes are considered a deviation from the norm established by the nuclear structure: she becomes an Other to the homogenous majority of schoolchildren and is pushed to the margin of her peer group, which ironically reflects a similar, historical, process taking place in the case of the Ainu people. These natives of Japan, "its abos, its Injuns" (37), a name which implies both the indigenous character of the Ainu and their ensuing exclusion and discrimination, had to retreat northwards in the face of the expansive civilization of the Yamato Japanese, and were eventually pushed as far as Hokkaido, the utmost peripheries of Japan. Like her alleged ancestors, the heroine falls victim to racial prejudice and aggression. The power of the group thrives on the helplessness of the victim, who has no other choice but to ignore her tormentors and seek refuge in the world of classical music and fairy stories written in English. Thus, Hisako, an excluded member of the community, adopts a semiotic system which is external to her native culture, as a means of defence against the violence of her classmates.

Moreover, in Hisako's case, music also becomes a medium of translation and communication, as the incomprehensible hostility of her peers and the resultant loneliness and pain of the girl are transcribed into the language of sounds produced by her cello, an instrument of European provenance. Rendered in the musical metalanguage of Hisako's private semiosphere, feelings and impressions from the outside world can be properly semioticized, internalized, and coped with, and only then imparted to others, which stresses the protagonist's growing separation from her environment and native culture. At one point, Hisako is assaulted by several school girls who keep her hands on a burning-hot radiator. As a result of the received wounds, she is unable to play her cello; significantly, however, she refrains from communicating the truth about the attack to her mother in words, insisting instead that it was an accident. It is only several weeks later at her audition for the Tokyo Music Academy that Hisako voices her suffering through the medium of music. Thus, one mediation system replaces another, i.e. the language of sounds replaces the system of verbal communication: "Because her hands were healed, she could use them to tell the judges how much it had hurt when they were forced on to the rough metal of the radiator; how much she had been hurt; how much her mother had been hurt; how much everything hurt" (39).

Later in life, the musical metalanguage assumes the same function in Hisako's encounters with foreign countries and cultures on her sea voyage around the world and when she experiences sensations which are alien to her. In such cases, she projects onto the outside world the norms of her own semiotic centre, modelling and absorbing the space around her through the medium of music. Moving within an unfamiliar space, like e.g. "Sal si puedes," a barrio in Panama City which she visits on her sea voyage, she familiarizes its strangeness by subordinating it to the metalanguage of her private semiosphere, as can be noticed in the following passage: "It was dangerous, sometimes frightening, quite lawless compared to Japan, but just so different. She felt alive. She tried to think of what music it would be good to play now, what composition she should take this mood to, so that the notes would sing and speak and take on resonances she hadn't heard in them before" (36).

The language of sounds also dominates and mediates the intimate world of Hisako's romantic relationship with Philippe, an officer from the French ship *Le Cercle*, whom she meets during the prolonged demurrage on Gatún Lake in Panama. The extraordinariness of the emotional and erotic experience is captured by Hisako by means of familiar musical concepts. The lovers' intimacy is here perceived in terms of a perfect union between a musician and his instrument, with Philippe being the cellist and Hisako the cello which he plays, thus producing sounds. Sometimes their physical closeness leads Hisako to believe that "she was the case and he the cello, fitted and nested and secure and embraced" (72), and Philippe's capacity for love is defined as "emotional and physical octaves" (71) he can encompass. The life of the female protagonist is inextricably linked with the element of water manifested in sea and seafaring, be it sailing, swimming, floating, or diving, which is imperative for the dynamic of Hisako's quest. For most of her life from childhood to maturity, the period presented in the Künstlerroman narrative, Hisako travels back and forth between her childhood home on the island of Hokkaido and the city of Tokyo on the island of Honshu, which constitutes the place of her education, professional career, and sexual initiation. The pattern of occasional leavings and returns becomes correlated with her youthful problems as well as her doubts and misgivings as a grown-up woman. Thus, transcending the boundary of the sea between the two spaces marks the sequence of important moments contributing to Hisako's growth as an individual. Accordingly, the sea voyage which she undertakes as a middle-aged woman is both the continuation and completion of her personal development. Its mythic quality is enhanced by the dreams mentioned in the title of the novel, both foreshadowing and elucidating the occurrences of the Panama story, but also excavating from the depths of the character's subconscious the past events and emotions she has been suppressing. The circular path of her voyage across the Northern Hemisphere represents her return to the roots (her abandoned Japaneseness), while the wheel of history comes full circle. Both narratives, therefore, present the single motif of continual homecoming.

The process of emergence of Hisako's Westernized self is accompanied by the protagonist's movement in physical space. Just as her Japanese self is slowly relegated to the position of the semiotic Other somewhere on the periphery of her personal semiosphere, so Hisako drifts away from insular Hokkaido and settles down in the country's political and cultural centre when she is granted a scholarship from the Tokyo Music Academy. Tokyo becomes a topographic foil to Hisako's culturally transformed identity, with the centre appropriated by the semiotic systems of Western culture, albeit surrounded by the peripheries of traditionally Japanese landscape. At this point, one can notice that owing to Hisako's connection to music, her private semiosphere undergoes gradual expansion, in both mental and geographical terms. From the tiny, enclosed space of the flat in the Susukino district of Sapporo, matched by the limited horizons of her school community, Hisako moves to the biggest city on the largest island of Japan, whose cultural space opens itself up to multifarious foreign influences. The capital represents everything a great Westernized metropolis can offer: Hisako has the opportunity to go to concerts, visit museums and galleries, which introduces her to the vastness of the world's cultural heritage.

Initially, however, it is her visits to the surrounding countryside, which has retained the atmosphere of old Japan (i.e. Hakone, Izu, and the Fuji Five Lakes), which are more entertaining and pleasant. This points to the tension within Hisako's world-picture, i.e. the clash of the native and alien semiospheres. While in the country, she can "climb things and go on ferries" (54), which means that she resorts to her old leisure activities, unconsciously transplanting her Hokkaido habits into the new life. Her return to Sapporo for holidays is like a trip down the memory lane: her mother often takes her for a walk in the woods and cornfields, like in the old days. Now Hokkaido appears to her eyes, fed on the exhausting wonders of the great city, "clean and clear and empty [. . .] and fairly deserted and unspoiled even compared to the countryside west of Tokyo" (55), which may as well apply to the island's unsullied Japanese identity and its traditional way of life. The holidays temporarily restore to the girl her lost sense of belonging. "She coped with Tokyo, she mourned for Hokkaido" (55), informs the narrator, commenting on Hisako's second year in the Academy.

With time, however, Hisako becomes increasingly alienated from "the dark island of her birth" (39) and its traditions. The megalopolitan and cosmopolitan capital stands in opposition to the parochialism of the northern peripheries, which constitute a rampart of old but now vulgarized Japanese values with its tradition of violence and prejudice, epitomized in the microcosm of Hisako's old school. The geographical relocation inevitably affects the character's perception of the space of home. Visiting the island after several years spent at the Tokyo Music Academy, she finds it difficult to relate to the world of childhood. Everyone and everything there seems aged (her mother and her old music teacher, Mr Kawamitsu), which underlines the temporal hiatus between Tokyo and Hokkaido, i.e. their respective modernity and backwardness. Hisako is detached from her old friends and scornful of the city's local colour and traditional entertainments like the famous ice festival in Sapporo.

This particular visit, which brings nothing but frustration, is followed by what can be interpreted as Hisako's attempt to definitely distance herself from her past and the space of origin. On her way back to Tokyo, on the canal separating Hokkaido and Honshu, Hisako throws her old cello into the sea. The reasons behind this act and its significance cannot escape us. It is very telling that the death of Hisako's father and the appearance of the old cello in Hisako's life coincide, if not in historical linear time then in the mythical cyclical order. Her father dies three months before her birth, the cello comes into her possession three months before her seventh birthday, bringing subtlety and peace to the heir of the old, militaristic culture, which perished in the blast of the nuclear bomb. The old cello, therefore, epitomizes Hisako's mediation between her own Japaneseness and growing Westernization, being both a reminder of Hisako's violent paternal heritage and of the girl's abandonment of her native culture for a life built around Western values.

The disposal of the old cello, though initially unsuccessful, as the instrument is recovered by the ferry crew, can therefore be seen as Hisako's attempt to free herself of the epitome of guilt at how enthusiastically she traded her national identity for the *gaijin* values. Curiously, she tries to accomplish this act of liberation on the borderland between the modern cosmopolitan centre and the traditional peripheries. Therefore the physical crossing of the boundary between the spaces is here symbolically coupled with her psychological passage from the burden of the past to the "rootlessness" of the future. Especially that in Tokyo she has left her new cello, bought in the capital and bearing no relation to the past, however hurtful it may be, which apparently gives Hisako a sense of guiltless eradication.

The protagonist manages to get rid of the ruined instrument in an act of violence and destruction by burning it weeks later on a hilltop north of the Fuji Five Lakes, which functions as yet another borderland between the traditional peripheries and the cosmopolitan centre of the capital. What has not been swallowed by the sea is finally consumed by the purifying flame, a ritual which will find its more powerful but inverse alternative in the lake of fire at the end of the novel. The old cello is "cremated [. . .] in its battered, twisted coffin" (80), its death marking her own rebirth as a new detached person. The smoke rising through the air is said to have "made Fuji itself tremble" (80), which only stresses the gravity of Hisako's deliberate breaking with the past. Making Fuji, the sacred mountain of the Japanese, witness this act of renunciation, and performing this very act in spring, the time of blossoming cherries, yet another symbol of Japan, is almost sacrilegious, and is frowned upon by the eternal and unforgiving nature.[15]

The process of Hisako's Westernization gathers momentum during her studies at *Todai* university, a vibrant international community, open to foreign students and encouraging leisure activities common to Western campuses, and thus quite pertinently perceived by Hisako as "the Harvard, the Oxbridge of Japan" (87). The heroine's life at the time develops practically in detachment from her past and native culture, there being no mention of her visits to Hokkaido within this period. *Todai*'s cosmopolitan atmosphere fosters Hisako's further immersion in the culture of the English-speaking countries, and the degree of her Westernization can be measured by her extreme fondness for and understanding of the specificity of English humour, here represented by the hilarious though often absurd *Monty Python's Flying Circus*, which her friends often find impossible to understand. She also differs from her fellow Japanese students in her carefree attitude towards education (87). The protagonist bases her absolute confidence for the future on the knowledge of *gaijin* words or a *gaijin* music box, i.e. English and the cello, which are actually epitomes of Western culture she has so enthusiastically embraced.[16] Even her first sexual experience is connected with

---

15   Years later Hisako visits the place only to find out that it has been turned into a picnic place, with plastic bins, barbecues, and Western pop music (161), which foregrounds the triumph of the Western way of life, ironically – its worst version.

16   The only link she seems to maintain with her native culture is through practicing Japanese sports like the way of gentleness, the open hand, archery, and kendo (87). Interestingly, these disciplines were also part of the samurai training and the exercise programmes for young people in the Meji period, which the nationalist propaganda saw as a means of upbringing in a spirit of the samurai tradition rather than a way of physical development (see Śpiewakowski, 1989: 103). However, she seems to practise Japanese sports not for the sake of tradition, but as a way of keeping her body in shape, apparently in compliance with modern fitness and beauty trends (she also swims, hikes, glides, and sails).

an alien culture – Hisako "decided to be seduced, and to let a *gaijin* do the seducing" (88).

An opportunity of Hisako's direct encounter with the West and its culture is thwarted unexpectedly by her inability to overcome a fear of flying when the NHK, the orchestra in which she plays, is about to board for a flight to the United States. A woman who managed to grow out of a snubbed and miserable "hairy Ainu" is now faced with the only thing innate to her that she cannot eradicate or control. It is an instinctive part, primeval in nature, which does not yield to the power of reason, and in this respect, constitutes the only manifestation of her real self which she has been trying to silence and conceal through cultural indoctrination. She experiences an unsettling feeling of discrepancy between her obligations as an adult professional and the uncontrollable "childish" fright with which one cannot debate. All arguments, explanations, and words of comfort offered by the other musicians are merely "a set of irrelevant symbols in a language that was not the reverberating note of her fear," and "[m]ere scrawls on a page pitched against the resonating physical chord of terror" (104), which emphasizes the fact that the whole experience cannot be expressed in terms of Hisako's internal semiotics. In the end, the orchestra leaves for America without her.[17]

The incident described above introduces yet another crucial motif, namely the latent conflict between Hisako and the culture which brought about the death of her father, i.e. the United States. Trying to convince Hisako to enter the plane, her friends from the orchestra tempt her with the prospect of seeing all the tourist attractions of the country, such as the Rocky Mountains, the Grand Canyon, the colours of autumn in New England, or the vertical cityscape of Manhattan. However, even the allure of such descriptions cannot help the protagonist to overcome her paralyzing fear. Finally, she is denied the opportunity to explore America and get to know the country through the contemplation of its natural wonders and countryside, or by making contact with American society

---

17   Taking into account her family's wartime experience and her later dreams filled with the Hiroshima symbolism, one may venture an opinion that Hisako's fear of flying has roots in her genetic memory, being indicative of her fear of the bomb dropped onto the city by the Superfortress bomber Enola Gay.

through music, which is a universal language of communication between people from different countries and cultures.

What is significant, Hisako also bypasses the States on her sea voyage from Yokohama to Europe twenty years later. At first, in order to placate her agent, Mr Moriya, who is worried about the prospect of her sailing through the war-engulfed Panama Canal, she proposes an alternative route through California, and then by train to New York, where she could take another ship to Europe. However, her contact with America is restricted to making a one-day stop in Honolulu, in the Hawaiian islands (which are outside the contiguous United States and whose population is mainly of Asian origin), which is laconically mentioned as the place of changing ships, from the *Gassam Maru* to the *Nakodo*. Some pages later we learn that the route was going to lead to Rotterdam via Panama and New Orleans (a city on the peripheries of the US, arguably more European in character than American), but the ship has been detained indefinitely on Gatún Lake. So the United States always remains outside the space of the character's peregrinations, which may reflect Hisako's unconscious avoidance of a peaceful confrontation with America.

The expansion of the space within which Hisako moves is thus stopped by the airport incident, as a result of which she turns inward both psychologically and topographically: she spends several days on Hokkaido, "unable to go out or see any of her old friends" (125). Finally, she goes on holidays during which she visits the most important places of Japanese history. However, the significance of her encounters with the ancient tradition of Japan eludes her. She finds the sites too crowded and noisy for her; she leaves many things unseen, the monuments intimidate her, she often feels weak, embarrassed, or plain foolish in the face of their grandeur and importance to which she cannot relate. This strange detachment indicates Hisako's ambiguous position vis-à-vis her native semiosphere, namely that of an insider and outsider at the same time. Her Westernization makes her unresponsive to Japanese culture, amidst which she is merely a tourist (125). In consequence, she does not benefit enough from her journey, which might have been a spiritual one. Paradoxically, it is only Hiroshima and Nagasaki – the places of violence and destruction, and thus of the reality which eludes representation – that wake Hisako from her stupor and where she emotionally reacts to the unimaginable suffering and the fate of her nation, which was so tragically connected with her own life (126). However, even while visiting the Hiroshima museum, she reads English captions instead of Japanese ones, which again underscores her detachment from her own country and her affinity with the Anglophone cultures.

Hisako keeps returning to Tokyo in ever-decreasing circles, which finally makes her realize that she is "only circling, in a holding pattern of her own" (128). The imagery which likens Hisako's movement in space to that of a plane waiting for clearance to land signals the impending catastrophe – her involvement in the demonstration at Narita airport and her murder of a riot policeman. Japan becomes a maze with the centre in Tokyo, and the closer she revolves around the capital, the nearer she gets to the confrontation, descending slowly but inevitably into the deepest recesses of her violent self.[18] A semiotic unity between Hisako and Tokyo becomes foregrounded, as they are both epitomes of post-war Japan – Westernized, with centuries of violent heritage overwritten by a new semiotic reality. Hisako's integrity is shaken by a repressed element of violence which underlies the layers of acculturation. By the same token, the mob violence at Narita airport becomes equally disruptive for the tamed and cosmopolitan space of Tokyo.

The scenes depicting Hisako's scuffle with the policeman alternate with passages presenting her peaceful tourist peregrinations. This narrative cross-cut contributes to the image of the protagonist's self as torn between her deeply-rooted predilection for aggression and a yearning for peace, but it is also indicative of the dichotomy implicit in the traditional culture of Japan, which on the one hand produced beautiful and sophisti-

---

18   This is one of several observations involving a circular movement that the narrator uses while referring to Hisako. When describing her hesitation as to how she should behave towards Philippe, her jealousy of other women he had contact with, and her insecurity about her own attractiveness, the narrator uses the following line: "And so she went round in circles on the trapped ship" (60). While diving, she and Philippe are described as swimming "round some of the islets nearby, circling the summits of the mostly drowned hills under the quicksilver carpet of waves" (59). Later in the novel, when she and Philippe are diving in Gatún Lake at night and get separated, Hisako thinks to herself that "she could try going in ever-increasing circles, until she found the line that led to the boat" (62). Also, while pondering over Sanae's marriage proposal, she keeps on thinking, "round and round" (179). Last but not least, the ship on which Hisako's fate comes full circle, is called exactly *Le Cercle*.

cated architecture and landscape designs, and on the other hand, relished warfare and hostility. The connection of the riots in Narita airport with the traditional culture of violence is aptly voiced by one of the passengers watching the event from the plane for whom it looks like "a medieval battle going on underneath; two armies; banners, smoke and fumes and lumbering cannon" (142).[19]

The observations above pave the way for the important conclusion that music and violence – a semiotic system of cultural mediation and the repressed element of the unmediated nature of man – are mutually exclusive in Banks's novel. The death of the policeman in what can be seen as a mythical threshold battle makes Hisako enter the underworld of pain and despair, which translates into her physical inability to play the cello. Hisako is taken to hospital. However, without the protective power of music and its familiarity the world around seems to her alien and unpredictable. Violence restricts the space expanded earlier by art and peace, which produces in Hisako the feeling of entrapment and constant danger. The character's awareness of her deadly potential manifests itself in her fear of earthquakes, which would make the ward ceiling collapse and bury her paralyzed under ferro-concrete beams. To keep the danger at bay, she sleeps sitting, propped by *gaijin* pillows, not lying down like a Japanese, as if shrinking from everything which would connect her to the violent heritage to which she has already succumbed. Her internal struggle finds its external representation in the polarity of the landscape and the tension between the Westernized centre and Japanese peripheries. "[I]f it wasn't cloudy or foggy, you could see Fuji," while "[i]n the evening, Tokyo blazed on the plain to the east" (138), the narrator reports Hisako's observations. This double image externalizes the character's struggle between a yearning for a return to the safety and peace of her previous Tokyo life and the traditional militant values which took control of her and made her guilty of homicide.

---

19   The same dichotomy is in fact implicit in the culture which Hisako confronts at the end of the novel, i.e. the United States of America. Being a dream tourist destination with its impressive cities, wheat fields, and natural wonders, at the same time it is shown in the novel as a ruthless player in the world politics, instigator of coups, attacks, and assassinations, whose authorities sacrifice people's lives for the sake of their overriding interests and political hegemony.

An unexpected visit of Mr Kawamitsu, Hisako's old cello teacher, who was the first to show her the beauty and serenity incarnate in music, restores peace to her world. Mr Kawamitsu brings with him a cello, and like in the old childhood days, he puts Hisako's hands on the instrument and teaches her how to hold it. It is Hisako's first encounter with a Stradivarius, which represents the beauty and magnificence of Western art, being the highest achievement of European violin-making. It also represents the timelessness of art, since it has managed, fragile as it is, to survive major human conflicts over two hundred and fifty years almost intact. An opportunity to play the archetypal instrument marks a renewal of Hisako's life as a musician and a human being. Significantly, the cello's arrival in Japan coincides with an act of violence: its owner was bringing it home at the time of the riots in Narita airport. For Hisako, directly involved in the demonstration and feeling guilty of the policeman's death, the cello is an envoy of peace, a consolation and a hope, fate's "undeserved balm" (142), which has taken away the emotional pain from her tormented soul and physical pain from her murderous hands. The instrument, therefore, functions as a psychopomp in reverse, as it helps her return from the world of the dead to the world of the living through the regenerative power of music. The weather on that day is significant, as this time Fuji is "invisible beyond the hills and inside the clouds" (139), which emphasizes the end of Hisako's inner struggle and her return to the culture of peace, along with a feeling of liberation, as "she felt as though she'd been untied, let loose" (140).

The Stradivarius becomes an epitome of Hisako's detachment from her native semiosphere, which can be noticed in the passages describing Hisako's sea voyage of the second narrative, when she sets off on a tour around the world. Her journey across the Pacific is marked with the hours spent playing the cello and the steadily subsiding influence of Japan. Just as the first narrative documents her gradual mental separation from Japan and its semiotic space, the second narrative takes her away from home also in geographical terms. On the ballasted tanker, the *Gassam Maru*, which the heroine boards in Yokohama, she is the only passenger among the Japanese crew. The life on board is dominated by almost military drill and formality of relationships in a strictly maintained hierarchy, in which her place is "that of honoured guest, with the privileges of an officer without the responsibilities" (26). The ship appears to her as clearly disconnected from the rest of the world, a "unit separated by its mobility" (26). On the one hand, it makes the voyage "an escape, an experience of freedom of a type and duration she'd never encountered before" (27); on the other hand, it emphasizes the fact that the vessel is in fact Japan in close-up, an island in the expanse of water.

In contrast to the ship's all-encompassing Japaneseness, Hisako's cabin functions as a Westernized subspace, suffused with the aura of the Stradivarius. The tension between the two worlds is made apparent from the start: the former seems to enclose upon the confines of her private space and hinder an immersion in the world of music by "the harshness of the cabin" (27), which considerably affects the sound of the cello. Hisako tries to improve the acoustics by sheets taped neatly to the walls, later replaced by cork tiles, which signifies the protagonist's attempts to keep the two worlds separate and maintain an uneasy truce between the inside and the outside. Within the boundaries of her cabin, Hisako is said to practice for hours, lost in the music and the touch of the old wood, oblivious of time. The seclusion gives her an opportunity to listen to herself as in her earliest days in the charge of Mr Kawamitsu. This comparison of her present and past situations further stresses a sense of isolation: in both cases, she inhabits an enclave of Western otherness surrounded by the expanses of the familiar.

The second ship that she boards is the *Nakodo* ("a go-between"), carrying Nissan limousines for the North American market. Its very name is indicative of its goal: to pass from the Pacific to the Atlantic, and thus traverse the boundary between the West and the East across the Bridge of the World, i.e. Panama. Additionally, the name underlines the ship's connecting quality. Hisako finds the ship "busier, more cosmopolitan and more interesting than the *Gassam*" (28), as she is surrounded mostly by foreigners: the Korean crew, Broekman (the second engineer from the RSA), and the one other passenger, Mr Mandamus, an Egyptian and "a friend of mankind, peripatetic expert in multitudinous fields and reputedly holder of degrees from universities on three continents" (25). Only the three senior officers are Japanese, which makes the atmosphere on board more relaxed and comfortable. Even the Captain, Endo, complies with the popular Western idea of a Japanese person, as he takes photographs of everything. Now Hisako's cabin is larger and wood-lined, which makes the demanding Stradivarius sound good in its warmth.

Strangely enough, the character's voyage, which was to take her away from her country, brings her to the land which resembles Japan. Watching the landscape and buildings around Gatún Lake on the Panama Canal, Hisako voices her surprise: "She had imagined low wastes of monotonous jungle, but here was a landscape of such variety of texture and shade, and such delicacy of proportion, she could almost imagine it was Japanese" (51). The quasi-Japanese order and subtlety of the above-water world of Gatún Lake is contrasted with the underwater abyss, which Hisako and Philippe explore while diving. The living space of the Panama isthmus overwrites the graveyard of older generations: down below is the remnant of life which ceased to exist along with the advent of technological progress, which culminated in the construction of the canal. The description of the silent underwater landscape which opens the novel mirrors the description of a similar, almost oneiric, landscape of destruction provided in the last chapter ("The Heart of the Universe"), whose image Hisako carries drowned deep but inescapable in her genetic memory, i.e. Hiroshima after the bombing. In her "flight" over the world which fell prey to man's ambitions and the expansionist inclinations of nineteenth-century politicians, she resembles her dead father, who, along with his unit, clambered through the ruins and dust of the city annihilated by human technological genius.

Gatún Lake forms an exceptional space on the canal route. It is an artificial reservoir of water, carrying ships for 33 kilometres in the middle part of their transit across the Isthmus of Panama. If Panama is considered by its inhabitants the Heart of the Universe, then Gatún Lake is the heart of the heart, which underscores its central position. Moreover, the lake forms an eye of water surrounded by hills, which makes its raised level difficult to access. The ship's transfer upwards is possible only through the enormous double set of locks which constitute the gates to the other side of the world. Watching the *Nakodo*'s passage up into Gatún Lake, Hisako perceives the ship's ascent in terms of some solemn religious ritual, whose divine calm and magnificence transfers itself to all passengers on the ship:

> [T]he deeply-eaved, oddly temple-like buildings set at the side of the artificial canyons of the locks, or perched on the thin concrete island dividing

> one set from the other; the feeling of procession as the ship made its way up towards the level of the lake, as though it was a novice being gently guided, prepared and anointed and clothed for some fabulous and arcane rite in the heart of a great basilica . . . (52)

The central and elevated position of the lake is associated in Hisako's impressions with its sacred character, as it is compared to the most important Christian temple where a probationer in a religious order is reborn to a new spiritual life. All these qualities turn Gatún Lake into a mythical Centre, an *axis mundi* where heaven and earth meet within a zone of the sacred. Describing the road into the Centre, Eliade calls it "arduous" and "fraught with perils," as it actually is "a rite of passage from the profane to the sacred, from the ephemeral and illusory to reality and eternity, from death to life, from man to divinity," while reaching the Centre "is equivalent to a consecration, an initiation" (1954: 18). Accordingly, when passing from the space of the profane to that of the sacred, Hisako's ship has to undergo a ritual of purification, which is duly registered by the heroine when "the gush of fresh water from the lock above wash[es] the Pacific's salt from the *Nakodo*'s keel" (52). The "divine" transfer into "absolute reality" (Eliade 1954: 17) is additionally reinforced by Hisako's sense of detachment from the goings-on of the outside world: "[E]verything made the war seem distant and irrelevant, and the fuss about threats against the canal and the ships that plied it somehow undignified and paltry" (52).

Within the sacred lacustrine space time becomes arrested, removing the passengers from the historical linearity of their voyage, which can be noticed in the case of Hisako, whose carefully planned itinerary has been irredeemably disrupted. Instead, the passengers of the three ships are trapped in the cyclicity of repetitive activities. The parties held every evening on one of the ships gather the "universal company," and become a ritual performed outside of time in the stasis of the lake between the two worlds, thus abolishing "profane time" and transferring the individuals into "mythical time" (Eliade 1954: 35):

> It was a Western cuisine night; each vessel had its own rhythm, and each played host to the officers and guests of the other two ships on a regular basis, sometimes with the addition of people from Gatún; shipping agents, canal officers, occasionally somebody from the consulates in Rainbow City or Colón. Tomorrow night they will all troop over to the *Nadia* for a dance and a native feast, eating local for a change. Last night on *Le Cercle*, with

Lekkas's Greek Banquet, had been a break in the cycle, which she and Philippe had appreciated, but still the pattern of meals, drink parties, dances and other social occasions helped to fill the time, while they waited for the war to run its course. Stagnant in the stalemate, only this ritualized consumption seemed to make much sense or offer a tangible link to the outside world. (29)[20]

Hisako's geographical return to the space of origin, at once familiar and unfamiliar, is here accompanied by her return to the past, which requires the heroine's descent below the surface of the lake, but also into the depths of her own subconscious. The Centre, as "the zone of absolute reality" (Eliade 1954: 17), invites dreams which function as bridges between the two worlds i.e. the upper- and underworld, the past and the present, the conscious and the subconscious. It is here that Hisako's past and memories, and her present experience become fused into a disturbing and meaningful oneiric patchwork. The recurrent motifs of the samurai, female pearl divers, destroyed cities, and exploding skies, alongside the landmarks of Japanese landscape and architecture, repeatedly bring into focus the semiotic reality of Japan, and extract from the depths of the protagonist's subconscious the related fears and dilemmas. Hisako's dreams not only become a stage on which the tragedy of Hiroshima replays itself time and time again but they also portend the impending confrontation between Hisako and the American mercenaries. The confrontation marks the climax of Hisako's trials in the *initiation* stage of her

---

20   Eliade postulates that ritualized nutrition (i.e. not arising from "pure automatism" but reproducing some primordial act) is not a simple physiological operation but it "renews a communion" and allows man to partake in a transcendent reality (1954: 4). "[A]n object or an act becomes real only insofar as it imitates or repeats an archetype," writes Eliade, which can be noticed in the passengers' feasting pattern, reproducing archetypal "rhythm" of each ship with its traditional cuisine for the sake of communal integration. According to Bakhtin, in the act of eating, the body transgresses its own limits: "it swallows, devours, rends the world apart, is enriched and grows at the world's expense" (1984: 281). Though Bakhtin's observation concerns the so-called "grotesque body," the encounter of man and the world, when "man tastes the world, introduces it into his body, makes it part of himself," can also be applied to the situation of the passengers. "The limits between man and the world are erased" (281), states Bakhtin, and a similar feeling is noticeable in Hisako's musings that "only this ritualized consumption seemed to make much sense or offer a tangible link to the outside world" (29).

quest, as the USA is presented in the novel as a mythical enemy, which is in the end symbolically defeated.

The showdown takes place in Panama, the country which throughout the centuries has been the battlefield between different nations (e.g Spaniards, Frenchmen, Englishmen, and Americans), and whose natural resources and favourable geographical location has always made it a tasty morsel for greedy and militant politicians. The history of Panama's relations with the United States, as we learn from Hisako's guidebook, to a considerable extent resembles that of Japan. The American extortion of the perpetual lease of the canal zone in 1903 mirrors the so-called opening of Japan under the threat of bombardment from the US ships under the command of Commodore Matthew C. Perry in 1854, an event which marked the first instance of power politics between the two countries. The Convention of Kanagawa eventually opened two Japanese ports to US trade and finished Japan's 200-year policy of seclusion.[21] As a result, the country entered the history of Western civilization and its semiotic space, which accelerated Japan's economic and social development, but also involved it in the realpolitik of the time.[22] And Hisako reveals the awareness of this interrelationship while talking to Dandridge, a CIA agent, thinking him to be the *jefe*, leader of the Panamanian guerrillas, for whom she is supposed to play her cello:

'We had strengths in our isolation, but it could not persist for ever. When we were . . . forced to change, we changed and found new strengths . . . or new expressions of the old ones. We tried too much; we tried to fit ourselves to the peoples outside; behave the way they did. We defeated China and Russia, and the world was amazed, and amazed too that we treated our prisoners so well . . . then we became . . . arrogant, perhaps, and thought we could take on America, and treat the . . . foreign devils as less than human. So we were treated the same way. It was wrong, but we were too.

---

21 For details see Hall 1979: 211-212.

22 Maruyama claims that centuries of Japanese isolation meant that "an awareness of equality in international affairs was totally absent" and international relations were perceived through the prism of the internal hierarchy. "Consequently," writes Maruyama, "when the premises of the national hierarchy were transferred horizontally into the international sphere, international problems were reduced to a single alternative: conquer or be conquered" (qtd. in Anderson 2006: 97). Cf. Śpiewakowski 1989: 105, and Hall 1979: 249-54.

Since then we have flourished. We have sadnesses, but [. . .] we can have
few complaints.' (120)

It is significant that Hisako's symbolical encounter with America, its attitudes and policies impersonated by Dandridge, takes place on the *Nakodo*. On the one hand, the ship's name (i.e. a go-between) implies a
possibility of dialogue between the two cultures, and on the other, this
possibility is denied by the fundamental imbalance of power between
their representatives coming into contact. Dandridge's attitude towards
the people in his power is one of scorn and superiority, which translates
into an exploitative and denigrating discourse, the most representative
example of which is his innuendo-dripping comment on the quality of
his Cuban cigar, "[r]olled between the thighs of *señoritas*" (121).

The private concert effects a transformation in the Westernized cellist. When asked by Major Sucre, one of the guerrillas, to play something for the *jefe*, she chooses an apparently Asian song, Tung Loi's
"Song of Leaving," but she does it unconsciously, not being sure why
this and not some classical piece. At this point, it appears, by changing
her music, Hisako begins to change the nature of her inner world, which
has so far been shaped and oriented by the values of Western culture.
The song about "the awakening of the woman and the dawning of the
day" (117) foreshadows Hisako's own awakening to the truth, both
about her captors and herself. When the ship is taken by the false guerrillas, she is forced to watch the hair-raising scenes of carnage: death of
the other passengers and her beloved Philippe, who are tied up, shot, and
grenaded, before she is herself abused and maltreated. However, it is the
destruction of the Stradivarius which turns out to be the most painful
wound. The death of the cello before Hisako's eyes, which once soothed
her pain and restored her to the world of the living, becomes equal to her
own demise. The heroine's private world of music and peace collapses:
the semiotic system of art, which "covers" and domesticates aggression,
crumbles, revealing the layers of unmediated reality of violence, and
triggering the shift and replacement of cultural codes of Hisako's private
semiosphere.

The heroine is taken under the deck of the ship and then locked in
the engineering workshop in complete darkness where she finally falls
asleep, which can be seen as her symbolical death. Like Jonah in the belly of the whale, she enters the world of her own subconscious, full of

primordial images connected with the memory of the Hiroshima bombing, bloodshed, and her own victimization. The dormancy of the heroine
in this makeshift sepulchre is like the calm before the storm, and precedes her resurrection as the lethal *force majeure*. Cairns Craig describes
the reborn Hisako as a "fear-inspiring and vengeful angel of death, im-
mune to all fear because she is beyond life" (2002: 34), which corresponds to the monomythic stage of the Master of Two Worlds. Transfig-
ured Hisako inhabits both the world of life and death, fear and fearlessness, human and inhuman, which finds a confirmation in the text when
Dandridge jokingly comments on Hisako's miraculous deliverance:
"Dead and kicking, huh?" (164). This is further corroborated by her
deadly equanimity in her methodical elimination of the enemies, a revenge which "could taste remarkably bland when you'd stopped feeling"
(159). Hisako's mood before the showdown is one of serenity: she feels
almost happy, resigned but oddly fulfilled, and at peace at last.

The change of Hisako's role, from an artist to an avenger and a warrior, is finally underscored by the change of attributes, as the instrument
of creating music turns into a weapon: she drives the Stradivarius' metal
spike like a vampire stake through Major Sucre's heart. The heroine duly "takes the toys from the boys," picking Uzi's and Kalashnikovs in the
course of her killing spree. Alongside male weapons, with which she
kills her tormentors like a Rambo,[23] Hisako also dresses like a guerrilla,
which is reminiscent of the re-investment motif in the monomyth. "She
didn't mean to impersonate a soldier, she was just sick of the torn, soiled
yukata. She wanted to be clothed again" (152), we read Hisako's
thoughts. However, it cannot be denied that a stolen uniform and beret
make her look androgynous, as if the world of violence she entered as a
participant endowed her with masculine traits and obliterated her gender.

Significantly, in Hisako's case, the element of water, traditionally associated with femininity, changes into the element of fire, associated

---

23 She comes close to the image of the lonely avenger, impersonated by Sylvest-
    er Stallone, overhung with an Uzi fitted with a silencer, and Sucre's Kalashni-
    kov with a nightsight, a Bowie knife, several extra magazines, with her hair
    held by the strip of yukata for convenience (152-6). Hisako Onoda's solitary
    fight also brings to mind the campaigns led in the Philippine jungle by a Japa-
    nese soldier of the same surname, Hiroo Onoda, who refused to surrender un-
    til 1974, thinking every attempt to convince him that the war was over to be a
    ruse (see Śpiewakowski 1989: 104, and Kawaguchi 2007).

with masculinity (cf. Biedermann 2005: 243), as she replays and subverts the destruction of Hiroshima, whose victims this time are the Americans caught in the blazing circle. The mirroring scenes of the *Pikadon* and its immediate aftermath involving Hisako's father, and those of the fire on Gatún Lake and the American soldiers unable to escape their death, are juxtaposed in one chapter, at the beginning and at the end of it. The same chapter contains the memory of baby Hisako being tangled in her own umbilical cord and her eventual coming into the world by Caesarean section, performed by the same surgeon who diagnosed her father's cancer several months earlier. Her conception, therefore, coincides with her father's death – her birth, in turn, signifies the father's rebirth in the body of his progeny with the heritage of violence flowing in her veins. By the fusion of the violent and mutually resounding images from the past and present, a connection is established between wartime suffering and current violence, which gives evidence to Hisako's predicament of the orphan of the soldier-father, who will not be at peace until the score is settled and the suffering is avenged.

Hisako's last dream on Gatún Lake brings the image of a lake full of blood and a sky full of fire, and of the globe being struck by a great lever, which she can see from outer space. The world "rang false and shattered, disintegrating into all the separate states and creeds, beliefs and prejudices that had riven it over the years, blowing like seeds from a flower" (184), observes the protagonist, vocalizing the awareness that the unity of the world is only illusory, something (super)imposed on the seething diversity underneath and on our true identities we cannot forsake in the name of the uniform whole. The ritual of destruction, i.e. replaying the Hiroshima bombing in which Americans are victims and she is a victimizer, performed in the heart of the universe out of vengeance and in the form of suicide, which are the cornerstones of the traditional samurai system of values (Hisako is aware of the suicidal nature of her revenge, she even refers to herself as having a feast before *seppuku*), brings the renewal of her culture. Her suppressed Japanese self is recovered from oblivion and reclaims the semiotic centre, dictating its own metalanguage and extending it onto the whole semiotic space of the protagonist. And so, Hisako's inner world of dreams filled with Japanese symbolism is ultimately projected upon the world of the Western hemisphere, as a result of which the outside world becomes symbolically subordinated to the heroine's subjective (viz. subconscious) vision. Like the lever in her dream shattering the seeming uniformity of the world, she has to destroy her false identity in order to give a lease of life to her true Japanese self, and be reborn through flames like a mythical phoenix which in the end swims off towards the rising sun.

4.3. The Virgin, the Mother, the Crone: the Return of a Mythical Woman in *The Business*.

Rejecting the corporate western world of big money and glamorous lifestyle in favour of love and communal responsibility in a small impoverished kingdom in the Himalayas, Kathryn Telman, the heroine of *The Business*, deliberates:

> Why am I doing this? Because it seems like the right thing to do. [. . .]
> This makes it all sound far too selfless. Actually there's a lot of self in this. All the same, part of me is recoiling in horror at all this. [. . .] Because in one way of looking at it, this is just another example of the same old sad self-sacrificial martyrdom crap I've lamented in my gender throughout my life. We have spent so many generations thinking of others, thinking of our families and thinking of our men, when all they do in return is think of themselves. Just in the last few generations, finally able to control our own fertility, have we been able to act more like men and contribute more with our brains than our bodies. I loved being part of that. [. . .] And yet here I am going back on all that, or seeming to. (2000: 388-9)

Kathryn's reflection perfectly summarizes the conflict implicit in her fate as a woman, as it juxtaposes her intellectual development and self-realization in the public sphere with her traditional feminine function of care and nurture as carried out in the space of the domestic. This ambiguous status, which is contingent upon her individual ambitions on the one hand and her biological drive on the other, in the end translates into the dualistic model of the heroic journey employed in the novel, where the "hard" male world of great business, great politics, and even greater corruption is pitted against the "softer" feminine dimension of romance and fairy tale.

In terms of its organizing plot, *The Business* is a techno-thriller set in the upper echelons of the business world. The protagonist, Kathryn, works as a senior executive in a powerful transglobal organization, the eponymous Business, whose origins date back to the Roman Empire and whose current objective is the purchase of its own state to gain a seat in the United Nations. In the course of her private investigation, Kathryn finds out that some of her superiors are making private money on the company-owned chip factory in order to accomplish their own far-reaching goals on the international stage. Unexpectedly, Kathryn discovers herself to be a pawn in another conspiracy devised by several senior officers. She is to be traded as a wife to the enamoured Prince Suvinder Dzung from Thulahn, to ensure his cooperation on turning the country into the company's new headquarters and pushing it on the path of technological development. Now the heroine has to not only resolve the case of the internal fraud and bring it to the attention of the Executive Board but also turn the project concerning her future and that of Thulahn to the advantage of both, against the Business's initial plans.

In broader terms, however, *The Business* traces Kathryn's life from childhood to adolescence and adulthood, the beginning of which is marked by her meeting with Mrs Telman, a Level Two executive in the Business, who saves the gifted eight-year-old from penury in the Scottish slums and later adopts Kathryn after the death of her biological mother. As a result, Kathryn enters the world of the Business and makes a name for herself as a market analyst whose job is to "keep abreast of current and incipient technological developments" (14). She grows into a work-devoted, money-making hi-tech specialist, living in luxury and without major personal commitments among other self-serving business people. At the same time, she reminisces with nostalgia about the warmth and care she received from her mother. She also occasionally voices her deep-seated yearning for a romantic relationship with an honourable man, which is hard to fulfil in a world revolving around money and power. By her anticipated acceptance of Suvinder's marriage proposal, Kathryn is bound to become the new queen of Thulahn, thereby taking on the responsibility of protecting her new nation against the dangers of progress epitomized in the Business and coming to terms with her female role of wife and potential mother.

Seen in this light, Kathryn's journey combines elements of two models of the heroic quest. The first is the traditional (Campbellian) monomyth, with its threshold crossings, battles, helpers, and enemies, wandering about in the labyrinth of lies, and the discovery of the truth. This part is here represented by the events of the thriller plot taking place in the Western world of trade, politics, and advanced technology, and follows a

typical adventure formula (for details see Cawelti 1976: 39-41). The
other model of the heroine's quest is proffered by the gender-specific
heroic journey, which goes beyond the investigation plot, and comes to
encompass Kathryn's Bildung narrative. Within the second paradigm,
the heroine progresses geographically, from the Scottish slums to the
"lost" Himalayan dukedom, and spiritually, from selfishness to responsibility, as she forsakes her worldly career for the fulfilment of traditional feminine dreams.

In her book *In a Different Voice: Psychological Theory and Wom-
en's Development* (1982), Carol Gilligan distinguishes three principal
stages of the woman's development, which she defines as a "sequence in
the development of the ethic of care" (qtd. in Erickson 2006: 105). This
includes the "selfish" stage, the "care" for other people, and the stage of
"universal care." In the first stage, which results from the feeling of disconnection and abandonment, the woman's self becomes the sole object
of her concern. The second stage finds its expression in the woman's acceptance of responsibility and "a maternal morality that seeks to ensure
care for the dependent and unequal." Such a change from egoism to the
sense of obligation to others is tantamount to "social participation" and
reflects the "conventional feminine voice." The third stage is marked by
the idea of care being expanded "to include both self and other" (105).
Thus, a balance is struck between egoism and obligation, and the shift
takes place "from goodness to truth:" a woman reconsiders the notion of
responsibility, "juxtaposing the concern with what other people think
with a new inner judgment" (106).

Another study contributing to an understanding of the gender-
specific heroic journey is Susan A. Lichtman's *Life Stages of Woman's
Heroic Journey: A Study of the Origins of the Great Goddess Archetype*
(1991), which, as Erickson observes, proposes such stages of the woman's development as the Virgin, the Mother, and the Crone, which correspond to Gilligan's stages of selfishness, care, and universal care. The
Virgin stage, according to Lichtman, constitutes the beginning of "a
journey of self-actualization that begins in adolescence and progresses
through adulthood toward psychological and spiritual wholeness of the
individual" (qtd. in Erickson 2006: 107). The Mother stage is tantamount to an acceptance of "personal responsibility for the present as
well as for the future." The woman commits herself to the improvement

of life and the perpetuation of the community – this stage is therefore characterized by creation or giving birth, not only to children but also things. As a woman's right of passage, the Mother stage leads to that of the Crone – a figure with "the ability to see and understand the past and the future, [. . .] interpreting for those younger the lessons and values of human life and human mortality" (109). The three archetypes determined by Lichtman find their realizations in the character of Kathryn and the women she meets on her life journey. Kate's biological mother, Mrs Telman, and the Queen Mother from Thulahn are not only representative of particular traits revealed by the woman at the successive stages of her development but they also exert an important influence on the development of the protagonist and her perception of the world.

The story of Kathryn Telman, or rather Katie McGurk, starts in a poor working-class neighbourhood in Coatbridge, in a dysfunctional family, with her drunkard father absent and her mother falling for abusive partners and struggling to make ends meet. The girl, deprived of proper care, has to look after herself, peddling "dainties" in the streets, engaging in scuffles and vulgar shouting matches with other kids, and dreaming of becoming a hairdresser in the future. At the same time, Kathryn is exceptional: at the age of eight and a half, she reveals a knack for doing business and an extraordinary mathematical talent, which attracts Mrs Telman's attention and finally contributes to the girl's rise from a life of poverty in the poor council estate to a lucrative job in a great multinational concern.

With the benevolent interference of Mrs Telman, who like a Fairy Godmother brings the girl under her protective umbrella, the young heroine is transferred from the world of pain, shortages, and social determinism into the sphere of make-believe for modern ambitious women, where "there might be a lot of other things [Kathryn] could be" rather than a hairdresser (30). Crossing the first threshold of the heroine's mythic journey, which is synonymous with crossing the boundary between two distinct spaces of signs, involves a transformation and a trial. On her first visit to Mrs Telman's elegant hotel apartments in Edinburgh, Kathryn is washed, examined, given new clothes (the equivalent of the divestiture and re-investment motifs of the monomyth), and she has to perform tasks which prove her quality – mathematical exercises and IQ tests, as befits a modern fairy tale.

Initially, Kate still lives with her biological mother, a poorly educated and prematurely aged Scottish woman, seen by Kate as "wee and dumpy" (30), in their old house near Glasgow. However, Kate is also favoured by elegant raven-haired Mrs Telman, who has an aura of magic and the unknown about herself. "[She] always seemed about six inches taller than she really was," says Kathryn, and she also notes that the woman's accent "sometimes sounded American, English, or tantalizingly foreign and exotic" (30). Kathryn, therefore, functions between two poles represented by the two female figures: the topographically and mentally limited world of her Glasgow quarter, and the limitless, geographically undetermined greater world, which will shape her horizons in the future. Mrs Telman appears in their house every few months, bringing gifts to her two wards, and through her benevolent mediation the old space of Kate's home becomes ordered, stable, and no longer inimical. Mrs Telman helps to improve the life of Kathryn's family, organizing the girl's education and finding her mother better paid jobs, thanks to which the latter can perform her maternal role properly. The child duly notices numerous changes taking place around her, pointing out the lessening discrepancy between reality and the language of its description with childlike naïveté: "I found I had a lot fewer uncles than I'd thought I had, and Mother stopped walking into doors" (33).

Kate's mother and Mrs Telman represent two clearly distinct facets of the woman's life: the one centred around childcare, the toil of everyday existence, and self-sacrifice; the other based on the awareness of one's needs, freedom, and self-actualization, but also on sympathy and understanding of life and the world. Thus, they may be considered the Mother and the Crone respectively. During her conversation with Level One executive Tommy Cholongai, Kathryn recalls the love, care, and protection against the evil of the world that she got from her mother despite their poverty (it returns several times in the novel as a memory of her mother hugging her close to her breast). At the same time, she observes that Mrs Telman was to her "like a mother [. . .], more like an aunt, perhaps" (158). According to Lichtman, the Crone is to the Virgin a "guide, teacher, or mentor" (qtd. in Erickson 2006: 109), and Kate stresses on several occasions the support and guidance received from Mrs Telman. Mrs Telman represents the healthy balance between selfishness and self-denying sacrifice for others, and she helps Kathryn avoid the pitfalls of life which absorbed her biological mother:

> If it hadn't been for that piece of luck I'd probably still be in the west of Scotland. I'm thirty-eight. By now I'd have had three or four kids knocked out of me, I'd weigh another twenty or thirty pounds, I'd look ten years older, I'd smoke forty a day and eat too much chocolate and deep-fried food. If I was lucky, I'd have a man who didn't hit me and kids who weren't doing drugs. Maybe I'd have a few high-school qualifications, maybe not. There's an outside chance I'd have gone to university, in which case it might all have been different. I might be a teacher or a social worker or a civil servant, all of which would be socially useful but wouldn't let me live the sort of life I've come to appreciate. (129)

By comparing her present life with a life which she might have lived, Kate juxtaposes two world models: one recognized in her former Scottish community, in which gender is a semiotically significant determinant, and the other, advocated by the Business, in which gender lies outside the symbolic system. Significantly, Kate links the failure of her alternative life in Scotland with the professions of a teacher, social worker, or civil servant, all of which involve care and responsibility for others, and are traditionally considered women's domains because they apparently appeal to women's nurturant side. In contrast, Kathryn's corporate life defies such gender stereotypes, as she is "helping to make a case for [her] half of the species being worth more recognition than that due to a womb alone" (389). This often involves behaving selfishly or thinking like a man, which is usually one and the same thing, and Kate, like her male colleagues, can enjoy the luxury of speedy promotion, immediate financial gratification, freedom of choice, and no personal commitments.

Interestingly enough, Kate perceives the Business in terms of a community in which everyone depends on "the support and co-operation of everybody else" in order to attain individual goals (140), which are, however, utterly egoistic. For this reason, her only loyalty is to the company, her identification with the Business being stressed by the use of the pronoun "we," and the company's profit is her chief interest, to which are subordinated all human emotions, including empathy and care. This can be noticed in her reaction to the news of destruction caused by Hurricane Mitch in Central America: "Part of my mind scanned a mental list of company assets in the area, wondering how we might be affected, while my conscience shook its metaphorical head and tried to dredge up some human sympathy for the victims from the depths of my corporate soul" (16).

As exemplified by the passage above, the worldview based on the values of profit and economic expansion takes precedence over the truly communal ethos of nurture and fellowship, which also implies the hegemony of the public over the private sphere. Activating the selfish and acquisitive part of human nature, the Business at the same time lays claims to everything its employees have gained during their lifetime's work, the fortunes of individual executives being in the end the property of the organization. "[I]t is impossible to bequeath all you've made to your offspring or, indeed, anybody else who isn't one of us" (90), remarks Kathryn, making it clear that the company torpedoes all loyalties based on emotional or family bonds, except for the purely self-centred corporate loyalty to itself. Similarly, the executives above Level Six must renounce all religious beliefs and national affinities, their only dedication being to Mammon, not to a God or a flag (50).

As such, the Business fosters Kathryn's professional and financial fulfilment, but it keeps her away from the obligations she could have outside the institution, thus preventing her social inclusion. For the most part of her adult life Kathryn seems to avoid the qualities implicit in the Mother archetype, represented by her biological mother, which involves mental and physical sacrifice, and she clings to the initial stage of the pattern, the Virgin, "insulating" herself from her feminine core. She voices this awareness towards the end of the novel, when she ponders over her fondness for flying, and traces its origin back to her adolescent flight from Italy to her mother's funeral:

> And was this whole thing about planes born in that other flight back after catastrophe, and did it go deeper than that, to layers of insulation I'd been wrapping around myself all my life, to all the hierarchies of contacts and business associates and good reports and executive levels and salary increments and pay-off guesses and colours of credit cards and classes of aircraft cabin and higher-level interest rates and even friends and lovers I'd collected around myself over the years, not to keep the world away from me, because people were the world, but to keep me away from me? (294)

The death of her mother at Easter marks Kathryn's detachment from her natural female path, and her entrapment in the Virgin archetype. Kathryn's sense of detachment is very physically manifested in the girl's partial hearing loss which afflicts her on the plane to England, and which she calls "that strange, numb knowing that [she] was cut adrift from [her] mother for ever" (293). Her drifting apart is further emphasized by the resemioticization of her identity, as her surname is changed after she is adopted by Mrs Telman and her estranged husband from America.

In her adult life, Kathryn lives in the public sphere connected with her job. Her activities are mapped by mobile and satellite communications and the Internet, which defy all political and geographical boundaries, and as such resemble the expansiveness and elusiveness of the Business itself – they are everywhere and nowhere. Kathryn has no permanent abode, which would foster equally permanent commitments and responsibilities for another person. A holder of two passports, British and American, she is committed to neither country, spending one-third of the year flying from place to place. She has a house in California, but she occasionally stays in the Business's apartments in Glasgow or London, as well as in her foster-uncle's house at Blysecrag. The only people she can call family are associated with the company (Mrs Telman, Uncle Freddie), and her relationships, based on sex rather than love, are also with people who work for the Business, like her chauffeur, Raymond. Even Kathryn's affection for Stephen Buzetsky, a married colleague, initially shows signs of an egoistical fascination with an unattainable male paragon, and her sexual desire is expressed in the business terms of profit and satisfaction, governing the corporate sensibilities (78).

Significantly, Kathryn's female quest leads her through three places which are connected with the dynamics of her affiliation with the Business and her growing affinity with Thulahn, namely the Blysecrag mansion in Yorkshire, the Business's headquarters at Chateau d'Oex in Switzerland, and the royal palace in Thuhn, each of which resonates with cultural references, relying on processes of either literary or filmic mediation, or a combination of both. Blysecrag is a lavish, grand-scale Gothic dream come true, a cross between Mervyn Peake's Gormenghast and Shirley Jackson's Hill House. Its "small but formidable" housekeeper, Mrs Heggies, "with grey bunned hair, a steely stare, lips the colour and fullness of a small elastic band, artificial eyebrows and a voice to etch titanium" (43), seems to be taken alive from yet another Gothic novel, Daphne du Maurier's *Rebecca* (or rather its film version), her prototype being Mrs Danvers. By the same token, the castle in Switzerland, which "looks like it can't decide whether it really is a chateau or a

Schloss" (353), is "chocolate-box pretty," much in the Disney style. It is not surprising, therefore, that Chateau d'Oex is suffused with oneiric fairytale atmosphere in the vein of *Beauty and the Beast*, with the staff "gliding around," "materializing and dematerializing at will," who make Kathryn's bags disappear "apparently of their own volition," and her coat slip "silently and almost unnoticed" from her shoulders. Kathryn describes her state as "dreamlike," as everything seems "dissociated from reality," and she feels uncertain of what is happening to her in the end (354). However, the place only foregrounds the irony implicit in the presentation of the Business. Spectral and intangible as an organization, with its records and imaginary treasures stored in a dreamlike castle, whose major part is hidden in the ground like an iceberg, the Business's world appears to be a false fairly tale. Kathryn has to disentangle herself from it before she can start her life in Thulahn, within the world of her own fairy tale played out on the roof of the world.

It is only her visit to Thulahn, the small mountainous realm in Asia, which makes Kate resume the abandoned quest for wholeness of her female self. At one point, the place is called Shangri-La, and humorous as this naming may seem, it points to important qualities of the state. Like the Himalayan utopia from James Hilton's *Lost Horizon*, Thulahn is almost entirely isolated from the outside world and difficult to access (the flight is dangerous and crossing the high mountain passes on foot practically impossible). Thus, it is virtually unaffected by the evils corrupting modern societies: it has not only retained its unspoiled landscape but also its moral integrity and traditional way of life. All the above qualities make it a kind of earthly paradise, the Centre comparable in its essence to Gatún Lake in *Canal Dreams*, where the protagonist has meaningful dreams, and where her quest for self finds an (un)expected resolution. Deprived of the luxury and comforts of the two other places, Thulahn allows the heroine to experience life through all her senses (away from the telecommunications, gadgets, modern conveniences, even clothes, which mediate her Western identity), which testifies to its archetypal nature.

However, Thulahn is an endangered paradise, as the Business wants to take over the country, changing irrevocably both the landscape and the way of life in the realm, thereby subjecting it to a different semiosphere – the technologically oriented culture of the West. In comparison with the isolated Buddhist realm, where life has for centuries revolved around such values as "family, faith, farms and fealty" (230), the Business comes across as expansive and developing in time, having no communal obligations and serving only its own economic interests. In Kathryn's view, the organization, which recognizes no political authority and inhabits no single geographical location, stands for Reason, Rationality, and Progress (139), while in Western culture, which the company epitomizes, "science is the religion that works" (268). The secretive ways of the corporation and its hidden agenda, which correspond to the unlimited range of its activity, are here contrasted with the open-hearted attitude of the Thulanhese and their wide smiles, despite the limited space occupied by their country.

As opposed to the other Business members, Kathryn possesses a dual perspective: on the one hand, she is a committed executive in her corporation, while on the other, she reveals a capacity for understanding differences. This double criterion (along with her being the object of Suvinder's love) proves decisive in nominating her as the Business ambassador in Thulahn:

> 'We need someone whom we can trust. That, of course, means someone in the business whom we know to be profoundly committed to it. [. . .] But we also need someone who can see things from a perspective outside the company, someone who will feel sympathetic towards the people of Thulahn. Someone who will be able to empathise with them, and advise us how best to incorporate their needs and wishes with those of the company itself.' (162-3)

As such, Kathryn resembles Isis Whit and Hisako Onoda in that she is the boundary character, which determines her perspective of both an insider and outsider of her culture. This position fosters dialogue with the semiotic Other, which is made explicit in Kathryn's easy adjustment to the Thulanhese ways in dress, eating habits, and even behaviour (see 248-9), to such an extent that she forgets to put on her executive clothes when returning to Britain. The dialogue between the West and its ethnic Other is best represented in Kathryn's relationship with Dulsung, a small Thulanhese girl, whom Kathryn presents with her guardian netsuke monkey, standing for her professional luck in the competitive business world. In return, she receives a little home-made wire-and-silk flower, which she comes to treat as a talisman, a bit of the mountainous paradise protecting its bearer in the outside world. Kathryn's transformation as a result of her contact with Thulahn is eventually underscored by her acknowledgement of the superiority of Thulahnese wild, untamed nature over the "compromised," man-made "civilization" of Swiss mountains, which she once appreciated (351).

If Kate's encounter with Mrs Telman contributed to her personal growth and gave her opportunities normally unavailable to her sex, in Thulahn Kathryn meets a woman who sacrificed her worldly career to become the guide and protector of the isolated land. The old dowager, Suvinder's mother, is in fact the Honourable Lady Audrey Illsey, an English aristocrat, who married Suvinder's father in 1946 and came to live in the small insignificant kingdom in the mountains. The dwelling of the Queen Mother, who functions as the other Crone in this heroic cycle, can be accessed through several protective boundaries of winding Himalayan roads, sturdy doors, dark incense-filled halls, and a host of faithful guardians, her ladies-in-waiting and the big Chinese bodyguard, Mihu. The presence chamber of her palace, which also serves as a big royal bedroom, houses in its centre yet another mountain: the Queen's high, pyramidal bed with a purple canopy, which the dowager never leaves (223-4).

Kathryn has to ascend its steps in order to talk to the bed-ridden, aged woman, who proves a formidable opponent to the Virgin coming in the person of the progressively oriented young executive. But it is also an eye-opening experience, as the Queen verbalizes all the doubts concerning Thulahn's introduction to the world of progress that eventually beset Kathryn after her affinity with the place has grown stronger. In reply to Kathryn's enthusiasm concerning the Business's offer to improve Thulahn's infrastructure, provide better water supplies, education, and medical care, the old Queen rationally observes:

> 'They have water. No one dies of thirst. They have all the education they need. Do you need a degree to walk behind the plough? No. And health? It will always be hard to live here. It's no place for the weak. We all have to die, young woman. [. . .]'
>
> 'I . . . think it would only be right to offer the Thulahnese people a choice as well.'
>
> 'A choice of what? Will they want television? Burger bars? Jobs in factories and supermarkets? Salaries in offices? Motor cars? They will doubtless choose all that, if they're offered it. And before you know it we will be just the same as everywhere else and we'll have homosexuals,

AIDS, socialists, drug-dealers, prostitutes and muggers. That will be progress, won't it, Miss Telman?' (230-1)

It is interesting that the figures of Mrs Telman and the old Queen become linked in Kathryn's consciousness: the recollection of the girl's
conversation with her adoptive mother about the unfairness of the world
immediately precedes her terrifying dream about the dowager, for whom
she is looking in the smoke-filled corridors of the dark, cold palace,
while being chased by dangerous lisping wraiths. Despite their difficult
conversation the day before, Kathryn unconsciously attributes protective
qualities to the Queen's figure, the qualities which extend both to the
Crone's endangered realm and to Kathryn herself, trapped in the as yet
unrealized conspiracy of Mr Hazleton.[24] In both cases, it is the Business
which turns out to be the source of potential danger. Kathryn's fear of
being caught by the demons is first and foremost a fear of becoming
"one of them; [. . .] consigned to wander the hollowed-out palace for ever" (238). Therefore Kathryn's flight from the "dark wraiths of pain" in
search of the dowager can also be interpreted as her attempt to break free
from the confines of the Virgin archetype, here synonymous with her
dedication to the Business and the hollowness of her personal relationships. Embarking on a quest for her suppressed feminine side would take
her to the Mother stage and let her escape from the selfishness of her inner world to "the world outside" (238), with emotional commitments
and responsibility for others.

Consequently, the bringing together of the two Crones of the novel
serves a particular function: it accentuates the duality implicit in the protagonist's development. Whereas Mrs Telman is a guardian who opens
to Kathryn the whole wide world of individual freedom and opportuni-

---

24   The perilous consequences of the Business's plans concerning Thulahn are
     communicated through another dream Kathryn has on her way back to Scot-
     land after uncle Freddy's car accident. Now she dreams about the old Queen
     being pushed out of her bed into the abyss below the palace by her Chinese
     bodyguard, who now looks like Hazleton's security chief. The east wind that
     the bodyguard lets into the chamber makes the bed's canopy swell like a huge
     sail, which helps to move the whole construction towards the terrace, and out
     into the precipice, symbolically representing the abyss of the Western semio-
     sphere into which the country is being pushed. Thus, the greatest obstacle,
     namely the conservative and insightful critic of the novelty, is removed along-
     side the tradition she represents.

ties of self-fulfilment ("the freedom always to behave selfishly, or always to do what a man would do in the circumstances" [389]), the old Queen represents the conservative standpoint, which upholds traditional lifestyle and hierarchies but also advocates what Kathryn calls "the freedom to do what seems right to [her] from first principles" (389), namely yielding to the call of her own womanhood and its propensity for nurture. Mediating between those two extremes, Kathryn has an opportunity to ensure an equilibrium between the Business and Thulahn, which she admits in a conversation with her friend Lucy, explaining the motives behind her acceptance of the post in Thulahn and, predictably, Suvinder's marriage proposal:

> I'm doing it because he's in a position of real power in a place I hardly know but I'm already half in love with. And he is a good man. But there's going to be so much change there. Not as much as some people were expecting, but a hell of a lot, and I don't know that Suvinder can handle it all by himself. I don't think he thinks he can, either. And I'd worry about who'd be advising him. Don't you see, Luce? For the first time in my life I can really do some good. Or fail in the attempt. (391)

Kathryn's acceptance of her female journey makes the heroine abandon the international scene and move to the small and far-removed kingdom and into the domestic sphere. It entails her conscious shift from the path of self-gratification to a more rewarding life of sacrifice and nursing. Her fulfilment of the mythical patterns of femininity means at once a rejection of the male-oriented world of business and its subordination to Kathryn's rediscovered communal perspective: by becoming the Queen of Thulahn, Kate will assume the role of a defender of the monarchic state against the Business's overly radical investment plans. The protagonist's quest is brought to a successful resolution; a distant call of the wedding bells heralds Kathryn's official involvement in the life of Suvinder and his country, and her prospective role as mother, both to the royal heir and the nation entrusted to her care. Last but not least, the prospective marriage and professional cooperation are reflective of semiotic dialogism, as they bring together two persons who stand at the boundary: a westernized Himalayan prince and a Scot who is increasingly "going native" (351), which offers a possibility of reconciliation between custom and novelty, between modernity and tradition.

***

The heroic quest of the female characters in *Whit*, *Canal Dreams*, and *The Business*, although embarked on for the sake of external objectives (the search for a lost relative, the pursuit of musical career, and an investigation into a financial scam, respectively), in the end comes to represent the heroine's path of maturation and development. It becomes a journey towards the true self and autonomy from the demands and dangers posed by a patriarchal order (Isis Whit); a journey to wholeness and balance as a person after a life-long trauma (Hisako Onoda); or, finally, a journey to the nurturant side of the self which is effected by the heroine's return and commitment to the space of the community (Kathryn Telman). However, in all of these versions of the female Bildungsroman the quest is accomplished with relation to the cultural and ethnic Other.

The quest formula not only creates an opportunity for the character to show her "heroic" qualities but also emphasizes the tension between the quester's subjective world-picture and the outside world which is the stage of her geographical and spiritual peregrinations. The pilgrimage to the unholy lands in *Whit*, the sea voyage to the mythical centre in *Canal Dreams*, and the air travel to a mountainous utopia in *The Business*, all involve a confrontation of the woman's native or proper semiosphere, with its particular modes of thinking or values, and various manifestations of an alien semiosphere lying beyond its borders. The encounter invariably takes the form of a conflict between the mythical and historical order, with the heroine functioning as the carrier of mythical consciousness. The latter finds its reflection in Isis's sectarian outlook as opposed to the secular thinking of contemporary Britain, in Hisako's dreams of Japaneseness as opposed to Western culture and its political domination, and in Kathryn's matriarchal yearnings, which cannot be accommodated within the masculinized and progressive Business world. Within this framework, the three female characters are shown as actively modelling outside reality in compliance with their personal worldviews and hidden desires, finally subordinating the male-dominated, historical world to the feminine power of myth.

CHAPTER 5

Apocalyptic Worlds
A Song of Stone, Complicity, and *Dead Air*

In the blueprint universe of *The Wasp Factory*, the protagonist inhabits an island which still bears traces of the cataclysmic events of World War II – bunkers, shells and unexploded bombs, which turn its grounds into a post-apocalyptic space. However, the island is also an arena for another war, namely Frank's war against nature, which is fought locally but ceaselessly, without pity or remorse. On the one hand, the war-torn landscape of the island is a mirror image of the psychological landscape of the hero, which has been turned into a wasteland in the wake of his personal catastrophe. On the other hand, it is also representative of Frank's body, which has become a scarred and ravaged battlefield of the war waged by his scientist father against Frank's biological sex.

Seen in this light, *The Wasp Factory* ushers in another set of novels in which the apocalyptic functions as the dominant factor of semiotic mediation both with respect to the public semiospheres in which the characters are immersed and to the inner landscapes of their private worlds. The apocalyptic appears here in different manifestations: as a war cataclysm putting an end to society, the individual, and the very text in *A Song of Stone*; as the ideology of selfishness and exploitation which wreaks havoc on personal memory and the country's social and economic structure in *Complicity*; or as a terrorist attack which brings into focus the emotional wasteland of the media society in *Dead Air*, while also dramatizing Baudrillard's claim of the end of representation. Whereas *A Song of Stone*'s semiotic locale is a nameless dystopian world, *Complicity* and *Dead Air* are firmly set in contemporary cultural and political reality: Britain after years of Conservative government and London in the aftermath of Al-Qaeda's attacks on the WTC.

The space as semioticized by the characters in the wake of the apocalyptic events (especially in the case of *A Song of Stone* and *Complicity*)
is one of violence, disintegration, and death. The foundations of the old
symbolic order are shaken, its social laws and moral values being obliterated by new ideologies and hierarchies which hide the underlying degeneracy, barbarism, and overwhelming sterility of humankind. The
characters are faced with a disturbing rift between the old and the new,
which makes them mediate between their position as the inheritors of the
past and the creators of the present. In *A Song of Stone*, Abel makes desperate but ineffective attempts to save the pre-apocalyptic world inside
the walls of his family castle against the disintegrating force of apocalyptic chaos brought from outside by the female lieutenant and her soldiers. In *Complicity*, Cameron and Andy find themselves stranded in the
post-apocalyptic wasteland of capitalist society, whose consumerism,
violence, and moral degeneration invade and disrupt the characters' inner worlds. In contrast with *A Song of Stone*, the space of the past offers
no refuge, as it is the locus of personal traumas which make impossible
the characters' life in the present. In *Dead Air*, Ken Nott and Celia Merrial escape from the emotional wasteland of modern society and the catastrophes of their times, broadcast and relayed by the media, into the
regenerative private world of mystery and romance. Whereas the world
presented in *A Song of Stone* and *Complicity*, irredeemably shattered and
diseased, is doomed to perish as a result of war or due to its own infertility and degradation, the post-apocalyptic wasteland of *Dead Air* is finally regenerated by love, truth, and humanity, and by the characters' return
to the invigorating space of homeland.

5.1. King Arthur in Distress: Post-apocalyptic Transgressions in *A Song of Stone*[1]

In *A Song of Stone* (1997), his ninth mainstream novel, Iain Banks takes
the motif of war as a cataclysm, already employed in *The Wasp Factory*
and shows an apocalypse in the making. Set in an unknown quasi-
European country whose realities resemble the first decades of the twentieth century, though in fact "[t]his could be any place or time" (1998:

---

1   Parts of this analysis appeared previously in Blaim A. and L. Gruszewska
     Blaim. (eds). (2012). *Spectres of Utopia: Theory, Practice, Conventions.*
     Frankfurt am Mein: Peter Lang.

272), the book depicts a nation in the state of complete political, social, and moral disintegration. The war, which left the land and its humanity at the mercy of plundering raids of itinerant soldiers, constitutes a critical moment in the history of the society and a turning point in the personal history of the novel's narrator, Abel, and his beloved Morgan. While taking flight from the hostilities, the two aristocrats are captured by a band of soldiers under the command of a female lieutenant and are brought back to their family castle. The heirs of the noble line become helpless marionettes in the hands of the victorious rabble and they are made to witness the demise of all things familiar.

The war in *A Song of Stone* constitutes a moment of rupture between two distinct temporal dimensions. The split of the world into what was before and what came after is underscored by the use of tenses in Abel's narration. The present tense, by which the character relates his current vicissitudes, is here juxtaposed with the past tense, which is the medium of memory. Such a juxtaposition highlights the gulf between the new post-apocalyptic reality and the world of the past buried under the ruins. At the same time, the present tense, used for describing the war-torn reality, evokes a feeling of time arrested, reminiscent of Kermode's concept of "time-between," which Abel's mind traces between the first pages of the novel and the moment of his own death. In consequence, the end of the individual corresponds with the universal End (cf. Kermode 1967: 25), while the reconfiguration of the semiotic fabric of the culture is mirrored by the demise of Abel's private world.

The conflict which has wasted the country's body politic and its landscape has led to military chaos, disrupting previous social relationships and, as a result, obliterating all known axioms and points of reference which used to determine social and cultural semiosis. The old laws and morals have collapsed and a new semiotic context has emerged, one in which social mechanisms are reduced to the law of the jungle and the survival of the fittest. Lacking a political, moral, or religious centre, which could dictate its norms to the entire semiosphere, the new world suffers from increasing disintegration and the fluidity of boundaries, be they physical, social, or moral, which renders the space transgressive and contributes to its post-apocalyptic quality.

The disruption of social life and its civilized mechanisms is accompanied by the devastation of the landscape. The land is marked by explosions and by the wheels of military vehicles, its roads and settlements being ravaged by plundering troops and trudging refugees.[2] Except for a few clearly defined landmarks, e.g. the castle, the forest, the windmill, which are connected by the road traversed by refugees, the space is inchoate in nature: barren and darkened, it shows signs of the season (onset of wintertime), whose deathly connotations add weight to the common carnage and destruction. The devastating effect of war is reinforced by various belongings left behind by the retreating humanity which represent the refugees' former civilized lives and private worlds now disintegrated by the external chaos. At the sight of the abandoned vehicles Abel makes a mental note: "All speak of the crowds who've passed this way, discarding these metal carapaces like tender-bodied crabs on the floors of seas, moulting off their past anatomies. We weave through their lifeless desolation like a needle through a frayed tapestry of ruin" (139-140).

The above-quoted comparison of the refugees to crustaceans shedding cuticle emphasizes the general devolution of humankind in the aftermath of the conflict. It is just one of many references to the debased condition of the human species, now frequently perceived in terms of its animal or material qualities. Animal imagery is often used with reference to the lieutenant's soldiers. Young Karma sleeps on the floor guarding the lieutenant's chamber door like a faithful dog. Yet another soldier, Verbal, is "obedient as any hound" (63) when he drops down to the ground at the lieutenant's command to enable her to fire at a flock of birds at the hunt. Already at the beginning of his acquaintance with the lieutenant, Abel learns that the dead medic from her unit was nicknamed Vet, which at the same time points to his credentials and demonstrates the degradation of his patients in the new order of things.

---

2   On the one hand, the refugees are alive in the devastated country like blood running through the veins of the organism, on the other, they reflect the death of the land, as their presence on the roads resembles "a scramble of dry leaves before the coming storm" (88). Moving through the landscape, they bring death to nature, their trail being marked by bared and broken trees hacked and splintered "as though by massed gunfire" (88) to make camp fires. Therefore, instead of creative, their relationship with space is destructive be-cause space is no longer theirs but alien and depersonalized, and thus a fit target of man's hostility and abusive actions.

The dehumanizing effect of the new post-apocalyptic reality can be noticed in the inexorable loss and resemioticization of identity, again the most striking example being the lieutenant's soldiers, forced to adopt masks behind which they can conceal their civilized (or civilian) selves. They are stripped of various qualities, such as their real names, which used to define them as individuals and anchored them in their previous identities from before the war. Instead, the soldiers in the lieutenant's unit are given nicknames indicative of their most distinctive traits, e.g. Deathwish, Psycho, Mr Cuts, Kneecap or Tootight, and thus become types rather than flesh-and-blood people. They are born again into the post-apocalyptic world, becoming "another person, after training" (42), as the lieutenant aptly sums up, and they can reclaim their pre-apocalyptic selves only through death.[3]

Yet another group afflicted by the terrifying process of depersonalization are the refugees, the nameless inhabitants roaming the equally nameless land. They lack individuality like a moving shapeless matter. They are perceived *en masse* through their shared predicament as a "stream," a "surge," a "flow [. . .] stretched and unbroken" – a primordial image of biological matter (4-5). The loss of individuality goes hand in hand with the refugees' objectification, which is here synonymous with their increased vulnerability in the dystopian world of savagery, as they resemble "paper-people, [. . .] all linked, all similar, [. . .] fragile, flammable, disposable – by their nature demanding some suitable ill-use" (5).[4]

---

3   At some point, the lieutenant confesses to Abel that she has forgotten the real name of every man in the squad, but that she remembered the old civilian name of the dying soldier Half-caste the moment she kissed him before shooting him out of mercy. It seems therefore that once the soldiers' part in the war is over they lose their adopted wartime identities and regain their real selves as human beings. The lieutenant's own nickname, Loot, may be an abbreviation of her function, lieutenant, "loot" and "Lieut-" carrying the same phonetic quality (especially in American English). However, the name may also imply the practice of pillaging and appropriating someone else's property, which seems rather pertinent in the light of capturing Abel's castle by the lieutenant and her gang.

4   The above passage sounds even more convincing after we recall Elana Gomel's observation concerning the apocalyptic body: "But most of all it is a suffering body, a text written in the script of stigmata, scars wounds, and

Though being equally vulnerable to the violence of war as the sad peregrine crowd, the two aristocrats stand out from the rest of the degraded dispossessed humanity. Their refined attire and the horse-drawn carriage speak of the world they still carry with and within them. Abel and Morgan are firmly attached to the pre-apocalyptic world of the ancien régime, in which signs and cultural codes had their fixed and recognizable referents, in which people used to be recognized by their names and various trappings signalling their affiliation with a particular family or social group, as well as through their rootedness in a particular place. That world, which no longer exists, is here confronted with the semiotic chaos of the post-apocalyptic new order ruled by vagrant wannabes with fake names, motley garment, and murderously acquired military ranks, of whom the lieutenant is a prime example.

Through the lieutenant the fragmented and unstable quality of the post-apocalyptic space acquires a tangible essence, which is already noticeable in her appearance. Her shabby attire, like that of her subordinates, is a semiotic patchwork of many different types of uniforms which communicates nothing about the side she used to be on in the war. When she is told that the castle of Abel and Morgan was taken by another group of soldiers a few days before, she asks about their uniforms, "Any better than ours?" (13). The question clearly implies that now, after the regular troops have turned into outlaws trying to survive in the lawless world, the uniform's distinguishing trait is its state of repair rather than its official design, colour, or badges. The lieutenant is a product of the current revolutionary times: her plebeian roots could once have been a hindrance to her social ascent; however, after the collapse of the traditional social hierarchy, they rather accelerate her career. Abel thus comments on that: "Our lieutenant's is a spirit freed by the reordering implicit in this general disorder; a beneficiary, so far, of the conflict. That which has dragged us down has buoyed her up" (68).

The novel's exclusive use of first names, like Abel and Morgan, not only underscores the primordial quality of the devolved world but is also indicative of the post-apocalyptic chaos, in which cultural or mythical paradigms are disrupted. Abel's name proves as much significant as

---

sores. Any apocalypse strikes the body politic like a disease, progressing from the first symptoms of a large-scale disaster through the crisis of the tribulation to the recovery of the millennium" (2000: 406).

subversive: named after the biblical son of Adam and Eve, he also becomes a victim of a fratricidal strife (the war which has ravaged the
country is, after all, a civil war). However, in contrast to his namesake
from the Book of Genesis, he is not an innocent victim. The meeting on
the road initiates an ongoing tension between the nobleman and the lieutenant, who like Cain intends to take over Abel's privileged position. In
a spectacle of appropriation and exclusion, which is enacted in Abel's
family castle, his powerlessness as a hostage is countered by his sustained challenge to Loot's authority, which culminates in his murder of
the lieutenant, thus defying any clear-cut biblical correspondence. A
similar misleading symbolism of proper names can also be noticed in the
castle's government, where the Arthurian legend is subverted and the
name Arthur is given to an old servant while Abel becomes the brother
and lover of Morgan. The characters' names, therefore, indicate a new
post-apocalyptic beginning, which is in fact the pivot of several beginnings – pseudo-biblical, implying the origin of humankind, and pseudo-
historical or pseudo-legendary, going back to the beginning of Britain –
which here occur simultaneously without the benefit of several millennia.

The post-apocalyptic transgression observable on the level of signs
and cultural codes also takes place in the sphere of sexuality and traditionally understood masculinity and femininity. Being biologically female, the lieutenant reveals those characteristics which are culturally associated with men, and especially with the paradigm of aggressive masculinity commonly displayed by soldiers in times of military conflicts
(cf. Craig 2002: 17-18). Her ruthlessness, androgynous aura, indomita-
ble will, lack of squeamishness, and lust for power make her a natural
leader of her male subordinates, who respect her and follow her blindly.
Abel, on the other hand, who is biologically a man (and socially a lord
of the manor), engages in ineffective philosophizing, not being able to
undertake any constructive actions to ensure his freedom or protect his
home from invasion and appropriation. "I feel I should be doing something assertive, dynamic [. . .] but I think I do not have the character required for such heroics," he self-consciously observes (83).[5]

---

5 Interviewed by Kate Kelman in *Cencrastus*, Iain Banks describes Abel as follows: "The only thing he has any control over is his language or how he ex-
   presses himself. [. . .] He is by no means a man of action, he tries to be, but

"Nothing is stable in Apocalypse," writes Tina Pippin, "especially gender and desire" (1999: 122), a sentence which may serve as a perfect commentary on the sexual complexities among the three characters. In his dream preceding the patrol's return from a reconnaissance on which the lieutenant has taken his sister, Abel fantasizes about Morgan, seeing her body as a landscape, a land he would possess and make his own, as if in need to reassert his slipping lordly authority. The undermining of Abel's physical space as well as his gradual disinheritance by the forces of chaos finds its reflection in the disturbed world of his subconscious. Abel describes himself as "a ship without way, pitched and driven by swell and gust," while Morgan's body remains a "distant memory, like a misty glimpse of land" (94). Several pages later, we are presented with an image of the lieutenant sleeping in the library, on which Abel remarks: "A map of our lands lies crumpled beneath her head, her curled, bedraggled hair, hovering like a dark cloud above us all" (114). These two scenes underscore Abel's progressive deprivation of everything he owns, Morgan and the land being metaphorically equated in that they once belonged to Abel, and now they are claimed by the lieutenant, along with Abel's old riding boots, "another pair of refugees abducted from [their] past" (114).

Loot's victorious entry into the castle marks the invasion of Abel's private world by the new, reconfigured public order, which, despite its coercive character, is also proof of dialogism effected across the semiotic boundary. The closed space of the castle with its ancient hierarchies, codes of dress, behaviour, and aristocratic pastimes, is breached by the element of an alien semiosphere, as the soldiers begin to use the "cellars, stores and rooms" (27), which were once used by nobility. Moreover, Loot begins to take over Abel's role as a master of the staff. Dressed in a

---

makes a mess of it" (1998: 21). The question of the language used by the protagonist and the combination of various styles employed by Banks in the novel have drawn the attention of John D. Owen, who observes: "Here is another contrast in the book, between the richness of his descriptive prose and the grittiness of his writing about the troop as they go about their business. The writing seems to echo the dichotomy between the central characters – the colourful but fading aristocrats against the sharp focus of the Lieutenant, whose edges slowly erode as she is drawn in by Abel and Morgan. She takes on some of their colour only to discover the deadly decay that such a gift brings with it" (1998).

jacket of Abel's old relative, she plays a gracious lord to the old servant Arthur, who brings a tray with Abel's best champagne into the castle courtyard. When later Abel informs the lieutenant about Arthur's death, she appears truly saddened and offers her help with the funeral, which Abel considers a usurpation of his prerogatives: "If anyone ought to feel aggrieved it is I; he was my servant and she has no right to assume my role in this, even if I have chosen not to play it to its limits; it is my right to underplay it, but not hers to understudy me" (115).[6]

Abel's helplessness against the intruders inside his house and against the forces of post-apocalyptic chaos attacking it from outside translates into a slow disintegration of his mental balance, as the castle in *A Song of Stone* represents the "genealogical and the psychological fortress of the self" (Craig 2002: 38). Thanks to the preserving power of the ancient walls, Abel's line has been allowed to perpetuate in the generative cycle, attaining a quasi-eternal form of existence through works and achievements.[7] The lieutenant and her soldiers, on the other hand, rootless and

---

6   The relationships between the characters in the post-apocalyptic world of A Song of Stone, and particularly the tension building up between Abel and the lieutenant, may owe much to Iain Banks's supposed employment of the medieval theory of the four elements, according to which Abel would be associated with water, Morgan with air, the lieutenant with fire, and the castle with earth. This information is given by Richard Puchalsky in his discussion of the novel at <http://groups.google.com/group/rec.arts.books/msg/545cf64d4de845ba>, and Cairns Craig writes, also in the context of this particular work, that "the archetypal elements of life – earth, air, fire and water – provide much of symbolic development of Banks's writing" (2002: 38). Although I have not been able to find another mention of the elements theory as specifically applied in A Song of Stone, the symbolism of the four elements is rather manifest in the construction of the characters and places. For an in-depth discussion see Pisarska 2012a: 282, note 6.

7   The castle has retained its focal position, even in the changing historical and social circumstances. By reason of its status as an aristocratic residence, it was the pivot of culture and refinement, and the place of gatherings of the noble society. With time it became increasingly removed from social focus, as its inhabitants grew alienated from their sphere by the introduction of baseness and perversity into their life. Socially peripheral, however, the castle remains the centre of Abel and Morgan's private world. Along with the lieutenant's takeover, it loses its exclusiveness and intimate quality and becomes again the centre of defence and communal existence, one integral place in the all-

disinherited of the past, belong to the earthly order in which all things have their end, and where time is a destroyer, not a preserver. Their presence in the castle disturbs its eternal pattern, the old stones seem somehow "lessened, brought down, reduced to something expressible in only time and matter" (123), and thus exposed to the cataclysm ravaging the land. The earthly pattern of living and dying insidiously replaces the castle's being forever and thus undermines the basis of Abel's own existence.[8]

The lieutenant's presence in the aristocratic nest is thus a subversion in social terms and a breach of the internal – viz. *eternal* – principles of this space, a desecration best represented by the officer's feasting on a table covered by a flag with the family's coat of arms. The offensive sight, however, makes Abel go back to another desecration of the flag which took place several years before, when he spilt his semen onto its embroidered coat of arms after an incestuous intercourse with Morgan. The memory of the faded unicorn on which Morgan fell asleep at the time emphasizes not only the post-apocalyptic disruption of the castle's symbolism, in which Abel replaces Arthur as Morgan's mate. It also stresses the contamination of innocence between the two siblings and the transgression of the code of propriety observed by their own caste. Thus,

---

consuming chaos. By its permanence and illusory sturdiness, the castle attracts not only the weary soldiers but also refugees seeking sanctuary. Paradoxically, in the world forsaken by God the castle begins to play a similar role to that of the nearby cathedral, which was destroyed by heavy guns several months before (82).

8   Therefore the castle, with its long line of inhabitants, constitutes existing evidence of the transition stage between what Frank Kermode calls earthly time (*nunc movens*), with its beginning and end, and eternity (*nunc stans*) with its "perfect possession of endless life" (1967: 71), i.e. the aevum. According to Kermode, the concept of aevum, which originally referred to the position of angels in Christian thought, completes the once absolute distinction between time and eternity by introducing the third order used in relation to the cycle of life and generation to which the human species is subject, and which is the only form of eternity given to man. "The concept of aevum," writes Kermode, "provides a way of talking about this unusual variety of duration – neither temporal nor eternal, but, as Aquinas said, participating in both the temporal and eternal. It does not abolish time or spatialize it; it co-exists with time, and is a mode in which things can be perpetual without being eternal" (72). For the complete discussion see Kermode 1967: 67-89.

the castle turns out to have been the site of transgression much earlier, effected, however, by its noble inhabitants. From this perspective, the seemingly different characters mirror one another, as they reveal equally destructive transgressive potential: the lieutenant poses a threat to the sanctified social order of old, whereas Abel and Morgan represent the moral corruption eating it from inside, the collision of oppositional semiotic orders being invariably spatialized with reference to the castle. The same interdependence is noted by David B. Livingstone in his review of the novel:

> Abel is, he leads us to believe, a paragon of civility and virtue – dignified, refined, almost absurdly well-spoken, a lover of art and culture, a last vestige of order and decency in a world gone mad. But Abel, we soon learn, doth protest too much; he and the strangely-silent Morgan may have more in common with the barbarism that menaces them than they realize, or would care to admit. For every manifestation of violence and ugliness that erupts around them, there seems to be an eruption of a corresponding internal sickness and spiritual rot. Abel may in fact be a man of his times, with all the taint that that entails, in spite of his professions to the contrary, and it is these spiritual malignancies which may have set the cataclysm around him in motion, and which may completely destroy him. (1998)

Consequently, the world of the past appears in many respects as contaminated and transgressive as the world of the present. The degenerate incestuous practices of the two aristocrats are the most extreme example of the moral corruption ravaging the castle long before the war; however, they are not the only one. Abel and Morgan were witnesses to the hostility between their mother and father and they were forced to take sides in domestic conflicts. The parents' incompatible characters and different expectations resulted in their extramarital liaisons, disruption of family life, and the siblings' separation. Moreover, the world of the past saw the collapse of religion and suffered from the lack of regenerative contact with God.[9] The only faith in Abel's childhood was "the true faith of immaculate hygiene" (51) inculcated into him by his mother as a sign of their aristocratic superiority over commoners. This fanatical cleanness, however, produced an adverse reaction and as a thing to be opposed it

---

9   In the last moments of his life Abel recalls the day when the castle chapel was excised on the order of his father and how he and little Morgan stood on the altar looking out at the countryside through the hole left after the "stained, dogmatic stillness" (278) of the chapel's great rosette.

only led to the perversion of the son's natural instincts and his growing fascination with filth and debasement.

As a result, Abel's perception is mediated by a combination of his class bias and his conviction of being outside conventional morality. He therefore contests the symbolic system of the public semiosphere while upholding another one, which transgresses the former's norms. Paradoxically, what his mother tried to achieve through her insistence on cleanness, Abel later executes through debasement. Degradation in sex of himself and his partner, accomplished by means of all sorts of perversity within the confines of their private world becomes a means of the lovers' elevation and distinction from the "cosy ordinariness" and "unthinkably smug normality" of intercourse between other couples:

> I have decided, however coldly, that for any of this life, this passing thought of mind, this wisp of purpose in all the surrounding, universal chaos to have value, to be worth anything at all I – we – must evade such mundane pursuits and set ourselves apart as much in the staging of that customary act as in our dress, habitation, speech or subsidiary manners. Thus have I degraded both of us in order to set us equally as far apart from the lowly as my imagination can devise, hoping – by these indiscretions – to make us both discrete. (72)

The new revolutionary order brought to the castle by the lieutenant may, at least initially, offer a promise of renewal, purging the deathly decadence of Abel's world with the purifying power of the new fiery mistress. Despite their apparent brutalization, the lieutenant and her men follow certain basic principles and retain some vestigial morality in the immoral post-apocalyptic world. The leader is loyal to her soldiers, and vice versa, and shows genuine interest in the well-being of the castle servants (unlike Abel, who does not even know the surname of his lifelong retainer, Arthur, to put it on the old man's tombstone). Loot displays a great propensity for action, which is manifest in the sortie against the enemy group threatening the castle with bombardment. Moreover, despite their crudeness, the lieutenant and her men seem to possess a clear sense of justice, punishing the crimes against the poor and the weak.[10] In the new times, when energy, the ability to fight, clear aims, and occasional ruthlessness are necessary to "make a more lenient re-

---

10   It happens, for example, in the case of the man who stole milk from the orphanage whose charges had been crucified on telegraph poles.

gime easier to maintain" (84), the lieutenant proves a better leader and defender than the passive and decadent aristocrat seeking the refuge of his mind.

However, the diseased influence of the old order proves in the end more powerful than the energy of the apocalyptic change represented by Loot, as the plebeian lieutenant and her minions gradually succumb to the lure of ancien régime, and instead of a revolution we have only a further affirmation of the previous decay. The regenerative fire, which could have burnt out the moral malaise and the spiritual lifelessness of the degenerate line, turns into a senseless desire for the power which at once thrives on and underpins the existing decadence. By the same token, the lieutenant's lust for Morgan remains unproductive and the infertile incest between the siblings is replaced by an equally sterile lesbian attraction. The newcomers, therefore, become heirs to the old corruption, and the malady is allowed to perpetuate and feed on the overwhelming barbarity of the new times, which finds its confirmation in the dreary carnival of the victory feast.

All possible boundaries are transgressed that night, all relationships subverted and hierarchies disrupted among the general devastation effected by the drunken rabble. Dressed in the evening dresses and other formal attire of Abel's ancestors, the mob reflects in a distorting mirror the colourful participants of the balls and parties held in the room in the past. The victory is celebrated through succumbing to sensual pleasures and the release of all moral restraints: the guests eat and drink in excess, copulate by the walls, and wreak havoc on the castle's collections like a troop of monkeys only dressed as humans. The scene of general mayhem and grotesqueness is also representative of the irrevocable disintegration of social relationships based on tradition and determined by birth. The death of the old world, so far preserved meticulously within the castle walls, finds its gloomy reflection in the fate of the old wood-brown globe depicting the ancient world, which is removed by the soldiers from its stand and kicked about in the ballroom.

Among the carnivalesque (dis)order, the lieutenant appears dressed in Abel's suit with Morgan at her side, who without demur lets herself be led to the dance floor by the newly established lord of the castle. Meanwhile, Abel's role is expanded from that of waiter to that of pianist providing entertainment to the frolicking bunch. Eventually, like a carnival king turned clown, he is dethroned and subjected to ridicule and humiliation at the hands of the jeering crowd: a helmet is thrust upon his head, and he is dropped down into the well, sitting in the bucket. The loss of distinctive traits by Abel and Loot, and their adoption of each other's characteristics bring the characters' eventual downfall and the disintegration of the space they both want to retain or make their own – the castle. Just as the lieutenant lays her parvenu claims to Abel's ancient heritage, gradually dispossessing him of everything he owns and becoming a caricature of the lord, the aristocrat also abandons his pacifist stance, so out of place in a time of war, and finally resorts to violence, contributing to the lieutenant's death in the mill. His newly-acquired role registers with him, and he calls himself "one the lieutenant would be proud of, one like her, a murderer now, like her filmy spirit, like a wraith returned, [. . .] one become soldier" (257). The transgression of his natural way makes Abel uncertain of his own identity, with the nagging question popping up in his mind, "Did I kill her by being different, or the same?" (260), which may point as much to his own immersion in the murderous new reality as to the lieutenant's "aristocratic" corruption.

Instead of the eternal cycle bringing chaos, resulting in a change of beliefs and renewal of the entire civilization, as Yeats once postulated,[11] the war apocalypse in *A Song of Stone* involves only the escalation of barbarity, which brings death to the last remnants of beauty found among the general ruin and causes further degeneration of the world. With the destruction of the castle and the treasure of human thought within it, the eternity of Morgan and Abel's line ceases to exist, but the world of the dying parents cannot be saved by their progeny. The relationship of Abel and Morgan has brought their line to a halt, as by reason of its degenerate nature it could bear only degenerate fruit.[12] "Ro-

---

11   "Love war because of its horror, that belief may be changed, civilization renewed" (qtd. in Forster 2003: 630).

12   Their sex was deprived of procreation and their decadence bred nothing but death, which Abel admits in his last hours by recalling the moment when Morgan presumably bore a stillborn child: "And you, my dear, you created our most fitting statement [. . .] by that one bloating of your own, when you gave birth to death" (276). Similarly, Morgan's same-sex intimacy with the lieutenant must remain sterile, and like previously such love can articulate only another "still utterance" (276).

mance, or our belief in it, is our genuine undoing" (279), goes a dour comment of the dying Abel, which underscores the subversion of the romantic pattern of life-death-regeneration in the novel. The only life after death available to him and his drowned sister is that of the decaying matter which serves as humus to other living species – "productive death" which swells inside "dead beasts" (276).

Therefore the correspondence that Abel suggests between his own suffering and Christ's sacrifice, while awaiting his execution at the hands of the lieutenant's gang, sounds hollow if not absurd. Both his life and death are meaningless; his enforced and ineffective heroics have saved nobody and nothing, and he will leave no heritage behind, only "dust, particle and wave-form" (279). His body stretched on the muzzle of the cannon called the Lieutenant's Prick is a mockery of Jesus' crucifixion, and it is only an empty sign in a world from which religion is banished and in which there can be no resurrection – the truth whose dreadful metaphor is the cannon replacing the cross. And Abel himself is aware of the emptiness of his comparisons, which have no grounding in spiritual life, as he sneers at ancient beliefs in life after death and different visions of paradise, which used to give comfort and strength to those awaiting their end.

In his study of post-apocalypse, James Berger claims: "The apocalyptic text announces and describes the end of the world, but then the text does not end, nor does the world represented in the text, and neither does the world itself" (1999: 27-8). But the world of *A Song of Stone* and the very text do perish in its narrator's private apocalypse. The present tense in Abel's mouth gains dramatic tension, the words are uttered nervously and impatiently, and the allusions follow one another in the last tumultuous affirmation of the retreating world, as if in anticipation of its inevitable end:

Let me die, let me go; I've said my piece, refused to make it, and now – is that the dawn? Is this some sleep, or do I dream, or can I now hear reveille and the bugle's closing call? – I face my future, turn my back on a lifetime's desolation and on these dumb persecutors and am duly raised, brought up again, elevated glorious and triumphant to skies the colour of blood and roses, sneer at the dice that tumble (yes, yes; die! Die! Iacta est alea, we who are about to die despise you), laugh at cheers that rise, buoying me, and with that salute my end. (280)

The text has ended. There is nothing more to be said.

5.2. From Virtual Reality to the Waste Land: Public Apocalypse and Post-traumatic Syndrome in *Complicity*

"It's a wasteland. My kingdom is gone" (1994: 261), observes Cameron Colley, the protagonist of *Complicity*, when he discovers that deprived of his masterly guidance, the realm he painstakingly created in a computer game has been overrun by bandits and destroyed beyond hope or redemption. With this wistful comment he unconsciously voices his own condition in the world he has come to inhabit. Cameron lives in the aftermath of Thatcher's government, which completely changed the socio-economic realities of Great Britain and caused the destruction of the old way of life. The game *Despot*, played by his character, serves as a metaphor of the social policy and aggressive capitalism promoted by the Conservative governments of the day, in which Cameron has also had his role. Therefore the failure of the character's actions in virtual reality is directly translatable into his bankruptcy in the real world, turning the latter into the post-apocalyptic wasteland of human hopes and endeavours.

In terms of plot, *Complicity* follows the formula of a thriller whose protagonist, Cameron Colley, a journalist from an Edinburgh-based newspaper *The Caledonian*, gets wind of a scandal among the upper echelons of British politics.[13] In the course of his investigation, he becomes unconsciously implicated in a series of psychopathic murders and assaults which appear to have been encouraged by his militant article about Tory policy. In the article he proposed certain extreme steps and measures which should be taken against venal MPs, conservative judges, and aggressive capitalists. And now the punishment is being duly administered by someone who acts like the suggested Real Avenger or Radical Equalizer, and lets the corrupt ones taste "their own medicine" (108).[14]

---

13   See Horsley 2005: 185-8 and 2009: 226-7. Cf. Pisarska 2008a: 149-58.

14   The interlacing of the individual and collective perspectives within the post-apocalyptic world of *Complicity* is underscored by the duality of the novel's narrative voice. The reader is presented with two subjective points of view, which alternate and ultimately contribute to the emergence of a unified narrative whole. Most of the novel is narrated by Cameron Colley, his commentary delivered in the present tense for describing both past and present events. The scenes of crimes committed by Andy are presented from the perspective of the

Apocalyptic Worlds 269

Cameron must confront an extremely eligible opponent, his best friend, Andy Gould, a veteran of the Falklands War, disillusioned with the outcome of Thatcherite reforms and the general moral decay of their times. As both a designer of the conspiracy tracked by Cameron (the project ARES) and a serial killer with a purpose, Andy piles insurmountable obstacles in Cameron's way and the latter, manipulated by his sinister double, has to prove his innocence and protect Andy's prospective victims.

On a deeper level, though, *Complicity* presents "personal traumas within a firmly established historical context" (Horsley 2005: 186), as Cameron and Andy live in the aftermath of their private apocalypse: as adolescents, they were assaulted by a paedophile. The man raped Andy, for which the boys clubbed the abuser to death with a branch and threw his body into a forgotten tunnel. Accomplices in the murder, they were forever tied to one another by the terrible secret, becoming victims and criminals at the same time. The traumatic experience, whose memory Cameron has suppressed but which is still vivid in the memory of the abused Andy, has left its indelible mark on the psychological landscape of both men. Their predicament calls to mind Berger's observation about the link between trauma and apocalypse:

> Events took place, catastrophic and defining in political, physical, and moral senses – but they will not be or cannot be remembered or represented. Events occurred and seem to leave no trace – and yet the entire landscape is an immaculate tombstone bearing a misleading epitaph. The landscape must be read. It is a sign, or rather a symptom. Trauma is the psychoanalytic form of apocalypse, its temporal inversion. Trauma produces symptoms in its wake, after the event, and we reconstruct trauma by interpreting its symptoms, reading back in time. [. . .] Both apocalypse and

---

offender, who addresses himself as "you," which evokes a disquieting feeling of a split personality. The ongoing alternation of I-you passages only emphasizes the relationship existing between the two friends: Cameron and Andy function as two sides of the same coin – after all, the "I" and the "you" ultimately make up the "we" of the society. Whereas Cameron writes in protest against the mendacious and corrupt ruling class and their ferocious capitalist policy, Andy implements his theories and purges the two of depravity in the spectacles of bloodshed and destruction (Craig 2002: 53). This divided nature of the narrator into a disillusioned loquacious journalist and the shadowy and violent Equalizer adds considerably to the reader's insecurity about the identity of the criminal and underscores the novel's pervading theme of our shared guilt in society's crimes.

trauma present the most difficult questions of what happened "before," and what is the situation "after." The apocalyptic-historical-traumatic event becomes a crux or pivot that forces a retelling and revaluing of all events that lead up to it and all that follow. (1999: 48)

The above passage summarizes both the historical trauma of post-Thatcherite society and the personal trauma of the two friends, as in both cases the nature of the catastrophe can only be determined by sifting and examining the "debris" the cataclysm left in its wake. The post-apocalyptic landscape which "must be read" in *Complicity* is as much national as it is individual, and its disintegrating influence renders impossible any form of creative modelling of space. Just as the outside world of aggression, consumerism, and loveless dissipation invades and infects the character's private world (Cameron), the character's personal wasteland is projected violently onto the outside semiosphere (Andy), turning the latter into the mirror image of the shattered innerscape.

T. S. Eliot's seminal work *The Waste Land*, recalled in the opening passage of this analysis, is far from being a mere random quote, as it offers a major reference through which we can read the vacuum of contemporary life presented in Banks's novel (Craig 2002: 73). The humanity from Eliot's poem, caught in the ennui of repetitive activities and loveless and unproductive relationships, is subject to death-in-life (cf. Brooks 1993: 130), while their world, deprived of the regenerative power of myth and religion, undergoes a progressive disintegration.[15] Likewise, the capitalist society of the early 1990s depicted by Banks in *Complicity* suffers from moral and spiritual degeneracy, being driven by material pursuits and infertile sexual lust. The world mediated by late capitalist ideology is shown as irredeemably infected with corruption and aggression, from which there is no escape, and the new order – built on the ruins of the bygone world – offers no hope of true fulfilment or regeneration.

The world depicted in Eliot's *The Waste Land* is the survivor of the Great War and a disillusioned witness to the atrocities and senseless death that humankind inflicted on itself in what has long been considered one of the most devastating events in history. Similarly, the country pictured in *Complicity* is an heir of the prolonged period of hostility and

---

15   For a comprehensive study of Eliot's *The Waste Land* see Gruszewska 1996: 95-148.

panicky fears associated with another war, the Cold War, whose deadly reminder can be noticed in the Trident nuclear submarines stationed in the Faslane Naval Base in Scotland's Gare Loch. Cameron, who watches the passage of one such menacing beauty in the first chapter of the novel, perceives the presence of the lethal weapon amidst the Scottish landscape in terms of infestation, as the ship appears to him "the biggest, blackest slug in all the world" (11). The unwanted nuclear parasite is part of the UK's Independent Deterrent, whose maintenance after the fall of communism seems to Cameron "pointless" and "even more of a waste" (15). However, it is not only the misuse of public money that Colley seems to have in mind.

The nuclear arsenal, epitomized in the passage of the Vanguard, represents a constant possibility of violence among the nations, which keeps the entire world in the grip of terror and thwarts its regeneration. Therefore the Vanguard's "grossly phallic shape" (12) has nothing to do with life and reproduction – it is able to "incinerate a few tens of millions of Russian men, women and children" (15), which makes Cameron liken the ship to a "potentially city-fucking, country-fucking, planet-fucking prick sliding up between the thighs of the loch" (16). The use of sexual imagery in this context stresses the violent quality of the submarine. On the one hand, its passage is like a violation of the countryside, and Cameron notices that it looks too big to fit through the narrows into the uterus of the lake (needless to mention its environmentally "unfriendly" radioactive warheads). On the other hand, filled with the Navy seamen (a clear pun on "semen," ventured by Cameron), it can breed nothing but death and violence.

Interestingly, in the world of *Complicity*, military violence is continually mentioned in the context of the economic changes that swept Britain and the Western world in the 1980s, which links the question of war with the devastation wreaked by late capitalism. Cameron, for instance, can see a connection between the arms build-up during the 1980s, whose part is also the Vanguard, and the collapse of the Soviet Union, gone bankrupt under the pressure of military competition, which allowed Western businesses to enter "those enticing Eastern markets [which] opened juicily up" (15). As a result, once hostile cultures have been brought into dialogue, in which the communist semiosphere has been breached and restructured by the social and economic ideologies mediating the Western outlook. The Cold War, therefore, is perceived by Cameron as nothing short of a "trade" war (cf. Brooks 1993: 136 on war in *The Waste Land*), which revealed the economic supremacy of the United States and its allies. As such, it is yet another facet of the capitalist system, which has been laying waste his own country for over a decade.

Ironically, the era of Thatcher's reforms is described in *Complicity* as a kind of war as well. While talking about his own involvement in the policy of the period, Andy calls himself "a loyal trooper in the children's crusade to recover the lost citadel of British economic power" (141), which underscores not only his and the society's initial faith in Thatcherism but also the potential of the new ideology to devour its own believers. At the same time, the Thatcherist era is connected with its own military conflict, the Falklands War, which also forms a part of the traumatic socio-political tapestry of modern Britain in *Complicity*. Andy, who took part in the hostilities, remembers them as a slaughter-house brought about by the inefficiency of the officers but also as an individual and national tragedy out of which the Conservative government made its political capital. The patriotic sentiment which surged across the country at war – the "squaddie culture" (212), so criticized by Andy – helped to recapture "Maggie's surrendered popularity" (141) after her first term in office, which in turn enabled the Conservatives to hold power and pursue their policy on the home front for another eight years.

The country seen by the characters is a site of ruin left in the wake of the "catastrophe" effected by the Tory policy, which changed the industrial complexion of the country. Supplanting the heavy industry with more profitable branches of the tertiary and quaternary sectors, it consequently triggered an increase in unemployment and social pathologies in the impoverished districts. The wasteland brought about by the Conservative governments is thus described by Andy:

> Here we are and we've had our experiment; there's been one party, one dominant idea, one fully followed plan, one strong leader – and her grey shadow – and it's all turned to shit and ashes. Industrial base cut so close to the bone the marrow's leaking out, the old vaguely socialist inefficiencies replaced with more rabid capitalist ones, power centralized, corruption institutionalized, and a generation created which'll never have any skills beyond opening a car with a coat hanger and knowing which solvents give

you the best buzz with a plastic bag over your head before you throw up or pass out. (141)[16]

Ironically, the economic radicalism of the country's political centre, which produced the landscape of waste and degradation, was awaited by Andy and others as "a breath of clean new air" and "a shock to the system" (140-1), able to revive the country incapacitated by the post-war consensus in British politics. However, instead of the renewal, "that promise, trimmed-down fitness" (140), incarnated in the idea of Thatcherism, has turned the old world into a graveyard overwritten with the order of the New Right. It resulted in the collapse of tradition and the disruption of communal life, leading to the rise of consumer society, in which people are driven by selfishness and greed, where no one cares for another, and where the rich and empowered commit acts of barbarism against the poor and the weak, all this in compliance with the ideology promoted by the political centre.

At one point, Cameron observes jokingly: "I am surrounded by selfish bastards I thought were my friends" (187). The remark, meant as a playful criticism directed at Andy and his other friend William Sorrell, who both voted Tory, comes to acquire sad undertones with regard to their circle. The novel continually asserts that the macrocosm of Anglo-American capitalism with its self-aggrandizing philosophy and mercantile values is reflected in the microcosm of the social framework in which Cameron functions. The four friends: William, his wife, Yvonne, Andy, and Cameron are all in their own ways complicit in the aggressive mechanisms of the new era and their destructive social consequences. The world they inhabit is a blighted artifice of their collective mediation, their joint enterprise, which is either an emanation of their personal hopes and desires, or the golden calf which they criticize but whose temptations they cannot resist.

The apparent normality of the new system, which they have all helped to fashion each for his or her own reasons, and which has, after all, allowed them to become successful in their respective professions, in fact conceals omnipresent corruption and decay, defying any rational

---

16   In the interview by Richard Tallaron, Banks says of *Complicity*: "If that book reeks of hatred for the Tories, and the odious, corruption-saturated, greed-obsessed culture they have brought to fruition in these isles over the last one and a half decades then it has not all been in vain . . ." (1996: 143-4).

approach: "The point is there is no feasible excuse for what we've done, for what we have made of ourselves. We have chosen to put profits before people, money before morality, dividends before decency, fanaticism before fairness, and our own trivial comforts before the unspeakable agonies of others" (301).[17] Andy's disillusioned words point to the fact that the inhuman mechanisms of the new era cannot be explained in terms of traditional ethics, as the latter no longer applies in a world in which individual ambition and economic pursuits have become a universal law. The ruling principle of the new order, in which one man's selfish drive is pitted against another man's greed and folly, naturally presupposes fierce competition and the survival of the fittest. The ideology of capitalism is best verbalized by its prominent representative William, who perceives the prehistoric hunt for mammoths and contemporary hunt for money in terms of evolution. In his view, he who is the most successful stands at the top of the food chain, and the cooperation between humans allows their leader to exercise better control over the group and use the subjects' work for his own benefit (220), which underscores the barbarity of the capitalist system and the modern degradation of humanity to its primitive evolutionary scheme (cf. Craig 2002: 75).

In the climate of money pursuit and self-gratification, human relationships remain hollow. The world cannot be redeemed by love or sacrifice because it is an emotional wasteland where people are merely consumers motivated by self-interest and comfort, trading such values as love, friendship, and fidelity for a sense of personal satisfaction and profit. Even if higher feelings do appear, like Cameron's love for Yvonne, they are unwelcome and thus must be suppressed, undergoing a steady dissipation among appearances and erotic games which undermine their value. Similarly to Eliot's *The Waste Land*, where the landscape of human relationships remains barren, sterility also becomes an affliction of the society depicted by Banks (cf. Craig 2002: 74). Neither Yvonne's marriage with William nor her clandestine affair with Cameron bring the parties involved genuine happiness or produce offspring,

---

17   Andy's words echo Lee Horsley's comment on a "rift in the familiar order of things," with which the noir protagonist is frequently confronted, "a recognition that apparent normality is actually the antithesis of what it seems to be: it is brutal rather than benign, dehumanized not civilized" (2009: 11).

who could be testimony to the productivity of the parents' sexual lust. Just like emotions, the erotic sphere also undergoes degeneration, providing space for a subversion of natural functions. Sex is not a responsibility and a means of regeneration but a toy to be used for idle entertainment and fulfilling violent fantasies.

Ironically, in the capitalist reality of modern Britain, the only permanence and meaning can be found in commercial relationships; therefore, they increasingly replace emotional attachment between people. The Sorrels, who enjoy their comfortable life of successful business people, treat their marriage as yet another profitable business contract, remaining an item "even if [they] do stray now and again" (217). However, marital licence has its boundaries, and every breach of contract entails relevant sanctions, which Yvonne vindictively underlines: "[I]f he ever gave me AIDS I'd give him a Colombian necktie" (217). William, on the other hand, demands the custody of the Mercedes in case Yvonne should leave him, and this is the only custody possible because in their relationship, discussed in terms of terminal illness and barbaric execution methods, there can be no children to nurture. The commercial nature of the Sorrels' marriage comes to light towards the end of the novel when Andy imparts to Cameron William's plans of "trading in Yvonne for a more up-market, user-friendly model, preferably one with her own title and a daddy in serious big business or the government" (303). But the husband's commodification of his wife only mirrors Yvonne's own commodification of her journo lover. When Cameron reveals to her the story of his unsuccessful attempt to bed Andy's sister, Clare, Yvonne ruthlessly jokes like a good capitalist employer: "I could have given you a reference, Cameron" (207).

Instead of producing children, the adults of *Complicity* behave like children, escaping from adult responsibility into the barren fantasy world offered by the products of globalized capitalism. "When in doubt, shop" (218), says Yvonne at one point, and the same motto can be attributed to her journo lover. Cameron, always so vocal about his Labour sympathies, retreats into the world of material comforts, where feeding one's senses with all sorts of stimulants is the basic principle, and where substances replace God and offer an epiphany (47). By the same token, he escapes into the world of computer games whose rules mirror those shaping the reality of the 1980s and early 1990s, i.e. violence and nuclear warfare in *Xerium*, or aggressive capitalism and strong leadership in *Despot*. Immersed in virtual reality, he throws icons "about [his] empire like thunderbolts" (55), changing the geographical and industrial landscape as he sees fit. He resorts to bloody military campaigns, executions, and religious worship of himself in order to reinforce his hegemony and drugs his adversaries into obedience, which, ironically, reflects his own narcotic immersion in the ethos of Thatcherism and the consumerist culture of the day.

Cameron's recourse to various chemicals in controlling his emotional balance as well as his escapist activities and childlike dependence on the products of the new era emphasizes the character's inner disturbance, which translates into the disorderly and temporary nature of the space of his home. Cameron's flat is cluttered with papers, empty cigarette packets, and hi-tech electronic gadgets, which reflects the invasion of the outside world into his private life. The activities he pursues within the space of home – playing computer games all night, taking drugs, smoking cigarettes, eating junk food and washing it down with alcohol – which should be one of peace and regeneration, stress the character's unhealthy and ruinous lifestyle and underscore the progressing devastation of his internal space. The only mail he receives is either advertising or bills, with no personal correspondence, which would speak of human bonds. There is a heap of clean laundry on the bed, which Colley has no intention of removing, because it gives him a feeling that there is someone with him, a thought he finds "comforting and sad at the same time" (29), which highlights his loneliness as a person.

In the face of the universal decay of human relationships and moral integrity, even the Highlands, the place of traditional Scottishness and communal spirit, have lost their regenerative power, as if stricken by the same malaise as the rest of the country. In the party organized by Andy, which gathers together the locals and the travellers, Cameron can see only xenophobic hostility and divides between some clean-shaven short-haired local lads and New Age hippie tourists, which makes him remark sourly that the party "emulsifies rather than combines" (144). Moreover, the Highlanders even behave disrespectfully and violently towards themselves. This is proved by the attitude of Howie, who entertains the guests with stories of how he battered his wife before she escaped to one of the women's refuges. Tradition, therefore, assumes the form of prejudice, either against the strangers or women, while people's private lives succumb to the (inter)national dynamics of power and submission. Similarly, the more remote regions of Scotland in *Complicity* serve as yet another representation of the bygone world crumbling under the unstoppable advance of globalized capitalism. It is especially conspicuous in the case of Eilean Dubh, the dark isle, comprising mostly the family burial ground, which becomes William's official legacy. The gravestones, coming from various epochs and belonging to people of different age and social status, form an exclusive domain of death which cannot be defeated by the word of God, because his chapel, deprived of divine mystery and turned into a tourist attraction, lies in ruins. Its symbolical opening to heaven is substituted by its very literal opening to the sky, as the building has no roof and thus also lacks the cross which must have once towered over the place. Now instead of the cross, the symbol of Christ's death and resurrection, and the redemption of mankind, there is William standing on the chapel's ruined wall and looking over the place through his binoculars (283). The house of God has become a house of man, the revealed faith has been supplanted by the false religion of greed and egoism whose advocate is the island's new owner.

The macabre clash between the old funeral tradition and William's mercantile world-picture is conveyed in his conversation with Cameron and Andy, when he reveals that he used to run boat trips from the hotel to the island, which resulted in a fracas between the funeral party and the tourists who were having a barbecue. The collapse of traditional values in the face of profit-making, which wipes out not only the sense of the communal and the sacred but even the terror of death, is best encapsulated in Cameron's comment delivered in an imitation of Southern American English:

> 'Kinda morbid for a graveyard, isn't it, Bill, old buddy? Couldn't ya kinda liven it up a bit, know what I mean? A few neon gravestones, talking holograms of the departed, and – hey – let's not forget a flower concession stand featuring tasteful plastic blooms. A ghost-train ride for the youngsters; necro-burgers made with *real dead meat* in coffin-shaped polystyrene packs; high-speedboat trips in the funeral barge used in *Don't Look Now*, the movie.' (280)

The same retreat of the old order and the invasion of the new globalized worldview take place in language, which fails as a medium of denoting reality (Craig 2002: 69-70). Just as the landscape after Thatcherite reforms was appropriated by new profitable US-based businesses (e.g. the establishment of the Silicon Glen in Scotland as a reflection of the Silicon Valley in California), traditional Scottish names also undergo "readjustment" to linguistic norms under the influence of standardized British and American English. The desemantization of space is metaphorically underscored by a game played by Frank Soare, Colley's friend from *The Caledonian*, who enjoys working with his computer spell-check on the names of places in Scotland. In the course of such orthographical "check-up," Colonsay becomes Colonic, Carnoustie – Carousing, Kirkton of Bourtie – Kickoff of Blurted, and Milltown of Towie – Molten of Toil, their real meanings and idiosyncrasies lost to the levelling power of official speech (cf. Todd 1996: 153).

The drive to standardization, which marks the subjection of all semiotic codes to the hegemony of the semiotic centre, begins to affect the semiotic peripheries and their particular thought patterns. Cameron himself, driving past the signs announcing the upcoming Euro-summit, comments with annoyance on his reconstruction of reality in accordance with the mediating system of "normative" language: "I don't know how they've done it but the typography on the signs makes *me* want to pronounce the word Edin-burg, and I *live* in the place, for God's sake" (175). The ultimate proof of how language has ceased to signify in the new reality of changes and improvements is provided by the sign "Strome Ferry – no ferry" near Andy's hotel, which reveals the paradox of the place's traditional name when the new road has made the ferry transport obsolete (Craig 2002: 70). Paradoxically, Cameron's own language suffers from a similar overuse of the new at the expense of the old, as he insistently resorts to the present tense narration while describing both present and past events. The present tense narrative, which emphasizes the character's immersion in the ethos of Thatcherism and the consumer culture of the day, is first and foremost Cameron's method for detaching himself from a childhood catastrophe – the murder committed by Andy and himself.

According to Craig, Colley's first-person account serves a double purpose: "to preserve the purity of the past by not allowing it to be seen through the experience of adulthood, and a denial that childhood events can still be present in the shaping of adult consciousness" (2002: 58). It is especially noticeable in Colley's perception of the space of his childhood, linked in his mind with the town of Strathspeld: he insistently tries to keep its memory idyllic through self-imposed selectivity. Already in the first chapter, Cameron reveals this evasive attitude when a dream takes him to that fateful summer: "Running through the woods, I'm 13 years old and while I'm running I'm also looking at myself from outside [. . .] *I've been here many times before and I know how to escape from it*" (22, emphasis added). The same situation takes place during Colley's visit to Andy's hotel, when insidious drunken dreams make him return to the day of the assault and "the running-through-the-woods dream" but he "*get[s] away from it*" (143, emphasis added). On the next night, the situation repeats itself: "I dream of Strathspeld, and the long summers of my childhood passed in a trance of lazy pleasure, ending with that day, running through the woods (but *I turn away from that memory, the way I've learned to over the years*" (147, emphasis added).

Cameron's avoidance of past events is contrasted with Andy's excellent memory and his constant awareness of the past (see 143).[18] Andy literally lives in the world of the past, materialized in the shape of the old decrepit hotel, which represents its owner's distance from the centre of the modern capitalist semiosphere and its ideology of success, wealth, and consumerism. Andy's position is one on the semiotic periphery, in the geographical, political, and economic sense, while the hotel, open to the corroding power of time and to destructive elemental forces, turns into the metaphor of the past ravaged by the unrelenting present. The sullen landscape and the devastated hotel provide a suitable climate for Andy's "burnt-out, fed-up, pissed-off mood" (138). Andy has been subject to physical and emotional suffering: the rape, a battle wound and the massacre of his soldier mates in the Falklands War, the premature death of his beloved sister as a result of medical negligence, and his own bitter disappointment with the disintegration of the country instead of its rebirth. The accumulation of traumatic experiences has produced a gaping wound and made Andy lead a life of a recluse, "drinking too much, getting wrecked most nights, [. . .] fishing from his dinghy, walking in the

---

18 Even after his winter accident, when he has spent ten minutes in the freezing water without oxygen, Andy seems "as bright and intelligent [. . .] as he'd been before, remembering details from earlier in his childhood and performing above average in the memory tests the doctor gave him" (161), which further emphasizes the incredible resilience of Andy's memory.

hills, and just lying in bed sleeping while the hotel [. . .] crumbles quiet-ly around him" (78).

The retreat of the suffering hero whose land's disease reflects his own physical and spiritual wounds makes Andy resemble the Fisher King from the Arthurian cycles (cf. Craig 2002: 73), who is also the key figure of Eliot's *The Waste Land*. As in the case of his legendary prede-cessor, Andy's "wound" has also caused his impotence. Andy's present life of "not really doing anything" (76) constitutes a depressing antithe-sis of his former active life as a serving soldier, a prosperous business-man, and an intrepid traveller who toured America on a Harley, cruised the Caribbean in a yacht, and went on a trans-Saharan trip. The hotel in the Highlands is like a castle which the Fisher King leaves in order to fish in the nearby loch, and when Cameron calls Andy one day and asks what he has been doing, the latter duly replies: "Nothing much. Bit of fishing" (74).[19] In this case, the groin wound which afflicts the Fisher King assumes a very tangible form, as Andy's "disability" is his own "sterility." Andy's implied sexual attraction to Cameron led to the only sexual act between the friends – the act of masturbation in the grass – and resulted in Andy's semen being carelessly squandered and brushed off Cameron's hand against the leaves and blades of their childhood par-adise (cf. Craig 2002: 73-4). The unproductive desire for Cameron was followed by the violent anal rape, which brought only pain and guilt and has impeded Andy's other relationships. When asked by Cameron about his sex life, Andy's answer – "I lost interest in all that stuff" (75) – em-

---

19   For the explanation of the Fisher King symbolism see *From Ritual to Ro-mance* by Jessie Weston (1920: 107-29). In *The Waste Land* Eliot creates a purely Christian version of the legend in which he combines the figure of the Fisher King with that of his saviour Percival, a Knight of the Round Table who roams the world in search of the Grail (see Gruszewska 1996: 144). The fusion of the king and the knight is also noticeable in Andy Gould, who first takes part in the "children's crusade" of Thatcherism and then, frustrated and defeated, retreats to his forlorn castle in the north. Moreover, the name "An-dy" is an abbreviated form of "Andrew," which means "manly" and which is also the name of the patron saint of Scotland (cf. Mcleod and Freedman 1995). Thus, Andy's impotence (his being "unmanly") may point to the impo-tence of Scotland in the new post-apocalyptic order, which coincides here with the Fisher King symbolism.

phasizes his own sterility and the deathly squalor of the world around him. Freedom from the past and the regeneration of himself and his kingdom is impossible in Andy's case. The character cannot be healed and his world regenerated because the painful past to which his wound is tied cannot be forgotten or put to rights. Being both a victim and a supporter of the ideology of power and exploitation, which he suffered on a personal level through childhood rape and whose different facet he helped to promote on the national level, Andy turns into the Real Avenger from Cameron's article, executing his friend's hollow postulates in the form of violent and semiotically meaningful actions. He keeps score of capitalist transgressions and metes out immediate punishment: "That's like Judgment Day; it never fucking comes. And I want justice *now*" (301). Whereas Cameron continually escapes from the memory of his personal catastrophe into the refuge of the present, Andy transforms the world of the present into the space of his private and universal vengeance, accelerating the end of the sick kingdom instead of its rebirth (cf. Craig 2002: 74). Paradoxically, Andy is the product of the very society he now punishes. Cameron calls Andy the "prince of reprisal, this jealous, vengeful, unforgiving son of our bastard commonwealth of greed" (289), because the latter has developed into menace both through personal hurt and in response to the barbarity and mendacity of the new system of government, which produced despair instead of hope. "[I]n that climate of culpability, that perversion of moral values, nothing, *nothing* I have done has been out of place or out of order or wrong" (301), Andy admits in the end. Blaming his murderous actions on the influence of the outside world, which encourages ruthlessness and aggression, Andy points to a feedback existing between the post-apocalyptic space and his own subjective mediation, which results in madness instead of sanity, in destruction instead of creation.

Therefore, while avenging society's wrongs, Andy picks his victims from the model representatives of the new world of selfishness and greed:

> All of them had all they could ask for in life, but they all wanted more –
> which is okay, I suppose, it's just a failing, you can't kill people for that
> alone – but they all treated people like shit, literally like shit; something
> unpleasant to be disposed of. It was like they'd forgotten their humanity
> and could never find it again, and there was only one way to remind them

of it, and remind all the others like them, and make them feel frightened and vulnerable and powerless, the way they made other people feel all the time. (297)[20]

In the space of post-apocalyptic reconfiguration, in which words increasingly lose their denotative function, Andy makes each murder into a sign, as the nature of the victim's transgression is communicated through the manner of his death. Cairns Craig comments:

> Andy is engaged in bringing language and reality very directly back into contact with each other [. . .]; his victims [. . .] are turned into texts. Thus the editor is not just thrown out of a window, he is "spiked" like a journalist's story; the judge who is lenient to rapists is raped, the doctor who failed to diagnose Clare's illness is dissected and the officer who failed to lead his men effectively is stood on a plinth designed for a war memorial. [. . .] The language which they deform in order to mask their crimes [. . .] returns to take vengeance by transforming them into a language that advertises the truth they have tried to conceal. (2002: 71-2)

By means of graphic violence inflicted on the key representative of the mendacious system, Andy shakes the society out of complacency with the illusion that is Thatcherite Britain. He delivers "a shock to the system" in the same way as he delivers one to the game-obsessed Cameron, who is transferred from the position of an observer and a demigod of virtual reality to the status of a participant in the game that *is* reality. By implicating Cameron in his own violent actions, Andy makes his friend aware of the fact that violence is real and barbarity can be found within the boundaries of civilization.

Through Andy's mediation, Cameron's memory of the apocalyptic events returns to him in the end. However, the recovery of memory about the childhood tragedy is not synonymous with coming to terms with the past. Rather it makes the hero aware of his inability to create his own space of normal life in the present (cf. Craig 2002: 73). On his re-

---

20   Scott McCracken notices that in contrast to Cameron, whose life represents internal disorder but external order, Andy "has apparent internal coherence, but creates external disorder." He commits his crimes "in a state of perfect mental control," but the results of his violence have "all the excessive paraphernalia of body-horror: penetrations, punctures, insides coming out, the drip of the terrified maid's urine on the floor, and the gory details of the victim's death" (1998: 145).

lease from arrest, Cameron watches the crowds in the streets of Edinburgh and realizes his exclusion from their common life:

> [I] know these people don't feel free, I know they're all hurrying along or sitting there worrying about their jobs or their mortgages or being late or an IRA bomb in the nearest litter-bin, but I look at them and feel a terrible sense of loss, because I think I've surrendered all this; the ordinariness of life, the ability just to be part of it and take part in it. I want to hope that I'm being melodramatic and everything will settle back to the way it used to be, before all this ghastliness, but I doubt it. In my guts I feel that, even if everything goes the best it possibly can for me, my life has changed completely and forever. (240)

Instead of peace and regeneration, the retrieved memory brings also the character's recognition of the unspeakable atrocities and devastation which prove his world unredeemable. Like the "ferryman" or the "boatman," Andy takes Cameron to the gun battery off Cramond, which for the journalist turns into a trip down to his personal inferno. Knocked unconscious by the "angel of death," Cameron is forced to return to the memory of "the man-made earthly black hell" (289) in Iraq during the first war of the Desert Storm campaign, where he was sent as a war correspondent eighteen months before. The "old devil *meme*" (201), activated by the agent of the past, replays in Cameron's head the picture of the land shattered by explosions and consumed by fire, in which the blood of the earth burns in vain in bombed oil wells and the blood of men is shed without mercy. The apocalyptic sight of the destroyed landscape and the macabre evidence of the civilian slaughter encountered by Cameron on the Basra Road make the words die on his lips and the language, which is his journalistic tool, fails as a medium of grasping and shaping reality, which eludes all mediation. The witness is incapable of articulating his horror in any other way but silence:

> I did have my chance, it was put right there in front of me practically screaming at me to *fucking write something* – I couldn't do it; couldn't hack it as a hack; I just stood there, awestruck, horrorstruck, absorbing the ghastly force of it with my inadequate and unprepared *private* humanity, not my public professional persona, not my skill, not the face I had laboured to prepare to face the sea of faces that is the world.
>
> And so I was humbled, scaled, down-sized. [. . .] I was reduced to a numb, dumb realization of our unboundedly resourceful talent for bloody hatred and mad waste, but stripped of the means to describe and present that knowledge. (290)

Cameron's recollection of his own inability to put into words the unimaginable destruction and suffering of war seems only ironic when we recall his enthusiasm while being engaged in the virtual atrocities of the game *Xerium*, whose world could be controlled by dropping nukes and riding the mushroom cloud. The one-time cyber-hero, now "humbled, scaled, down-sized" in the face of the horror of bloodshed and waste, is allowed to experience the cold touch of death, proving true Andy's jeering comment that he is not "gung-ho enough" (136) to play the reality game.

The post-apocalyptic space in *Complicity* defies the characters' efforts to create the zones of refuge and make their lives meaningful, or to forward their subjective world-pictures other than by destruction and violence. Instead, the forces of deadly chaos filter into the inner world of man, subjecting his body and mind to the slow but inevitable process of death. Just as Andy is incurably sick in his spirit, Cameron turns out to be incurably sick in his body. At the end of the novel, Colley is diagnosed with lung cancer, a tumour "the size of a tennis ball" (311) in his chest, which is a tangible manifestation of the corruptive and diseased influence of the world he inhabits and inhales with cigarette smoke.[21] The closing paragraphs show Cameron, the fitting hero of the sinister space, sniffing coke and smoking cigarettes. His body already turned post-apocalyptic, he continues his damaging practices to accelerate rather than prevent his end. "What the fuck. Screw the world, bugger reality" (313), asserts the journo laughing under his breath, but he only proves one final time that in the world of sustained degeneration and emotional wasteland, "screwing" brings no life or promise of renewal.

---

21   It is also the ultimate proof of his complicity in society's crimes which produced the cancer that is Andy, which, as Cairns Craig notices, Colley is nursing "like a growth within himself, just as Andy nurses Colley's words within himself as the justification of his own demented actions" (2002: 63). Finally, they are one not only in the mind but in the body as well. These last scenes of the novel are narrated by Cameron, who, like Andy before, addresses himself as "you," further stressing their shared guilt and bringing their alternating voices into a single narrative in an ultimate act of complicity.

5.3. On-Screen Catastrophes and Post-apocalyptic Romances in *Dead Air*

The third and last novel discussed in this chapter, *Dead Air* (2002), presents the reader with the events taking place shortly before and after 11 September 2001, the date which has been commonly recognized as apocalyptic in the history of the modern world. The impact of this day lies not only in the tragic toll of nearly 3,000 deaths, but most of all in the universal feeling of solidarity it provoked around the globe. In their essay entitled "Worlds in Collision," which discusses the cultural and political causes and ramifications of the attacks, Ken Booth and Tim Dunne observe:

> It is curious how a specific date – not a year, but a specific month and a specific day – have almost universally come to define a world historical crisis. The signposts of world affairs in the twentieth century were fixed in particular places: Sarajevo, Munich, Suez, Cuba, Vietnam and the rest. In the case of the attacks on the World Trade Center and the Pentagon it is as if we instantly understood that the meanings of these 'events' were global, beyond locality, an out-of-geography experience. September 11 was a place we all shared. (2000: 1)

Chris Jenks, in his book *Transgression* (2003), applauds the world's response to the tragedy:

> Within a relatively short space of time there was a burgeoning and near global reaction. A violation had occurred, some line had been crossed. There was a growing consensus that a boundary, perhaps even a universal moral boundary, had been overstepped. Just as it was once voiced that there would be no more art or poetry after Auschwitz, September 11th began to slip into the language as a metaphor for irrevocability. Things would never be the same again. People across religions, across nations and across ideologies registered grand transgression. Western politics now sought, strategically, to capitalize on existing alliances and to affirm new ones. The World (more or less) was to be at war with terrorism. Through this transformational cycle the social process moved to completion: the fracture gave rise to repair; the violation generated consolidation; the individual act of deviance summoned up a collective response. (1-2)

And Jill Bennet thus comments on the global reaction – including that of Londoners – in her perceptive essay "The Limits of Empathy and the Global Politics of Belonging:"

Having watched the tragedy unfold from London, before travelling to New York a few days after the attacks, it seemed to me that in some quarters, at least, the impact was felt as profoundly in London as in parts of the United States. If this was, indeed, a global tragedy and an attack on trade, the devastating impact in the financial heart of London – where many had lost friends and colleagues – brought this home. While many commentators would argue that citizens of the United States suffered a kind of "collective trauma," it is also the case that the personal trauma of loss – not directly experienced by most Americans – affected bereaved families in many nations. The economic fallout of the tragedy also had a devastating impact worldwide. The term "national trauma," frequently used by the U.S. media in relation to September 11, is, then, something of a misnomer, insofar as it dramatically understates the reach of the tragedy. (2003: 131-2)

For the protagonist of *Dead Air*, Ken Nott, a DJ in one of London radio stations, September 11 comes to signify, allegedly, a kind of caesura as well, splitting his own and other people's lives into the *before* and the *after*. The acknowledgement of this dual perspective comes in the opening paragraphs of the novel, when the memory of himself being kidnapped one drunken night brings yet another flashback:

All of [it] actually happened not far from here (here where we're starting; here where we're picking up our story precisely because it was like a start and the end of something, a time when everyone knew exactly where they were), all of it probably within sight, if not a stone's throw, of this raised *here*. Maybe; there's no going back to check because the place where we're starting's not there any more. (2009a: 3)

In the passage Ken returns to the fateful wedding party three weeks earlier, which ended up in the guests' watching the horrific scenes of destruction in New York, repeatedly shown by all TV channels. The "raised *here*" is in fact ambiguous as it may refer both to the venue of the reception, i.e. a loft on the eighth floor of the building which was pulled down shortly afterwards, and to the WTC, with nothing left of it but Ground Zero.

The first chapter brings several persistent images of New York and America which foreshadow the terrorist attacks. As a result, the two seemingly distinct realities become superimposed: the London scene functions as a dwarfed reflection of the New York occurrences. The apartment in which the party takes place is said to have been turned into "a big New York style loft" (5), and its owners, Kulwinder and Faye, intend to leave for New York the following day and stay at the Plaza

Hotel in Manhattan. The impending tragedy is further prefigured by the apple with a piece bitten off (an obvious reference to the name "Big Apple" denoting New York), whose gradually browning flesh mirrors the progressing destruction in the heart of the city. The fall of the solitary fruit, which tumbles off the parapet, hits the asphalt and "explode[s] in a highly satisfactory manner" (18), is a sinister herald of the collapse of the Twin Towers. The thoughtless act is followed by the fall of another two apples which Ken and his girlfriend throw down at once, one each. This develops into a regular game, involving most of the guests. Like excited children, the players drop fruit, bottles, furniture, and household appliances, at the same time camcording the whole enterprise with exhilaration (21-3). The scene of the merry mayhem presents in the distorting mirror the absolute pandemonium of the WTC, with people jumping from the fire-consumed offices only to meet their death upon hitting the ground, which was recorded by TV reporters, and then broadcast repeatedly all over the world with morbid tenacity.

The national apocalypse becomes international when it starts living its own life in the media, undergoing the process of fictionalization. In a society feeding on Hollywood action movies, accustomed to on-screen killings and explosions, the response to the apocalyptic images of perfectly cinematic quality comes as no great surprise:

> 'Where's Superman? Where's Batman? Where's Spiderman?' 'Where's Bruce Willis, or Tom Cruise, or Arnie, or Stallone?' 'The Barbarians have seized the narrative.' 'Fuck, the bad guys are re-writing the scripts . . .!' '*Challenger* and Chernobyl were SF, Aum Shinrikyo and the Tokyo Underground was manga; this is a disaster movie directed by Satan.' (33)

While commenting on the above passage, Marie Odile Pittin-Hédon states that Banks initiates the plot of *Dead Air* by using the September 11 events as "reality-based peripeteia that will only serve it insofar as it allows the narrative voice an outburst that [. . .] reverses the order of prevalence between reality and fiction" (2006: 259). Hence the viewers' desperate call for the most famous superheroes, who would save the day as if in another American blockbuster. The need for imaginary saviours clearly indicates that the WTC apocalypse, represented through visual media in Hollywood style, becomes part of pop culture (cf. Pittin-Hédon 2006: 260). It can be watched, recorded, and replayed like a movie in the privacy of one's home, and the activity involves the same fascination and expectations as those regarding a moving picture, as well as an inevitable projection of the fictitious reality on the immediate realities of the viewer:

> [W]e kept going out onto the terrace to look at the Canary Wharf towers. Tall against the skyline less than a mile away, half expecting to see them hit by a plane and crumble with the same awful grandeur as the first tower. 'It's Pearl Harbour II,' we said. 'They'll fucking nuke Baghdad.' 'I can't believe this. I just can't believe I'm seeing this.' (33)

Being the stuff of pop culture and mass information, the 9/11 apocalypse is inevitably trivialized into becoming an article of consumption, like the 5,000 red T-shirts by DKNY with the Twin Towers on them, mentioned by Ken's lover Celia (32), which, although touching in their manifestation of solidarity, are most of all items on sale.

The tragedy and the ensuing public debate spawn numerous programmes in which the attack on the WTC can be forever recycled and on which television, radio stations, and the press can thrive for months to come. It is also true for *Capital Live!*, and especially Ken's shows, in which September 11 provides fuel for comic relief on air, with Ken humorously challenging the gravity of the recent crisis (see 32). However, September 11 is not the only tragedy which ends up as a target of jibes and out-of-place remarks on air. Images of earlier apocalyptic events pop up in the novel, most often as factual crutches for Ken's political jeremiads, or in the form of over-beer chat aimed at impressing friends or picking up women. One of these spectacular speeches comes right after he has been invited to a TV show in order to confront a Holocaust denier, one Lawson Brierly from America:

> 'What I said was, these namby-pamby Holocaust revision people didn't go *remotely* far enough. It wasn't just the Holocaust that didn't happen, it wasn't just the death camps that were faked; the whole of the Second World War is a myth. Occupation of Paris? Battle of Britain? North African Campaign? Convoys and U-Boats? Barbarossa? Stalingrad? Kursk? Thousand-bomber raids? D-Day? Fall of Berlin? Singapore? Pearl Harbour? Midway? Hiroshima and Nagasaki? *None* of it happened! All special effects and lying. Guys of a certain age; you remember how close those Airfix Spitfires and Lancasters looked to the real thing you saw in the film footage? That's because *they* were just models *too!* All the old airfields, the concrete tank traps, a few so-called bomb-sites; they were built after the war.' (63)

In his exaggerated clownish speech Ken unwittingly touches upon the subject of apocalyptic representation. The already quoted passage about the Hollywood superheroes emphasizes the role of the visual media in the (re)construction of the image of reality. At this point, the "real thing" from wartime newsreels is reduced to military aircraft models made by young boys, in this way detracting from its authenticity and adding substance to the fictitiousness of the televised simulacrum, turning the latter into the only existing reality.[22] As Jean Baudrillard writes in "The Anorexic Ruins," "[e]verything has already become nuclear, faraway, vaporized. The explosion has already occurred; the bomb is only a metaphor now . . . in a certain way there is no life anymore, but the information and the vital functions continue" (qtd. in Berger 1999: 71). By the same token, Berger postulates that in the twentieth century "[m]ost of the unimaginable, the unspeakable, has already happened, and continues to happen. And, paradoxically, while unimaginable, it is at the same time quite visible. The apocalypse is on television all the time, as a fait accompli, as 'news'" (1999: 80-1).

Although *Dead Air* opens with the images of the WTC tragedy, except for a few scattered references, the subject is practically absent from the main narrative. In his *Guardian* review of *Dead Air*, Steven Poole complains about the novel's failure to take full advantage of the impact that September 11 had on British public opinion and might have had on the characters themselves:

> Looming over the whole book is the shadow of the al-Qaida attacks of last September: the opening party ends with the news of the World Trade Centre collapse; and the dustjacket portrays a clever visual analogue of the event, with a plane flying over two chimneys of Battersea power station. But the novel does nothing with it; it is merely set-dressing. (2002)

Despite its genuine or alleged structural flaws, *Dead Air* seems to reflect without idealization the true effect the attacks had on the lives of indi-

---

22   The mediated apocalypse of *Dead Air* echoes Baudrillard's claim of the "illusion of the end," in which events "drift unpredictably towards their vanishing point – the peripheral void of the media." As a result, "we no longer have the pulsing of events, but only the cardiogram, have neither representation nor recollection of them, but merely the (flat) encephalogram, neither desire nor enjoyment of them, but only the psychodrama and the TV image" (2001b: 258).

viduals in the long run. After the doom-laden pictures had run their course in the world media, the life of the viewers came back to normal. Banks's novel provides evidence to the fact that people are responsive only to a tragedy that is served in the audio-visual wrapping as "news," played and replayed in the homes all over the world, yet their interest finally abates as in the case of a film replayed all too often.[23] At the same time, they remain oblivious of the plight of thousands of nameless victims which exists in the form of statistics but has not been (re)presented in the form of media coverage, as "images and symbols" (402). This truth is verbalized by Kenneth at the end of the novel, shortly before he faces John Merrial, a powerful gangster and the cuckold husband of his beautiful lover, Celia, an occurrence which functions as the real turning point in Ken's life and results in the character's unexpected illumination:

> It's because there was a reliable-sources statistic that Phil discovered the other day; that every twenty-four hours about thirty-four thousand children die in the world from the effects of poverty; from malnutrition and disease, basically. Thirty-four thousand, from a world, a world-society, that could feed and clothe and treat them all, with a workably different allocation of resources. Meanwhile, the latest estimate is that two thousand eight hundred people died in the Twin Towers, so it's like that image, that ghastly, grey-billowing, double-barrelled fall, repeated twelve times every single fucking day; twenty-four towers, one per hour, throughout each day and night. Full of children.
>
> We feel for the people in the towers, we agree with almost any measure to stop it ever happening again, and so we should. But for the thirty-four thousand, each day? Given our behaviour, and despite the idea we're

---

23   The limited political influence of September 11, which may as well describe its influence on the personal lives of ordinary people, is matter-of-factly summed up by Colin Gray: "Because the now global media lives by what appears to be new 'news', any dramatic event is liable to be retailed as the herald of a new era. The dramatic quality of an event, however, is not an entirely reliable guide to its significance. September 11 may score a perfect ten for shock effect, indeed it could have been inspired by a Hollywood storyboard, but really what does it signify for the future of world politics? [. . .] It may be worth my mentioning the fact that if the actual (the First and Second World Wars) horrors of the twentieth century failed to effect radical change in the means and methods of world politic, it is hardly likely that isolated terroristic atrocities, no matter how televisual, would succeed in their turn" (2002: 226-7).

supposed to love our children, you could be forgiven for thinking that most
of us just don't give a damn. (402-3)

The passage reverberates with the words written by the leader writers of
the *New Statesman* not long after the attacks. The journalists tried to put
the WTC tragedy in the right perspective by quoting merciless statistics
concerning the death toll among children dying each day of diarrhoea
which was caused by the lack of a clean water supply.[24] The very title of
the article, "Never forget the other Terror," was inspired by the writings
of Mark Twain, who on the basis of his study of the political situation in
Europe in the 1790s, differentiated between two "Reigns of Terror:" one
which meant "the horror of swift death," and the other which involved a
"lifelong death from hunger, cold, insult, cruelty and heartbreak." The
first "inflicted death upon a thousand persons," the second "upon a hundred million" (Booth and Dunne 2002: 6).

Coinciding with the political crisis lived and relived in the media, yet
entirely disconnected from it, is the protagonist's personal crisis which
proves destructive to his former life but, more importantly, brings the
promise of renewal and hope. Although at the party Ken is yet unaware
of the attacks in New York, he suddenly finds the throwing game less
appealing than it was "in the old days," explaining that he liked it more
before the participants switched from fruit to heavier artillery, and lost
their "amateur status" (23). The comment may in fact reveal more than
is put into words, and reflect the character's subconscious fear of change
and the demands which life makes on a grown-up man, to which one of
his friends replies, "You can't live in the past, Ken. [. . .] We should be
proud we were there at the start" (24). This observation clearly accentuates a growing awareness of the end of "the old days" and of the coming
of the new era, which will diametrically change the character's personal
world, but it is also a reference to Ken's immature ways and his clinging
to the life of non-commitment.

---

24   Banks himself commented on the catastrophes in an interview for *The Guar-*
     dian: "You know all the horrors that go on in the world, the sheer numbers
     that die of malnutrition, and compared to that, 2,800 in one day in New York
     is not that big a deal. And yet it was, because it was deliberate, it was a terro-
     rist spectacular, it was obscene, and traumatic for so many people who had no
     connection with anyone involved" (Brooks 2002).

Ken's life has for a long time been a sequence of pub crawls, occasional flings which he can rarely talk about without embarrassment or falling into trouble, and numerous excesses. He owes his career to his foul mouth and irresponsible actions, dismissing the problems he causes himself and the station with a boyish nonchalance. A Scottish expatriate in London, he dwells on the *Temple Belle*, a boat rented to him by his radio station, *Capital Live!*, which only emphasizes the flotsam nature of his present existence, which like a boat can be moored and unmoored at will. Ken appears to be aware of it when he describes occasional DVD sessions or football matches on TV watched with Craig, his Scottish childhood friend, an IT specialist in one of London-based companies: "Those tended to be the nights I came along and Craig and I got the chance to relive an adolescence that he – a father and effectively a husband at eighteen – had quit maybe too abruptly and I – arguably dissolute, still alone but variously entangled at thirty-five – had never quite shaken off" (102).

In contrast to Ken's youthful non-commitment and life cluttered with trivialities, Craig has both feet on the ground: he has a stable, well-paid job, owns an elegant three-storey family house in Highgate, tries to save his struggling marriage with Emma, and is a doting father to his daughter Nikki. But Ken's carefree attitude is juxtaposed not only with Craig's professional and personal responsibility but also with Celia's maturity, which can be attributed to unpleasant experiences in the past and years of living behind a mask. In addition, Ken's youthful stance also manifests itself in his inability (or rather refusal) to come to terms with the surrounding world: the reality which he inhabits and refers to in his numerous asides appears as abominable and in constant need of improvement. There are many things around him which he despises and cannot accept, from politics to media and lifestyle, to his own radio station, and the "shite" they play every day. On one occasion his girlfriend, Jo, points to his general dissatisfaction with the world: "'There is just so much you hate, Ken. Your life, your working life; it's, like, full of stuff and people and things and organizations you just can't stand. [. . .] Jesus. Is there *anything* you like, without qualification?'" (201-2).

Ken's malcontent perception of the surrounding space goes hand in hand with his self-proclaimed role as an advocate of truth in a corrupt and immoral world. But the truth he advocates is his own truth, rational-

istic and Eurocentric, which he would like to become a common principle. His attitude is well summed up by Celia when she calls him "a colo-
nialist of the mind" who believes in "the justified imperialism of Western thought" (224), denying other people the right to think differently
from himself. Moreover, his mission to expose the truth in the capacity
of a public commentator stands in sharp contrast with his private life,
replete with falsehoods, betrayals, and lack of unquestionable values (or
rather observance thereof), which sometimes makes him, also in his own
view, a despicable man.

Despite all the bustle in his social life, Ken's relationships, especially
those with women, are rather superficial. His only marriage ended in divorce due to his infidelity, he had a brief and sorely regretted episode
with the wife of his best friend, Craig, and he remains in a relationship
with Jo, whom he secretly cheats on and by whom he is cheated on in
return. The same is true for most of the characters from his London circle, with the notable exception of Craig, who is still in love with his estranged wife. Others, like Celia and John Merrial, though legally bound
to each other, have been living separate lives for a long time. The desert
of feelings among the Londoners finds a picturesque summation in the
chessboard metaphor, when Celia compares Ken and herself, and in effect all men and women, to two different coloured solitary bishops,
which Ken elaborates on pensively: "They could never connect. They
could slide past each other for ever, but never affect. They appear to inhabit the same board, but really they don't. Not at all" (226).

Accordingly, Ken's occasional glimpses of solitude from time to
time, followed by embarrassment about feeling sorry for himself (e.g.
the emptiness he feels during Celia's prolonged absence), are sympto-
matic of his subconscious longing for stability and genuine affection.
Instead, his life is one of unrewarding dissipation and aimlessness, holding the protagonist in the throes of living stillness with no progression.
The stasis within the character's personal space finds its evidence in various images of death and decay scattered in the universe of the novel,
which run in the background of the narrative, yet every now and then
reveal their disturbing ghoulish presence.

The river Thames, where the *Temple Belle* moors, the main artery
within the urban organism, at low tide uncovers waste and garbage reek-

ing of "ancient shit and things long dead" (68).[25] Somerset House, where, as Ed, another of Ken's friends, notices, they used to register births, marriages, and deaths, now has "an artificially cold heart" (214). The records which testified to the regenerative quality of the lives of people visiting the place have been replaced by an ice-rink, made by means of carbon dioxide instead of natural freezing (which may in fact stress both the lifelessness of modern times and the emotional dormancy of Kenneth, whose hibernating heart becomes finally awoken by the exotic skating creature that is Celia).[26] Moreover, there are numerous references to the death threats received by Kenneth, as well as to Celia's weird belief in her own partial death after she had been struck by lightning at the age of fourteen (37-8). The fire from heaven, which scorched the woman's skin and allegedly effected the split into two different Celias, one dead and one alive, may also be responsible for the woman's infertility, as if branding out her capacity for reproduction.

As can be noticed in the above observations, the lifelessness and inertia of the London space is connected with the disturbance in the binary nature of the four elements, which seem to be deprived of their regenerative power. After all, the action unfolds in the shadow of the eponymous "dead air," which acquires multiple meanings over the course of the novel. The first and most obvious of them is an interruption in a radio broadcast involving the lack of sound, the phenomenon which Ken refers to when talking about two DJs from Radio One who deliberately make pauses in order to sound funny (46). The "dead air" is therefore something opposite to "white noise," i.e. data with no meaning, which

---

25   The littered river in *Dead Air* is reminiscent of the Thames from "The Fire Sermon" in T. S. Eliot's *The Waste Land*, which carries waste and is connected with sexual pursuits devoid of love (ll.176-9).

26   The meaning of their names turns their affair into an ironic fusion of ancient tradition and pop-culture. The name "Celia" which is etymologically connected with the Latin word *caelum* (heaven), was often given to heroines in pastoral literature (not to mention Shakespeare's *As You Like It*). At one point, Kenneth spots his secret lover in an ice rink, jumping and spinning like "a fabulously exotic alien creature fallen into our mundane world from a higher reality" (209). On the other hand, the name "Kenneth" is of Gaelic origin and means "fire-born" or "handsome" (Mcleod and Freedman 1995: 124). However, in its shortened form, it brings to mind the male doll Ken, Barbie's plastic partner.

permeates the modern reality in which the characters live. The "white noise" is represented in the novel by repetitive news and media broadcasts of September 11, which are constantly on air but cease to be registered by the characters as meaningful information. The "dead air," on the contrary, is conspicuous, as it makes a breach in the "white noise," thus presumably capturing the attention of listeners/viewers suddenly experiencing silence around. Another meaning is obviously connected with stopping air traffic after September 11, and with the resultant "spooky" silence, as Celia calls it, not only in the sky but also in the city, deserted by some of its more affluent residents (33). In the light of the previous discussion, the radio term may also metaphorically encapsulate a period of deathly pause in Kenneth's life, which comes to an end after he falls in love with Celia and goes through a personally traumatic experience.

Kenneth's beloved, Celia, whose presence gives his heart another lease of life, has an aura of mystery and an almost palpable burden of painful experience around herself. The suffering is tangible in her case because it is imprinted on her skin in the form of scars: an unnatural fern-like pattern left by the lightning on one side of her body, and the marks on her forearm, which may be the evidence of a suicide attempt or drug injections (no wonder Kenneth describes her hair as being the colour of heroin [82]) or both. We also learn that John Merrial helped her through a very difficult time in her life when she was a model in Paris. He married her out of love but then he cooled towards her when he found out that she could not have children (120-1). The causes of Celia's infertility are obscure and never explained. Whatever its reasons, Celia's barrenness seems to match Kenneth's otherwise fruitless existence, and even if it is not a manifestation of death, it may be representative of the predicament of post-apocalyptic mankind and its inability to produce life.

Paradoxically, the meeting of the two misfits brings hope into their respective lives. Celia, whose name is etymologically connected with heaven, whose body is stigmatized by the light from the sky, and whose current life follows a peculiar kind of resurrection, is a Christlike figure in the novel's universe. She redeems Ken from a life of plastic and meaningless romances (and in the end, she literally saves his life in the confrontation with her husband), and gives him strength to overcome his limitations. As a result, the character who cannot (Kenn Nott) give himself entirely to another person, finds in his heart the ability to love, which he offers to the divine being along with a life of togetherness in an earthly peace. "At least I said I loved Ceel," he notices, "I told her, in the conventional three words. That's something that I got to say, maybe the last unforced thing I'll ever say" (403). The regenerative quality of their relationship finds its mirror image in the vegetation of Park Lane, which they watch during their first tryst, the "new growth of green and black and full of life and movement and promise" (120).

At this point it is worth recalling Pittin-Hédon's claim concerning apocalyptic disturbance in the "order of prevalence between reality and fiction" (2006: 259), as this process is here accompanied by the characters' partial removal from the harrowing dangerous reality into their private fantasy world of romance and eroticism. It results in the creation of two distinct universes in which the characters play completely different roles. The best example of such a hiatus is Celia. The fissure of her personal world in the past translates into the dichotomy of her present world, which she construes with masterly methodicalness. In public, she plays the role of a faithful wife and the mistress of an elegant house in Belgravia. In private, she becomes involved in an erotic-cum-romantic affair with a Radio DJ whom she meets by chance at a party. Her secret life can be compared to the fernlike pattern left by the bolt on the left side of her body, which never appeared in her official pictures when she was a model. Therefore, when she reveals to Ken that "covering things up is easy" (125), her words may imply much more than the superficial message. Just as the scar was a blemish on her otherwise perfect body and had to be concealed, so her affair with Ken is a flaw on her seemingly flawless wifehood (it is noteworthy that Ken is not allowed to leave a mark on her body, which could put her husband on their trail). "This has to be outside of real life, Kenneth. That way we can get away with it. [. . .] It is like a dream, no?" she tells her lover, when he offers to cover the hotel expenses and suggests spending a weekend together (129).

So instead of open public places like cinemas or restaurants, their relationship develops in various hotel rooms around London (where she arrives and departs dressed up beyond recognition), behind closed doors and curtained windows, in artificial light instead of daylight. Going to their first clandestine tête-à-tête, Ken is struck by "the whole cloak and dagger set up of their meeting" (115); he even suspects Celia of deliberate dramatization of her husband's evil intentions because it fulfils "some appetite for mystery" (115). He is drawn into the make-believe world of crime story and like it or not, he has to play by its rules: "My heart was thudding; I was half expecting muscled goons with eighteen-inch collars to burst out of the wardrobe, whack me on the back of the head, gaffer-tape my mouth and zip me into a body-bag . . . though, from the impression I had of the room from the desk lamp's weak light, this place was too posh for wardrobes; it had a dressing-room instead" (116).

The "dream" world is characterized by peculiar ritualization: it can be accessed only after a phone call from Celia and the delivery of a plastic hotel key card by a courier. During their first intercourse, Celia asks Ken to remain silent in order to create a propitious omen for their relationship (114). They usually meet on Fridays because she likes listening to his shows beforehand, and the circumstances of their encounters are always the same:

> Wherever it was I met Ceel, she was always there, always waiting, almost always reading a book – usually something recent I'd heard of: *White Teeth, Man and Boy, Bridget Jones's Diary*. Once it was *The Prince*, once *Madame Bovary*, and once the *Kama Sutra*, which she was reading for ideas we didn't really need. Twice it was *A Brief History of Time*. The room – suite – was always dark, always hot. There would be something light to eat if we wanted, and vintage champagne. It was a while before I realized the glasses we drank from were always the same ones, and that there would always be a different, spare glass present. She brought the crystal flutes herself; they belonged to her. (123)

Paradoxically, the space "outside of real life," or a dream, as Celia calls it, is pure and free of pretence. Only in a hotel room can she be herself, can she trust and be trusted, and live her life as she wants, whereas at home and around her rightful mate she has to watch her every step and keep up the appearances of a successful marriage. On the one hand, the whole affair seems illusory, even questionable, due to the long intervals between their meetings and the necessary aura of secrecy. On the other hand, the romance is gradually becoming the most important part in both their lives, eclipsing the things beyond.

Exciting as they may be, their trysts are also occasional, and neither of them can lay claims to the other side's feelings and the permanence of their relationship. The full realization of it strikes Ken while he is watching *Intimacy*, the fictionalized version of an affair like theirs, "about a couple who meet up every now and again in a filthy flat for sex, and remain strangers to each other" (134). The rules of engagement presented in the film, and by the same token Celia's and his, turn out to be Ken's greatest worry, because his feelings for the woman are not yet recognized but already genuine. Reality, therefore, proves even more disturbing than the film. At one point, during a longer separation from her, the same worry makes Ken project the criteria of the "dream" onto the separate world of Celia's marriage, and leads him to believe that she must have fallen in love with her husband again, or even hazard an unwarranted conjecture that he is just one of Celia's many secret lovers (333).

A desire for fictionality runs deep in the protagonist. It is signalled as early as his first encounter with Celia, at a party organized by Kenneth's boss, Sir Jamie. He joins her on the balcony, looking at the city below and an advancing storm:

> Lightning. Much later I thought it ought to have been lightning that lit the scene, that it had been that sort of storm and when I first saw her standing there it was courtesy of a flash of lightning, which lit up the Mysterious Figure in the Shadows. But it wasn't. Just the lights of the storm-pressed city. Sometimes reality isn't Gothic enough. (83-4)

Accordingly, when his interest in Celia skating in Somerset House is noticed by her husband, Ken thinks to himself while at the same time frantically trying to find a way out of the situation, "Oh shit, why the *fuck* wasn't life a computer game where you could go back and re-live the last few minutes and make a different choice?" (211). The following conversation with John Merrial depicts on a verbal level the conflict between the two so far separate worlds, unexpectedly brought together. Kenneth has to mediate between his role of Celia's lover and that of a stranger, in order to avoid disastrous consequences which may result from the encounter, and thus a potential breach in their private world:

> 'We were never introduced, but I think I saw you, now you've been pointed out to me.'
>
> 'I believe we were,' I said. I'm fucking your wife, I'm fucking your wife, I kept thinking, some suicidally insane bit of my brain wanting to blurt it out, to just say it, to get this over with, to make the worst that could happen actually happen and not have to keep imagining it.
>
> 'How's Jamie?' he smiled.

> 'Fine. Last time I saw him.' Which was at the same party, come to
> think of it; the party where I met your wife and snogged her and felt her up
> and agreed to this patently suicidal affair in the first place. (212)

The novel confronts both the reader and the protagonist with situations
which show what happens when reality proves too akin to fiction, eventually surpassing the latter's dramatic impact. It is not only true in the
case of the Al-Qaeda attacks executed in the vein of Hollywood action
blockbusters, which function as a fictional starting point for the entire
story, but also in the case of Ken's vicissitudes as a radio performer.
Kenneth stages his every show in *Capital Live!* by breathing his true
opinions and prejudices into it with an extremely vocal but in fact only
faintly registered sense of responsibility for his words and actions. However tongue-in-cheek his programmes are, they earn him not only irate
phone calls from various groups and organizations that feel insulted, but
also a very realistic danger to his life. Despite all Ken's neglect, the
death threats he receives for offending other people's beliefs may come
true, which he himself admits after being kidnapped. By the same token,
a bad thriller-like dream about himself being handcuffed and Jo being
raped by some masked attackers functions as a premonition of the attack
effected by Merrial's people, and as grim evidence that reality can be the
most disturbing of nightmares.

The above observation is best put to the test in Chapters 9-11, which
describe the nightmares realized. First, the truth about Ken's one-night
stand with Craig's wife comes out, and he faces one of his greatest fears
in life – the possibility of losing not only a good loyal friend but also
Craig's family, Emma and Nikki, whom he considers his own. What follows is a drunken night of self-pity and longing for Celia, when he accidentally calls the land line number in the Merrials' house and leaves a
message with explicit sexual content on the answer-machine. In this
light, Ken's pleas to God, whom he has never believed in anyway, sound
amusing and contradict the nature of the world he inhabits, as he actually
is living a nightmare, and a very real nightmare at that:

> I want to Undo. I want to press F1 or go to the relevant menu with a mouse
> arrow and Undo, totally fucking Undo what I did last night, rewind the
> tape, oh yes, wipe the chip, reformat the disk, rewind that fucking little
> deadly tape or whatever the hell it was sitting in a house less than a mile
> away from here, rewind and erase. Better still, take it out and fucking burn

> it and mash the ashes into a fine paste and flush it all down a waste dispos-
> al unit somewhere in Outer fucking Mongolia. (355)

For want of better options, Ken is forced to break into Celia's house in order to erase the tape, and his ill-fated burglary has all the planning and execution one can come across in heist films or caper stories: from a key in the artificial stone in the back garden, to the alarm number and a closed study with a treasure inside, topped with the untimely arrival of the owner and his Scandinavian bodyguard. The narrative unfolds before the reader's eyes with every minute detail of the surroundings and the burglar's behaviour registered like a picture on a film. The dramatic heist plot is here effectively balanced by hilarious, if rather offensive, scenes of Kenneth emptying his bowels in John Merrial's toilet, and his self-mocking internal monologues, which turns the whole story into a criminal comedy in the vein of Guy Ritchie or Quentin Tarantino. This pictorial technique is all the more justified when we realize that a part of Ken's snooping around the house has been recorded by a security camera in the corridor and then watched by the house owner. Unwittingly, Ken has become a hero in an amateur production, but he will get his deserved applause from the flesh-and-blood audience that he feared in the first place.

The moment of crisis, Ken's personal apocalypse, is literally a descent into the underworld, with "darkness black as night, the darkness of an infinite pit" and the black water smelling of something "dead and rotten" (404), the images clearly representative of death and burial. Waiting for the guilty hero is the sombre lord of the underworld ready to execute the character's last judgement. Ken is spared nothing: he is manhandled and beaten by Merrial's men and utterly humiliated when he defecates into his pants in front of the woman he loves and her dangerous cuckold husband. The confrontation in the underground car park is also the turning point in the life of Celia, who must challenge her husband in order to save her incautious lover and win her own future away from Merrial's dodgy business. It is in the Astramax car park, in her own view, that the worlds of two different Celias have converged, bringing an appreciable change: "It was meant to happen on my birthday, but it happened then instead. That was a strong event. It pulled matters towards it, distorting things sufficiently" (434-5). The cross-over of her two alternative lives, dramatic as it may have been, has also made her one and whole again.

In conclusion to her article, Pittin-Hédon projects her sinister vision of "a gradual darkening of the material" used by contemporary Scottish writers, Banks with his *Dead Air* among them (2006: 260). True as the statement may appear for the most part of Banks's novel, it cannot be accepted in its entirety when considering *Dead Air*'s ending, which offers a tentatively optimistic outlook. The novel ends with the image of the two lovers visiting Scotland, Kenneth's home, a month before their flight to Celia's home in Martinique. Their new relationship begins in March, when nature awakens, and develops along with the changing seasons, and for both of them time starts anew. It is a beginning in many respects (e.g. Ken's friendship with Craig, in which they are "kind of starting from scratch" [435]) but also a return to the space of childhood forsaken for a career in the greater world. Ken's return to his roots takes place in Scotland's "late-summer glory" (436), when the land is lush with vegetation and vibrant with the energy of life. Accordingly, the poetics of post-apocalypse gives way to the articulation of faith, trust, and sincerity, which, alongside love, seem to be the saving graces of "this fractured, fallen world [. . .] constructed for ourselves, and our heirs," as Ken describes it in one of the last paragraphs (436). The invigorating summer rain falling on the heads of the carefree couple adds a final note to the newly-found harmony of the world and its regeneration, painting the lovers' future with a truly brighter palette.

***

The last model established by the blueprint novel, the model of Apocalyptic Worlds, introduces a new quality in the characters' relationship with the world. Namely it shifts the centre of gravity from the creative modelling of space by the characters to the deterministic influence of space on the characters, which they can only partly resist. In the novels discussed in this chapter, it is the outside world which constructs the character, thwarting his mediating attempts and drowning him in its own chaos, which is especially noticeable in the dystopian universe of *A Song of Stone* and the political wasteland of *Complicity*.

In *A Song of Stone*, the character's withdrawal into the inner spaces of thought and memory, or those connected with art and tradition, fails as a medium of redemption, because the inside eventually proves as degenerate as the outside, perpetuating moral decay and stasis. For Abel, the appropriation and the ensuing destruction of the family castle, which represents the pre-apocalyptic order based on the notion of class hierarchies, puts an end to his own life and narrative. In *Complicity*, the characters escape from the chaos of modernity into their private worlds, structured, paradoxically, around the products of the diseased external semiosphere – substances, violent sexual fantasies, and computer games (Cameron); or they become outcasts to the degenerate world, punishing its wrongs by equally degenerate acts of murder (Andy). The disease of the world penetrates into the character's personal space literally and metaphorically, infecting it with its cancerous corruption or with hatred and thirst for revenge. The disintegration of the world is also visible on the level of language, which undergoes desemantization and fails as a denotative medium, succumbing to the power of globalization.

Only the last of the novels discussed, *Dead Air*, offers hope and a promise of renewal. It shows the characters living in the world in which apocalypse has become an unceasing media broadcast, its original catastrophic impact dissipated in the repetitive sensationalism of journalistic accounts. The society, desensitized to catastrophes by the omnipresent violence in the media (e.g. Hollywood blockbusters), is an heir, if more optimistic, to the society depicted in *Complicity*, afflicted by the same crisis of human relationships, flawed morality, consumerism, drug abuse, and an "artificially cold heart." The characters, Ken and Celia, construct their secret world of love and tenderness – their private romantic movie – within the expanses of the outside world of death and violence. The translation of the character's secret enclave of love into the empirical world is possible only through experiencing their personal apocalypse which remains outside the media coverage. The victory of their love, won at the price of pain and humiliation, unshackles their world from the grip of death and ushers in a period of regeneration and vitality, bringing reality once again under the creative power of individual vision. At least so the story goes. Ironically, the happy ending of the romantic scenario which underlies the narrative of Ken and Celia is yet another cinematic cliché. It seems, therefore, that the world of fiction in the end becomes subordinated to the requirements of Hollywood cinema.

CHAPTER 6

Coda: *The Quarry*

Banks's last novel, posthumously published in 2013, eludes easy categorization. On closer examination, it becomes obvious that *The Quarry*
(2013) does not follow one particular spatial paradigm among the four
models characteristic of Banks's mainstream prose but rather fuses them
all. As such, it bears a strong resemblance to *The Wasp Factory*, also
echoing other themes and motifs which feature prominently in the blueprint novel – e.g. the father/son relationship, the secluded northern locus,
the quest for the feminine, the conflict between rationality and superstition, or the real and the imaginary, and the narrative delivered from the
perspective of a socially inhibited youth.

Published several days after Banks's untimely death of cancer, *The
Quarry* explores the experience of life lived in the shadow of a terminal
disease. Its protagonist is an autistic youth who lives with his misan-
thropic father, Guy, a cancer victim, in a ramshackle house shaken by
the activity of the nearby quarry. The plot revolves around a visit of
Guy's university friends, Hol, Pris, Ali, Rob, Paul, and Haze, now in
their late thirties, one fateful weekend. Being a courtesy call paid to a
dying mate, the group's arrival is also connected with a search for an old
videotape containing, as it is gradually revealed, an embarrassing porn
movie which they made as students of the Film and Media Department.
As the friends meet again, old grievances and uncomfortable secrets
come to light, showing the flimsiness of bonds and loyalties. Contrary to
Banks's initial intention, the novel became a testimony to his own predicament, as fiction turned into reality when the author was diagnosed
with cancer about ten thousand words before completing the manuscript
(Wark 2013).

Kit, the protagonist and narrator, in many ways resembles Frank
Cauldhame, the social attitudes of both being determined by their re-

spective physical and psychological conditions. Frank distances himself from the community as a result of his alleged castration, treating the outside world with a combination of superiority and fear. Kit's alienation from the community is due to Asperger syndrome, his attitude oscillating between self-appreciation, or even boastfulness, as he is fully aware of his exceptional intelligence, and the recognition of the world's prejudice towards his "difference:"

> Also it helps that I'm very clever, if challenged in other ways. Challenged in this context means that I am weird, strange, odd, socially disabled, forever looking at things from an unusual angle, or however you want to put it.
> Most things, I've come to understand, fit into some sort of spectrum. The descriptions of myself fit into a spectrum that stretches from 'highly gifted' at one end to 'nutter' at the other, both of which I am comfortable with. One comes from understanding and respect, while the other comes from ignorance and fear. (Banks 2013: 1)

Kit remains on the periphery of the public semiosphere because he does not conform to the accepted "norm" of social behaviour as defined by medicine, psychology, and law, which makes the public institutions and local authorities question his ability to live on his own and perform "the full range of adult responsibilities" (82). His case is not considered individually; rather, Kit is treated as one of the challenged group who do not come up to the social yardstick and who must be therefore supervised by the normative majority. Such an indiscriminate perception of his condition prevails and cannot be changed, despite the testimonies to the contrary made in court by Mrs Willoughby, a social worker, and Holly (Hol), Guy's friend from London. Functioning as the social Other, Kit himself keeps the outside world at a distance. He is reluctant to leave the house, save the need for weekly shopping, preferring instead the solitude of his bedroom where he plays computer games.[1] At one point Kit ob-

---

1   Kit's activities (much like Frank Cauldhame's) are characterized by increased ritualization or small obsessions. The most striking example is the protagonist's regular walk round the garden consisting of exactly four hundred and fifty-seven steps, a number which is a prime and which highlights Kit's obsessively mathematical mind (51-4). Equally "weird" is his focus on maintaining one hundred kilos of weight (17). Moreover, the boy schedules his showers according to a seasonal timetable, displays a bizarrely methodical approach to shopping and food preparation (going to shops on particular days or looking

serves that he has never been part of "any given gang, group or clique" (246), which he finds useful, as the outsider's perspective on things is more comprehensive and more detached than that of the insider. Such a standpoint, however, comes at a price. "'Yeah, you see more but you feel less'" (246) is Hol's reply to that, which points out the lack of emotional involvement and empathy on the outsider's part, and thus that person's alienation from communal bonds and collective life.

Connected with Kit's emotional detachment is his inability to grasp the nuances of interpersonal communication, which seriously impedes his interaction with other people. Paradoxically, his extraordinary intelligence, which is of help in such matters as learning things, repairing electronic equipment, planning the everyday logistics of his and Guy's life, or using computers and the Internet, constitutes an obstacle to a successful exchange between him and others. Guided by reason, Kit rationalizes all life phenomena, regarding human emotionality as intervening with mutual understanding, as people "*should* know what they think, and express it properly" (4).[2] This attitude, which stems directly from Kit's disorder and presupposes that one should always tell the absolute truth regardless of circumstances, is made explicit in his early conversation with Hol, who teaches Kit about the importance of the context in which people communicate, a thing which Kit finds problematic (2). Context determines meaning as much as words, and communication between people is never merely verbal. Rather it depends on the circumstances in which it occurs, non-verbal signs and gestures, and even on what the other side chooses to leave unsaid. Kit's cleverness is juxtaposed by Hol with a different kind of cleverness, namely emotional intelligence, "[e]mpathising with others, getting on with people, intuiting what and how they think" (4).

---

for sales in order to get better prices or save time), things which for an average person seem irrelevant or plain paranoid. It is also worth mentioning Kit's unusual devotion to recycling. The latter obsession highlights both the protagonist's focus on his inner life and his connection with the larger global community.

2 Kit's attachment to reason and rationality differentiates him from Frank Cauldhame, immersed in his realm of superstition and magic. Paradoxically, however, the characters' respective beliefs alienate them from their communities in the same measure.

Holly explains to Kit that such signs as tone of voice or facial expression enter into verbal communication and are interpreted by the other side as signifiers of a particular kind of signified: instead of conveying patience, as Kit intended, they give the interlocutor the impression of scorn and superiority (3). "Get the procedure right, Kit; your comms protocols need refreshing" (56), says Hol when Kit fails to provide a satisfactory response to her utterance, and the computer imagery of her remark carries more significance than it may appear at first glance. Kit has to learn how to respond to another person's message: understanding emotions, as he himself asserts (6), yet unable to naturally feel for the Other, he has to master a set of culturally accepted reactions which a person without his psychological limitations develops as a natural response to other people's expectations through years of socialization. Like a computer, he learns and updates his communication skills – he memorizes certain phrases mentioned by Hol and then uses them, depending on the situation.[3]

The Quarry's focus on the nuances of interpersonal communication calls to mind Lotman's idea of the semiotic act as an act of communication whose participants must be able to recognize the languages (or codes) used by their culture and know the ways of decoding messages "written" in those languages. The communicating sides, therefore, must have some previous semiotic experience and choose to approach messages as potentially meaningful, while an act of communication always involves a translation of the message from a foreign language into our own (cf. Lotman 1990: 123-40). This makes the process of *semiosis* at once objective and subjective, mechanical and personalized. By issuing a response, the addressee lets the addresser know that the message has been received and understood (or misunderstood), thus revealing their familiarity with the mediating mechanisms of culture or society as well as the limits of their own perception. Apart from his self-avowed inability to translate both the verbal and non-verbal content of the message

---

3   This happens for example in his conversation with Pris when instead of the natural response of saying nothing, Kit comments on Pris's plans to meet her boyfriend with "That's nice," which is "one of those pointless phrases" he heard from Hol (55). At one point he himself recognizes his affinity with artificial intelligence: "[L]ike a computer I struggle with some stuff that normal people find easy to the point of not thinking about it" (281).

successfully, Kit very often remains the addressee while failing to become the addresser in the act of communication, the one-sidedness of which is addressed by Hol in the following way:

> 'You just say *something*, Kit,' she told me, when I protested that usually these misunderstandings occurred when I had nothing useful to say in return to something I'd just been told. 'A nod, or a grunt, would be an absolute minimum, or an "Uh-huh". Just a "Really?" or "That's nice", or "I see", or partially repeating what you've just been told, or thinking it through a little so that if they say they're going out you ask, "Anywhere exciting?" or suggest they take a brolly cos it's pissing down. You don't just stare blankly at them. Apart from anything else these meaningless replies are like saying "Roger", or "Copy that"; you're letting people know that you received their message. If you don't use them you're getting the whole communication thing wrong. (55)

Hol's lecturing Kit on the importance of bilateral communication and emotional intelligence is ironically contrasted with the way in which signs are manipulated by Guy and his friends so as to elicit a particular response or conceal the truth behind their actions and intentions. Probably the most striking example of such a false mediation is the couple Rob and Ali, two "corporate bunnies" (63), whose job involves abusing the semiotic mechanisms underlying social communication and parasitizing emotional intelligence for the purpose of financial profits and career development. Hol's advice to Kit about "[e]mpathising with others, getting on with people, intuiting what and how they think" (4) finds its sinister equivalent in the corporate programme of discovering people's expectations and responding to them appropriately in order to build a favourable image for the company (97-8).

Interestingly, similar image-building takes place on a smaller scale among the members of the group, revealing their respective pretences to being someone else and their yearning for acceptance, respect, or admiration. Such a tendency can be noticed in Hol's dropping of her northern accent to make herself sound "less provincial, less identifiable, more neutral and bland" (7). Only the term of endearment "love," with which she refers to Kit, is pronounced by her in a genuine "Ay-oop" accent (7). Even more obvious and ironic is Hol's carefully constructed image of a socialist and advocate of communitarian values criticizing the rapacity of banks, corporations, and governments. This stance is compromised when it is revealed that she has embezzled Kit's deposits to pay her own expenses and has borrowed money from Rob and Paul, whom she has often censured as servants of greedy capitalism. Another example of the manipulation of signs can be noticed in Guy's histrionic self-fashioning in the past. He used to drive a hearse, occasionally dressing in a top hat, a frock coat, a black cane, and dark glasses, which made him look like a rock star and was supposed "to prove how wacky and eccentric he was" (127). Years later, his declared misanthropy, which he voices on the farewell recording addressed to his mates, is disproved by his fear of death and his helpless rebellion against the world going on without him after he is gone (170-1).

The play of appearances goes even deeper, undermining the bonds of friendship and loyalty among the members of the group. Apart from marked differences in their political outlooks, careers, and lifestyles, the group seems to be internally antagonistic, the "friends" competing against each other, resenting each other, or fearing each other's negative opinion. Paul, who is a corporate lawyer, bribes Kit into giving him a missing video tape which all of them wanted to get before the others had a chance to see it. Haze makes a pretence of having a career; however, in the meantime, he tries to wangle small amounts of money from his mates and even Kit, which makes Hol observe ominously: "'Just because you'd trust someone with your life doesn't mean you can trust them with your money'" (85). Hol, in turn, seems to silently resent Ali for taking Rob away from her exactly at the moment when she felt there could be something between them. Ali's violent reaction to the news that Rob has lent money to Hol, who is after all their mutual friend, without his wife's knowledge may have less to do with Ali's concern about Rob's separate bank account and more with his past attraction to Hol, of which Ali may have been aware. Moreover, Ali's attitude towards the others is often tinged with a degree of superiority; in her view, Pris "run[s] a couple of homes for pensioners stinking of urine," while Hol "write[s] about films nobody watches in magazines nobody reads" (145). Ali's manipulative and imposing way of soliciting Kit's help in her search for the embarrassing video cassette makes the boy suspicious, as her arguments about the disadvantage of women, who always have more to lose than men, contradict her pushy "male" behaviour.[4] Last but not least, the disturbed

---

4   Kit does not want to react like a sexist to Ali's statement on gender inequality;
     however, the combination of coquettishness and bullying in her demeanour

communal dynamics of the group proves especially noticeable in the case of Pris, who is afraid that her well-educated, successful, and highly critical mates will not approve of her new boyfriend, Rick, who is a simple telephone engineer. For Pris, the group constitutes a point of reference against which she "calibrates" her life and choices, always measuring herself against them, which she admits in a conversation with Kit (246), and for which she is vocally and rather aggressively reprimanded by Rob during the fateful last evening at Guy's house. Verbalizing and confirming Pris's fears of the group's unfavourable opinion of Rick (308), Rob unwittingly lays bare the mechanisms of social interaction, in which offensive or unacceptable reality is often cloaked in euphemisms, understatements or white lies which serve the purpose of communal unification. The implied discrepancy between what people think and what they say echoes Holly's earlier teachings about context and Kit's justified doubts about the veracity of interpersonal communication.

As in *Stonemouth*, the communal past as well as various distortions and abuses of existing social codes are brought to the surface through the media of film, television, and camera recordings. The most important in this respect is the lost VHS cassette, which contains a porn movie shot by the group with themselves as actors. The video from their carefree, uncompromising youth could jeopardize their present image of successful and respected professionals: Paul's political aspirations, Rob and Ali's future as, ironically, their company's image builders, Haze's already uncertain job prospects, Pris's trustworthiness as a social worker, and Hol's reputation as a film critic. As Paul tells Kit, the tape contains "ample footage to get [them] all as fully disgraced and as fired as [their] respective employers might deem fit" (266). At the same time, while capturing bygone days and immortalizing transitory moments, the cinematically mediated past reveals its striking difference from the present, foregrounding change, process, and degeneration over time. "Back then they all looked young and fresh," observes Kit while talking about Guy and his friends' appearance in their youthful productions, which his father has occasionally shown to visitors. "You can see how they've changed from the people they were then to the people they are now,

---

makes him suspicious. The scene shows a conflict between the social convention of political correctness and Kit's inner conviction of Ali's insincerity and egoism, whether she is a woman or not.

though I don't know that you'd have been able to guess exactly how they would age" (43).

While conveying the uncomfortable truth about a person's past and mediating people's perception of the passage of time, film as a medium enters everyday life in *The Quarry* through evocative imagery and language. In this way, someone's imaginative construct, his/her authorial representation of reality, becomes a semioticizing filter for a collective image of the world, which can be noticed in Kit's reaction to Paul's offer of a financial reward in case the boy should find the missing tape: "I'm fairly sure the one time I ever heard mention of a 'finder's fee' was in the Coen brothers's film *Fargo*, and I seem to recall things didn't turn out too well for the person who expected to be on the receiving end of one" (94). As a medium, film also shows a degree of contamination by its creator or producer and thus advocates particular ideologies, as, in Hol's view, is the case with Hollywood blockbusters like *The Hobbit*. In this production, a particular world-picture, first mediated by literature, is later remediated by cinema, its message reshaped and updated to the expectations of contemporary audiences for the financial benefit of the producers.[5] No wonder Holly calls *The Hobbit* "a piece of disproportionate, self-indulgent wank with values driven entirely by the needs of the studio and the distributors, not the original story" (61). It is also interesting that one mediation is described in Kit and Holly's conversation through a reference to another cinematic mediation, as she calls *The Hobbit* Peter Jackson's *Phantom Menace*, an apparently negative judgement with which Kit does not agree.

---

5   Equally significant for the discussion of cinematic mediations is Hol's article on paintings being produced according to Hollywood's criteria concerning films. In Hol's view, the *Mona Lisa* would be too "dull and dowdy" to be considered a finished product by film-makers (159). It would have to go through several drafts before turning into "a dusky maiden [. . .] wearing a low-cut wrap with a smouldering, alluring look and an exotic bloom in her long black tresses" (160). Finally, as Hol predicts, Leonardo's famous model "would look like something you were embarrassed your grandad bought in Woolworths in the early seventies" (160). Interestingly, the passage atrributed to Hol is extracted in a practically unchanged form from Banks's earlier novel *Dead Air*, where it is delivered by Ken Nott, a radio DJ, in a conversation about the credibility of representation in Hollywood films (2009: 325-6).

Film imagery is also used by the characters in order to highlight the propensity of the human mind for wish-fulfilment, which results in a construction of alternative or counterfactual versions of reality. With such wishful mediations human beings exorcise painful reality, deceiving themselves and others by what Hol calls "miraculist thinking." Trying to disprove the fantasy of romantic love, Hol develops her argument by taking aim at the general tendency among people to look for extraordinary and improbable solutions:

'All I'm saying [. . .] is that the same belief – that if everybody would believe in this or behave like that, everything would somehow come right: that there'd be no more of all the bad stuff, or at least an absolute minimum of it – is closely related to the idea of romantic love and that . . . that conviction that if only this person will love me, will agree to us being together – for ever – then my life will be perfect, and all will be well. You know; happy till the end of time, till the mountains crumble into the sea, till the rivers turn to dust, etcetera, blah. [. . .] Yeah, but even after you're together with your perfect person [. . .] you still have to accept you continue to live in the real world, and there will always be problems in it, and even perfect couples – who, obviously, do completely exist – have arguments and disagreements and, at the very last, *risk* growing apart over time.' (196)

In its essence, such a miraculist fantasy of one true love is similar to the wish-fulfilment fantasy offered by Hollywood productions like *Independence Day*, *Star Wars*, and *Lord of the Rings*, as it advocates a method of dealing with reality in a way which precludes any rational approach but welcomes an overnight improvement of the world due to some wondrous intervention (196-7). However, according to Hol, the betterment of reality takes place slowly and painstakingly, with repeated effort and sacrifice, over generations and without end. The world develops, as she puts it, through "the usual but eventually steady progress of human morality and behaviour, built up over millennia; [. . .] the spreading of literacy, education and an understanding of how things really work, through research and the dissemination of the results of that research through honest media" (197).

A similar scepticism is expressed by Kit with reference to the miraculous nature of a grand mediating system of human culture, namely religion, which remains outside Kit's private semiosphere, whose centre is built around the metalanguages of rationality and science. Within the limits of Kit's semiotics, the relationship between signs and their referents has an empirical foundation, and the generation and attribution of meanings is done on the basis of evidence. In religion, on the other hand, as Kit observes, there is no "robust proof," only "claims in old books about miracles happening [. . .] written ages after the events they describe" (173). Interestingly, Kit questions the reliability of the media in representing reality, be it yesterday's newspapers or holy books (173), as the report is always coloured or distorted, either by the author's subjective perception or the ideology to which he/she subscribes. For Kit, religion is clearly nothing other than a collective fantasy whose feasibility relies on the agreement of a large number of people to believe in the same thing without proof (174). Taking Kit's argument further, such people function in two parallel dimensions – one determined by scientific evidence and the other by mass delusion. As a result, the scientific and religious outlooks cannot be reconciled. The former relies on verifiable knowledge where findings of various disciplines "fit together" and support "clearly provable physical laws and mechanisms" (175); the latter depends on faith, which Kit considers madness and which is "an area that's been fenced off as out of bounds, not subject to the rules about proof and likelihood" (175).

Ironically, a combination of "mad" faith and miraculist thinking can be found in people's attitude towards death, which happens to everyone and yet is universally denied and treated as a taboo. Addressing other people's advice to think positively, Guy notes bitterly:

> 'Because people are pissed-scared. That's why. Because nobody wants this to happen to them, and so they think, Well, it just *won't* happen to me. If they're God-botherers they think it's because their made-up God loves them and they won't get it because they don't deserve it. If they're not God-botherers they just think that it'd be different for them. If *they* got a whiff of anything ending in "oma" they'd escape its clutches with one mighty fucking bound through the sheer power of positive thinking. So they tell you to think positively, as though that's going to help with a metastasising cancer rampaging its way through your fucking body.' (169)

What can be detected in Guy's raving account is our collective tendency to put a spell on reality: each of us lives in a bubble of his/her own belief in God's or the universe's benevolence towards themselves while death, diseases, accidents, or other misfortunes happen to someone else. Whether it is divine providence or our own wishful thinking, we use both to mediate the harrowing reality which otherwise escapes our understanding. This self-delusion finds additional expression in the notion of heroism attributed to a struggle against cancer. As Guy puts it, it is always a "brave battle," never "a cowardly battle or just a resigned one" (169), as if it is only through resistance, however delusional it may be, that human death can acquire any meaning at all.

The notion of alternative worlds is further explored by Banks through the concept of virtual reality. Early in the novel Kit observes:

> In a sense I don't really live here. The place where I really live is HeroSpace.
>
> Obviously, I do live here; this is where my body and my brain are, where sleep happens and real food has to be consumed and bodily functions experienced and coped with, where other people and officialdom have to be encountered and managed and so on... But over the years that has all increasingly started to feel like the part of my existence that just has to be got through with the minimum of fuss so that I can get back to the really important part, which is my life on-line, and especially my life in HeroSpace.
>
> It's as though what we call reality is the boring motorway journey to the exciting place where you actually want to be – something to be borne, even suffered, so that you can get to the place where you can do the things you really want to do. Like going on holiday, in other words. (35)

The virtual world and the empirical world in Kit's case are clearly separated and linked to his two different identities, a situation which again foregrounds his similarity to Frank Cauldhame, who is caught between reality and the world of his own imagination. In the real world Kit is an autistic youth from the north of England who shies away from worldly bustle and too much human contact, hiding in the solitude of his derelict house by the quarry. The scale of Kit's activities is limited to a few shops in the nearby city of Bewford and less frequented places like the local bridge, from which he enjoys watching the scarce traffic below and occasional jams. In the online game, on the other hand, he roams the vast futuristic world of computer animation in the body of a warrior-avatar, seeking "quests, battles, honour and treasure" (36) among millions of other players. The game offers its own inner levels of reality and simulacrum in the vein of *The Matrix*, with people lying in pods in gigantic cities and dreaming their lives while intelligent machines try to destroy both the dreamers and the awakened heroes defending them. The reason why many players find HeroSpace so attractive, Kit suggests, is that the life dreamt by those in pods may in fact be the life we live in the real world, and only upon awakening can we become aware of and fully enter the unmediated reality of HeroSpace (36-7). Significantly, Kit's attachment to the real and the rational applies as much to the physical as to the virtual worlds, which prevents him from labouring under the above delusion. "[W]hat looks like reality is reality," he asserts, "and HeroSpace, much though I love it and sometimes wish it was real, is just a game" (37).

While recognizing the difference between reality and the computer-generated construct, Kit notices the game's superiority to the world of everyday affairs. Despite their number, complexity, and steady evolution, the governing rules of HeroSpace are "definite and clear" (36), which apparently appeals to Kit's orderly nature and systematized thinking. Moreover, the game gives him the ultimate experience of things (i.e. trials, wars, and sweeping victories) which in the real world could prove fatal or simply impossible to accomplish (this aspect of the relationship between the real and the game has been fully explored in *Complicity*). However, paradoxical as it may sound, the most important quality of the game is that it allows Kit to be his true self (36). On the one hand, it offers a graphically appealing illusion in which he can hide his condition and enjoy safe anonymity; on the other hand, it is in the game that he can fully express himself, freely fashioning his avatar and its actions away from the institutional restrictions and domestic obligations which weigh on his life in the physical world. The game allows Kit to be part of a worldwide community, in which over the years he has "accrued status, power, combat experience, loot, respect and even comrades and friends" (36), which is contrasted with his reclusive Northumbrian existence.[6]

However, the two worlds, real and virtual, interpenetrate, their respective elements undergoing translation into the languages of the different semiotics. Just as Kit's inner world is expressed in terms of signs proper to a computer game – the type of character, diction (like, for ex-

---

6   The semiotic boundary which both separates and connects the real and the virtual, the limited and limitless, the spaces of solitude and communality is provided by the broadband connection, which he calls his "secret, high-speed tunnel out of the house into the rest of the real world, and those beyond" (102).

ample, swearwords used by his avatar), action, etc. – Kit's operations in the escapist online fantasy bring real profits, as Kit sells the points he has accumulated in the game to other players. Thus, the seemingly immeasurable value of his virtual heroics is expressed through hard and tangible currency. Significantly too, like the reconfiguration of his status between the worlds from a recluse and an outsider to a chief player and a guru among gamers, Kit's real-life relationship with Holly undergoes a translation to the laws of the virtual world. While in reality Holly often acts as Kit's guide and teacher through the meanders of social interaction, online it is Kit who is Holly's guide, as she follows him through the world of HeroSpace as his Voy, watching and learning from the master of the game and relying on his advice in order to avoid potential pitfalls. Ironically, the game offers a representation of the ugly side of their relationship in reality, which Kit discovers only at the end of the novel. As a Voy, Hol relies and parasitizes Kit's skills to move through the virtual world, just as she takes advantage of his trust and uses the money she was supposed to manage for him. The Internet medium is used to further highlight the breach of trust in the scene in which Hol logs in to the game to show the others the swearwords of Kit's invention, which may as well be summed up by Kit's earlier comment on Holly's presence in his game which makes Kit feel "a little like [his] privacy has been invaded" (150).

Apart from visual media like TV, cinema, and the Internet, reality in *The Quarry* is often conveyed and manipulated through verbal accounts and storytelling, as is the case in *The Wasp Factory*, but also in *Walking on Glass*, *Whit*, and some of the novels discussed in the Community Worlds chapter. Particularly striking in this respect is Guy's treatment of the family past and especially Kit's mother. The protagonist's provenance is patrilineal, as he does not know who his mother was, an ambiguity which makes his predicament again similar to that of Frank Cauldhame, who also has no memory of his mother and therefore constructs his image of her on the basis of what his father decides to reveal. In Guy's numerous versions of the past, Kit's mother is

an emigrated-to-Australia ex-barmaid from a long-closed pub in Bewford; a married, middle-aged member of the aristocracy somewhere between one-hundred-and-fiftieth and two-hundredth in line to the throne; a disgraced Traveller girl now settled quietly in County Carlow (which is in Ireland); an American exchange student from the Midwest with hyper-strict parents, belonging to some bizarre religious cult; or possibly just some random girl/conquest he promptly forgot about even at the time, who literally abandoned me on his doorstep one evening. (83-4)

As in *The Wasp Factory*, where Frank's condition is connected to a quasi-mythical event of godly castration, Kit's appearance in Guy's house and life has a fairytale quality reminiscent of George Eliot's *Silas Marner*. Kit was allegedly found by Guy as "a warm bundle inside the front porch" and was only unwrapped by his father in the kitchen – hence the boy's nickname Kitchener, in short Kit (84). Whereas Guy's fatherhood is unquestionable, as it has been proved scientifically by DNA tests, the figure of the mother remains a verbal creation, an elusive metamorphic being of Guy's making. It is this immaterial being to whom Kit tries to give a material shape over the course of the novel, perusing old issues of the local paper and questioning Guy's female friends, Ali, Pris, and Hol, about his mother's identity. The quest for the feminine which is excluded from or remains peripheral in the altogether masculine environment, which in *The Wasp Factory* results in the rediscovery of Frank's femininity, is orchestrated in *The Quarry* as Kit's pursuit of the maternal amidst Guy's multi-layered mystification.

Mediation of the past through storytelling can also be observed in the case of Guy's own history and especially his student years. Raised on his father's stories, Kit has always had a rather negative impression of Guy's university performance; therefore, when talking to Hol about the possibility of his own studies, Kit assures her that he will not be discouraged by "Dad's bad example" (214). It is only Hol who puts him in the picture about Guy's fortunes as a student and his near graduation which was only prevented by his failure to show up for the viva. On this occasion, Hol draws Kit's attention to his father's talent for equivocation. Apparently Guy did not take the final exam because he either went to the Orkneys to watch the aurora borealis or he went to the Atlantic to surf on big waves. "He told me both stories within a couple of weeks at the time," remembers Hol, "and I never did find out which was the truth. If either" (215).

At one point Holly comments on Guy's acting skills and his real keenness for directing, which in the relationship with other people, and especially his own son, takes the form of manipulation. Guy "directs" Kit's life, first by denying him full knowledge of his provenance, which

Kit sees as "part of the act" and Guy's desire "to mess with [his son's] head" (250), and second, by withholding important information about their financial situation and Kit's inheritance in case of Guy's death (255). Interestingly, the most effective means of communication between Guy and Kit are old servant bells, a remnant of the family's bourgeois past, by means of which the economic relationship of master and servant is projected onto the relationship between father and son. In many ways Kit's role as his father's nurse resembles the work of a servant, as he does a number of tasks for Guy, ranging from the preparation of his father's food to cleaning him after he uses the toilet. His dedication and work, however, are taken for granted and left not only without remuneration but also, frequently, without one good word. Guy justifies his harsh treatment of Kit with a desire to toughen him up and prepare him for a life when his father is gone, an intention which seems doubtful to Kit: "Guy being who he is, that could just be an excuse" (45). The strain of the task and the state of constant alertness to Guy's call makes Kit develop a behavioural reaction – Kit compares himself to Pavlov's dog, feeling a jolt of fear every time he hears Guy's bell (23). Although he is a dutiful son and a dedicated nurse, Kit reciprocates Guy's lies and egoism with secrets of his own, and he finds refuge in his bedroom, which he calls his "haven" and "citadel" (101), a phrasing echoing *The Wasp Factory* (see Banks 1984: 128) and the division of the house between Angus's and Frank's respective spheres of influence.

Ironically, Kit lives in a dying world whose epitome is the derelict Willoughtree House with its blocking doors, creaking floors, loose window frames, faulty plumbing and bad chimneys. The physical disintegration of the family house is reflective of the steady degradation of family relationships over the decades: the divorce of Guy's parents, the estrangement of the fathers from their sons in both generations, and the lack of a nurturing mother. The family life, as observed by Kit, as well as the entire family space have been pending towards a catastrophe, the devastation of the outside world gradually afflicting Guy's inner space: "Maybe there's always been something in Guy's life that was falling apart. Until finally, as well as the house and the car and whatever else, the thing falling apart ended up being himself" (128). If the decrepit Willoughtree House comes to represent Guy's diseased and dying body (an externalization reminiscent, for example, of the relationship between the castle and the protagonist in *A Song of Stone*), the nearby quarry, whose advent towards his estate Guy has been trying to stop for a number of years, turns into the metaphor of his cancer, the excavations causing constant tremors to the house's already flimsy structure and undermining the cliff on which the house is situated. It is not surprising, therefore, that the death of the owner coincides with the end of the house, as the quarry eventually devours the place, leaving only a gigantic hole (326).

One of the most poignant scenes in the novel is one in which the group, having scoured the house in search of the missing videotape, are burning old things and rubbish amassed by Guy over the course of his life. Watching the blazing pyre, Kit observes with ominous perspicacity:

> It's like a river, I think suddenly. It starts small and hesitant, becomes bigger, quicker, more assured as it grows, bursts with power and fury in its prime, then returns to slow, meandering quietness towards the end, eventually giving itself to nothing, recycled into its constituent parts. [...] [T]his is like looking at an image of our own lives, our own abandoned histories, our own past, baggage and legacies; all that hoarded meaning going up in smoke and flame, reduced to no more than bulk fuel for a mindless chemical reaction. (281)

The imagery of water and fire, signifying transience and destruction, respectively, has something apocalyptic about it, which is further underscored by the sight of Guy looking at the flames consuming his past while holding on to his stick with his thin emaciated hands. But it is also an ironic commentary on a life lived in the past, with its useless creeds and ideologies which, like Guy's pessimistic rant on global idiocracy or Hol's Marxist jeremiads, convince only their authors. In his speech intended as a farewell message to his friends, recorded on the missing porn tape, which he throws into the quarry and which Kit notices and recovers on one of his walks, Guy raves about the evils of society – its greed, inequality, violence, and growing stupidity caused by exposure to visual media. He finds the situation catastrophic and unbearable, which allegedly makes him happy to leave this degenerate world. However, it is Rob's oft-repeated phrase that the world has changed which in the end rings truer than Guy's unproductive bellyaching addressed to his friends and which, paradoxically, seems to underlie the message of the novel. Despicable and uncompromising as his final outburst may appear, Rob is probably the only character who fully realizes the inevitability of transformation and the need to move on. "Patterns, ways of life, economic circumstances, ways of doing business and making things: they all change, and if you don't move with the times, the times just roll over you and bury you" (254), he observes, unwittingly foreshadowing the end of Guy and his disintegrating house on the cliff.

In the final chapter of the novel we learn that after Guy's death the Power of Attorney action against Kit has been dropped and the protagonist, deemed capable of looking after himself, moves into Hol's flat in London. Frank Cauldhame, long incapacitated by Angus's lies and his own fear, is in the end resolved to depart from the crumbling house ruled by the father to the unpredictable outside world. Like Cauldhame, Kit also leaves his home in northern England and tries to find a place for himself in the metropolis. "I can't decide if I want to move back up here at some point, or not," muses Kit in the end. "I miss it, but Hol says sometimes missing somebody is just a natural part of your life, and doesn't mean you absolutely have to go back to that person or place" (325). What Banks seems to tell us in the closing paragraphs of *The Quarry* is that after death there is still life and there is memory, even though there may be no going back.

CONCLUSION

The analysis contained in this book reveals that there exists a drive among Banks's characters to perceive, interpret, and thus (re)construct the world in accordance with their personal worldviews. Such an individual mediation can be attributed to three major reasons. Firstly, the act of forwarding one's own world-picture functions as a medium of escape from the outside world which is frequently seen by the character as a negatively marked space – hostile, disintegrated, suffocating, exhausting, chaotic, immoral, etc, creating instead a space which yields to individual control. Secondly, by semioticizing "objective" reality into idiosyncratic world models, the characters can familiarize or domesticate the surrounding world in order to make it more meaningful or comprehensible, or to ensure their own place within its borders. Thirdly, the act of subjective mediation is used to manipulate other characters and the fabric of the perceptible reality in order to achieve one's own ends, or challenge (usually in some radical way) an unsatisfactory vision of the world. These three functions, three intentions on the part of Banks's characters, are visible in various degrees in each of the four spatial models, sometimes in combination, at other times with a discernible predominance of one particular function.

In the blueprint novel, *The Wasp Factory*, all three functions appear simultaneously and can hardly be distinguished as separate motivators. Frank withdraws from the frightening and hostile outside world, which he blames for his emasculation, into the refuge of his own insular realm. His self-devised substitute identities let him accept and give meaning to a life of disability, while the modelling of space resulting from his apperception (i.e. interpretation of reality in connection with his traumatic experience, gender bias, and primitive religion) ensures his place in the world as an "unchallenged lord of the island and the lands about it" (139). At the same time, Frank is shown as continually fighting against the encroachments of the external world on his domain (the Sacrifice Poles, the cache system) or trying to subordinate the public space to the codes of his private semiotics by eliminating unwanted people or killing off animals. While Frank as a child manipulates the fabric of reality in order to deceive adults and hide his deliberate murders, the protagonist's own life turns out to be a consequence of his father's alternative world-picture, his patriarchal scientific mediation, which is based on the verbal manipulation of the past events and the physical manipulation of his daughter's body.

In the Alternative Worlds, the escapist, familiarizing, and manipulating functions seem to be employed in various degrees, the characters' relationship with the world, whether it is one of affinity or contestation, being developed in connection with literature and the space of dreams. Grout struggles to escape from the reality of London by reading speculative fiction, which mediates between the fabricated world of his imprisonment and the allegedly true dimension of greater reality. Distancing herself from the sequence of lost games, Ajayi studies languages of the Earth and reads the books which form the castle walls, which consequently leads to the familiarization of the alien and prisonlike world of the castle, the meaning of which is now literally readable. In the case of Graham, the filter of the romance convention fosters his identification with the great city, while his own life appears as more meaningful. Slater and Sara's individual mediations of reality have the function of manipulating Graham, Sara's jealous husband, and their own parents, but they also challenge the conservative world-picture determined by conventional morality, in which their incestuous relationship is considered abominable and has to be concealed. In the second novel of the type, *The Bridge*, Lennox's dream life as John Orr is a medium of the character's escape from the nightmare of his physically and emotionally draining Edinburgh existence to a world which is under his exclusive control. There he can freely shape his appearance, social status, and emotional relationships, in compliance with his prejudices and desires. In *Transition*, the concept of mediation is connected with the act flitting, a mental and imaginative process catalyzed by septus, which results in the per-

son's transfer between the many worlds of the multiverse. Operating
through the medium of another person's body, the agents undergo an adjustment to the governing semiotics of the target world, whose future
can be then influenced and manoeuvred into conformity with the vision
of history promoted by the Concern.

In the novels of the Community Worlds, the familiarizing function is
given predominance, with other functions being present only marginally,
and the characters' mediation of the world is effected either verbally or
by means of gardening or music.[1] In *The Crow Road*, Kenneth
(re)constructs elements of the surrounding world through his tales of
magic and myth. Acquainting the children of the family with the origin
of Scottish landscape and its peoples, Kenneth mediates his kids' and
nephews' image of national space, helping them notice their own place
in the history of Scotland. His brother Rory, on the other hand, personalizes the space of his peregrinations in India, writing a travelogue in
which the experience of the exotic lands is channelled through his Western consciousness. Later, trying to make sense of his sister's premature
death, Rory dramatizes reality in the form of a fictional account. In *The
Steep Approach*, the protagonist in search of his own place within the
clan, turns to the family estate in Somerset, shaping it as his own paradisiacal kingdom, cultivating the land, and drawing the maps of his dominion. Stranded in the alien world of London, he repeats the process of
domesticating and personalizing his space by farming the home garden
in Richmond and then helping to cultivate the public space of Kew Gardens. In *Espedair Street*, the familiarizing and escapist functions of mediation become intertwined in the character of Danny Weir, whose relationship with the outside world develops in connection with music. Giving expression to his inner unmediated desires, music makes possible his
communication with the band members and his audience. Initially, music offers the protagonist a means of escape from his poor neighbour-

---

1   There are several examples of the manipulating function of mediation in the
     Community Worlds. In *The Crow Road*, Fergus McHoan produces signs ai-
     med at convincing Kenneth that his brother Rory is still alive, whereas, in fact,
     Rory has been killed by Fergus, afraid that the truth of his uxoricide will come
     to light. In *The Steep Approach*, Winifred conceals the truth of the incestuous
     relationship between Irene and Blake, producing a fabricated version of the
     family history, letting Alban believe his real father is Andy McGill and mani-
     pulating her grandson's life accordingly.

hood to the international scene; later, however, it becomes the medium of his liberation from the confinement of St. Jute's and into a life within the community in Arisaig. It is only in *Stonemouth* that the manipulative function of mediation comes to the fore, involving a distortion of the communal past and the character's present by means of technology and verbal accounts. Even if it aims at uncovering "the truth," the intention behind the representation is felt as inherently misguided or wicked. Last but not least, mediation is noticed in the very functioning of Stonemouth, where the surface of communal values rests upon the criminal core built around profit and domination.

In the Mythical Worlds, the process of world-mediation is connected primarily with its familiarizing or escapist functions. Isis filters the space of her peregrinations through her sectarian and mythological consciousness, due to which the road to London turns into a pilgrimage to Babylon(don), rife with perils but religiously significant and domesticated by familiar sectarian concepts. Hisako escapes from the world of violence connected with traditional Japanese culture into her private world (re)constructed around Western values. With the help of her Stradivarius, the protagonist of *Canal Dreams* on the one hand creates an insulation against her Japaneseness, and on the other, domesticates the territories encountered on her sea voyage to Panama, choosing a type of music which would suit the new experience. In the case of Kathryn, the interplay of the two functions is more complex. The protagonist's childhood transfer into the Business fairy tale for modern ambitious women, which involves a life of freedom and self-accomplishment, ensures her escape from the poor neighbourhood and the woes of traditional femininity, connected with nurture and self-sacrifice. However, it is only her adult and fully conscious choice of a life in the primitive utopia of Thulahn as the queen both of the country and of her private fairy tale which results in Kathryn's escape from the male-oriented world and in the domestication of the suppressed female element in herself.[2]

---

2   Interestingly, the manipulating intention behind the characters' mediation of reality is revealed by the men whom Isis, Hisako, and Kathryn meet on their way. In *Whit*, Grandfather Salvador falsifies his past and constantly amends the holy book of *Orthography*, which provides a theological and customary underpinning of Luskentyrianism, in order to retain and take advantage of his power as the Founder of the sect. Similarly, Isis's brother Allan, despite the

The characters of the Apocalyptic Worlds construe their subjective world-pictures so as to escape from the world of hostility, violence, corruption, meaningless relationships, and physical and psychological devastation, which defies any form of domestication or meaning-making. However, in contrast to the characters from the previous models, the escapist efforts of apocalyptic heroes to create personal enclaves of safety and harmony remain largely futile, as the outer world filters into their inner worlds, subjecting them to its relentless disintegrating power. In *A Song of Stone*, Abel's internal world is inextricably linked with the space of his family castle, which constitutes the only place of fragile order in the overwhelming chaos beyond its walls. The disintegration of the place under the rule of the lieutenant and its subsequent collapse in flames put an end to Abel's own life and his increasingly hazy narrative. In *Complicity*, Cameron's mental escape into the world of the "now," which is mediated by the present tense of his narration, ensures an unstable and ineffective rampart against the encroachment of the catastrophic past (memory of the sexual assault, murder, and the hair-raising images of the Gulf War). Similarly, his escape into drug and computer addiction causes only further havoc and disease in his body and mind, as his inner space becomes subordinated to and thus manipulated (without him being conscious) by the languages of domination and self-gratification which govern the public semiosphere. Andy, on the other hand, challenges the world-picture of the new capitalist order, which he helped to create but which appears to him now as at once breeding and thriving on multifaceted corruption. An exile from the semiotic centre, he resorts to degenerate methods and violence, which only emphasizes his extreme mental disturbance and makes his own vision of the world equally unsatisfactory as the target of his attacks. Only in *Dead Air*, the characters' escape into their personal secret space of love and mutual commitment,

---

appearance of moral rectitude, is in fact a self-serving manipulator jealous of Isis's position as a Leapyearian, who concocts a plot aimed at discrediting her in the eyes of the Order. In *Canal Dreams*, the CIA officer Dandridge designs a mystification in which his CIA agents act as Panamanian guerillas and kill all the passengers on the three ships on Gatún Lake. In *The Business*, Mr Hazelton not only devises a way of stealing from the organization but also contrives a plot of trading Kathryn to Prince Suvinder as his future wife in return for his consent to turn his country into the Business's headquarters.

mediated by the rules of various film genres, offers a way out from the deathly thrall of the modern wasteland and its televised catastrophes.

In *The Quarry*, in which neither of the four models predominate but they all merge to an indistinguishable degree, one can also detect the three functions of mediation appearing in a similar measure. Kit escapes into the futuristic world of HeroSpace, which gives him freedom from the restrictions he grapples with in reality as an autistic person – both physical, resulting from his condition, and institutional. In the guise of an avatar warrior and thanks to his exceptional intelligence, he becomes a major player and authority in the world's game, which is contrasted with his position of a "challenged" teenager, considered by doctors and authorities to be incapable of living on his own. His status in cyberspace gives him a sense of respect and accomplishment, needless to mention financial resources, which allow him and his terminally ill father to get by in the real world. The manipulative function of mediation can be noticed in Guy's stories concerning Kit's mother but also in his differing accounts of his own life. However, the most striking example in the novel can be found in the mechanism of social interaction, in which meaning-generation through the use of social conventions, language, and non-verbal signs can involve truth as much as deception, leading either to the consolidation of the community or to the domination of one person or group by another.

In Banks's fiction, spatial archetypes lack their fixed qualities. Space cannot be described in terms of distinctive features because its evaluation changes depending on the character's perspective. Perhaps the most striking example of space which in different novels is endowed with different characteristics is the family house or estate. Though often presented as dysfunctional, threatening the character's identity and happiness, rife with conflicts and moral turpitude (*The Wasp Factory*, *The Steep Approach*, *A Song of Stone*, *Walking on Glass*, *Whit*), it is equally often presented as a source of love, permanent values, personal and national identity, and regeneration (e.g. *The Crow Road*, *The Steep Approach*, *Espedair Street*, *The Business*, *Whit*, *Stonemouth*). Similarly, rural Scotland and the Highlands may be at once regenerative (*The Crow Road*, *Espedair Street*) and afflicted with decay (*Complicity*, *The Steep Approach*). The inner city or council estates may be seen by the characters as suffocating, violent, and impeding their development (*Espedair*

Street, The Business), but also giving hope and ensuring renewal and genuine fellowship (*Espedair Street, The Steep Approach, Stonemouth*). London in *Walking on Glass* is an urban dystopia, a city of simulation, and the Tormentors; in *Whit* it is a den of iniquity but also unexpected alliances, while in *Dead Air* it is a post-apocalyptic wasteland, which, however, can be redeemed by friendship and love. Finally, in *The Quarry* London becomes a destination where the protagonist chooses after the demise of his family home, and where he finds independence and opportunities for self-realization. In *The Business*, Kathryn Telman falls for the simplicity and moral superiority of the Himalayan state over the world of money and technology, but the latter also has its own merit: the hysterical supportiveness of her friend Luce, the loveable naivety of Uncle Freddy, the vulgar heartiness of Jeb Dessous, or the quaint chivalry of Steve Buzetski. Paradoxically, the characters' versions of reality which oppose those mediated by official culture are not always safe for themselves or others. The fantasy realm of *The Wasp Factory* offers the character refuge but simultaneously imprisons him/her in its violent cycle; Lennox's fantasy of the Bridge gets out of control and dooms Orr to a journey through lands shaken by war; Mrs Mulverhill's idea of the many worlds' contact with alien civilizations turns her into an outcast of the Concern by defying its policy of universal isolation; Hisako's Westernization and pacifist stance prove ineffective and self-defeating when confronted with the world's savagery; and Danny Weir's musical experiments cost his two friends their lives.

Examining the trajectory of the characters' movement, one inevitably comes to a conclusion that in practically all cases, the movement is circular, which appears to be a typical pattern in Banks's fiction. It involves not only circling in space, but also the character's constant return to some moment in time, the cycle of myth in which the character is caught, the turn of events he or she is subject to, as well as entrapment in pointless wandering. In *The Wasp Factory*, for example, Frank's movement in space is visible in his daily rounds of the island, occasional walks to and from Porteneil, and his shuttling between the loft with the Wasp Factory and the outskirts of his realm. His life, moreover, is caught in the cyclical time connected with the repetition of the deadly ritual and the reiterative pattern of perennial war. Last but not least, the recovery of the protagonist's femininity is tantamount to her physical and psychological return to the outside world, where she belonged before her alleged castration.

Although the circular pattern is present in all the four models, in each of them it has a different purpose and significance. In the Alternative Worlds, it underscores the character's imprisonment but also a possibility of breaking free from his or her confinement. Graham's walk takes him to Sara's flat but also documents his entrapment in the conventions of romance. At the end of the narrative, he is back to where he started, heading for home and being again in the world of the mundane where people are hostile and where there is no romance. Grout wanders about London and back to his room cluttered with SF books, being caught in the repetitive pattern of manic activities which would help him survive in the alien reality. In the end, he "shifts" from the prison of London to a mental hospital and to a condition of amnesia, but he is at least free of his previous draining paranoia. Quiss and Ajayi wander around the labyrinth of the castle vertically and horizontally, and Ajayi's reading of the novel which starts with the first line of Graham's narrative effects the structural return of the whole text in the form of the Moebius strip. In *The Bridge*, the circular movement of the character and the narrative takes place on every ontological level, and the text's descent to the level of the Barbarian and its final ascent to the level of the Edinburgh narrative matches Lennox's immersion into his coma and his final re-emergence to consciousness, when the novel forms a closed circle. Finally, in *Transition*, after a long series of "flittings" between various points of view, the text returns to the Unreliable Narrator from the Prologue, who assures the reader, right before the novel's end, that "it's a start" (404).

In the Community Worlds, the circular movement involves the pattern of separation and reintegration (from and into the family/neighbourhood/country), as a form of return to some original, proper state. Prentice, who is in conflict with his father, circles around his family base and returns home after Kenneth's tragic death in order to effect a belated reconciliation with the latter's memory. Rory, who distances himself from home and Scotland and travels to exotic lands, ultimately finds his resting place at the bottom of a Scottish loch. *The Crow Road*, moreover, advocates the idea of the cycle of life, in which "death is not all loss," which is reflected in the baptism of baby Kenneth at the end of the novel. The same circular movement of the character with respect to the space of home occurs in *The Steep Approach*, *Stonemouth*, and *Espedair Street*, with the additional return of Danny Weir to his creative powers.

In the Mythical Worlds, the circular movement predictably presupposes an adjustment to cyclical time and ritual, as well as the employment of the single mythological invariant of *separation – initiation – return* in the plot of the heroic quest. Its purpose to a large extent coincides with that of the previous model; however, it also involves a return after a meaningful journey and a triumph of the female element. Isis Whit travels from the North to the South and back to the North, away from her Order and back to its fellowship and regeneration in truth. Kathryn leaves the childhood space of motherly love and nurture and circles in space and airspace in her adult life only to reach the childlike ideal of home in Thulahn. The circling movement is perhaps best represented in the journey of Hisako, which not only involves the recurrence of primordial violence, but also the protagonist's frequent circling in space. It can be noticed in the holding pattern of her wanderings around Japan with a continual return to Tokyo, her shuttling between Hokkaido and Honshu at some pivotal moments of her life, as well as the final sea voyage around the world and the confrontation on the ship *Le Cercle*, which spurs Hisako's return to Japan and its traditional culture.

In the Apocalyptic Worlds, the circular trajectory takes the form of the deadly reiterative pattern of destructive activities which stresses the impossibility of the character's liberation and the renewal of the world. In *Complicity*, Cameron is imprisoned in the repetition of the same harmful activities – drug taking, game playing, acting on his and Yvonne's sexual fantasies – which reflect the pointlessness of existence and cause only further decay. He is also increasingly forced to return to the memory of childhood trauma and his terrifying experience in the Gulf War, which marks his entrapment between the hell of the past and the present wasteland. Abel in *A Song of Stone* escapes from the castle only to be brought back to it and meet his own end. His descent in the social hierarchy finds its ironic reversal in his final elevation when he is shot up in the air by the fire of the great gun. Only the last novel of the model, *Dead Air*, implies the return of the world to "normal" and its rebirth through love and suffering.

Even *The Quarry*, which seems to be the most linear of all Banks's narratives, reveals the typically Banksian circularity, first, by depicting the friends' return to the area in which they lived in youth and second, by showing Kit's entrapment in a cycle of ritualized activities performed in the confines of the disintegrating home. Significantly, the ending of the novel, which brings the death of the protagonist's father, also marks Kit's symbolic re-unification with his mother, whose name and address he learns from Guy's lawyer. Last but not least, Kit's departure for London echoes the overall message of Banks's novel about the inevitability of change in the world, which is a sign of its repetitive and cyclical nature.

In his first novels, *The Wasp Factory* and *Walking on Glass*, which are clearly indebted to the poetics of postmodernism and its ontological and epistemological uncertainties, Banks toys for the first time with a grand theme of literature which is the conflict between appearance and reality, showing the truth as dependent on an individual perspective and thus impossible to be learnt in its entirety. At the same time, in Banks's fiction the truth is considered indispensable for identity-making and personal freedom, themes which come up regularly in his later novels of the communal and mythical type: *The Crow Road*, *The Steep Approach*, *The Business*, or *Whit*, as well as in his last novel, *The Quarry*. Being "a rather old-fashioned story teller" (Rennison 2005: 18), Banks also advocates the importance of family roots and national background for individual development, but also the necessity (rather inevitable) of fusing tradition and innovation: an observance of communal values and heritage on the one hand, and looking forward into the future of progress and technology on the other (*The Bridge*, *The Crow Road*, or *The Business*). Another message which can be read in Banks's novels is the importance of individual involvement and active resistance to all forms of injustice and exploitation: social, sexual, and political. "Washing one's hands didn't work two thousand years ago, and it doesn't work today" (256), says Banks through the mouth of his frustrated character in *Complicity*, warning us readers that by passive acceptance of "our collective dream, our corporate imagery" (*The Bridge* 281), we may all wake up one day in the post-apocalyptic wasteland.

Banks's works are often novels of purpose which allow him to preach his own political creed. The author was famous for his socialist stance and unreserved dislike of the Tories,[3] as well as for his opinions concerning nuclear weapons and the evils of American imperialism, to which he gave voice in *Complicity, Dead Air*, and *The Steep Approach*. He also repeatedly criticized the use of torture, which he took up as a motif in *Transition*.[4] Despite his constant frustration as a political writer and a moralist, he always treated it as his mission. In an interview with Chris Mitchell for the *Spike Magazine* Banks revealed:

> People usually just ask me 'What are you *on?*' You can't be too prescriptive about what a writer does, but it's important to me to get these ideas into the books, just for my own peace of mind, so that I feel I'm not just doing this to make money, I'm not just writing pageturners for people to skim through, put aside and forget. Like anybody else, I want to make the world a little more like the world I'd like to live in, sad though that is. (2000)

Although the mission to improve man and the world can be read in all of Banks's mainstream novels, the author played his utopian dreams on a truly universal scale in the far-future scenarios of his science fiction monolith, the space opera cycle *The Culture*. The socialist egalitarian utopia of the Culture is sensitive to the suffering of the weak and the poor, refrains from violence, fights superstition, and ensures social and material welfare by resorting to the power of limitless artificial intelligence (MacGillivray 1996). And it fulfils, if only in fiction, Banks's dream of a truly communitarian society "with a generosity of spirit" (Burnside 2009), which he believed could be materialized in Scotland. The analysis of *The Culture*, however, must necessarily stop at this point, as the sheer volume of the enterprise would require a separate book.

---

3   In the interview with Lev Grossman, Banks revealed that when he was a child, he had shocked his parents by declaring himself more British than Scottish: "It was a lot to do with things like the BBC, the GPO and the NHS. Institutions with three letters. So much of that stuff has been or is being privatised. That has kind of destroyed what Britain meant to me" (2008).

4   In an interview for *The Sunday Times*, Banks stated: "I think what comes out of *Transition* is that torture should always be absolutely illegal. Murder is illegal; there is a commandment that says you shalt not kill, yet we still have army chaplains. There are lots of loopholes but you should only torture if you're so convinced you're doing the right thing that you are prepared to suffer the consequences and the consequences should be absolute" (Burnside 2009).

Bibliography

Abramowska, Janina. (1978). "Peregrynacja." *Przestrzeń i literatura.* Ed. M. Głowiński, A. Okopień-Sławińska. Wrocław: Zakład Narodowy im. Ossolińskich. 125-58.

Adams, Douglas. (1995). *The Hitch Hiker's Guide to the Galaxy: A Trilogy in Five Parts.* London: William Heinemann.

Alegre, Sara Martín. (2000). "Consider Banks: Iain (M.) Banks's *The Wasp Factory* and *Consider Phlebas.*" *Revista Canaria de Estudios Ingleses* 41: 197-205.

Anderson, Benedict. (2006 [1983]). *Imagined Communities. Reflections on the Origin and Spread of Nationalism.* London, New York: Verso.

Bachelard, Gaston. (1994). *The Poetics of Space.* Trans. M. Jolas. Boston: Beacon Press.

Bakhtin, Mikhail. (1984). *Rabelais and His World.* Trans. H. Iswolsky. Bloomington and Indianapolis: Indiana University Press.

Banks, Iain. (1986). *Walking on Glass.* London & Sidney: Futura Publications.

Banks, Iain. (1987). *The Bridge.* London: Pan Books & MacMillan.

Banks, Iain. (1989). *Canal Dreams.* London: Macmillan.

Banks, Iain. (1994 [1990]). *The Wasp Factory.* London: Abacus.

Banks, Iain. (1996 [1994]). *Complicity.* London: Abacus.

Banks, Iain. (1996). *Whit, or Isis amongst the Unsaved.* London: Abacus.

Banks, Iain. (1998). *A Song of Stone.* London: Abacus.

Banks, Iain. (2000). *The Business.* London: Little, Brown.

Banks, Iain. (2003 [1990]). *Espedair Street.* London: Abacus.

Banks, Iain. (2005 [1993]). *The Crow Road.* London: Abacus.

Banks, Iain. (2007). *The Steep Approach to Garbadale.* Little, Brown.

Banks, Iain. (2009a [2003]). *Dead Air.* London: Abacus.

Banks, Iain. (2009b). Preface. *The Wasp Factory*, 25th anniversary edition. London: Abacus. ix-xi.

Banks, Iain. (2009c). *Transition.* London: Little, Brown.

Banks, Iain. (2012). *Stonemouth.* London: Little, Brown.

Banks, Iain. (2013). *The Quarry.* London: Little, Brown.

Baudrillard, Jean. (2001a). "Simulacra and Simulations." Trans. P. Foss, P. Patton, P. Beitchman. *Selected Writings*. Ed. M. Poster. Stanford: Stanford University Press. 169-87.

Baudrillard, Jean. (2001b). "The Illusion of the End." Trans. C. Turner. *Writings*. Ed. M. Poster. Stanford: Stanford University Press. 254-65.

Bell, Eleanor. (2004). *Questioning Scotland: Literature, Nationalism, Postmodernism*. Basingstoke: Palgrave Macmillan.

Bennet, Jill. (2003). "The Limits of Empathy and the Global Politics of Belonging." *Trauma at Home: After 9/11*. Ed. J. Greenberg. Lincoln and London: University of Nebraska Press. 132-8.

Berger, James. (1999). *After the End. Representations of Post-Apocalypse*. Minneapolis and London: University of Minnesota Press.

Biedermann, Hans. (2005 [2001]). *Leksykon symboli*. Trans. J. Rubinowicz. Warszawa: MUZA SA.

Binns, Ronald. (1991). "Castles, Books, and Bridges: Mervyn Peake and Iain Banks." *Peake Studies* 2.1: 5-12.

Boheemen, Christine van. (1987). *The Novel as Family Romance. Language, Gender, and Authority from Fielding to Joyce*. Ithaca and London: Cornell University Press.

Booth, Ken and Tim Dunne. (2002). "Worlds in Collision." *Worlds in Collision: Terror and the Future of Global Order*. Ed. K. Booth, T. Dunne. Houndmills, New York: Palgrave Macmillan. 1-23.

Bradford, Richard. (2007). *The Novel Now: Contemporary British Fiction*. Blackwell Publishing.

Brewster, Scott. (2006). "Beating, Retreating: Violence and Withdrawal in Iain Banks and John Burnside." *Ethically Speaking. Voice and Values in Modern Scottish Writing*. Ed. J. McGonigal, K. Stirling. Amsterdam – NY: Rodopi, 179-98.

Bridgwood, Christine. (1986). "Family romances: the contemporary popular family saga." *The Progress of Romance. The Politics of Popular Fiction*. Ed. J. Radford. London and New York: Routledge & Kegan Paul. 167-93.

Brooks, Cleanth. (1993 [1968]). "*The Waste Land*: Critique of the Myth." *T. S. Eliot: The Waste Land*. Ed. C. B. Cox, A. P. Hinchliffe [1968]. Houndmills: Macmillan. 128-161.

Brooks, Libby. (26 August 2002). "The Word Factory." *The Guardian*. <http://www.guardian.co.uk/books/2002/aug/26/fiction.iainbanks>. 24 October 2006.

Burnside, Anna. (13 September 2009). "Iain Banks: the man who fell to earth," *The Sunday Times*. <http://www.thesundaytimes.co.uk/sto/culture/books/article18458.ece>. 26 February 2010.

Butler, Andrew M. (1999). "Strange Case of Mr Banks: Doubles and *The Wasp Factory*." *Foundation* 76: 17-26.

Campbell, Joseph. (2004 [1949]). *The Hero With A Thousand Faces*. Princeton and Oxford: Princeton University Press.

Cawelti, John G. (1976). *Adventure, Mystery, and Romance: Formula Stories as Art and Popular Culture*. Chicago and London: University of Chicago Press.

Cohn, Dorrit. (1978). *Transparent Minds. Narrative Modes for Presenting Consciousness in Fiction*. Princeton: Princeton University Press.

Colebrook, Martyn. (2010). "'Journeys into lands of Silence': *The Wasp Factory* and Mental Disorder." *Demons of the Body and the Mind. Essays on Disability in Gothic Literature*. Ed. R. B. Anolik. Jefferson, North Carolina, and London: McFarland & Company, Inc. 217-26.

Colebrook, Martyn. (2010). "Reading Double, Writing Double: the Fiction of Iain (M.) Banks." *Bottle Imp* 8: 1-6. <http://www.arts.gla.ac.uk/ScotLit/ASLS/SWE/TBI/TBIIssue8/Colebrook.pdf>. 25 March 2013.

Craig, Cairns. (1999). *The Modern Scottish Novel: Narrative and the National Imagination*. Edinburgh: Edinburgh University Press.

Craig, Cairns. (2002). *Iain Banks's* Complicity*: A Reader's Guide*. New York, London: Continuum.

Craig, Cairns. (2004). "Scotland and Hybridity." *Beyond Scotland: New Contexts for Twentieth Century Scottish Literature*. Ed. G. Carruthers, D. Goldie, A. Renfrew. Amsterdam, New York: Rodopi. 229-53.

Craig, Cairns. (2004a). "Beyond Reason – Hume, Seth, Macmurray and Scotland's Postmodernity." *Scotland in Theory: Reflections on Culture & Literature*. Ed. E. Bell, G. Miller. Amsterdam – New York: Rodopi. 249-80.

Craig, Cairns. (2005). "Player of Games: Iain (M.) Banks, Jean-François Lyotard and Sublime Terror." *The Contemporary British Novel Since 1980*. Ed. J. Acheson, S. C. E. Ross. Edinburgh: Edinburgh University Press. 229-39.

Craig, Cairns. (2006). "Devolving the Scottish Novel." *A Concise Companion to Contemporary British Fiction*. Ed. J. F. English. Blackwell Publishing, 121-40.

Daamen, Roel. (2006). "A Confluence of Narratives: Cultural Perspectives in Postmodernist Scottish Fiction." *Cultural Identity and Postmodern Writing*. Ed. T. D'Haen and P. Vermeulen. Amsterdam: Rodopi. 119-48.

Dannenberg, Hillary P. (2008). *Coincidence and Counterfactuality: Plotting Time and Space in Narrative Fiction*. Lincoln and London: University of Nebraska Press.

Davison, Carol Margaret. (2009). "Monstrous Regiments of Women and Brides of Frankenstein: Gendered Body Politics in Scottish Female Gothic Fiction." *The Female Gothic: New Directions*. Ed. D. Wallace, A. Smith. Basingstoke: Palgrave Macmillan. 196-214.

Dean, Jeremy. (n.d.). "Jeremy Dean talks with the very calm, but very exciting novel-
    ist." *SCRAWL*. <http://homepage.virgin.net/questing.beast/scrawl_banks.htm>.
    21 March 2010.
Dodou, Katherina. (2006). "Evading the dominant 'reality' – the case of Iain
    Banks's *Walking on Glass*." *Studia Neophilologica* 78.1: 28-38.
Eliade, Mircea. (1954). *Cosmos and History. The Myth of Eternal Return*. Trans.
    W. R. Trask. New York: Harper & Row Publishers.
Eliot, Thomas Stearns. (1975). *The Complete Poems and Plays of T. S. Eliot*. Lon-
    don: Faber and Faber.
Erickson, Leslie Goss. (2006). *Re-Visioning of the Heroic Journey in Postmodern
    Literature: Toni Morrison, Julia Alvarez, Arthur Miller, and* American
    Beauty. Lewiston, Queenston, Lampeter: The Edwin Mellen Press.
Erll, Astrid and Ann Rigney. (2009). "Introduction: Cultural Memory and its Dy-
    namics." *Mediation, Remediation, and the Dynamics of Cultural Memory*.
    Ed. A. Erll, A. Rigney. Berlin, New York: Walter de Gruyter. 1-12.
Finney, Brian. (2006). *English Fiction after 1945: Narrating a Nation*. Houndmills:
    Palgrave Macmillan.
Forster, R. F. (2003). *W. B. Yeats. A Poet*, vol. 2. Oxford: Oxford University Press.
Frazer, Sir James George. (1994). *The Golden Bough: A Study in Magic and Reli-
    gion*. Ed. R. Fraser. Oxford, New York: Oxford University Press.
Frazer, Robert. (1994). Introduction. *The Golden Bough: A Study in Magic and Re-
    ligion*. By Sir James George Frazer. Oxford, New York: Oxford University
    Press. ix- xliii.
Freud, Sigmund. (2010). *Delusion and Dream*. Trans. H. M. Downey. New York:
    Moffat, Yard & Co., 1917. Bartleby.com, 2010. <http://www.bartleby.com/2
    87/>. 15 May 2012.
Freud, Sigmund. (2010). *The Interpretation of Dreams*. Trans. and ed. J. Strachey.
    New York: Basic Books.
Frye, Northrop. (1976). *The Secular Scripture. A Study of the Structure of Ro-
    mance*. Cambridge, Massachusetts, and London, England: Harvard Universi-
    ty Press.
Frye, Northrop. (2000 [1971]). *Anatomy of Criticism: Four Essays*. Princeton and
    Oxford: Princeton University Press.
Gardiner, Michael. (2009). "Arcades – The 1980s and 1990s." *Edinburgh Compan-
    ion to Twentieth-Century Scottish Literature*. Ed. I. Brown, A. Riach. Edin-
    burgh: Edinburgh University Press. 181-92.
Gifford, Douglas. (1996). "Imagining Scotlands: The Return to Mythology in Mod-
    ern Scottish Fiction." *Studies in Scottish Fiction: 1945 to the Present*. Ed. S.
    Hagemann. Frankfurt am Mein: Peter Lang. 17-49.
Gomel, Elana. (2000). "The Plague of Utopias: Pestilence and the Apocalyptic
    Body." *Twentieth Century Literature* 46.4: 405–33.

Gray, Colin. (2002). "World Politics as Usual after September 11: Realism Vindicated." *Worlds in Collision: Terror and the Future of Global Order*. Ed. K. Booth, T. Dunne. Houndmills, New York: Palgrave Macmillan. 226-44.

Grossman, Lev. (29 February 2008). "Iain Banks: *The Matter* Interview." *Time Tech*. <http://techland.com/2008/02/29/iain_banks_the_matter_intervie/#ixzz0dwo54bvo>. 2 April 2008.

Gruszewska, Ludmiła. (1996). *Wizje i re-wizje w poezji Thomasa S. Eliota*. Lublin: Wydawnictwo UMCS.

Guriewicz, Aron. (1976). *Kategorie kultury średniowiecznej*. Trans. J. Dancygier. Warszawa: Państwowy Instytut Wydawniczy.

Hall, J. W. (1979). *Japonia od czasów najdawniejszych do dzisiaj*. Trans. K. Czyżewska-Madajewicz. Warszawa: Państwowy Instytut Wydawniczy.

Hart, Francis Russell. (1978). *The Scottish Novel: From Smollett to Spark*. Cambridge: Harvard University Press.

Head, Dominic. (2002). *The Cambridge Introduction to Modern British Fiction, 1950-2000*. Cambridge: Cambridge University Press.

Hoggard, Liz. (18 February 2007). "Iain Banks: The novel factory." *The Independent*. <http://www.independent.co.uk/news/people/profiles/iain-banks-the-novel-factory436865.html>. 20 January 2010.

Horsley, Lee. (2005). *Twentieth-Century Crime Fiction*. New York: Oxford University Press.

Horsley, Lee. (2009 [2001]). *The Noir Thriller*. Houndmills: Palgrave Macmillan.

Hühn, Peter. (2009). Introduction. *Point of View, Perspective, and Focalization: Modeling Mediation in Narrative*. Ed. P. Hühn, W. Schmidt, J. Schönert. Berlin, New York: Walter de Gruyter. 1-8.

Hutcheon, Linda. (1996 [1988]). *The Poetics of Postmodernism: History, Theory, Fiction*. New York and London: Routledge.

"Isis – Goddess of the Throne." *The White Goddess Pagan Portal*. <http://www.thewhitegoddess.co.uk/the_goddess/isis_-_goddess_of_the_throne.asp>. 27 April 2013.

Jenks, Chris. (2003). *Transgression*. London: Routledge.

Jones, Stephen R. (2004). "Action at a Distance: Narrative Structure and Technique in Iain Banks's *Whit*." *Studies in Scottish Literature* 33/34: 372-86.

Jordan, Michael. (2004 [1993]). *Dictionary of Gods and Goddesses*. Second Edition. New York: Facts on File.

Jung, C. G. (1991). *The Archetypes and the Collective Unconscious*. 2nd edition. Trans. R. F. C. Hull. London: Routledge.

Kawaguchi, Judit. (16 January 2007). "Hiroo Onoda." *The Japan Times*. <http://www.japantimes.co.jp/life/2007/01/16/people/hiroo-onoda/#.UaddNdhr24o>. 20 March 2013.

Keen, Suzanne. (2006). "The Historical Turn in British Fiction." *A Concise Companion to Contemporary British Fiction*. Ed. J. F. English. Blackwell Publishing. 167-87.

Kelman, Kate. (1998). "A Collision of Selves: Kate Kelman interviews Iain Banks." *Cencrastus* 60: 19-22.

Kermode, Frank. (1967). *The Sense of an Ending: Studies in the Theory of Fiction*. New York: Oxford University Press.

Kincaid Speller, Maureen. (2000). "No Man Is An Island: The Enigma of *The Wasp Factory*." *Steam Engine Time* 1: 28-9. <http://efanzines.com/SFC/SteamEngineTime/SET01.pdf>. 15 April 2013.

Kopaliński, Władysław. (2003). *Słownik mitów i tradycji kultury*. Warszawa: Oficyna Wydawnicza RYTM.

Kuehl, John. (1989). *Alternate Worlds*. NY and London: New York University Press.

Leishman, David. (2009). "Coalescence and the fiction of Iain Banks." *Études écossaises* 12: 215-30.

Livingstone, David B. (1 December 1998). "Iain Banks: *A Song of Stone*." *Spike Magazine*. <http://www.spikemagazine.com/1298banks.php>. 2 April 2008.

Lotman, Juri. (2009). *Culture and Explosion*. Ed. M. Grishakova. Trans. W. Clark. Berlin, New York: Mouton de Gruyter.

Lotman, Yuri. (1990). *Universe of the Mind: A Semiotic Theory of Culture*. Trans. A. Shukman. London, New York: I.B. Tauris & Co. Ltd. Publishers.

Lurkar, Manfred. (2004 [1987]). *The Routledge Dictionary of Gods and Goddesses, Devils and Demons*. London and New York: Routledge.

Lyall, Roderick J. (1993). "Postmodernist otherworld: postcalvinist purgatory. An approach to *Lanark* and *The Bridge*." *Etudes Ecossaises* 2: 41-52.

Lyotard, Jean-François. (1984). *The Postmodern Condition: A Report on Knowledge*. Trans. G. Bennington, B. Massumi. Minneapolis: University of Minnesota Press.

Łotman, Jurij. (1977). "Zagadnienia przestrzeni artystycznej w prozie Gogola." *Semiotyka kultury*. Ed. E. Janus, M. R. Mayenowa, S. Żółkiewski. Warszawa: Państwowy Instytut Wydawniczy. 213-65.

Łotman, Jurij. (1984). *Struktura tekstu artystycznego*. Warszawa: Państwowy Instytut Wydawniczy.

Łotman, Jurij and Boris Uspienski. (1998). "Mit-imię-kultura." *Historia i semiotyka*. Trans. B. Żyłko. Gdańsk: Słowo/Obraz terytoria. 63-80.

Macdonald, Kirsty A. (2011). "'This Desolate and Appalling Landscape': The Journey North in Contemporary Scottish Gothic." *Gothic Studies* 13.1: 37-48.

MacGillivray, Alan. (1996). "The Worlds of Iain Banks." *Laverock* 2, *The Association for Scottish Literary Studies*. <http://www.arts.gla.ac.uk/ScotLit/ASLS/Laverock-Iain_Banks.html>. 15 February 2009.

MacGillivray, Alan. (2001). *Iain Banks'* The Wasp Factory, The Crow Road *and* Whit. *Scotnotes* 17. Glasgow: Association for Scottish Literary Studies.

Macmurray, John. (1969). *The Self as Agent*. London: Faber and Faber.

Macmurray, John. (1995 [1961]) *Persons in Relation*. London: Faber and Faber.

Malcolm, David. (2000). *That Impossible Thing. The British Novel 1978-1992*. Gdańsk: Wydawnictwo Uniwersytetu Gdańskiego.

March, Cristie L. (2002). *Rewriting Scotland*. Manchester and New York: Manchester University Press.

Marshall, Andrew G. (22 September 1998). "Revelations: I thought that only bad writers made money. Iain Banks, London, 1983 (Interview). *The Independent*. <http://www.independent.co.uk/arts-entertainment/revelations-i-thought-that-only-bad-writers-made-money-1199822.html>. 28 January 2010.

McCracken, Scott. (1998). *Pulp: Reading Popular Fiction*. Manchester: Manchester University Press.

McHale, Brian. (1987). *Postmodernist Fiction*. New York and London: Methuen.

McKenzie, Simon. (1995). "Scottish writer Iain Banks spoke with Simon McKenzie," *Time Off*. <http://www.enthea.org/phlebas/text/banksint10.html>. 15 April 2013.

Mcleod, Iseabail and Freedman, Terry. (1995). *The Wordsworth Dictionary of First Names*. Ware: Wordsworth Editions Ltd.

McMillan, Dorothy. (1995). "Constructed out of bewilderment: stories of Scotland." *Peripheral Visions. Images of Nationhood in Contemporary British Fiction*. Ed. I. A. Bell. Cardiff: University of Wales Press. 80-99.

Meletinsky, Eleazar. (2000). *The Poetics of Myth*. Trans. G. Lanoue, A. Sedetsky. New York and London: Routledge.

Middleton, Tim. (1995). "Constructing the Contemporary Self: The Works of Iain Banks." *Contemporary Writing and National Identity*. Ed. T. Hill, W. Hughes. Bath: Sulis Press. 18-28.

Miller, Gavin. (2007a). "Iain (M.) Banks: Utopia, Nationalism and the Posthuman." *The Edinburgh Companion to Contemporary Scottish Literature*. Ed. B. Schoene. Edinburgh: Edinburgh University Press. 202-9.

Miller, Gavin. (2007b). "Beyond Make-Believe: Play in the Science Fiction of Iain (M.) Banks." *Playing the Universe. Games and Gaming in Science Fiction*. Ed. D. G. Mead, P. Frelik. Lublin: Maria Curie-Skłodowska University Press. 47-65.

Mitchell, Chris. (11 July 2000). "Iain Banks: *Whit* and *Excession*: Getting Used To Being God." *Spike Magazine*. <http://www.spikemagazine.com/0996bank.php>. 2 April 2008.

Muir, Edwin. (2000 [1993]). *An Autobiography*. Edinburgh: Canongate Classics.

Nairn, Thom. (1993). "Iain Banks and the Fiction Factory." *The Scottish Novel Since the Seventies: New Visions, Old Dreams*. Ed. G. Wallace, R. Stevenson. Edinburgh: Edinburgh University Press. 127-35.

Nairn, Tom. (2004). "*Break-Up*: Twenty-Five Years On." *Scotland in Theory: Reflections on Culture and Literature*. Ed. E. Bell, G. Miller. Amsterdam – New York: Rodopi. 17-33.

Nash, Cristopher. (1987). *World Games: The Tradition of Anti-realist Revolt*. London and New York: Methuen.

Ness, Patrick. (26 September 2009). "*Transition* by Iain Banks." *The Guardian*. <http://www.guardian.co.uk/books/2009/sep/26/transition-iain-banks-book-review>. 15 February 2013.

"Never forget the other Terror," *New Statesman* (5 November 2001). <http://www.newstatesman.com/node/141548>. 28 April 2013.

Oswell, David. (2006). *Culture and Society. An Introduction to Cultural Studies*. London, Thousand Oaks, New Delhi: Sage Publications.

Owen, John D. (1998). "*A Song of Stone* by Iain Banks." *Infinity Plus*. <http://www.infinityplus.co.uk/nonfiction/stone.htm>. 2 April 2008.

Petrie, Duncan. (2004). *Contemporary Scottish Fiction*. Edinburgh: Edinburgh University Press.

Pippin, Tina. (1999). *Apocalyptic Bodies: The Biblical End of the World in Text and Image*. London: Routledge.

Pisarska, Katarzyna. (2007). "A Heroine's Quest for Self: the Poetics of Monomyth in Iain Banks's *Whit*." *Zeszyty Naukowe t. 3*. Lublin: Wyższa Szkoła Społeczno-Przyrodnicza. 79-100.

Pisarska, Katarzyna. (2008a). "In Search of a Formula: Iain Banks's *Complicity* as a Modern Noir Thriller." *Margins and Centres Reconsidered: Multiple Perspectives on English Language Literatures*. Ed. B. Klonowska, Z. Kolbuszewska. Lublin: Towarzystwo Naukowe KUL. 149-58.

Pisarska, Katarzyna. (2008b). "Worlds in a Loop: Iain Banks's *Walking on Glass*." *Structure and Uncertainty*. Ed. L. Gruszewska Blaim, A. Blaim. Lublin: Maria Curie-Skłodowska University Press. 201-19.

Pisarska, Katarzyna. (2012a). "After the End of All Things: Iain Banks's *A Song of Stone* as a Post-apocalyptic Dystopia." *Spectres of Utopia*. Ed. L. Gruszewska Blaim, A. Blaim. Frankfurt: Peter Lang. 247-55.

Pisarska, Katarzyna. (2012b). "Living a Dream within a Dream: Iain Banks's *The Bridge*." *The Lives of Texts: Exploring the Metaphor*. Ed. K. Pisarska, A. S. Kowalczyk. Newcastle upon Tyne: Cambridge Scholars Publishing. 83-113.

Pisarska, Katarzyna. (2012c). "Music as a Colonizing Other in Iain Banks's *Canal Dreams*." *Música-Discurso-Poder*. Ed. M. de Rosário Girão Santos and E. M. Lessa. Braga: Universidade do Minho. 201-20.

Pittin-Hédon, Marie Odile. (2006). "Re-imagining the City: End of the Century Cultural Signs in the Novels of McIlvanney, Banks, Gray, Welsh, Kelman,

Owens, and Rankin." *The Edinburgh History of Scottish Literature*, Vol. 3. Ed. I. Brown. Edinburgh: Edinburgh University Press. 253-62.

Pittock, Murray. (2008). *The Road to Independence? Scotland Since the Sixties*. London: Reaktion Books.

Poole, Steven. (14 September 2002). "It's all in the initial: *Dead Air* by Iain Banks." *The Guardian*. <http://www.guardian.co.uk/books/2002/sep/14/shopping.fiction>. 2 April 2008.

Puchalsky, Rich, discussion of *A Song of Stone*. <http://groups.google.com/group/rec.arts.books/msg/545cf64d4de845ba>. 20 September 2011.

Punter, David. (1999). "Heartlands; Contemporary Scottish Gothic." *Gothic Studies* 1.1: 101-18.

Rees, Jasper. (8 January 1998). "Interview: Iain Banks: Alice Cooper, Pink Floyd, the Stones . . . Iain Banks? The monster of rock that never was." *The Independent*. <http://www.independent.co.uk/life-style/interview-iain-banks-alice-cooper-pink-floyd-the-stones-iain-banks-the-monster-of-rock-that-never-was-1137365.html>. 20 February 2013.

Renan, Ernest. (2009). "What is a Nation?" Trans. M. Thom. *Nation and Narration*. Ed. H. K. Bhabha. London and New York: Routledge. 8-22.

Rennison, Nick. (2005). *Contemporary British Novelists*. London and New York: Routledge.

Riach, Alan. (1996). "Nobody's Children: Orphans and their Ancestors in Popular Scottish Fiction after 1945." *Studies in Scottish Fiction: 1945 to the Present*. Ed. S. Hagemann. Frankfurt am Mein: Peter Lang. 51-83.

Robertson, James. (1989/90). "Bridging Styles: A Conversation with Iain Banks." *Radical Scotland* 42. <http://www.enthea.org/phlebas/text/interv4.html>. 15 April 2013.

Rosenthal, Daniel. (25 April 1999). "How we met: Iain Banks & Fish." *The Independent*. <http://www.independent.co.uk/arts-entertainment/how-we-met-ian-banks--fish-1089637.html>. 2 April 2008.

Sage, Victor. (1996). "The politics of petrifaction: culture, religion, history in the fiction of Iain Banks and John Banville." *Modern Gothic. A Reader*. Ed. V. Sage, A. G. Lloyd-Smith. Manchester and New York: Manchester University Press. 20-37.

Schoene, Berthold. (2007). "Going Cosmopolitan: Reconstituting 'Scottishness' in Post-devolution Criticism." *The Edinburgh Companion to Contemporary Scottish Literature*. Ed. B. Schoene. Edinburgh: Edinburgh University Press. 7-16.

Schoene-Harwood, Berthold. (1999). "Dams Burst: Devolving Gender in Iain Banks's *The Wasp Factory*." *Ariel: A Review of International English Literature* 30.1: 131-48.

Shelley, Mary. (1999 [1993]). *Frankenstein or The Modern Prometheus*. Ware: Wordsworth Editions Ltd.

Smith, Evans Lansing. (1997). *The Hero Journey in Literature: Parables of Poesis.* Lanham, New York, London: University Press of America, Inc.

Smith, G. Gregory. (1919). *Scottish Literature: Character and Influence.* London: MacMillan and Co. Ltd.

Stevenson, Randall. (2004). "A Postmodern Scotland?" *Beyond Scotland: New Contexts for Twentieth Century Scottish Literature.* Ed. G. Carruthers, D. Goldie, A. Renfrew. Amsterdam, New York: Rodopi. 209-28.

Stevenson, Randall. (2006). *The Oxford English Literary History: Volume 12: 1960-2000: The Last of England?* New York: Oxford University Press.

Śpiewakowski, Aleksander. (1989). *Samuraje.* Trans. K. Okazaki. Warszawa: Państwowy Instytut Wydawniczy.

Tallaron, Richard. (1996). "Iain Banks." *Études écossaises* 3. 141-8.

"*The Wasp Factory* at 20." (February 2004). *The Banksoniain* 1: 7-8. <http://efanzines.com/Banksoniain/Banksoniain01.pdf>. 12 April 2013.

"*The Wasp Factory* at 25." (February 2009). *The Banksoniain* 14: 6-7. <http://efanzines.com/Banksoniain/Banksoniain14.pdf>. 12 April 2013.

Todd, Richard. (1996). *Consuming Fictions.* London: Bloomsbury.

Toporow, Władimir. (1977). "O kosmologicznych źródłach wczesnohistorycznych opisów." Trans. R. Maślanko. *Semiotyka kultury.* Ed. E. Janus, M. R. Mayenowa, S. Żółkiewski. Warszawa: Państwowy Instytut Wydawniczy. 103-46.

Uspienski, Boris. (1998). "Percepcja czasu jako problem semiotyczny." *Historia i Semiotyka.* Trans. B. Żyłko. Gdańsk: Słowo/Obraz Terytoria. 19-51.

Walker, Marshall. (1996). *Scottish Literature Since 1707.* London: Longman.

Walker, Maxton. (8 September 2009). "Even at my age I still have something to prove." *The Guardian.* <http://www.theguardian.com/global/2009/sep/08/iain-banks-transition>. 15 October 2012.

Walters, James. (2008). *Alternative Worlds in Hollywood Cinema: Resonance Between Realms.* Bristol, Chicago: Intellect.

Walton, James. (3 September 2009) "*Transition* by Iain Banks: review." *The Telegraph.* <http://www.telegraph.co.uk/culture/books/bookreviews/6132913/Transition-by-Iain-Banks-review.html>. 15 October 2012.

Wark, Kirsty. (9 June 2013). "Author Iain Banks: In his own words." *BBC News Scotland.* <http://www.bbc.co.uk/news/uk-scotland-22780003>. 20 July 2013.

Watson, Roderick. (2007). *The Literature of Scotland.* Basingstoke: Palgrave MacMillan.

Weston, Jessie L. (1920). *From Ritual to Romance.* Cambridge: Cambridge University Press.

Wilson, Andrew. (1994). "Iain Banks Interview." *Textualities.* <http://textualities.net/andrew-wilson/iain-banks-interview/>. 19 June 2008.

Witt, R. E. (1997). *Isis in the Ancient World.* Baltimore: Johns Hopkins University Press.

Yoke, Carl B. (1987). Introduction to *Phoenix from the Ashes: The Literature of the Remade World*. Ed. C. B. Yoke. New York: Greenwood Press. 1-12.

Zgorzelski, Andrzej. (2004). *Born of the Fantastic*. Gdańsk: Wydawnictwo Uniwersytetu Gdańskiego.

Index

Mediated Fictions

Studies in Verbal and Visual Narratives

Series Editors: Artur Blaim and Ludmila Gruszewska-Blaim

Vol. 1 Katarzyna Pisarska: Mediating the World in the Novels of Iain Banks. The Paradigms of Fiction. 2013.

www.peterlang.com